Michele Hulbert

Staff for this Book

EDITOR
Michael Blow

ASSOCIATE EDITOR
Ralph K. Andrist

ART DIRECTOR
John J. Conley

COPY EDITOR
Barbara Leish

PICTURE EDITORS
Linda Sykes
Alice D. Watson
Kristi N. Witker, *Assistant*

ASSISTANT EDITORS
Linda Cooper
Lynne Parsons

CONTRIBUTING EDITOR
Nancy Lindemeyer

PICTORIAL RECONSTRUCTIONS
Cal Sacks

EUROPEAN BUREAU
Gertrudis Feliu, *Chief*
Mary Jenkins

AMERICAN HERITAGE
PUBLISHING CO., INC.

PRESIDENT
Paul Gottlieb

GENERAL MANAGER, BOOK DIVISION
Kenneth W. Leish

EDITORIAL ART DIRECTOR
Murray Belsky

"America," from an allegory of about 1600
METROPOLITAN MUSEUM OF ART, ESTATE OF JAMES HAZEN HYDE, 1957

The AMERICAN HERITAGE
History of The
Thirteen Colonies

ELGII
IÆ NEC NON

ABULA
mendata
isscher
schenk Iun:

ERDAM
ttans

E. t'gevangen huys F. de H. Generaels huys G. t'Gerecht H. de Kaeck I. Compagnies Pachuys K. Stadts Herberch
307 308 309 310 311

Netherland and New England by Nicolas Visscher, about 1655

The AMERICAN
HERITAGE
History of The
Thirteen
Colonies

By the Editors of
AMERICAN HERITAGE
The Magazine of History

Editor in Charge
Michael Blow

Narrative
Louis B. Wright

Pictorial Commentary
Ralph K. Andrist

Published By
American Heritage Publishing Co., Inc.

Book Trade Distribution By
McGraw-Hill Book Company

New Amsterdam seen from the south: an inset from a map of New

times. What was different in the fifteenth century was the increasing demand for goods that previously had been restricted to the wealthy. More people now could buy more goods, and merchants and shipowners struggled to supply the demand.

The Crusades, which in practice turned out to have many more objectives than the rescue of the holy places from the Saracens, had brought Europeans into contact with Eastern cultures and given them an acquaintance with luxuries that until then were little known in western and northern Europe. The Venetians particularly had profited from the Crusades. They exacted high prices for conveying warring knights to the East, and they loaded their returning galleys with expensive commodities collected from Cairo, Alexandria, and other Mediterranean ports. Whatever the turn of politics and war, the Venetians usually managed to make a profit. Genoa on the west coast of Italy also developed into a great seaport and a rival of the Queen of the Adriatic. Venice and Genoa established bases and imposed their rule at various points in the Mediterranean as they expanded their trade between the Near East and distant European markets.

But by the end of the fifteenth century Venice and Genoa were both in trouble. Their traditional trading routes and bases were threatened by the Ottoman Turks, who had supplanted the Seljuk Turks, the Arabs, and the Moors as the dynamic bearers of the banners of Islam. Previously, Venice had been able to reach an accommodation with the Seljuk Turks of Asia Minor, and she had contrived arrangements with the Mamelukes of Egypt. Genoa had also made favorable trade agreements in the Mediterranean before the rise of the Ottoman Turks. By the end of the century, however, all this had changed. The Ottoman Turks, a virile, warlike, and highly organized military power, swept into Egypt and Asia Minor, conquered the Mamelukes, overthrew the Seljuks, and pushed on into the Balkans. They were temporarily diverted in 1402 by the attack on their rear from other Asiatic invaders under Tamerlane, but this nomad's power was short-lived, and the Ottoman Turks managed to take Constantinople in 1453. Moving into Europe, they marched to the very walls of Vienna before they were stopped, and none knew when they might resume their advance.

Worse still, the Turks now developed sea power. Before this time they had been an army of horsemen, but after they captured Constantinople their sea power steadily increased. Corsairs flying the Turkish flag lurked in all the principal seaports of North Africa. Many of the bases and colonies of Venice and Genoa surrendered to Turkish naval commanders. A crowning insult to Christendom occurred in 1480, when Muhammad II captured the Italian town of Otranto and set up a market for the sale of Christian slaves. By 1565 the Turks even laid siege to Malta and only narrowly failed to capture it. The great days when the Venetian war galleys ruled the Mediterranean and Venetian merchants held a monopoly of the trade in Eastern luxuries were over before Columbus set sail.

Venice and Genoa still managed to bring in some luxury goods and even contrived to trade with the enemy—if only on his terms. But the prices of Eastern luxuries rose until they were frequently exorbitant. It is small wonder that merchants all over Europe were hopeful of discovering new routes to India, to the Spice Islands, and to the riches of other lands in the Far East.

For generations, Europeans had depended upon the East for spices and drugs. The Crusaders had acquired a taste for luxuries and a liking for dates, raisins, preserved fruits, candied melons, and other delicacies enjoyed by their enemies, the Saracens. The Moors in Spain had also introduced many of the good things of the East, and Spaniards had learned from their conquerors about a life more civilized than northern Europeans had known.

Although the Turks in the eastern Mediterranean were a dynamic force in the fifteenth century, the power of Islam as represented by the Moors, an Arabic-speaking people of mixed blood and Muslim faith in North Africa, was on the wane. A small Moorish kingdom still held sway in Spain, but ten years before Columbus's first voyage, Christian Spain began its final war against the Moors, which ended in 1492 with the surrender of Granada, the last Muslim stronghold.

At the same time, Portugal had carried the war against the Moors into Africa. In 1415 the Portuguese captured Ceuta on the African mainland opposite Gibraltar and used it as a base for further operations. The occupation of Ceuta was an important step in Portugal's development as a maritime and trading nation. The man who raised the Christian standard over the walls of Ceuta was Prince Henry, later to be called by the English—somewhat erroneously, for he made no voyages himself—"Prince Henry the Navigator," because of his encouragement of maritime affairs.

A World to Take

When Christopher Columbus set out from Palos, Spain, on his momentous voyage of discovery on August 3, 1492, western Europe had changed little since the age of Dante and Chaucer. An uneasy torpor, characteristic of the late Middle Ages, lay over most of Europe. The Church still exerted its authority over Christendom, but its strength was uneven and its hold often tenuous as rebellious sovereigns defied the popes, or as venal popes forfeited the respect of the pious. Few states had rulers who sat securely on their thrones and held sway over united nations. The modern state had not yet evolved, although it was slowly taking shape in England, France, Portugal, and Spain. Italy and Germany remained complexes of independent or semi-independent cities and principalities. The emperor of the Holy Roman Empire could hardly be said to rule, but he held a suzerainty over an amorphous portion of Central Europe. The pope and the emperor were often at odds and sometimes at war as each contended for dominion over territories in northern Italy and neighboring regions. Christendom was poised between two eras, the medieval world, with traditional patterns of thought, and the modern age, with revolutionary changes that within a century would affect every phase of life.

One of the most powerful influences at work was the expansion of trade brought about by the increasing demand for commodities from the East. The buying power of most of Europe had been slowly developing throughout the century as farming and sheep raising improved, industries expanded, and the silver mines of eastern Europe poured more bullion into the money market. The increasing flow of money started an inflationary spiral that was given additional impetus as the discoveries and conquests of the Spanish conquistadors in the New World sent another stream of silver and gold to Europe. Money was becoming more plentiful, the demand for goods in all the principal marts was keen, and prices were rising. These conditions stimulated merchants and shippers in many cities, some of which grew rapidly in the late fifteenth and early sixteenth centuries.

Trade, of course, had been the lifeblood of many European communities since early

North America (at top of map) was still only poorly known but a powerful magnet for adventurers when Guillaume le Testu, a French chart maker, drew this map of the North Atlantic in 1555.

9

An episode during the French and Indian War: British boats, each armed with a single cannon, defeat a ten-gun French ship of war at Fort La Galette on the St. Lawrence. The action, in August, 1760, led to the fall of the fort and enabled the British army to advance down the river. The artist was Thomas Davies, English officer and painter.

sions of dynastic wars. Although English land claims stretched to the Pacific, the thirteen colonies actually occupied only a relatively narrow and highly vulnerable strip of land along the Atlantic seaboard. And, for the most part, the colonists were left to fend for themselves against the imperial troops of France and Spain. In the end British regulars in force came to their aid, but what really enabled them to hang on were the roots they had thrust into the land. The Spanish had come to the New World in search of gold and silver, the French to mine the riches of the fur trade. The people who settled the English colonies were far from being oblivious to these attractions, but most of them came determined to stay, and they were not about to be pushed out.

This tenacity enabled them to endure, but not to prevail. That took something else—a sense of common purpose—and not surprisingly it was a long time coming. The colonists, after all, differed enormously in nation-ality, religion, even in language. From the beginning they were a fragmented group more apt to pursue independence in diversity than in union. But eventually there came a time when colonists began to consider themselves not English or Dutch, not Virginians or New Yorkers, but Americans, and, as Americans, willing to sacrifice regional interests to common goals. As John Adams observed, there had been a "change in the principles, opinions, sentiments and affections of the people," and this was "the real American Revolution."

When the colonists came to grips with their destiny, it was because they had finally realized that liberty and responsibility go hand in hand. No single event brought about that awareness; no single reason—the struggle for survival or the search for identity—can explain it. If we are to understand how the colonies became one nation, and the colonists one people, it is well that we examine the whole story, from beginning to end.   *The Editors*

Introduction

It all began in 1492 when Christopher Columbus sailed west to find a new route to the Indies and stumbled onto an unknown continent along the way. But if the origin of the colonial period was accidental, the ending was not. The representatives of the thirteen colonies who approved the Declaration of Independence in 1776 charted a collision course by design, fully aware of the obstacles in their path and the risks they were taking.

The events that led up to their decision took place over a period of nearly three hundred years. Looking back, the wonder is that it all came to a head so quickly. For a century after its discovery, the New World was little more than a lode to be mined by adventurers seeking quick profits. Not until the end of the sixteenth century were serious efforts made to establish permanent colonies. Even then, the perils of the journey and the threats of starvation and Indian attack kept settlement down. Many colonists turned

back when they discovered that life in America was not quite what the promotional tracts of land developers made it out to be.

But gradually the settlers came, sinners and saints, spurred by the fear of religious persecution in part, but above all drawn by the hope of owning land. They were a mixed bag: English Separatists from Leiden, French Huguenots, Dutch burghers, Mennonite peasants from the Rhine Valley, a few gentleman Anglicans. But they shared a quality of toughness, and they made the land feel their determination.

America was not a tranquil place to build a home. The settlers found themselves immersed in almost continuous conflict as the great European powers maneuvered for power in the New World. Foreign policy made in London, Paris, Madrid, and The Hague turned America into a battleground for more than a century.

It is worth remembering that the English colonies were always the underdogs in these frontier exten-

Turkish forces try to board Venetian ships in a contemporary woodcut of the 1499 Battle of Zonchio. By such harassment, long continued, the Turks blocked old trade routes to the East.

The Portuguese, who had developed a mercantile society interested in trade, were eager to expand their commercial ventures. With a firm foothold on the shores of Africa, it was natural for them to think of expanding into that continent. The push into Africa had the irresistible appeal of a godly crusade sweetened with profits. The Portuguese as well as other Europeans convinced themselves that they had a mission to convert the heathen—especially when the missionary effort would produce material rewards. If God in his infinite mercy permitted the Portuguese to capture unbaptized Africans who could be sold into Christian bondage, loss of liberty was a small price for these heathen to pay for salvation. Thus the Portuguese—and all the slave traders who came after them—salved their consciences for trafficking in human souls.

In 1418 Prince Henry established a residence looking out to sea on Sagres Point, near Cape St. Vincent. Learned men with a knowledge of the sea found a welcome at Sagres, which became a curious combination of religious order and school of navigation. As Grand Master of the Order of Christ, Prince Henry had funds available for voyages of discovery, and he sent out exploring expeditions that annexed the Madeira, the Azores, and the Cape Verde Islands to Portugal. Expeditions under his sponsorship sailed down the African coast, and before his death in 1460 his captains had gone as far south as Senegal and had brought back gold, ivory, and—until forbidden by Prince Henry—slaves.

Africa was promising, but neither the discomfiture of Islam, nor the conversion of the heathen Senegalese, nor the trade in pepper, ivory, and slaves was enough to

11

While King Ferdinand gazes symbolically across the ocean, Columbus reaches the New World. This 1493 woodcut was one of the earliest attempts to portray Indians.

satisfy the Portuguese. Stories of the riches of the East stirred them to further action. They must find a way to India. Prince Henry's explorers had gone far enough around the western hump of Africa to convince themselves that they might reach India by rounding that continent, and the opening of that route became their aim. A Portuguese land traveler named Pedro de Covilhão set out in 1487 upon a journey that eventually took him from Cairo to Aden and across the Arabian Sea to Calicut on the coast of India. He was the first Portuguese to visit Goa. Although Covilhão decided to settle in Abyssinia, he sent back a report of the opportunities for trade with India.

In the same year that Covilhão departed, Bartholomeu Dias sailed from Lisbon on a voyage that took him around Africa to a point on the east coast near the Great Fish River and Mossel Bay. Observations and information picked up by Dias strengthened his belief that In-

dia could be reached by sea, but lack of provisions made it impossible for him to test his theories. In December, 1488, he returned by way of the cape on the tip of Africa, which he called the Cape of Storms and King John II of Portugal renamed the Cape of Good Hope.

When Dias docked at Lisbon, the Genoese navigator Christopher Columbus was there and made notes concerning the voyage. In 1484–85 Columbus had laid a proposal before King John II to reach the East by sailing west and had found that monarch interested. King John, even more keenly than Prince Henry before him, was concerned with maritime exploration and trade. He encouraged chart makers, seamen, and pilots until Portugal became the foremost center in Europe for maritime information and enterprise. King John had put off Columbus in 1485 because two of his own captains had a project for sailing westward that promised to cost him less than the Italian's proposal. When nothing came of this endeavor, he once again gave some encouragement to Columbus. But when Dias came back with news that India could be reached without sailing to the west, King John lost interest in the Genoese's plans.

Since Portugal had a monopoly of African commerce and the Cape of Good Hope route, Columbus realized that Spain might be more receptive to exploration of "the Great Ocean Sea" (the Atlantic). He returned to Spain, where he had earlier appealed to Ferdinand II of Aragon and Isabella of Castile, whose marriage in 1469 had led to a united Spain. At the same time, he sent his brother Bartholomew to London to lay his proposal before King Henry VII.

In 1488, as Columbus struggled to gain a new hearing from the Spanish sovereigns, Bartholomew tried to interest the thrifty Tudor monarch in a western voyage of discovery. Although no direct evidence remains of Henry's dealings with Bartholomew, Columbus's son Ferdinand later wrote that the English king was sufficiently interested to keep up negotiations until news of Columbus's successful voyage reached him. Another early source, the Spanish historian Gonzalo Fernández de Oviedo, asserted that Henry's counselors ridiculed Bartholomew's idea of sailing westward to the Indies and that Henry declined to support the project. What is certain is that Henry VII missed the opportunity to be the first to gain a foothold in the Western world by right of discovery. It is also certain that Bartholomew applied to Charles VIII, king of France, and that France also turned him down.

Until 1492, Christopher met with no more encouragement from the Spanish rulers than Bartholomew had received in England and France. Ferdinand and Isabella were preoccupied with the last crusade against the Moors, and pious Isabella was more concerned with driving the last of the Muslim warriors out of Spain than she was with distant islands and lands beyond the Ocean Sea. Columbus had to wait. In the meantime, learned scholars appointed by the sovereigns to appraise Columbus's "Enterprise of the Indies" reported that his plan was not feasible, and that if he ever reached the other side of the Western Sea, as the Atlantic was also called, he would never get back.

His patience exhausted, Columbus determined to shake the dust of Spain from his feet and once more apply to the king of France for help. But before he had crossed the Spanish border, friends interceded with Queen Isabella, who again sent for Columbus. He found the queen preoccupied with the siege of the Moors in Granada and once more had to wait through frustrating delays. When Granada fell on January 2, 1492, Columbus carried a banner in the procession that

celebrated the final victory over the Muslims in Spain. But still the queen refused to back the Enterprise of the Indies, and it was not until April, 1492, that the two sovereigns finally put their assent into written orders that gave Columbus three ships and empowered him to make his voyage.

On August 3, 1492, Columbus, with ninety men in three caravels, the *Santa María*, the *Pinta*, and the *Niña*, sailed from the port of Palos. Strong in their Christian faith, Columbus and his men took holy communion in the gray dawn, asked God's blessing on their enterprise, and sailed away on an expedition that would change the world. Queen Isabella had seized an opportunity that John of Portugal, Henry of England, and Charles of France had rejected, and for this she would gain for Spain an empire that would be the envy of the rest of the world.

The long voyage of the three ships, the discouragement of the sailors, and the final landfall on October 12, 1492, probably at San Salvador (Watling's Island) in the Bahamas, is a story too often told to need retelling. Columbus believed that he had reached one of the outermost islands of Asia and that Japan (then known as Zipangu) lay close by. He had read his Marco Polo, studied a letter and chart by the Italian Paolo Toscanelli that showed the land mass of Asia reasonably close, and absorbed other geographical lore of his day which taught that the Western Ocean was much narrower than it is, and that Japan was much nearer to Europe than even the Atlantic seaboard of North America. When his long voyage ended in the Bahamas, he was certain that he had found the western route to the Indies, a belief to which he clung through three more voyages of discovery.

When Columbus returned to Spain after exploring Cuba, Hispaniola (Haiti), and other islands and leaving a garrison on Hispaniola, he reported to his sovereigns that he had found the westerly route to the Indies and had discovered islands where gold mines clearly existed. He himself had collected gold nose plugs, a few pearls, and stories of vast quantities of gold to be found on the next island. The search for that elusive source of gold, just beyond the next inlet, just over the next mountain, was to be a will-o'-the-wisp that would lure men to fateful destinations for generations to come. The news of Columbus's safe return to Palos in March, 1493, carried by letter to the rulers of Spain, brought an invitation from the two sovereigns to come to Barce-

Since no authentic portrait of Columbus existed, engraver Theodor de Bry made this one from imagination to embellish a 1596 map.

lona, where they were holding court. Columbus made a triumphal journey across Spain in April and was received by the king and queen in great state. He drew up a plan for colonizing the new territories and began preparations for a second expedition. The age of western discovery had begun.

So accustomed are we in the modern age to the instant dissemination of news that we find it hard to realize that all Europe did not immediately learn of Columbus's voyage. For Europe it was more significant than modern man's penetration of outer space; yet many parts of Europe had to wait months and even years for word of the discovery. In the ports of Spain and Portugal, it is true, sailors and ship captains talked of the western voyage. Italian merchants, ever on the watch for news that would affect commerce, wrote home of the return of Columbus from exploring islands off Asia, and the Portuguese in particular renewed their own maritime activities. But outside of the Iberian Peninsula and Italy, news of Columbus's first voyage traveled slowly, and only gradually did the event kindle the imaginations of people elsewhere.

In the meantime, Spain had taken steps to ensure her possession of the lands that Columbus had discovered, or that others might find, in the West. The reigning pope, Alexander VI, was a Spaniard, born Rodrigo Borgia. The Spanish sovereigns sent a mission to persuade him to issue a bull favorable to Spanish interests. The bull, called *Inter Caetera* (1493), drew a line from Pole to Pole one hundred leagues west of the Cape Verde Islands. It gave Spain all heathen lands beyond the line and left to Portugal the lands to the east. Portugal complained that her own interests were damaged, and she succeeded in negotiating with Spain the Treaty of Tordesillas (1494), which shifted the line to 370 leagues west of the Cape Verde Islands. This new boundary ran through eastern South America, giving Brazil to Portugal. The rest of the world was thus excluded by papal decree from sharing in the spoils of discovery; but eventually French, Dutch, and English explorers ignored the Line of Demarcation and began probing the coastline of the New World.

Portugal, in the meanwhile, was preparing to exploit the Africa-to-India route. On July 8, 1497, ten years after Bartholomeu Dias had demonstrated that ships could reach India by sailing around the tip of Africa, Vasco da Gama sailed from Lisbon with four vessels, bound for India. Da Gama's voyage, the theme of one of the greatest of Portuguese epics, Luiz Vaz de Camões's *Os Lusiadas*, took two years and established not only the sailing route for future voyages to India but also the essential trading plan that the Portuguese were to follow. Da Gama made contacts in Calicut, an important spice port, learned that trading with India would have to be more sophisticated than bartering the trinkets desired by African natives, and returned with a cargo of cinnamon and pepper. Trade with the East via the Cape of Good Hope had begun, and the Portuguese set about establishing naval bases to protect their interests. Portugal's attempt to maintain a monopoly of the Indian trade, especially in spices, was reasonably successful until the rise of the English and Dutch East India companies in the early seventeenth century.

All Europe envied the Portuguese for their monopoly of the eastern trade by way of the Cape of Good Hope, and every maritime power hoped to find some other route to the wealth of Asia. For many long years after

14

Columbus's time, even after it was clear that a vast land mass blocked the way to the East, explorers continued to search for some strait that would lead into the Great South Sea and thence to Japan and China. Explorers became professional adventurers ready and willing to serve under any ruler with the means to hire them. From Italy and Portugal came professional geographers, navigators, pilots, map makers, and other maritime specialists ready to offer their skills in the best market.

Such a professional geographer was Amerigo Vespucci, who gave his name to the New World. Vespucci began his career as a commercial agent employed by the Medici of Florence and in 1492 was sent to Seville on business concerning ships' supplies. Fascinated by the new science of geography and navigation, Vespucci applied himself to study and became a proficient observer on four voyages of discovery, which he accompanied as a specialist in geography rather than as a commanding officer. It was he who first realized that

the new discoveries were a previously unknown continent and not part of Asia.

After his second voyage with Alonso de Ojeda in 1499, an expedition that discovered the pearl fisheries off the coast of Venezuela, Vespucci returned and entered the service of Portugal. In 1501 he went with Nuño Manoel's expedition that explored the coast south of Brazil. The findings of this voyage led experts to believe that a passage to the ocean beyond might be discovered at the tip of South America, just as a passage had been found around Africa. Vespucci accompanied a fourth voyage of discovery to Brazil and finally returned to Spain, where he received an appointment in 1508 from the Casa de Contratación (or India House) in Seville as pilot major, that is, chief pilot and instructor in navigation, a post that he retained until he died in 1512 of malaria.

Vespucci's reputation was made by his reports. Although some of his claims of personal accomplishments

Vasco da Gama (left, from an early painting), first to reach India via the Cape of Good Hope, ended his days as viceroy of India. Above, Amerigo Vespucci is pictured in a detail from the 1507 map in which the name "America" was first used. Many printings of the map popularized and established the name.

were exaggerated, he was a keen and accurate observer, and he wrote well. His descriptions of the coasts he visited provided information that other explorers could use, and these reports, in the form of letters, quickly got into print. They formed part of the first popular collection of voyages, Fracanzano de Montalboddo's *Paesi Novamente Retrovati* ("The Newly Discovered Lands"), published at Vicenza in 1507, a popular work that soon went through a number of editions in Italian, French, and German.

In that same year a German geographer and map maker, Martin Waldseemüller of the College of St. Dié in Lorraine, published two maps, with an explanatory introduction entitled *Cosmographiae Introductio*, which included Vespucci's letters. Waldseemüller tentatively named the southern part of the new lands, shown on his map as an island, "America" for Amerigo Vespucci. Waldseemüller's work became popular throughout Europe. The name he had given South America at length attached itself to the whole of the New World, and Amerigo Vespucci's name thus was made immortal.

A voyage that marked the climax of the early stages of exploration was the first circumnavigation of the globe, undertaken by Ferdinand Magellan, a Portuguese nobleman who had served in India under the Portuguese viceroy Affonso de Albuquerque. Having fallen into disfavor in Portugal, Magellan offered his services to the king of Spain, Charles V, whom he persuaded to outfit an expedition under his command to seek the spice islands of the East by sailing around South America. A fleet of five ships with some two hundred and seventy men sailed from Sanlúcar on September 20, 1519. More than a year later, on October 21, 1520, after exploring the coastline of South America, Magellan discovered the strait that is named for him.

The wind and currents in this strait are notorious among seamen for consistent malevolence, and Magellan spent nearly forty racking days trying to make the passage. Finally, with three ships surviving, he reached the Pacific on November 28, 1520. He was the first European to emerge in "the Great South Sea," an expanse of water that would have terrified him had he known its extent. Sailing northwest, he found only an endless sea until at last, on March 6, 1521, he reached the green isles of the outlying Marianas. Food and water were nearly gone, and the men were ragged, hungry, and thirsty. But, after refreshing themselves, they pushed on to the Philippines. Intervening in a tribal war, Magellan

was killed there on April 27, 1521, and Juan Sebastián del Cano took command.

One of the three surviving ships proved unseaworthy and was burned. In the other two, the explorers sailed to Borneo and the Moluccas, where they loaded a cargo of the precious spices that they had come to find. One vessel now turned about and sailed for Panama; it was ultimately wrecked. In the other, the *Victoria*, Cano sailed across the Indian Ocean, rounded the Cape of Good Hope, made a landfall on the Cape Verde Islands, where the Portuguese intercepted him and took off thirteen men, and ultimately reached Sanlúcar on September 7, 1522, with eighteen survivors out of the two hundred and seventy who had sailed three years before.

Though Magellan did not live to see its conclusion, his imagination and skill had planned the momentous voyage that demonstrated the possibility of sailing around the earth. (This circumnavigation also proved that the oceans were of far vaster extent than Columbus and most of his contemporaries had ever dreamed.) Spain had found a route to the Spice Islands and had established a claim to an empire in the Pacific that she would not relinquish until the United States took the Philippines in 1898. The way to Asia around South America proved too long, stormy, hazardous, and costly to make it practicable for the spice trade, but Spain contrived to develop a trade between the Philippines and the west coast of America. For many years, galleons from Manila brought rich cargoes to Mexico, whence they were distributed to other markets.

With the circumnavigation of the globe begun by Magellan, the extent of the world was established, and geographers could make their maps with more accuracy and assurance. The nature of the great land mass between the Atlantic and the Pacific was at last realized. Though explorers would continue to seek a northwest passage to Asia, they now knew that a long voyage separated them from Japan and China. The New World was now known to be two vast continents, although their extent and treasures remained unknown, to be discovered by later explorers.

Even before Magellan's expedition, Spanish adventurers had heard rumors about gold and pearls to be had for the taking on the coasts of the new lands. Although few had penetrated the mainland and the islands of the Caribbean, some who had landed on the Isthmus of Darien (now Panama) heard stories of a people to the westward so rich in gold that they kept it

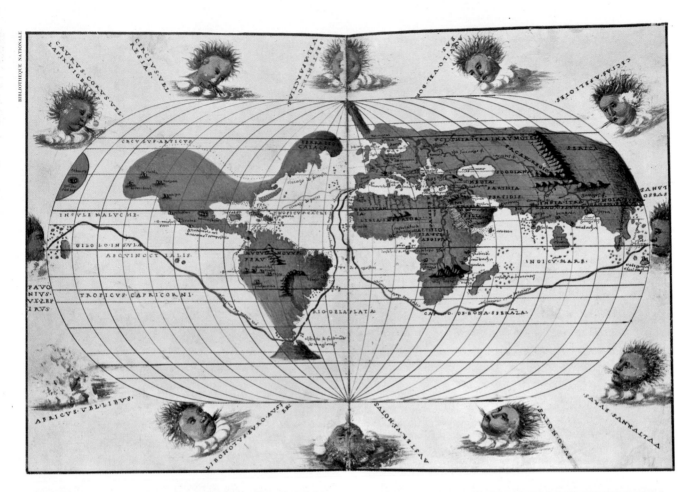

A 1536 map (top) shows Magellan's round-the-world path, and also marks out the Spanish route across Panama to Peru. Immediately above is a French version of the map of Magellan's strait sketched by Antonio Pigafetta of Magellan's crew. At right is Magellan as a 17th-century English map maker thought he might have looked.

FERDINAND MAGELLANUS.

stored in baskets. An adventurer who gave credence to these tales was Vasco Nuñez de Balboa, who organized an expedition to seek this wealth. Beating his way through the underbrush of the Isthmus on September 25, 1513, he came upon a small hill, which he climbed to get a better view. What he saw stretching without limit before him was the Pacific Ocean. Thus from "a peak in Darien" the first white man caught a glimpse of the ocean that Magellan's expedition would cross seven years later.

With Balboa on this expedition was one Francisco Pizarro. On that September day he stood with Balboa, looked out upon the Pacific, and considered tales of a people down the west coast whose humblest utensils were made of gold. Balboa was not fated to reach this wealth. He was executed on a charge of treason in January, 1517, with Pizarro presiding at his execution. Fourteen years later, Pizarro embarked on an expedition that seized the Inca of Peru, forced him to gather an enormous ransom of gold, and then treacherously murdered him.

In 1519, two years after Balboa's execution in Darien, Hernando Cortes marched from the coast of Mexico, where he founded Vera Cruz, to Tenochtitlán (now Mexico City), the capital of the Aztecs, whose emperor was Montezuma. The palaces of the Aztec emperor, resplendent with flowers, gold, and silver, and the enormous temples where insatiable gods required huge numbers of human sacrifices astonished the Spaniards, who reported that the Great Khan himself could show no greater wonders.

At first welcomed as gods by the Aztecs, the Spaniards soon earned their hatred. On the night of June 20, 1520, the Aztecs rose and drove them out of Tenochtitlán, Montezuma's sacred inner city, situated in the middle of a lake. Many Spanish soldiers were so burdened with gold that they were swept from the causeway leading to the mainland and drowned.

Eventually Cortes recaptured the city and sent most of its gold to Spain. In 1528 he himself went to receive the thanks of the Spanish Emperor Charles V. The capture of Montezuma's treasure, greater than any previously found, and the story of his fabulous empire spread throughout Spain and the rest of Europe. Soon swarms of adventurers were pouring into Mexico. Cortes had laid the foundation of the Spanish empire in America, and Mexico quickly became its most valued region. Spain would reap a golden harvest from its Mexican

mines, and bullion from the New World would maintain its armies and support its economy.

The known sources of gold, silver, and pearls in Central America and Mexico concentrated Spanish attention upon the Caribbean and adjacent regions. But the Spaniards did not totally neglect the rest of America. In 1513 Juan Ponce de León, who had made a fortune in gold and slaves as governor of Puerto Rico, explored the mainland of Florida. He is best remembered be-

Cortes (in left panel, under the "18") enters Mexico City, where Emperor Montezuma (right panel, in high crown) welcomes him in full panoply. At that time the Aztecs still believed that Cortes was Quetzalcoatl, the white god for whose return legend had prepared them. However, Spanish greed disillusioned them and led to war. The paintings are entirely imaginative, for they were done by a Spanish artist 179 years after the event.

sippi. Crossing the Mississippi River, his group went as far west as western Arkansas before doubling back to the Mississippi. At this point de Soto died and was buried by his men in the river to keep the Indians from learning that their leader was dead. Luis de Moscoso took command of the expedition, which then wandered into Texas, perhaps as far as the Trinity River, returned to the Mississippi, made its way to the river's mouth, and thence sailed around the coast to Vera Cruz, which it reached in 1543.

De Soto's expedition was almost incredible in distance covered and hardships endured, but an even more astonishing exploration was made in 1540–42 under the leadership of Francisco Vásquez de Coronado, who went in search of the legendary Seven Cities of Cibola and of an elusive Indian city called Quivira. This expedition pushed north from Mexico and into what is now Arizona, New Mexico, Texas, Oklahoma, and western Kansas. One of Coronado's lieutenants discovered the Grand Canyon, and the expedition made contacts with the Zuñi, Pueblo, and Plains Indians. Indeed, it was a Plains Indian, given to spinning tall tales about the rich city of Quivira, who led the Spaniards over long, dusty trails until they reached a point near modern Wichita, Kansas, to find only villages of seminomadic Indians. The Seven Cities of Cibola, reported to be laden with gold, turned out to be Indian pueblos near the present city of Santa Fe, New Mexico. Coronado returned to Mexico a disappointed and ruined man. But although he had found no gold, he had shown the extent of the vast land, for expeditions subsidiary to the main one had explored to the west as far as Southern California and gained information about a region that would ultimately be settled by the Spaniards.

The intoxication of treasure hunting, which had become a Spanish mania soon after Columbus reported gold and pearls on the islands that he had discovered, profoundly affected Spanish activities in the New World. The visible evidence of the wealth of Mexico

cause of the story of his search for a fountain of youth, but he had other, more realistic, aims. In 1521 he attempted to settle a colony in Florida, but hostile Indians forced the expedition to retreat to Cuba, where Ponce de Léon died.

Somewhat later, in 1539–42, Hernando de Soto, who had been in Peru with Pizarro, led an exploring expedition across Florida and into the future states of Alabama, Georgia, the Carolinas, Tennessee, and Missis-

*Coronado –
See
"American
History
Illustrated
February, 1976
pg. 4*

19

*Spanish mistreatment of Indians was notorious, and this grisly
picture of De Soto's cruelties in Florida had real basis in fact.*

that Cortes contributed to Spain stirred adventurers
into a fever of eagerness to sail to the New World.
Every swordsman from Andalusia to Estremadura believed that he could make his fortune in the New
World. Such news could not be confined to Spain, and
soon other countries were eying Spain's monopoly with
envy and planning ways to circumvent the Line of Demarcation set by Pope Alexander VI, dividing the heathen world between Spain and Portugal. Ultimately
these two countries would have to recognize, however
grudgingly, the rights of other countries. A king of
France would demand to see the will of Father Adam,
that he might know how Adam had disposed of the
patrimony of his children. And others, less concerned
with Father Adam or the pope, would simply go out
and claim a part of the New World.

Although the news of Columbus's first voyage may at
first have had small repercussions in northern Europe,
the most knowledgeable seafaring people were aware of
its implication. During the fifteenth and sixteenth centuries, trained pilots, geographers, and navigators of
various nationalities, but particularly technicians from
Italy and Portugal, followed the news of maritime
events. These professional men were constantly hatch-
ing new schemes of exploration and were eager to enter
the service of whichever monarch would support them.
Thus it was that John Cabot of Genoa, a merchant
naturalized in Venice, went to Bristol and in 1496 offered his services to Henry VII of England. Later his
son Sebastian served England and then Spain, where
he was pilot major for many years before finally returning to England.

It is significant that John Cabot went to Bristol, for
Bristol at this time had the most daring and enterprising
of English mariners. For many years they had been
sailing around Ireland to Iceland for fish, and they had
penetrated the misty seas of the northwest, perhaps as
far as the fishing banks off Newfoundland. Since they

were a closemouthed race of men, intent upon keeping trade secrets to themselves, no one can be sure how far the men of Bristol sailed. Some scholars believe that they may have reached the shores of Newfoundland and the mainland of North America before Columbus's first voyage. Other enterprising fishermen from Brittany and the Bay of Biscay may also have discovered the Newfoundland banks and adjacent regions. Certainly they were active in the decade after 1492, and by the early years of the sixteenth century, Portuguese, English, French, and Spanish fishermen were beginning to swarm to Newfoundland, which became a neutral ground for fishermen of all countries.

Stories of two mysterious islands to the west of Ireland had long circulated among maritime folk of northern Europe. The nearest of these mythical islands, Antilia, was the Island of the Seven Cities that figured in medieval legend. The other, the island of Brasil, lay farther to the west, and it was this island that the discoverers of Newfoundland thought they had found.

Medieval legends also told of voyages to islands in the West by St. Brendan, an Irish priest, by Welsh Prince Madog, and others. The only voyages that are historically verifiable, however, were those made by Irish monks to Iceland, and those by the Norsemen, who superseded the Irish on Iceland and continued on to Greenland, where they settled colonies. Norse sagas tell of Vikings going to the mainland of America. That Norsemen made contact with North America at intervals after the occupation of Iceland and Greenland in the tenth century is fairly well proved, but they made little use of their discovery except to procure timber.

The stories of lands in the Western Sea prompted activity by Bristol explorers around 1480 and possibly before. John Day, an English merchant trading in Spain, wrote to someone, possibly Columbus, in 1497–98, reporting that men from Bristol had found the island of Brasil sometime before Cabot's first voyage. This letter, found in the archives at Simancas, Spain, in 1956, reinforces the belief that Bristol men had made discoveries in the northwest probably as early as 1480, when other records show that voyages of discovery were going out of Bristol.

Since the Bristol men were concerned with fisheries and not with trying to find the Spice Islands and a short route to Asia, only fishermen were very much interested in a discovery of "Brasil" or Newfoundland. It took John Cabot, with his dream of finding a quick north-

westerly passage to China, to arouse King Henry VII. Precisely when Cabot reached Bristol has not been determined, but John Day's letter indicates that Cabot made a voyage of reconnaissance that came to nought in 1496, soon after he received a patent from the king. This patent, granted "to our well-beloved John Cabot, citizen of Venice, and to Lewis, Sebastian and Sancio, sons of the said John," authorized them "to sail to all parts, regions and coasts of the eastern, western and northern sea, under our banners, flags and ensigns, with five ships or vessels of whatsoever burden . . . to find, discover and investigate whatsoever islands, countries, regions or provinces of heathens and infidels, in whatsoever part of the world placed, which before this time were unknown to all Christians."

To Cabot and his sons and their heirs forever, the king gave the right to seize and govern such lands of the heathen as they could conquer, but he required them to acknowledge themselves vassals of the king of England and to pay over to the king one fifth of the profits from each voyage. Cabot thought that Asia lay before him in the northwest, and he envisioned a sequence of profit-

The Vikings were the first of several peoples who braved northern seas to search for western lands. These three, ignoring a huge fish, appear in a 12th-century painting.

able voyages that would follow the opening of the route.

We know little about the 1496 voyage except that it failed. Of the second voyage, in 1497, a little more is known. Cabot sailed in May from Bristol in a small bark, the *Matthew*, with eighteen men according to one account, twenty according to another. At least two were Bristol merchants who may have sailed in northern waters before. Since this was to be a voyage of reconnaissance rather than of trade, a tight little craft and a small crew of experienced seamen sufficed. After clearing Ireland, Cabot first sailed north, then turned westward, and on June 24 made a landfall, naming the spot Prima Tierra Vista. The precise location of this first-seen land remains a mystery, but historians lean to the theory that it may have been somewhere on the coast of Maine, or if not there, on Nova Scotia. Cabot and his

men went ashore and claimed the land for King Henry VII of England, ceremoniously planting a cross and the banners of England, the pope, and St. Mark, the patron saint of Venice. Thus did Cabot pay homage to God, his royal patron, the head of the church, and his adopted city. Vague as the precise geographical details are, this voyage was of paramount importance to England, for it was upon Cabot's formal taking possession of the land that England later based her claim, by right of discovery, to North America.

Cabot made a phenomenally rapid fifteen-day passage from the easternmost cape of the mainland to Bristol and arrived about August 6. Few Atlantic crossings for the next century exceeded this one in speed, and it gave renewed hope of a short route to the East.

The success of Cabot's reconnoitering voyage caused

Olaus Magnus put monsters in his 1539 map of the northern seas not as decorations but to instruct mariners. Magnus believed the weird creatures really existed and based his pictures on a mixture of observation, hearsay, and imagination. On the map Norway is at the right, the Faeroe Islands in the center.

a stir in mercantile circles, and he himself cut a great figure, so that he "esteems himself at least a prince," according to a letter from the Milanese ambassador in London, Raimondo de Raimondi de Soncino, to Lodovico il Moro, Duke of Milan, dated December 18, 1497. "Perhaps . . . your Excellency, it may not weary you," Soncino wrote, "to hear how his Majesty here has gained a part of Asia, without a stroke of the sword. There is in this Kingdom a man of the people, Messer Zoane Caboto [John Cabot] by name, of kindly wit and a most expert mariner. Having observed that the sovereigns first of Portugal and then of Spain had occupied unknown islands, he decided to make a similar acquisition for his Majesty."

Another voyage to exploit the discovery that Cabot had made was already being planned, Soncino reported.

"Before very long they say that his Majesty will equip some ships, and in addition he will give them all the malefactors, and they will go to that country and form a colony. By means of this they hope to make London a more important mart for spices than Alexandria. The leading men in this enterprise are from Bristol, and great seamen, and now they know where to go, say that the voyage will not take more than a fortnight, if they have good fortune after leaving Ireland."

Already in 1497 the excitement of discovery had taken possession of men in Bristol and London, as it had in Spain and Portugal. Soon no port in western Europe would lack eager mariners ready to adventure into the Western Sea.

The voyage that Cabot was planning began probably in May, 1498, when a fleet of four or five ships, pro-

visioned for a year and containing articles of trade, sailed from Bristol. Somewhere in the vast ocean Cabot and his ships were lost. What happened to the vessels, no man knows. Some slight evidence points to English ships as far south as the Caribbean in 1498, but records of Cabot's last voyage are lacking. His voyage of 1497, however, had done enough to give England a claim to a portion of the New World that she would one day assert. But that time was still far distant.

But England had not heard the last of the Cabots. John Cabot's son Sebastian made a voyage in 1508–9, about which little is known. He was seeking the elusive Northwest Passage that for years to come would be a magnet for many seamen. He may have reached Hudson Bay, but the voyage was a failure. In 1512, while serving in Spain with Lord Dorset, who was leading an army allied with that of King Ferdinand, Sebastian obtained permission to enter the service of Spain, and four years later he became pilot major of Spain. After a long career, part of which he spent exploring the South Atlantic, he returned to England in 1548 and in 1553 was one of the organizers of a joint stock company designed to find a northeast passage to India and Cathay. In that year Cabot planned the voyage of Stephen Borough (or Burrough) that rounded the North Cape and made contact with Russia. Cabot became governor of the company formed by Borough, which developed trade with Russia and for that reason came to be known as the Muscovy Company.

With the interest in explorations demonstrated by Henry VII, it is surprising that England waited nearly a century before making any effective attempt at colonization. Although Henry had promised John Cabot some convicts to serve as colonists, there is no evidence that any attempt at settlement was made. Bristol fishermen, it is true, increased their activities on the Newfoundland banks, but that was common ground for all Europeans. English colonization was subordinated to other political events in Europe.

Because England's break with Spain late in the reign of Queen Elizabeth was so dramatic, we are inclined to think of England and Spain as traditional enemies during the centuries of expansion overseas. Actually, for long periods in the sixteenth century, England and Spain were friends, if not allies. Henry VII had dared to encroach on what Spain claimed as her rights in the Western Sea only because, at the time, Spain was trying to induce England to assist in a war against France.

Henry VIII was not prepared to compete with Spain for distant goals in America. He was busy building up a navy for protection nearer at hand, and only occasionally would an enterprising merchant vessel venture into Spanish waters overseas. The brief Protestant reign of Edward VI was followed by that of Mary, who married Prince Philip, later Philip II of Spain. She made her policy subservient to that of Catholic Spain and of course did not wish to encroach on Spanish rights on the other side of the Atlantic. If Mary and Philip had had an heir, England might never have undertaken to colonize any portion of North America, and Latin America might have extended to French Canada.

Soon after Queen Elizabeth's accession in 1558, she began playing Spain against France. Faced with many domestic problems and with critical diplomacy in Europe, she could not at first afford to divert energy to overseas expansion. But her merchant marine was growing, and her seamen were becoming more enterprising. The day was not far distant when they would begin to penetrate Spanish waters on the western side of the Atlantic Ocean.

In the meantime, France had not been unmindful of opportunities overseas. Since France and Spain were frequently at war during the sixteenth century, France had no reason to be squeamish about violating Spanish rights in America. Seamen from Normandy and Brittany were already braving the North Atlantic to exploit the Newfoundland fisheries; early in the sixteenth century, some had ventured as far as the mainland.

A Florentine navigator, Giovanni da Verrazano, took service with Francis I in 1524 and made an extensive reconnaissance of the Atlantic seaboard from North Carolina to Maine. He was probably the first European to sail into New York Harbor. Verrazano continued to make voyages for the French, but in 1526–27, while exploring the West Indies, he was killed—and probably eaten—by Carib Indians. Verrazano's investigation of the North Atlantic coast gave a further impetus to French exploration of that region.

The ancient walled city of St-Malo in Brittany had become a nest of corsairs, and its seamen were among the most daring in France. In 1534 one of their leaders, Jacques Cartier, led an expedition to the shores of Newfoundland and continued on through the Strait of Belle Isle into the Gulf of St. Lawrence. Landing on the Gaspé Peninsula, Cartier claimed the land for France. After touching at Anticosti Island, he sailed back to

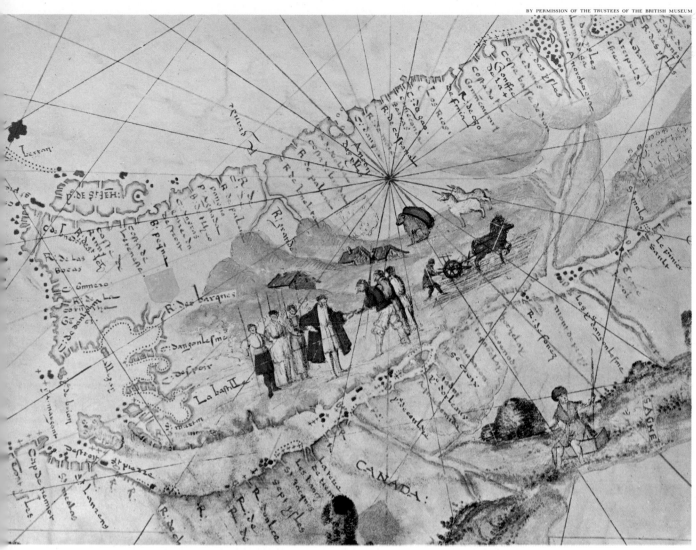

Jacques Cartier's discoveries in Canada are shown in a 1544
map that has south at the top. The map maker has also
pictured Cartier and French settlers on the bank of the St. Lawrence.

France and reported that he had discovered a fertile and fruitful land, suitable for colonists, and that he had also found an estuary, which he believed might open upon a sea route to Cathay. With this cheering news, the king authorized—and paid for—a second expedition of three ships that sailed in May, 1535.

This time Cartier sailed up the St. Lawrence as far as the Lachine Rapids and the site of Montreal. To his disappointment, he found that he was exploring a river that continually narrowed and not an estuary that led to the China Sea. A long and miserable winter spent near the present site of Quebec nearly ended the expedition, for many died of scurvy until friendly Indians taught them to drink a tea made from spruce needles. When warm weather at last returned, Cartier kidnapped a group of Indians and sailed for St-Malo, which he reached in July, 1536.

In 1541 Cartier led a third expedition to Canada, with colonization as its purpose. He sailed in May with five ships and landed near Quebec, where the settlers built their camp, planted turnips, searched for gold and diamonds, and prepared for the winter, which nearly proved disastrous. Cartier was disappointed and disgusted because Sieur de Roberval, a nobleman from

25

Picardy who had been appointed viceroy and was supposed to follow with additional men and supplies, had not appeared. Consequently, when spring came, he embarked his colonists and set sail for France. Calling at St. John's Harbor, Newfoundland, on June 8, he encountered Roberval with his ships, bound for the Canadian colony. Cartier, who had no intention of turning back, slipped away in the night and left Roberval to find his way to the deserted site where the colonists had wintered. Without experience or proper supplies for establishing a colony in the wilderness, Roberval's people suffered like the previous settlers, and about one third of them died during their winter in Canada. Finally, in 1543, the king ordered ships to bring back the miserable survivors. Thus ended the earliest French efforts to claim Canada for France.

A few years later, French Huguenots made an effort to gain a foothold in America, this time in Florida. Under the leadership of Jean Ribaut, a Huguenot sea captain from Dieppe, two shiploads of colonists sailed from Le Havre on February 18, 1562, and on May 1 they landed at the mouth of a river that they called the River of May, now the St. Johns. The country pleased them. The soil was rich, and magnificent trees grew in abundance. One tree covered with caterpillars led an observer to comment that the silkworms were bigger and more promising than those of France and augured the development of a silk industry. A stone inscribed with the royal arms was set up to claim the land for the king of France. Ribaut pushed farther north and finally made a settlement on what is now Parris Island, South Carolina. He called the harbor Port Royal and built a stockade named Charlesfort in honor of the new king, Charles IX. Leaving a garrison of thirty men, Ribaut sailed for his home port. After a few months of bickering and trouble, the garrison fashioned a makeshift craft and embarked for France. They endured terrible sufferings from thirst and hunger that is said to have ended in

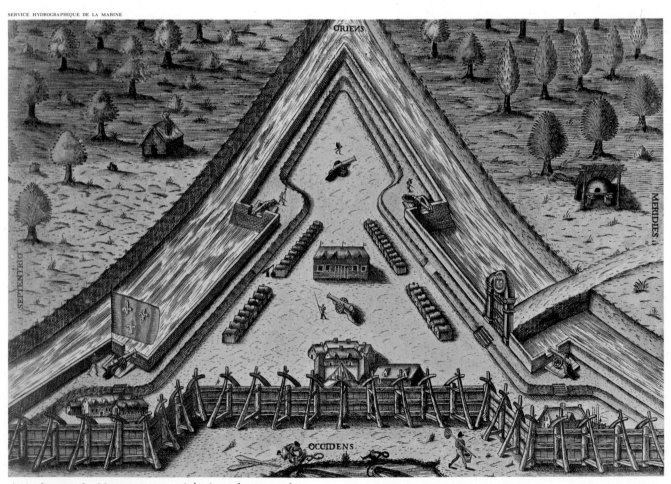

Artist Jacques Le Moyne was one of the few who escaped the Spanish massacre of Huguenots at Fort Caroline in Florida. An engraving from his painting of the ill-fated fort shows a triangular structure built of sod and timbers.

cannibalism before they were at last found by an English craft and carried prisoners to England.

French Huguenots were determined to plant a colony in Florida where their distressed religionists could find a refuge. Two years after Ribaut's expedition to Port Royal, René de Laudonnière, a nobleman from Poitou who had been with Ribaut, led a second group of Huguenot settlers to Florida. They landed on the south bank of the St. Johns River and established a settlement called Fort Caroline. Like the previous French colonial ventures, Laudonnière's settlement was soon on the verge of starvation, and by 1565 the hungry and quarrelsome settlers were planning to build a vessel in which to escape.

At this point one of the first of the English explorers on this coast, John Hawkins, sailed into the St. Johns River with a flotilla of four vessels. One of these he sold to Laudonnière, whose men were clamoring to return to France. Before they could sail, Jean Ribaut appeared on the St. Johns with seven ships and reinforcements. In the meantime, Pedro Menéndez de Avilés, named *adelantado* (governor) of Florida by Philip II, was ordered to sail for that land and drive out the Huguenots. He arrived off the mouth of a small river he named the St. Augustine in late August, 1565, and in early September he began fortifying a Spanish settlement there. After failing to force Ribaut to a fight, he marched overland, destroyed Fort Caroline, and slaughtered every Frenchman he captured. Over some, hanged from trees, he placed the inscription: "I do this, not as to Frenchmen, but as to Lutherans."

Ribaut, who had sailed with his fleet to attack the Spaniards at St. Augustine, met disaster. A September hurricane wrecked his ships, and he and his men who managed to get ashore were found by the Spaniards and slain. Out of the carnage, Laudonnière and Jacques Le Moyne, an artist who painted pictures of Florida life, managed to escape and ultimately reached France.

Menéndez, an able and ruthless soldier of Spain, successfully founded a colony at St. Augustine. He was also instrumental in sending an expedition to establish an outpost at St. Helena in South Carolina and a short-lived settlement on Chesapeake Bay. The French had been repulsed and Spanish influence extended; but France had served notice that she would claim a portion of the New World.

The appearance of John Hawkins on the coast of Florida in 1565 was symbolic of the growing activity of English seamen in western waters. For this development, England had the Hawkins family to thank, for they had been pioneers in attempts to reap profits from America. Old William Hawkins, a seaman and merchant of Plymouth, was said to have been much beloved of Henry VIII because of his knowledge of "sea causes." About 1530 he made a voyage to Guinea, on the West African coast, where he traded for ivory and slaves. The latter he took to Brazil and sold, thus beginning a traffic that would bring enormous profits in later times. He made two other voyages to Brazil with slaves and set an example for his son John, who further developed the slave trade with America.

Before 1560 John Hawkins engaged in the Spanish trade and made voyages to the Canary Islands, where he learned of the demand for Negro slaves in the Spanish possessions. In 1562 he organized an expedition of three ships that loaded slaves in Senegal and continued to Hispaniola, where he sold the slaves and took on a cargo of hides, sugar, gold, and pearls. Taking Spanish friendship for granted, he loaded an additional hulk with hides and sugar and shipped it to Spain. But Hawkins was a foreigner and an unlicensed trader in Spanish dominions overseas. The Spanish government was not willing to ignore Hawkins's activities and confiscated the ship. Even so, the voyage made such a profit from the sale of slaves that, with the support of Robert Dudley (later the Earl of Leicester) and the Earl of Pembroke, among others, he was able to organize a second expedition in 1564. He also obtained the loan of a royal ship, the *Jesus of Lübeck*. With four ships, Hawkins repeated his collection of slaves in Africa and this time sold them on the Venezuelan coast. After disposing of his slaves, he continued up the coast of Florida until he made contact with Laudonnière at Fort Caroline. Hawkins recognized the value of Florida as a land for raising cattle and producing other commodities.

Although this voyage showed a handsome profit and Hawkins was granted a coat of arms bearing the device of a "demi-Moor proper in chains," the queen and the Privy Council had to disavow responsibility for him after the Spanish ambassador made a violent protest. The council was even moved to prohibit him from making another voyage that he was planning. By 1567, however, Hawkins had got around the council's prohibition and was preparing another slaving and trading expedition. This time he had two royal ships, the *Jesus of Lübeck* and the *Minion*, and four other vessels. One of these was the *Judith*, commanded later in the voyage by Francis Drake, Hawkins's distant kinsman. While collecting slaves at Sierra Leone, the expedition plundered Portuguese vessels and obtained more than seventy thousand gold pieces. Hawkins sold most of his slaves in the West Indies and at Cartagena. Soon after, his fleet took refuge from a storm in the harbor of San Juan de Ulúa (modern Veracruz), port of entry to Mexico.

It was the bad luck of the English that a convoy of thirteen great ships of Spain arrived at this moment bearing the new viceroy of Mexico. Hawkins could have used his guns to deny entrance to the harbor, but he would have been bottled up. Therefore, on obtaining a promise of peace from the Spaniards, he permitted the convoy to sail in and anchor. On September 23, 1568, despite the truce, the Spaniards launched an attack on the outnumbered English. Only two ships escaped, the *Minion*, crowded with some two hundred men, and Drake's *Judith*, which sailed away without waiting to give aid to the *Minion*.

Lacking both food and space for so many men, Hawkins was forced to put approximately half of the company ashore on a desolate beach some two hundred miles north of Veracruz. Some marched into the wilderness and died at the hands of Indians or from starvation. Others found a Spanish settlement, surrendered, and were taken as prisoners to Mexico City, where they ultimately came before the dreaded Inquisition.

Three men claimed to have made their way to Nova Scotia, where a French fishing vessel picked them up. Their narrative, printed by Richard Hakluyt in the first edition of his *Principall Navigations* (1589), was omitted in later editions because of "certain incredibilities." Hawkins got back to England in the *Minion* on January 25, 1569. Many of his men, half-starved, had died on the terrible voyage home. Drake in the *Judith* had arrived three days before him.

The disaster at San Juan de Ulúa marked a turning point in English-Spanish relations, which hitherto had been relatively peaceful. Although English corsairs before this had occasionally plundered Spanish ships, as they had Portuguese craft, England had tacitly recognized Spain's rights in America and had made little effort to circumvent them. But after San Juan, English seamen were bitter against Spain. Furthermore, several score English prisoners were being held by Mexican authorities. Hawkins was determined to release them if he could. Although the queen could take no overt ac-

tion, she too was displeased. From this time onward, English corsairs multiplied, and though the queen might outwardly condemn their depredations, she gave them secret encouragement and shared in the spoil.

The experience that Drake gained at San Juan made him, like Hawkins, an inveterate enemy of Spain. Revenge gilded with Spanish gold was the purpose of a voyage that he made in 1572 to Panama and the adjacent region. For months, during the late summer, fall, and winter, Drake terrorized the coast of the Spanish Main. He pillaged towns and captured and destroyed shipping. In February, 1573, he marched across the Isthmus of Darien and got a view of the Pacific, which induced him to pray God that he might sail an English ship in that sea. When he got back to England in August, 1573, he had burned Puerto Bello on the Panama coast, destroyed many a Spanish ship, made his name a terror throughout the West Indies and Central America, and got rich in the bargain. Few voyages against the Spaniards could have been more satisfying.

But Drake had dreams of greater things, and in this the queen encouraged him. He confided in her a plan to sail around the tip of South America, following in Magellan's track, and to attack the Spanish possessions in the rear. He had observed enough to know that Spain was reaping a harvest of gold and silver on the west coast of South America, and that her towns were unprotected. The queen could not openly connive in this scheme, nor did she dare let even her most trusted minister, Lord Burghley, know about Drake's plan, for Burghley was intent upon keeping peace with Spain.

But Drake's description of the treasure waiting to be brought home in English ships was too vivid to resist. With its real purpose kept secret, the expedition was organized. Drake went in a ship of his own, the 120-ton *Pelican*; Captain John Winter commanded the *Elizabeth* of fifty tons; and there were three smaller vessels. On December 13, 1577, the squadron sailed from Plymouth. Only Drake and the queen knew its destination. Spanish spies had reported its sailing, but they thought that Drake was again heading for the Spanish Main. His men had been given to believe that they were going on a Mediterranean expedition, but after they left the Cape Verde Islands, they learned that the squadron was bound for the River Plate. There they captured two Portuguese vessels, from one of which they took a pilot, Nuño da Silva.

On the south coast of what is now Argentina, at Port

Thomas Cavendish, Francis Drake, and John Hawkins were probably the three greatest English sailors of their time. Drake and Cavendish both circumnavigated the earth.

St. Julian, Drake's squadron stopped for two months, and there Drake executed, after dining with him in friendly fashion, Thomas Doughty, a gentleman whom he charged with stirring up dissension and mutiny. Two small vessels no longer seaworthy were broken up, and the *Pelican*, the *Elizabeth*, and the *Marigold* sailed for the Strait of Magellan. In honor of Sir Christopher Hatton, a friend and investor in the voyage, Drake changed the name of the *Pelican* to the *Golden Hind*, that being the device on Hatton's escutcheon.

After making a fast passage of only sixteen days through the strait and entering the Pacific on September 6, 1578, Drake ran into prolonged violent weather. He lost the *Marigold* with all hands; later the *Elizabeth* turned back and eventually made her way to England. At long last, at the beginning of November, the *Golden Hind* found herself in smooth seas and was able to turn north and head for the golden treasure that Drake had promised his men.

By careful stages Drake made his way up the coast, searching for Spanish vessels as he went, plundering and taking what he wanted or needed but committing no cruelties upon the inhabitants. At Callao, in Peru, where he arrived on February 13, 1579, he got wind of a treasure ship, the *Cacafuego*, bound for Panama, which he overtook and captured. It was a rich prize, loaded with gold, silver, jewels, and precious stones to the value of 362,000 pesos. A few weeks later, off Acapulco, he captured another Spanish ship with its owner, a certain Don Francisco de Xarate, who, after being freed, made a report to the viceroy.

Drake, Xarate asserted, lived in great state, his food served with silver plate bearing his crest, his cabin sweetened with perfumes given him by the queen, and his meal hours enlivened by the music of violins. Nine or ten gentlemen who made up a sort of council dined with him and showed him great respect. The sailors and men-at-arms to the number of a hundred took pride in their weapons and kept them polished and clean. In short, Xarate gave an almost idyllic—and wildly exaggerated—picture of life aboard Drake's ship and described Drake as one of the greatest seamen alive.

With his vessel so heavily loaded with treasure that he dared take on no more, Drake sailed north and made a reconnaissance of the California coast. At a bay, probably just north of San Francisco, he set up a brass plate claiming the land for Queen Elizabeth and naming it New Albion.

Presumably Drake had hoped to find a passage in the north back to the Atlantic, but having failed in this, he set his course across the Pacific. During the long and dangerous voyage, he demonstrated exceptional skill as a commander and brought his ship safely home by way of the Cape of Good Hope. In the East Indies, he managed to find space for a quantity of highly prized cloves that added to the value of his cargo.

At last, on September 26, 1580, the *Golden Hind* dropped anchor at her home port of Plymouth. Drake sent his trumpeter to London to report to the queen the ship's safe arrival after a prosperous voyage, and the news quickly spread. The Spanish ambassador, furious at Drake's depredations, made vigorous complaints to the Crown, and Queen Elizabeth, with a show of justice, promised an investigation. She ordered Drake to report to her in person, which he did, and she sent a messenger to Plymouth to list the treasure and see that it was conveyed to the Tower of London for safekeeping. But Drake was first allowed to remove ten thousand pounds' worth for his own purposes.

The crew of the *Golden Hind* were questioned and testified that no Spaniard had been killed and none seriously injured in the capture of ships and the plundering of towns. As to the amount of treasure taken, everyone, including the royal messenger sent to list it,

29

CIVITAS S Dominici sita
in Hispaniola Indica Angliæ mag-
nitudine fere æqualis, ipsa urbis elegan-
ter ab Hispanis extructa, et omnibus
circumuicinis insulis iura dat.

After being knighted for his piracies against Spain, Drake
returned to his raiding with new vigor. A contemporary picture
shows his raid on Santo Domingo in 1585; Drake's fleet lies
at anchor while his army approaches the city walls from the left.

was vague. It was a huge amount, that much was certain, and the investors in the voyage stood to make a handsome profit. But first the queen had to answer the charges of the Spanish ambassador.

Queen Elizabeth probably guessed that Philip II was not ready for open war with England. He was not enthusiastic about the papal attacks on Elizabeth, designed to remove her from her throne, for the likeliest heir was Mary, Queen of Scots, widow of a French king and closely allied with France. An alliance of France and England under Mary was not to Philip's liking, and he was willing to endure freebooting attacks like Drake's rather than start a war that would be costly and unsatisfactory in its conclusion. So Philip let his ambassador bluster, while he sat in the Escorial thinking of some other plan to thwart Elizabeth the Heretic.

For her part, Elizabeth told the Spanish ambassador that she had already endured much from Spain. Spanish and Italian troops had stirred up a rebellion in Ireland, and Spanish interference in English affairs had cost her more than all the treasure that Drake had taken in America. By refusing to allow legitimate trade with the colonists in the New World, Spain and Portugal had brought upon themselves attacks by resentful seamen. Furthermore, the queen stoutly refuted Spanish and Portuguese claims to the whole of the New World by reason of any papal decree, and she asserted English rights to territory not already occupied by any Christian prince. Clearly she did not intend to punish Drake for his exploits, and she was not likely to turn over to Spain such a quantity of treasure as she now had safely housed in the Tower.

As if to underscore her reply to Spain, Queen Elizabeth ordered Drake to bring his ship around to the Thames, and there on the deck of the *Golden Hind* at Deptford on April 4, 1581, she dubbed him knight. No clearer evidence of her approval of Drake's attacks on the fringes of the Spanish empire could be given. From this time forward, England knew that the wealth of the New World was no longer exclusively Spain's. Her seamen had brought back stories of the riches that Spain had found across the Atlantic, and now Drake had returned with a ship loaded with treasure taken from Spanish ships and towns, tangible evidence of the prizes that the new land offered to daring men. In this way Drake's expedition stimulated a movement, already being promoted by men like Richard Hakluyt and Walter Raleigh, to colonize a portion of America.

31

England Stakes a Claim

Although the English were slow to challenge Spain's claims to the New World, a few farsighted Englishmen argued, as early as the 1560's, that England must seize a portion of America before it was too late. Ironically, their position was significantly advanced through the efforts of Jean Ribaut, the Huguenot sea captain from Dieppe. When Ribaut came home in 1562 after establishing a French colony in Florida, he found the civil war between Catholics and Protestants raging and fled to England. There in 1563 he published a treatise on Florida that stimulated interest in America and caught the attention of Queen Elizabeth, who was induced to look favorably upon a joint Anglo-Huguenot effort to succor the colony at Fort Caroline. To aid the colony, she lent one ship to a fleet of six under the command of Thomas Stukeley. Unhappily, Stukeley was a rogue and immediately turned pirate. His flotilla was used to prey on shipping in the Channel and elsewhere with little thought of colonizing, and the whole project became an embarrassment to the queen.

Although the Stukeley expedition was a fiasco, the fact that it could be organized indicates the growing English interest in colonial enterprises. Indeed, when John Hawkins sailed up the coast of Florida in 1565, he may have had some notion of planting a colony. Certainly Laudonnière, who was already there, feared that the English might prove competitors, and as badly as he needed help, he was unwilling for Hawkins to linger too long on that coast.

John Sparke, who accompanied Hawkins on this voyage, wrote an account that Richard Hakluyt published in his *Principall Navigations* (1589). In it Sparke described the fertility of Florida, its fruits and products, and its promise as a place for raising cattle. (Hawkins had discovered in the West Indies that trade in cattle hides could be extremely profitable.) Sparke was convinced that Florida was destined to be a great cattle country, but because individual investors in the New World were concerned only with immediate profits, he thought colonization of Florida was "more requisit for a prince, who is of power able to go thorow with the same, rather then for any subject." But Queen Elizabeth was not ready to go into the cattle business in Florida, and

Queen Elizabeth was fifty-nine years old when this portrait was painted in 1592. Although a supporter of colonization, she would not see a successful colony before her death in 1603.

Sparke's hint was ignored, although it had some merit.

Nevertheless, word was getting around in mercantile and shipping circles in England that profits were to be made in the New World, and that the time was ripe for England to assert its rights to land overseas by actually taking over some area not yet occupied.

The pioneer in English colonial ventures was Sir Humphrey Gilbert, a Devonshire man intimately associated with the merchants and seamen of the West Country, and a half brother of Sir Walter Raleigh. If Gilbert's actual success was negligible, his arguments and his propaganda were important in crystallizing opinion in the latter part of the sixteenth century, and his influence upon Raleigh helped to shape the views of that incipient imperialist.

About 1566, Gilbert wrote out his views of the advantages of seeking a northwest passage to China. His treatise was published ten years later as *A Discourse of a discoverie for a new passage to Cataia* (1576). Although his main purpose was to advocate the advantages of a short trade route to the East, which Gilbert maintained could be found in the northern waters of America, he took occasion to emphasize the advantages of founding colonies in the new land along the passage to China. Not only would trading posts with the Indians be profitable, but colonies in North America would provide opportunities for "such needie people of our Countrie, which now trouble the common welth, and through want here at home, are inforced to commit outragious offenses, whereby they are dayly consumed with the Gallowes." The notion that American colonies would be useful as an outlet for the surplus population would increase with the years, and the idea of ridding England of convicts by shipping them overseas would continue to attract the favorable attention of authorities at home. Long before Gilbert, Henry VII had promised John Cabot some "malefactors" if he needed settlers for the lands that he had discovered.

Before Gilbert could take any further steps to promote the search for a northwest passage to China, he, along with Walter Raleigh, Sir Richard Grenville, and other West Countrymen, became involved in efforts to pacify the rebellious Irish and to establish English colonies and "plantations" in Ireland. That experience helped him to develop ideas about American colonization. Sir Henry Sidney, Lord Deputy of Ireland, wrote to Lord Burghley that it would be costly for the government to foster a settlement in Ulster but that private

Sir Humphrey Gilbert

English soldiers return to camp after a fight with the "wild Irish." Attempts to colonize Ireland had only partial success, but they encouraged promoters like Gilbert and Grenville to try the same thing in America.

Sir Richard Grenville

speculators might be induced to undertake it. They would have to come well stocked and prepared, he warned, and "they must be so furnished with mony, apparell, victualle, and meanes to tyll the grounde, and seede for the same, as if they should imagine to finde nothinge here but earthe, And in dede Littell els shall they finde savinge only fleshe, and some beastes for careing of the grounde."

The proposals and efforts to establish English colonies in Ireland in the late 1560's and early 1570's kept alive the idea of colonies overseas and set Englishmen to thinking about similar undertakings in America. The wild Indians would be no greater hazard, some Englishmen thought, than the wild Irish, and the prospects for wealth across the Atlantic were greater. Colonial efforts in Ireland or America would not directly involve the government but would be made by private enterprise.

Gilbert left Ireland early in 1570, and although he was engaged in a variety of activities for the next few years, he retained an interest in exploration and overseas expansion. He was a shareholder in the Cathay Company, organized by Michael Lok, a London merchant, and Martin Frobisher, a sea captain who was convinced of the existence of a northwest passage to China. In his first voyage in 1576, Frobisher had discovered a gulf that he thought might be the entrance to a passage to the Pacific. Of more interest to some of his London promoters was a piece of rock that he brought home, for they mistakenly thought they found gold in it. A rumor spread that Frobisher had found a rich gold mine, and when the queen granted a patent to the Cathay Company, Lok and Frobisher had no trouble finding subscribers to the stock.

On a second voyage in 1577, Frobisher loaded his ship with ore that proved worthless, but before that fact was known, he had departed in May, 1578, on a third expedition. For a brief period, speculative fever swept London, and the stock of the Cathay Company rose spectacularly as investors dreamed of gold mines in North America, with colonies of workers to get out the ore. Then, when the bitter truth leaked out that Frobisher had brought back only worthless iron pyrites, "fool's gold," the Cathay Company went under. Frobisher returned from the third voyage with more worthless ore and news of the discovery of a strait later to be named after Henry Hudson.

While mercantile circles in London were still excited about the expeditions of the Cathay Company, Humphrey Gilbert applied to the queen and received a patent for a colonial venture in America. His charter gave him the right to settle, fortify, and govern any heathen land not already occupied by a Christian prince. It did not limit him to any specific region. Furthermore, his claim would extend for two hundred leagues—about six hundred miles—in every direction from the point of settlement. Such land as he should occupy would be ruled by him as a liege of the English sovereign, and such laws as he would impose would be consonant with English common law. The sovereign claimed one fifth of all the precious metals discovered. If Gilbert did not make a settlement within six years, the patent would lapse.

The first effort by Gilbert under this patent was made in the autumn of 1578, when he collected an imposing fleet of nearly a dozen vessels, one of which was commanded by Walter Raleigh. The expedition sailed in November for an unknown destination and returned in the spring of 1579 with a story of hardships, bad weather, and desertions of some of the vessels, and with nothing to show for the endeavor. The whole enterprise is shrouded in mystery. Some of the fleet apparently strayed off and turned pirate—buccaneering always seemed more enticing than the prospect of settling the wilderness. At any rate, in 1579, when Gilbert was planning a second expedition, the Privy Council required him to put up sureties for the behavior of his seamen.

But in Gilbert's opinion, settlements overseas were imperative if England expected to protect herself from the Spanish colossus. On November 6, 1577, before he had launched his first expedition, Gilbert had presented to the queen two discourses headed "How Hir Majestie May Annoy the King of Spayne." In one of them he offered to lead an expedition that would capture the foreign fishing fleet in Newfoundland and bring home the best ships loaded with fish, which could be sold in Holland. Gilbert suggested that this could be done under the cloak of a colonizing expedition, and that the queen could disavow responsibility by saying that it was the work of pirates. The second discourse recommended an attack on the Spanish West Indies. Again a colonizing expedition, ostensibly headed for the region of the St. Lawrence, could rendezvous in Bermuda and establish a base there, from which it could launch an attack on Hispaniola and Cuba. Clearly Gilbert planned to use colonization overseas as a means of weakening and destroying Spain's power and possessions in America and

hence her potential for attacking England at home.

In defense of his plans, he says in his first "Discourse": "I hold it as lawfull in Christen pollicie, to prevent a mischief betime[s]: as to revenge it to late, especiallie seing that god him selfe is a party in the common quarrells now a foote, and his ennemy['s] malitiouse disposition towardes your highnes, and his Church manifestlie seen, although by godes mercifull providence not yet throughly felt."

Eager as Gilbert was to get on with his overseas schemes, he had to be content for the time being with activities nearer home. In the summer of 1579, several of his ships tried to keep Spanish reinforcements from reaching the Irish rebels. When his sailors did not receive their pay, they seized his ships and turned pirate (Gilbert's ill luck in this respect was phenomenal). Eventually he recovered one small vessel, a frigate of eight tons called the *Squirrel*. The next spring Gilbert placed a Portuguese pilot, Simon Fernandez, in charge of the *Squirrel* and sent it on an exploring expedition to the North American coast. It made a landfall somewhere on the coast of New England and returned with a report on the Indians and other useful information.

The speed of the *Squirrel's* round trip and the data that it gathered encouraged Gilbert, but he was so hard pressed financially that he had to make assignments under his patent to other individuals, including Dr. John Dee, a geographer, scholar, and astrologer much interested in exploration. Dee wanted to pursue the Northwest Passage project, and he received from Gilbert the privilege of making discoveries and settlements above the fiftieth parallel of latitude, a privilege that Dee was unable to exercise immediately.

Though Gilbert was not able to send colonists to America at once, he hoped to license others to make settlements that he could eventually amalgamate under his governorship. They would in effect hold their land under him as tenants and pay quitrents to him, that is, rent in lieu of the services he could otherwise require of them. To this end he encouraged two Catholic leaders, Sir George Peckham and Sir Thomas Gerrard, to organize a project to establish a haven in America for loyal English Catholics who wished to worship undisturbed by restrictive laws. Sir Francis Walsingham, an ardent expansionist as well as a vigorous leader of the reformed faith, approved of this plan to rid the kingdom of troublesome Catholics and at the same time further the development of English colonies overseas.

*The mountain of Potosí in Bolivia, the richest silver
deposit ever found, sent a constant flow of wealth to
Spain, whose treasure ships were a favorite prey of
English buccaneers. An unknown artist, about 1584, has
shown mines, the processing plant, and pack llamas.*

By the summer of 1583, after much negotiation and
effort, Gilbert was able to organize a joint stock company known as the "Merchant Adventurers with Sir
Humphrey Gilbert," financed chiefly by the merchants
of Southampton, who received a promise that the colonists would use that port exclusively for their trade.
Peckham and Gerrard, who had been unable to organize
a separate venture, threw in their lot with Gilbert. On
June 11 the expedition of five vessels sailed from Southampton. Gilbert himself sailed in the 120-ton *Delight*,
captained by William Winter. Raleigh had contributed
a vessel of two hundred tons, the *Bark Raleigh*, al-

though he himself was not aboard and his vessel deserted two days out of port. Edward Hayes, chronicler
of the voyage, commanded the *Golden Hind*, named
after Drake's famous craft; and the other two vessels
were the *Swallow*, which later turned pirate, and Gilbert's little frigate, the *Squirrel*.

The fleet made for Newfoundland, where it arrived in
the early days of August. It was the height of the fishing
season, and thirty-six sail of fishing craft were in St.
John's Harbor when Gilbert arrived. There, on August
5, 1583, he went ashore, claimed the land in the name of
the queen of England, set up a post upon which he

37

nailed the royal arms in lead, announced himself as governor of the land for two hundred leagues around, and leased ground to the fishermen for drying their catch. He also promulgated certain laws: the religion of the territory was to be that of the Church of England (presumably the Catholics who had come along would quietly worship as they pleased); no one should dispute the rights of the English to claim the land under Gilbert's patent without risking the penalty of trial under the queen's law; and anyone who spoke to the dishonor of the queen should suffer the penalty of losing his ears and, if he were a shipowner, his ship.

Thus did Gilbert make manifest for the first time in the New World English law and justice. What the fishermen of various nationalities thought of these proceedings is not recorded, but they must have been puzzled and incredulous.

Gilbert now proposed to sail to the mainland, where he planned to establish his colony, but some of his men, including Captain Winter of the *Delight* and the captain of the *Squirrel*, refused to go any farther. After some wrangling, Gilbert let them depart in the *Swallow*, which had already proved an embarrassment by its piratical forays. He himself took command of the *Squirrel*, leaving his papers and documents in the *Delight*. The three ships made for the mainland, but somewhere on the coast of Nova Scotia, probably south of the site of Louisbourg on Cape Breton Island, the *Delight* ran aground and sank with all hands except for sixteen men who got away in the ship's pinnace. All of Gilbert's maps and papers went down in the *Delight*.

Short of supplies and with crews discouraged, the two remaining vessels headed for England. The sea was rough and the *Squirrel* by this time was none too seaworthy, yet Gilbert refused Captain Edward Hayes's advice to come aboard the *Golden Hind*. On September 9, Hayes again hailed the *Squirrel* and repeated his admonition, but Gilbert calmly replied, "We are as neere to heaven by sea as by land." That night the crew on the *Golden Hind* saw the lights of the *Squirrel* suddenly vanish. She and those aboard were never seen again.

Gilbert had paved the way, however, for further efforts to establish colonies by an expansionist group headed by Walsingham, Raleigh, Edward Dyer, and other prominent figures at court. Their propagandists were the two Richard Hakluyts: the elder a lawyer in-

This chart of England's south coast by an unknown artist of Henry VIII's time is not only handsome but accurate, and contains sailing instructions for mariners. These three sections—only part of the entire chart—show the coast from Land's End (left) to Exmouth, the region whence most early voyages to America, including those of Drake, Hawkins, and Gilbert, set out.

fluential with the London merchants, and his younger cousin, a preacher and the compiler of annals of voyages.

For several years the two Hakluyts had been diligently collecting information and making reports that would be useful to explorers and potential colonists. For Gilbert, in 1578, Richard Hakluyt the lawyer had drawn up notes on what an expedition ought to look for in a new country and the kind of place that ought to be chosen for a settlement. Hakluyt made it clear that Englishmen should look for a climate that would yield those products then being bought from England's enemies. If the heathen inhabitants of the new country would not allow the English to occupy the whole land, then an effort should be made to establish a base for friendly trade. "But if we may injoy any large Territorie of apt soyle," he adds, "we might so use the matter, as we should not depende upon Spaine for oyls, sacks [sherry], resignes [raisins], orenges, lemons, Spanish skinnes, etc. Nor uppon Fraunce for woad, baysalt, and gascoyne wines, nor on Estland [Eastland, or the Baltic] for flaxe, pitch, tarre, mastes, etc. So we shoulde not so exhaust our treasure, and so exceedingly inrich our doubtfull friendes as we doe." Hakluyt thus expressed a doctrine

that was to be repeated hundreds of times in the years to come: the necessity for England to find sources of those products that were not yet obtainable within a closed English system.

In 1579–80, while the fate of Drake's voyage around the world was still unknown, the younger Hakluyt had submitted to the queen a plan that was headed, "A Discourse of the Commoditie of the Taking of the Straight of Magellanus." He recommended seizing and fortifying the entrance to that gateway to the Spanish possessions on the Pacific side of America. A base should also be seized at Cape St. Vincent in Brazil. If the queen should find it inexpedient to send an expedition openly to do this, a notorious pirate, one Thomas Clark, might be induced to do it surreptitiously, taking jailbirds and other undesirables as settlers for the new bases. Two years after this report was submitted, Hakluyt the younger brought together his first compilation of travel narratives, his *Divers Voyages to America* (1582), dedicated to Sir Francis Walsingham's son-in-law, Sir Philip Sidney, who was himself interested in westward expansion. In his dedicatory preface, which was a plea for colonization overseas, Hakluyt commented: "I marvail

not a little (right worshipfull) that since the first discoverie of America . . . after so great conquest and
plantings of the Spaniards & Portingales there, that we
of England could never have the grace to set fast foot-
ing in such fertill and temperate places, as are left as yet
unpossessed by them." But, he continued, since Portugal had now been taken over by Spain and Spain's
own secrets uncovered by Englishmen like Drake, Hakluyt hoped that the "time approcheth and nowe is, that
we of England may share . . . both with the Spaniarde
and the Portingale in part of America, and other regions
as yet undiscovered." The compilation provided not
only narratives but a documented argument of the rights
of Englishmen to America, based on Cabot's discoveries
and other voyages.

A more elaborate statement of the value of colonization came from the younger Hakluyt's pen two years
after the *Divers Voyages*, when he presented to the
queen a document headed, "A particular discourse
Concerninge the greate necessitie and manifolde com-
modyties that are like to growe to this Realme of Eng-
lande by the Westerne discoveries lately attempted,
Written in the yere 1584 by Richard Hackluyt of Ox-
forde at the requeste and direction of the righte Worshipfull Mr. Walter Raghly nowe Knight, before the
Comynge home of his Twoo Barkes." This treatise, generally called "A Discourse of Westerne Planting," was
a closely argued pamphlet summarizing the reasons of
state that required England to seize and settle a portion
of the New World. Written at the behest of Raleigh, it
was designed to convince the queen and to provide
Walsingham with all the facts and reasons that he might
need in defending expansion overseas before less enthusiastic members of the government. The "Discourse"
was Hakluyt's most complete statement of the value and
necessity of colonization. Omitting nothing, he proved
that the economic, political, and spiritual welfare of
England demanded settlements overseas.

As the heading of Hakluyt's "Discourse" indicated,
Raleigh had sent two ships to America sometime before
the document was completed. In March, 1584, he had
received a patent similar to Gilbert's, except that Newfoundland, already claimed by Gilbert the previous
year, was excluded from lands that Raleigh might occupy. On April 27 he had dispatched from Plymouth
two vessels commanded by Philip Amadas and Arthur
Barlowe. They had spent two months exploring the
coast of what is now North Carolina and returned to

*Raleigh (above), though an able sailor, was mainly
a backer of others' voyages. At right, an engraving
of settlers approaching Roanoke Island in 1585
was based on a picture by one of the colonists.
It deserves study for its wealth of minute detail.*

Plymouth by the middle of September. The explorers
had claimed the land for England, and in honor of the
Virgin Queen, Raleigh named it Virginia. Pleased with
his exploit—and the compliment—Queen Elizabeth
early the next year dubbed Raleigh knight.

Barlowe wrote a lyrical account of the land between
Cape Hatteras and Cape Lookout. Grapes, he observed,
grew in profusion. The land was well wooded, game was
plentiful, and the fertile soil produced excellent corn,
peas, melons, cucumbers, and gourds. The Indians
whom they encountered were friendly and hospitable.
So pleased was Barlowe with their entertainment and
the fruitfulness of the country that he commented:
"Wee found the people most gentle, loving, and faith-
full, void of all guile, and treason, and such as lived
after the manner of the golden age."

This notion of the New World as a land where every
good thing grew in plenty and one could live off the
land with little effort quickly gained currency. It com-
ported with what the early promoters hoped to find, and

it absolved adventurers from the necessity of tedious labor. It also helped to bring about the undoing of many early settlers, who came unprepared and ill-equipped, mentally or materially, to deal with the wilderness.

Amadas and Barlowe brought back from Virginia two Indians, Manteo and Wanchese, who created great interest in London. After they had learned English, they were used to promote Raleigh's plan for a colonizing expedition, which he began immediately to organize. Raleigh would have gone himself, but the queen refused permission, and he had to give the command to his cousin, Sir Richard Grenville, who had already gained a corsair's reputation in privateering voyages against the Spaniards. With seven ships and a complement of nearly six hundred men, one hundred of whom were to be settlers, Grenville got under way in April, 1585. Ralph Lane, a professional soldier, went along as governor of the colony. John White, an artist, and Thomas Hariot, a scientific observer, were among the company.

Grenville's fleet took the southern route by the West Indies. In Puerto Rico and Hispaniola they traded with the Spaniards for supplies and livestock, seized a few Spanish vessels, and stole certain other commodities before heading north. One of the purposes of the colony was to establish a base for raiding Spanish shipping, and Grenville intended to keep in practice on the way. Indeed, Raleigh and his partners in the privateering syndicate expected to pay expenses and make a profit from prizes taken.

On June 26 the expedition reached Ocracoke Island on the North Carolina coast, but a month was consumed in exploring rivers and sounds in the region. At last, on July 29, they decided to settle on Roanoke Island, and for the next few weeks they were busy unloading the vessels, trading with the Indians, collecting information about the country, erecting huts, and preparing a settlement for the one hundred and eight men who were to remain. Grenville sailed away on August 25, leaving Lane in charge with a small pinnace and a few boats to use in further exploration.

41

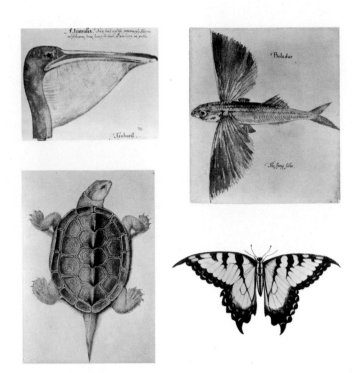

John White / Artist

John White's water colors have survived still bright, but the man himself is shrouded in mist. Nothing is known of him before 1585 or after 1593, and it is even possible that there were two John Whites. In 1585 he appears accompanying the first Roanoke colonists, commissioned by Sir Walter Raleigh to make drawings to use in stimulating settlement. It is generally accepted—though not absolutely proved—that he was the same John White sent by Raleigh in 1587 to establish what became the tragic Lost Colony. Among the colonists who disappeared without trace while White was away in England were his own daughter and his granddaughter, Virginia Dare, the first English child born in America. After 1593, when White, then in retirement, sent to Richard Hakluyt an account of his last voyage, he disappears from history. But his pictures remain; his Indian drawings are among the few realistic portrayals of the natives of the region. At right is White's map of the coast, bearing Raleigh's coat of arms. Above are four wildlife sketches: brown pelican, flying fish, swallowtail butterfly, and diamondback terrapin.

Lane and his colonists, despite all of Richard Hakluyt's sound advice, were ill-prepared as settlers. They were more eager to search for gold, silver, and pearls than they were to cut trees or to plant crops. Furthermore, the season was now too far advanced to hope for food crops until another year. They had to depend upon the Indians for corn and game, and already the English had created bad blood with the Indians by burning one of their villages in retaliation for the theft of a silver cup. All in all, neither the site chosen nor the actions of the settlers promised success. Furthermore, the colony was essentially a military base, and its inhabitants were men manning a garrison rather than settlers intending to stay and make a career in the new land.

That privateering was more profitable than colonizing was indicated by Grenville's success in taking a Spanish treasure ship on his way home, the *Santa Maria de San Vicente*, loaded with sugar, hides, cochineal, ginger, pearls, silver, and gold. The Spanish complained bitterly about the loss, which amounted, they claimed, to a million ducats. To Sir Francis Walsingham, one of the investors, Grenville admitted that each adventurer not only would get back the money that he had risked but would make "some gain." Queen Elizabeth is said to have received from this prize a casket of pearls. As principal backer of the expedition to Roanoke, Raleigh recouped his investment with some money to spare, thanks to his cousin Grenville's audacity at sea.

Theodor de Bry is believed to have engraved this self-portrait in 1597, a year before his death. Through his engravings De Bry brought to the world the art of John White (pages 42–43) and of Jacques Le Moyne (page 26), often painstakingly hand-coloring his work, like the map on page 41, which was based on a White original. At left is a White water color, at right a De Bry engraving from a similar White painting; it shows body markings of various Indian chiefs and illustrated a book by Thomas Hariot, who was with the first Roanoke colony.

44

While Grenville was searching for Spanish prizes, the members of the colony on Roanoke Island set about building a fort for defense against both Indians and marauding Spaniards. John White made maps and drawings of plant, animal, and human life. Thomas Hariot busied himself with scientific observations and notes for *A Briefe and True Report of the New Found Land of Virginia*, which he published in London in 1588. Ralph Lane, the governor, led exploring expeditions that he hoped might find a gold mine or a passage to the South Sea.

By the summer of 1586 the Indians, having decided that the white settlers whom they had at first welcomed were a threat to their security, plotted to starve them out by denying them food. In the open warfare that developed, Lane's men killed the chief of the Roanoke Indians and a number of his tribe. For the time, the danger from the Indians was lessened, but the garrison had to live in a state of siege, and food was hard to find.

Just when the morale of the colonists had reached its lowest ebb, a party stationed at Croatan Island, on June 8, 1586, caught sight of English ships offshore. These were vessels in a great fleet commanded by Sir Francis Drake, who had made a successful foray upon Spanish towns and shipping in the West Indies and Central America and had recently destroyed St. Augustine. On his way home, he had orders to check on Raleigh's colony. Finding the colonists ill-furnished and dis-

HARIOT, *A Briefe and True Report of the New Found Land of Virginia*, 1588

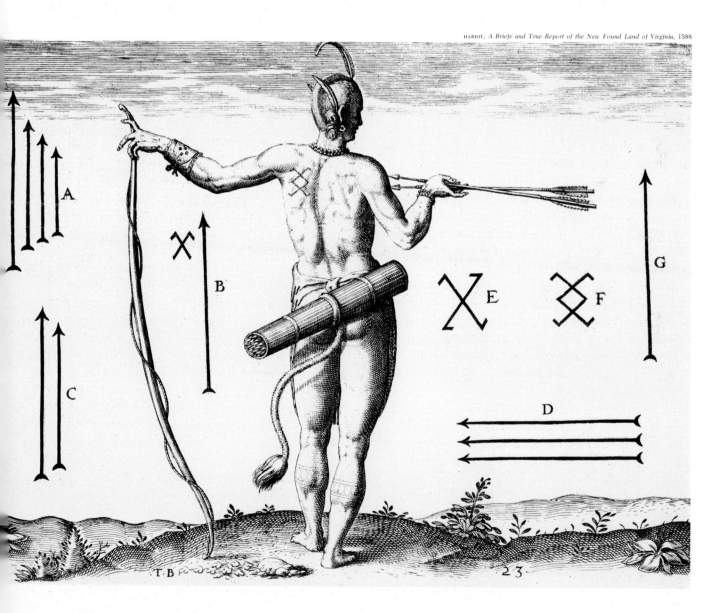

45

couraged, he at first offered them a ship but later agreed to take them home. Since supplies promised by Grenville had not arrived, Lane decided to embark his men, and they sailed away on June 18 or 19. A short time afterward, a ship with supplies sent by Raleigh arrived at Roanoke, but when its crew could find no settlers, they sailed back to England. A little later Grenville himself arrived with supplies and new recruits, but, finding the colony deserted, he left a token force of fifteen men on Roanoke Island and departed in search of Spanish prizes. The unfortunate fifteen men were later wiped out by the Indians—or they may have perished while trying to escape by boat.

Although most of the garrison who came back from Roanoke could not say a good word for "Virginia," John White and Thomas Hariot remained ardent propagandists for colonization. Raleigh himself was determined to make another attempt to establish a permanent settlement, not just a military garrison. To that end he planned an expedition that sailed on May 8, 1587, with John White as governor. Settlers were to receive a minimum of five hundred acres of land, which they would hold as Raleigh's tenants. Included in this expedition were women, wives of settlers, for this colony was intended to last and to perpetuate itself.

White, who was captain of the *Lion*, the largest of the three vessels that sailed, had Simon Fernandez, the Portuguese pilot who had been on the previous voyages, as master and pilot. White later complained that Fernandez displayed both carelessness and ignorance in guiding them through islands in the West Indies and in trying to find the site of the North Carolina colony. White hoped to stop at Roanoke, which he planned to leave in charge of Manteo, the Indian who had been taken to England by Amadas and Barlowe in 1584, while he himself would sail on to Chesapeake Bay, where he expected to establish a new City of Raleigh. But Fernandez apparently was more intent upon privateering than upon getting settlers to Chesapeake Bay, a fact that may account for his landing them on Roanoke Island despite White's protest. At any rate, in late July they found themselves on Roanoke, where they set about repairing the houses of the previous settlers. White had Manteo baptized a Christian and established friendly relations with his band, the Croatans, who themselves were hostile to the Roanoke Indians who had given Lane so much trouble. On August 18 John White's daughter Eleanor, wife of Ananias Dare, gave birth to a daughter, who was named Virginia. She was the first child born to English parents in America.

Supplies were so scanty and the prospects at Roanoke so bleak that the colonists begged White to return to England to procure reinforcements and aid. Accordingly, bearing a certificate that this was the wish of the colonists themselves, White set sail in a flyboat, while Fernandez went away in the *Lion* to look for prey that would be more profitable than lumber and sassafras (then valued as a drug), the only cargo visible on the coast of North Carolina. Left behind on Roanoke Island were one hundred and twelve colonists—eighty-four men, seventeen women, and eleven children.

White did not set foot on English soil until early November, but he at once began trying to succor the colony. Raleigh provided a pinnace, which White was to use for taking supplies to Roanoke while a larger expedition was being organized. But the pinnace did not sail, and in the spring of 1588, when Grenville got together a small relief expedition, the Privy Council refused to let him sail because of the impending threat of invasion from Spain. White was finally allowed two pinnaces, but he could not control his seamen, who turned to privateering as soon as they got out of sight of land. The vessel in which White sailed was badly damaged by a French privateer and had to return to port, and White himself was wounded. Once again, privateering thwarted colonial enterprise. By this time the threat of the Spanish Armada forced England to bend all her maritime efforts to defense.

In the early months of 1589, after the danger from the Armada was past, Raleigh resumed his efforts to do something for his colony in Virginia. He authorized a small stock company, chiefly of London merchants but including Richard Hakluyt the younger, to trade with the colony tax-free and to have rights of tenancy like those offered White's colonists under Raleigh's charter. The company would also have the responsibility of sending reinforcements to Roanoke. William Sanderson, one of Raleigh's men, purchased a ship to go to America, but nothing happened until the spring of 1590, when White was permitted to go with a privateering expedition that promised to land him at Roanoke.

In mid-August of that year, two vessels anchored off Oregon Inlet, not far from Roanoke Island, and White and some of the ships' company went in small boats to seek the colony. When they reached the site, they discovered that the houses had been dismantled but that

The defeat of the Spanish Armada in 1588 had a profound effect on the settlement of America, for the English no longer felt the same need for caution in the New World, and the Dutch, freed from Spain, also became colonizers. The picture is a detail from an engraving of the battle, made about 1615.

the palisade around the settlement was still standing. Some heavy guns remained, but smaller cannon had been taken away. Chests that the departing settlers had buried had been dug up and rifled by the Indians. Some of these contained torn papers, books, and pictures that White himself had left. On a tree were carved the letters CRO, and upon a palisade near the gateway was the word CROATOAN.

It had been agreed that an inscribed cross would be left as a sign of distress if the settlers had to leave under dangerous conditions. No cross was found, and no trace of any person was discovered, although White and his companions marched back and forth through the island while their trumpeter played English tunes to assure any Englishman hiding that they were friends. But no human, white or Indian, showed himself. Because of stormy weather, the search had to be abandoned without visiting Croatan Island, and the two vessels eventually made sail for England. White held to the hope that the colonists were living on Croatan with Manteo, the Christian Indian, but he was never again able to come to America to search for them.

Nor did Raleigh exert himself in the colonists' behalf. Raleigh's patent would expire on March 24, 1591, if he had not established a colony by that time, but so long as the colony that he had sent to Roanoke was "lost" and not destroyed, his patent would remain valid. For this reason it has been suggested that Raleigh was reluctant to discover that his colony had been wiped out. At any rate, he let the matter remain in doubt and was not disposed to invest additional funds during the 1590's in colonial enterprise.

The fate of the "Lost Colony" has remained a mystery and the theme of numerous legends. One of the most persistent is that the colonists, or some of them, were absorbed into the Croatan band. Long afterward, the Hatteras Indians, who may have been the same band, showed evidences of white blood and told of early white ancestors. Another theory, supported by reports of the early settlers at Jamestown, is that some of the colonists reached the Chesapeake Bay region and were killed there by Powhatan about the time of the arrival of the Jamestown settlers in 1607; others feel that Powhatan may have slain them on Roanoke. Still another possibility is that the colonists sailed away in their pinnace and were lost at sea, a suggestion that seems reasonable, since they carried away certain small cannon that they were known to possess. Whatever their

fate, they have made a lasting impression upon American literature and folklore.

If Raleigh's colony served no other purpose, it provided John White with an opportunity to make drawings and water colors of American life that profoundly influenced his contemporaries, and it induced Thomas Hariot to write a descriptive account of the colony that served as useful promotional material for many years. In 1590, Theodor de Bry, a Flemish engraver and publisher, brought out in his *America*, Part I, an edition of Hariot's *A Briefe and True Report of the New Found Land of Virginia*, illustrated with engravings based on White's drawings. These engravings helped to stimulate the imagination of Europeans for generations to come.

Raleigh did not abandon his colonial ambitions, but he never understood that the establishment of permanent colonies required more capital than he was willing or able to invest. To him colonies would be the means of personal aggrandizement and glory. He expected them to pay their way as a source of valuable commodities, and they were also to be used as bases for attacking his bitter enemy Spain.

The expansionists never ceased their propaganda for colonization. Richard Hakluyt the younger continued his collection and publication of expeditionary reports. To him colonization was a religion, and he and others who were like-minded continued to preach the gospel of overseas expansion. They were convinced that colonization would be for the glory of God and the benefit of the nation. The need to Christianize the heathen before Spain made them all papists was a constant theme and was combined with the promise that this pious enterprise would be certain to return handsome profits. Hakluyt and his colleagues emphasized the value of trade and the useful commodities certain to be found in the New World, citing Raleigh's expeditions in the early 1600's to the coast of North Carolina to load timber, sassafras, and other medicinal plants, which returned a profit on the London market.

Even Raleigh was beginning to sense that the products of the soil in the new territory might be profitable, but before he could make any serious efforts at renewing his colonial ventures in North America, Queen Elizabeth died in 1603, and King James I, at the behest of Spain, had Raleigh confined in the Tower of London on a charge of treason. Raleigh's personal activities in the colonization of North America were over. But the experiments he had fostered were soon to bear fruit.

In Their Words...

The Land They Found

History can be told in a number of ways—but never fully without the firsthand accounts of those who made it. When the participants speak in their own words, the characters of history emerge from legend and become real people in real situations rather than stock figures in patriotic tableaux. On these pages, and in three similar sections later in this book, some of those present during the discovery and settlement of the New World report on what they found, what they thought, the society they developed, and the contributions they made to the growth and maturity of the Thirteen Colonies.

*I*n A.D. 986, *Bjarni Herjolfsson and his crew of Norsemen, lost in the fog while sailing from Iceland to Greenland, became the first known white men to encounter North America. They sailed along the continent's northeastern coast for a number of days but did not land. That achievement was left to Leif Ericsson, who in 1000 became the first Viking explorer to set foot on the New World. A Norse saga tells the story.*

[Leif Ericsson and his men] now prepared their ship and sailed out to sea once they were ready, and they lighted on that land first which Bjarni and his people had lighted on last. They sailed to land there, cast anchor and put off a boat, then went ashore, and could see no grass there. The background was all great glaciers, and right up to the glaciers from the sea as it were a single slab of rock. The land impressed them as barren and useless. "At least," said Leif, "it has not happened to us as to Bjarni over this land, that we failed to get ourselves ashore. I shall now give the land a name, and call it Helluland, Flatstone Land." After which they returned to the ship.

After that they sailed out to sea and lighted on another land. This time too they sailed to land, cast anchor, then put off a boat and went ashore. The country was flat and covered with forest, with extensive white sands wherever they went, and shelving gently to the sea. "This land," said Leif, "shall be given a name in accordance with its nature, and be called Markland, Wood Land." After which they got back down to the ship as fast as they could.

From there they now sailed out to sea with a north-east wind and were at sea two days before catching sight of land. They sailed to land, reaching an island which lay north of it, where they went ashore and looked about them in fine weather, and found that there was dew on the grass, whereupon it happened to them that they set their hands to the dew, then carried it to their mouths, and thought they had never known anything so sweet as that was. After which they . . . [brought their ship up a river into a] lake, where they cast anchor, carried their skin sleeping-bags off board, and built themselves booths. Later they decided to winter there and built a big house.

There was no lack of salmon there in river or lake, and salmon bigger than they had ever seen before. The nature of the land was so choice, it seemed to them that none of the cattle would require fodder for the winter. No frost came during the winter, and the grass was hardly withered. Day and night were of a more equal length there than

Eric the Red, father of Leif Ericsson, as an Icelandic artist of the 1600's imagined him

in Greenland or Iceland. On the shortest day of winter the sun was visible in the middle of the afternoon as well as at breakfast time. . . .

[In exploring the island, they found abundant grapevines and grapes, and Leif told his crew,] "We now have two jobs to get on with, and on alternate days must gather grapes or cut vines and fell timber, so as to provide a cargo of such things for my ship." They acted upon these orders, and report has it that their tow-boat was filled with grapes. . . . Leif gave the land a name in accordance with the good things they found in it, calling it Vinland, Wineland; after which they sailed out to sea and had a good wind till they sighted Greenland and the mountains under the glaciers.

Grænlendinga Saga

The discovery of America in 1492 almost eluded Columbus. His men, a month and more than three thousand miles away from their last sight of land in the Canary Islands, were growing mutinous and demanding that he turn back. But land birds were flying overhead, and plants and branches floated past Columbus's three ships. After they weathered a near gale on October tenth and eleventh, so many indications of land appeared that the crisis was over. The following excerpts are taken from a contemporary summary of Columbus's journals, the originals of which are now lost.

The islands found by Columbus: a woodcut used when the report of his voyage was printed in 1493

The course was W.S.W., and there was more sea than there had been during the whole of the voyage. They saw sand-pipers, and a green reed near the ship. Those of the caravel *Pinta* saw a cane and a pole, and they took up another small pole which appeared to have been worked with iron; also another bit of cane, a land-plant, and a small board. The crew of the caravel *Niña* also saw signs of land, and a small branch covered with berries. Every one breathed afresh and rejoiced at these signs. . . . As the caravel *Pinta* was a better sailer, and went ahead of the Admiral, she found the land, and made the signals ordered by the Admiral. . . .

The vessels were hove to, waiting for daylight; and on Friday [October 12, 1492] they arrived at a small island of the Lucayos, called, in the language of the Indians, Guanahani [probably Watling Island]. Presently they saw naked people. The Admiral went on shore in the armed boat, and Martin Alonso Pinzon, and Vicente Yañez, his brother, who was captain of the *Niña*. The Admiral took the royal standard, and the captains went with two banners of the green cross, which the Admiral took in all the ships as a sign, with an F and a Y [Fernando and Ysabel] and a crown over each letter, one on one side of the cross and the other on the other. Having landed, they saw trees very green, and much water, and fruits of diverse kinds. The Admiral called to the two captains, and to the others who leaped on shore, and to Rodrigo Escovedo, secretary of the whole fleet, and to Rodrigo Sanchez of Segovia, and said that they should bear faithful testimony that he, in presence of all, had taken, as he now took, possession of the said island for the King and for the Queen his Lords, making the declarations that are required, as is now largely set forth in the testimonies which were then made in writing.

Presently many inhabitants of the island assembled. What follows is in the actual words of the Admiral in his book of the first navigation and discovery of the Indies. . . . "It appeared to me to be a race of people very poor in everything. They go as naked as when their mothers bore them, and so do the women, although I did not see more than one young girl. All I saw were youths, none more than thirty years of age. They are very well made, with very handsome bodies, and very good countenances. Their hair is short and coarse, almost like the hairs of a horse's tail. They wear the hairs brought down to the eyebrows, except a few locks behind, which they wear long and never cut. They paint themselves black, and they are the color of the Canarians, neither black nor white. Some paint themselves white, others red, and others of what color they find. Some paint their faces, others the whole body, some only round the eyes, others only on the nose. They neither carry nor know anything of arms, for I showed them swords, and they took them by the blade and cut themselves through ignorance. They have no iron, their darts being wands without iron, some of them having a fish's tooth at the end, and others being pointed in various ways. . . .

"All last night and to-day [October 22] I was here, waiting to see if the king or other person would bring gold or anything of value. Many of these people came, like those of the other islands, equally naked, and equally painted, some white, some red, some black, and others in many ways. They brought darts and skeins of cotton to barter, which they exchanged with the sailors for bits of glass, broken crockery, and pieces of earthenware. Some of them had pieces of gold fastened in their noses, which they willingly gave for a hawk's bell and glass beads. But there was so little that it counts for nothing."

Journal of the First Voyage

*J*ohn Cabot, a Venetian in the service of the king of England, made the first of two voyages to America in 1497 and returned convinced that he had reached the Orient. Actually, he had found Cape Breton Island and Nova Scotia. Cabot left no first-person accounts; his story is told in the words of his contemporaries.

Carib Indians navigate a raft and fish in West Indies waters.

The Venetian our countryman, who went with a ship from Bristol to find new islands, has returned, and says that 700 leagues hence he discovered mainland, the territory of the Grand Cham [Grand Khan, a reputed Oriental potentate]. He coasted for 300 leagues and landed; he did not see any person, but he has brought hither to the King certain snares which had been set to catch game, and a needle for making nets; he also found some cut trees, wherefore he supposed there were inhabitants. Being in doubt he returned to his ship. . . .

The King [Henry VII] has promised that in the spring our countryman shall have ten ships, armed to his order, and at his request has conceded him all the prisoners, except traitors, to go with him as he has requested. The King has also given him money wherewith to amuse himself till then, and he is now at Bristol with his wife, who is also Venetian, and with his sons; his name is Zuam Talbot [John Cabot], and he is styled the great admiral. Vast honor is paid him; he dresses in silk, and these English run after him like mad people, so that he can enlist as many of them as he pleases, and a number of our own rogues besides.

The discoverer of these things planted on his new-found land a large cross, with one flag of England and another of St. Mark, by reason of his being a Venetian, so that our banner has floated very far afield.

Letter of Lorenzo Pasqualigo to his brothers Alvise and Francesco, merchants in Venice, August 23, 1497

Ferdinand Magellan, with his discovery of a passage around South America and his voyage across the Pacific, 1519–22, showed that the Orient could be reached by sailing west. But the voyage proved so arduous and impractical that nations turned more of their energies to the colonization of the New World. This laconic account of the finding of the Strait of Magellan is by one of Magellan's crew.

This map from a 1603 book of voyages reduces the Strait of Magellan to a mere canal.

Leaving that place, we found, in 51 degrees less one-third degree, toward the Antarctic Pole, a river of fresh water. There the ships almost perished because of the furious winds; but God and the holy bodies aided them. We stayed about two months in that river in order to supply the ships with water, wood, and fish. . . . They were very good although small. Before leaving that river, the captain-general and all of us confessed and received communion as true Christians.

Then going to fifty-two degrees toward the same pole, we found a strait . . . whose head is called Capo de le Undici Millia Vergine [Eleven Thousand Virgins]. . . . That strait is one hundred and ten leguas or 440 miles long, and it is one-half legua broad, more or less. It leads to another sea called the Pacific Sea, and is surrounded by very lofty mountains laden with snow. There it was impossible to find bottom [for anchoring], but [it was necessary to fasten] the moorings on land 25 or 30 brazas away. Had it not been for the captain-general, we would not have found that strait, for we all thought and said that it was closed on all sides.

Antonio Pigafetta
First Voyage Around the Earth, 1525

For many generations the search went on for a northwest passage, a water route through North America to the Orient. One of the early seekers was Giovanni da Verrazano, a Florentine in the service of the French king, Francis I. In 1524 Verrazano explored the American coastline from the Carolinas to Nova Scotia, discovering New York Harbor on the way. On his return, he reported that North America was a good deal more solid than he had expected.

My intention was in this navigation to reach Cathay *and* the extreme east of Asia, not expecting to find such an obstacle of new land as I found; and if for some reason I expected to find it, I thought it to be not without some strait to penetrate to the Eastern Ocean. And this has been the opinion of all the ancients, believing certainly our *Western* Ocean to be one *with* the Eastern Ocean of India without interposition of land. This Aristotle affirms . . . which opinion is very contradictory to the moderns and according to experience untrue . . . it [the new land] shows itself to be larger than our Europe and Africa and almost Asia, if we estimate correctly its size. . . . All this land or New World . . . is connected together, not adjoining Asia nor Africa . . . it may join Europe by Norway and Russia. . . . It would therefore remain included between two seas, and between the Eastern and the Western. . . . I hope we shall have better assurance of this . . . that we may see the perfect end of this our cosmography, and that the sacred word of the evangelist may be accomplished: *Their sound has gone out into all* the earth. . . .

Giovanni da Verrazano
Report to King Francis I of France, July, 1524

On his first voyage to America in 1534, Jacques Cartier found what he assumed to be the entrance to a northwest passage. The next year he returned but discovered that his "passage" was a river, the St. Lawrence, which he explored as high as the site of Montreal. These excerpts are from a contemporary translation of his account of his trip.

The next day being the 19 of September [1535] we hoysed saile, and with our Pinnesse and two boates departed to goe up the river [the St. Lawrence] with the flood, where on both shores of it we beganne to see as goodly a countrey as possibly can with eye be seene, all replenished with very goodly trees, and Vines laden as full of grapes as could be all along the river, which rather seemed to have bin planted by mans hand than otherwise. True it is, that because they are not dressed and wrought as they should be, their bunches of grapes are not so great nor sweete as ours; also we sawe all along the river many houses inhabited of Fishers, which take all kinds of fishes, and they came with as great familiaritie and kindnesse unto us, as if we had beene their Countreymen, and brought us great store of fish, with other such things as they had, which we exchanged with them for other wares, who lifting up their hands toward heaven, gave many signes of joy: we stayed at a place called Hochelai, about five and twentie leagues from Canada [an Indian village on the site of Quebec], where the river waxeth very narrow, and runneth very swift, wherefore it is very dangerous, not onely for that, but also for certaine great stones that are therein: Many boates and barkes came unto us, in one of which came one of the chiefe Lords of the countrey, making a long discourse, who being come neere us, did by evident signes and gestures shew us, that the higher the river went, the more dangerous it was, and bade us take heede of our selves. . . . Upon the 28 of September we came to a great wide lake [Lake St. Peter] in the middle of the river five or sixe leagues broad, and twelve long . . . foure or five branches do compasse about five or six Ilands very pleasant, which make the head of the lake. . . . That day we landed in one of the saide Ilands, and met with five men that were hunting of wilde beastes, who as freely and familiarly came to our boates without any feare, as if we had ever bene brought up togither. Our boates being somewhat neere the shore, one of them tooke our Captaine in his armes, and caried him on shore, as lightly and as easily as if he had bene a child of five yeeres old: so strong and sturdie was this fellow. We found that they had a great heape of wild Rats [muskrats] that live in the water, as bigge as a Conny, and very good to eate, which they gave unto our Captaine, who for a recompence gave them knives and glassen Beades. We asked them with signes if that was the way to Hochelaga [Huron Indian village on the site of Montreal], they answered yea, and that we had yet three days sayling thither.

. . . There groweth also a certaine kind of herbe [tobacco], whereof in Sommer they make great provision for all the yeere, making great account of it, and onely men use of it, and first they cause it to be dried in the sunne, then weare it about their neckes wrapped in a little beasts skinne made like a little bagge, with a hollow peece of stone or wood like a pipe: then when they please they make pouder of it, and then put it in one of the ends of the said Cornet or pipe, and laying a cole of fire upon it, at the other ende sucke so long, that they fill their bodies full of smoke, till that it commeth out of their mouth and nostrils, even as out of the Tonnell of a chimney. They say that this doth keepe them warme and in health: they never goe without some of it about them. We ourselves have tryed the same smoke, and having put it in our mouthes, it seemed almost as hot as Pepper.

A Shorte and Briefe Narration (Cartier's Second Voyage), 1535–36

Indian hunter enjoys a smoke.

Hernando de Soto

*H*ernando de Soto, marching northward from Florida with six hundred men, became the first explorer to penetrate the interior lands of what would become the southern colonies. During the expedition's wanderings, 1539–43, they passed through Florida, Georgia, both Carolinas, Tennessee, Alabama, Mississippi, Arkansas, Texas, and Oklahoma. From accounts of the expedition came the first knowledge of the geography and of the Indian tribes of the region. This firsthand report was written by a gentleman from the town of Elvas, Portugal, who was a member of the expedition.

On the third day of May [1540], the Governor set out from Cutifachiqui [Yuchi town on the Savannah River]; and, it being discovered that the wish of the Cacica [chieftess] was to leave the Christians, if she could, giving them neither guides nor tamemes [carriers], because of the outrages committed upon the inhabitants, there never failing to be men of low degree among the many, who will put the lives of themselves and others in jeopardy for some mean interest, the Governor ordered that she should be placed under guard and took her with him. This treatment, which was not a proper return for the hospitable welcome he had received, makes true the adage, For well doing, etc.; and thus she was carried away on foot with her female slaves.

This brought us service in all the places that were passed, she ordering the Indians to come and take the loads from town to town. We travelled through her territories a hundred leagues, in which, according to what we saw, she was greatly obeyed, whatsoever she ordered being performed with diligence and efficacy. . . .

One day while on this journey, the Cacica of Cutifachi, whom the Governor brought with him, as has been stated, to the end of taking her to Guaxule [town, probably Creek Indian, in southern Alabama], the farthest limit of her territories, conducted by her slaves, she left the road, with an excuse of going into a thicket, where, deceiving them, she so concealed herself that for all their search she could not be found. She took with her a cane box, like a trunk, called petaca, full of unbored pearls, of which those who had the most knowledge of their value said they were very precious. They were carried for her by one of the women; and the Governor, not to give offence, permitted it so, thinking that in Guaxulle he would beg them of her when he should give her leave to depart; but she took them with her, going to Xualla [Cheraw village in Swain County, North Carolina], with three slaves who had fled from the camp. . . .

The Gentleman of Elvas
The Narrative of the Expedition of Hernando de Soto, 1557

*I*n 1565 Nicolas le Challeux was at Fort Caroline, the French outpost in northern Florida, when it was attacked by the Spaniards. All but a handful of defenders were massacred. Among those who escaped was Le Challeux, who wrote an account of his experiences as a colonist in a virgin land.

When we were settled there [Fort Caroline], I studied the form of the natives of the land. The men are straight and well proportioned, of a somewhat ruddy color. To me they seemed kind and gentle. I learned that in every village they have a king. What little clothing they wear is of leather, strangely decorated. Neither the men nor the women dress in any other garb, but the women are girdled with a little fringe or apron, made from the skin of some animal, to cover their shame. They are neither flat-

Huguenot with Florida Indian

nosed nor big-lipped, but their faces are round and full, their eyes clear and timid. Their hair is very long, and they bind it very neatly around their heads. This trussing of their hair serves as a quiver to carry their arrows when they go to war. It is marvellous to see how swiftly they can take the arrows into their hands and shoot them unbelievably straight and far.

As for their manners, they are dissolute. They do not instruct or correct their children. They will steal without conscience, and all that they can take secretly they count as their own. Every one has his own wife, and they keep the marriage bond with all rigor. They make war against adjacent countries, each of which has a different language. Their weapons are bows and arrows. Their houses are round, much like dove-cotes with foundations and structures of large trees, roofed over with palm leaves.

They have no fear of wind or tempest. Little flies, which they call *maringons*, annoy them often; to get rid of these vermin, they make small fires in their houses—especially under the beds. They say these flies sting cruelly, and those parts that are stung look like the flesh of lepers.

Among these savages nothing is so rich and fair as the feathers of birds, which are of various colors. They also prize little counters, made from the bones of certain fish and from green and red stones. They eat roots, fruit, herbs, and fish of various kinds. Their fish are very fat, and they cut out the fat to use instead of butter and sauce. They hang and dry the fish, which they call *boquarie* in their language.

They have no wheat, but they have an abundance of a certain seed [corn], which grows seven feet high. The stalk is thick like a cane, and the grain is as large as peas. The ear is a foot long, the color of natural wax. The way they use it is first to bruise and pound it to meal. Then it is mixed and made into *mygan*, which is like the rice we have in this country. It must be eaten as soon as it is made, because it cannot be kept and will quickly spoil.

In some parts of this country many bastard vines grow around the trees, but the natives do not press out the wine. Their drink, which they call *cassinet* [cassina] is made from mixed herbs and looks like the ale of our country in color. I have tasted it, and it did not seem strange to me. The countryside is hilly and thickly forested. This may be the reason for the abundance of wild animals, which they say will injure those who do not take great heed. I will not write much about those beasts I know of only by hearsay. There is enough for me to say of the things I have seen that I think worthy to be noted for posterity.

There are crocodiles, especially, which are often seen coming up on the sand in search of prey. We have observed many—a dead one in particular, which we ate. The meat was tender, white as veal, and had almost the same taste. It was killed by a gunshot, struck between two scales. Otherwise the crocodile is strong enough for any hits. His mouth is extremely large, and his teeth straight, like the teeth of a comb. . . . The lower jaw protrudes over the upper jaw, a monstrous thing; the mere sight of it strikes a man with fear.

I also saw a dead serpent in the woods, killed by one of our men. It had wings with which it might, at times, fly up from the ground. The savages cut off its head and carried it away with great diligence and care. I could not learn the reason. Some of our men thought that the savages did so because of some superstition. As far as I could see, they are not without some idea of Divinity. I conjecture that under circumstances they might easily become civilized and made honest. They could also be converted to holiness and sound religion—if God in His mercy should so ordain it.

Florida Indians killing an alligator

For as soon as the bell rang for prayers at our fort, they would be there, stretching up their hands to Heaven as we did, even with reverence and attentive ear.

Nicolas le Challeux
Narrative of Captain Jean Ribaut's last voyage in 1565

The English continued to put exploration before colonization. Martin Frobisher, questing for the illusory Northwest Passage, made voyages in 1576, 1577, and 1578. On Baffin Island he found a strait that he believed led to the East, and ore that his backers thought contained gold. Both ideas proved false.

Eskimo woman and baby, a John White drawing

They [the Eskimos] are men of a large corporature, and good proportion: their colour is not much unlike the Sunne burnt Countrey man, who laboureth daily in the Sunne for his living.

They weare their haire something long, and cut before either with stone or knife, very disorderly. Their women weare their haire long, and knit up with two loupes, shewing forth on either side of their faces, and the rest foltred upon a knot. Also some of their women race [scratch] their faces proportionally, as chinne, cheekes, and fore-head . . . whereupon they lay a colour which continueth darke azurine.

They eate their meat all raw, both flesh, fish and foule, or something per boyled with blood and a little water which they drinke. For lacke of water they will eate yce, that is hard frosen, as pleasantly as we will do Sugar Candie, or other Sugar.

If they for necessities sake stand in need of the premisses, such grasse as the Coun-trey yeeldeth they plucke up and eate, not deintily, or salletwise to allure their stom-acks to appetite: but for necessities sake without either salt, oyles or washing, like brute beasts devouring the same. They neither use table, stoole, or table cloth for comlines: but when they are imbrued with blood knuckle deepe, and their knives in like sort, they use their tongues as apt instruments to lick them cleane: in doing whereof they are assured to loose none of their victuals.

They frank or keepe certaine dogs not much unlike Wolves, which they yoke to-gither, as we do oxen & horses, to a sled or traile: and so carry their necessaries over the yce and snow from place to place: as the captive, whom we have, made perfect signes. And when those dogs are not apt for the same use: or when with hunger they are constrained for lacke of other victuals, they eate them: so that they are as needfull for them in respect of their bignesse, as our oxen are for us.

Master Dionise Settle
The Second Voyage of Master Martin Frobisher, 1577

It was not until 1584 that an English expedition was dispatched with the specific mission of exploring the American coast. Then two ships, commanded by Philip Amadas and Arthur Barlowe, explored the coast of North Carolina. Barlowe reported their findings to Sir Walter Raleigh, who had financed the expedition.

The second of July, we found shole water, wher we smelt so sweet, and so strong a smel, as if we had bene in the midst of some delicate garden abounding with all kinde

*The coat of arms of Sir
Walter Raleigh's company*

of odoriferous flowers, by which we were assured, that the land could not be farre distant: and keeping good watch, and bearing but slacke saile, the fourth of the same moneth we arrived upon the coast, which we supposed to be a continent and firme lande, and we sayled along the same a hundred and twentie English miles before we could finde any entrance, or river issuing into the Sea. The first that appeared unto us, we entred, though not without some difficultie, and cast anker about three har-quebuz-shot within the havens mouth, on the left hand of the same: and after thankes given to God for our safe arrivall thither, we manned our boats, and went to view the land next adjoyning, and to take possession of the same, in the right of the Queenes most excellent Majestie, as rightfull Queene, and Princesse of the same, and after delivered the same over to your use, according to her Majesties grant, and letters patents, under her Highnesse great seale. Which being performed, according to the ceremonies used in such enterprises, we viewed the land about us, being, whereas we first landed, very sandie and low towards the waters side, but so full of grapes, as the very beating and surge of the sea overflowed them, of which we found such plentie, as well there as in all places else, both on the sand and on the greene soile on the hils, as in the plaines, as well on every little shrubbe, as also climing towardes the tops of high Cedars, that I thinke in all the world the like abundance is not to be found: and my selfe having seene those parts of Europe that most abound, find such difference as were incredible to be written. . . .

We remained by the side of this Island two whole dayes before we saw any people of the Countrey: the third day we espied one small boate rowing towardes us having in it three persons: this boat came to the Island side, foure harquebuz-shot from our shippes, and there two of the people remaining, the third came along the shoreside towards us, and wee being then all within boord, he walked up and downe upon the point of the land next unto us: then the Master and the Pilot of the Admirall, Simon Ferdinando, and the Captaine Philip Amadas, my selfe, and others rowed to the land, whose comming this fellow attended, never making any shewe of feare or doubt. And after he had spoken of many things not understood by us, we brought him with his owne good liking, aboord the ships, and gave him a shirt, a hat and some other things, and made him taste of our wine, and our meat, which he liked very wel: and after having viewed both barks, he departed, and went to his owne boat againe, which hee had left in a little Cove or Creeke adjoyning: assoone as hee was two bow shoot into the water, he fell to fishing, and in lesse then halfe an houre, he had laden his boate as deepe, as it could swimme, with which hee came againe to the point of the lande, and there he divided his fish into two parts, pointing one part to the ship, and the other to the pinnesse; which, after he had (as much as he might) requited the former benefites received, departed out of our sight.

Captain Arthur Barlowe
The First Voyage Made to the Coasts of America, 1584

In 1602 Bartholomew Gosnold and Bartholomew Gilbert came to Cuttyhunk Island, southwest of Cape Cod, and made the first English settlement in New England, though a very temporary one. John Brereton, "one of the voyage," who wrote an account of the expedition, was not only overwhelmed by the abundant and fruitful plant and animal life of Cuttyhunk but was also very favorably impressed by the Indians.

These people, as they are exceeding courteous, gentle of disposition, and well conditioned, excelling all others that we have seene; so for shape of bodie and lovely favour, I thinke they excell all the people of America; of stature much higher than we; of complexion or colour, much like a darke Olive; their eie-browes and haire blacke, which they weare long, tied up behinde in knots, whereon they pricke feathers of fowles, in fashion of a crownet: some of them are blacke thin bearded; they make beards of the haire of beasts: and one of them offered a beard of their making to one of our sailers, for his that grew on his face, which because it was of a red colour, they judged to be none of his owne. They are quicke eied, and stedfast in their looks, fearlesse of others harmes, as intending none themselves; some of the meaner sort given to filching, which the very name of Salvages (not weighing their ignorance in good or evill) may easily excuse: their garments are of Deere skins, and some of them weare Furres round and close about their necks. They pronounce our language with great facilitie; for one of them one day sitting by me, upon occasion I spake smiling to him these words: How now (sirha) are you so saucie with my Tabacco? which words (without any further repetition) he suddenly spake so plaine and distinctly, as if he had beene a long scholar in the language. Many other such trials we had, which are here needlesse to repeat. Their women (such as we saw) which were but three in all, were but lowe of stature, their eie-browes, haire, apparell, and maner of wearing, like to the men, fat, and very well favoured, and much delighted in our compane. . . .

John Brereton
Briefe and True Relation of the Discoverie of the North Part of Virginia, 1602

Martin Pring, destined to become a widely traveled ship's master, made his first voyage in 1603 in command of a ship sent to New England for sassafras. The place where he met the music-loving Indians he describes is not known with certainty; probably it was Plymouth Bay, but it may have been on Martha's Vineyard.

During our abode on shore, the people of the Countrey came to our men sometimes ten, twentie, fortie, or threescore, and at one time one hundred and twentie at once. We used them kindly, and gave them divers sorts of our meanest Merchandize. They did eat Pease and Beanes with our men. Their owne victuals were most of fish.

We had a youth in our company that could play upon a Gitterne, in whose homely Musicke they tooke great delight, and would give him many things, as Tobacco, Tobacco-pipes, Snakes skinnes of six foot long, which they use for Girdles, Fawnes skinnes, and such like, and danced twentie in a Ring, and the Gitterne in the middest of them, using many Savage gestures, singing Jo, Ja, Jo, Ja, Ja, Jo: him that first brake the ring, the rest would knocke and cry out upon.

Martin Pring
A Voyage set out from the Citie of Bristoll, 1603

In 1607 the first permanent English colony in the New World was established at Jamestown in Virginia. Many of the first settlers were impressed by the bounty of the land, yet the colony was almost stillborn. The selection of a swampy site for the col-

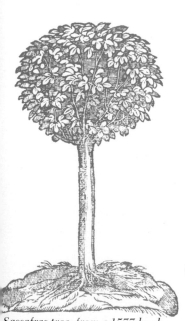
Sassafras tree, from a 1577 book

ony and the settlers' inability to get along with the Indians were the two principal reasons, as the following firsthand accounts indicate.

The six and twentieth day of Aprill [1607], about foure a clocke in the morning, wee descried the Land of Virginia: the same day wee entred into the Bay of Chesupioc directly, without any let or hinderance; there wee landed and discovered a little way, but wee could find nothing worth the speaking of, but faire meddowes and goodly tall Trees, with such Fresh-waters running through the woods, as I was almost ravished at the first sight thereof. . . .

The nine and twentieth day we set up a Crosse at Chesupioc Bay, and named that place Cape Henry. Thirtieth day, we came with our ships to Cape Comfort; where wee saw five Savages running on the shoare. . . .

The twelfth day [of May] we went backe to our ships, and discovered a point of Land, called Archers Hope, which was sufficient with a little labour to defend our selves against any Enemy. The soile was good and fruitfull, with excellent good Timber. . . . If it had not beene disliked, because the ship could not ride neere the shoare, we had setled there to all the Collonies contentment.

The thirteenth day, we came to our seating place in Paspihas Countrey, some eight miles from the point of Land, which I made mention before: where our shippes doe lie so neere the shoare that they are moored to the Trees in six fathom water.

The fourteenth day, we landed all our men, which were set to worke about the fortification, and others some to watch and ward. . . .

The fifteenth day of June we had built and finished our Fort, which was triangle wise, having three Bulwarkes at every corner like a halfe Moone, and foure or five pieces of Artillerie mounted in them, we had made our selves sufficiently strong for these Savages, we had also sowne most of our Corne on two Mountaines, it sprang a mans height from the ground.

George Percy
Observations, 1607

Title page from a 1609 booklet promoting emigration to Virginia

The place, on which the Towne is built, is a perfect Peninsulla, or tract of Land, all most wholly incompast with Water. Haveing, on the Sowth side the River (Formerly Powhetan, now called James River) 3 miles brode, Incompast on the North, from the east point, with a deep Creeke, rangeing in a cemicircle, to the west, with in 10 paces of the River; and there, by a smalle Istmos, tacked to the Continent. This Iseland (for so it is denominate) hath for Longitud (east and west) nere upo 2 miles, and for Lattitude about halfe so much, beareing in the wholl compass about 5 miles, litle more or less. It is low-ground, full of Marches and Swomps, which makes the Aire, especially in the Sumer, insalubritious and unhelty: It is not at all replenish'd with springs of fresh water, and that which they have in ther Wells, brackish, ill sented, penurious, and not gratefull to the stumack. . . .

Bacon's and Ingram's Proceedings

The land is not populous, for the [Indian] men be fewe; their far greater number is of women and children. Within 60 miles of James Towne there are about some 5000 people, but of able men fit for their warres scarse 1500. . . . The people differ very much in stature, especially in language. . . .

Some being very great as the Sesquesahamocks, others very little as the Wighcocomocoes: but generally tall and straight, of a comely proportion, and of a colour browne, when they are of any age, but they are borne white. Their haire is generally black; but few have any beards. The men weare halfe their heads shaven, the other halfe long. . . .

They are inconstant in everie thing, but what feare constraineth them to keepe. Craftie, timerous, quicke of apprehension and very ingenuous. Some are of disposition fearefull, some bold, most cautelous, all Savage. Generally covetous of copper, beads, and such like trash. They are soone moved to anger, and so malitious, that they seldome forget an injury: they seldome steale one from another, least their conjurers should reveale it, and so they be pursued and punished. That they are thus feared is certaine, but that any can reveale their offences by conjuration I am doubtfull. Their women are carefull not to bee suspected of dishonesty without the leave of their husbands.

Captain John Smith

Captain John Smith
A Map of Virginia, 1612

After exploring the outer end of Cape Cod and deciding against it as a place to settle, the Pilgrims entered Cape Cod Bay, where, in bitter weather on December 6, 1620, ten men set out in the shallop or ship's boat to make a complete circuit of the bay. The second day out, they fought a sharp but bloodless battle with Indians. After giving thanks to God for their deliverance, they continued their exploration and found the spot for their now historic settlement.

. . . From hence they departed, and costed all along, but discerned no place likly for harbor; and therfore hasted to a place that their pillote, (one Mr. Copplu [second mate of the *Mayflower*] who had bine in the cuntrie before) did assure them was a good harbor, which he had been in, and they might fetch it before night; of which they were glad, for it begane to be foule weather. After some houres sailing, it begane to snow and raine, and about the midle of the afternoone, the wind increased, and the sea became very rough, and they broake their rudder, and it was as much as 2. men could doe to steere her with a cupple of oares. But their pillott bad them be of good cheere, for he saw the harbor; but the storme increasing, and night drawing on, they bore what saile they could to gett in, while they could see. But herwith they broake their mast in 3. peeces, and their saill fell over bord, in a very grown sea, so as they had like to have been cast away; yet by God's mercie they recovered them selves, and having the floud with them, struck into the harbore. But when it came too, the pillott was deceived in the place, and said, the Lord be mercifull unto them, for his eys never saw that place before; and he and the m^r mate would have rune her ashore, in a cove full of breakers, before the winde. But a lusty seaman which steered, bad[e] those which rowed, if they were men, about with her, or ells they were all cast away; the which they did with speed. So he bid them be of good cheere and row lustly, for ther was a faire sound before them, and he doubted not but they should find one place or other wher they might ride in saftie. And though it was very darke, and rained sore, yet in the end they gott under the lee of a smalle iland, and remained ther all that night in saftie. But they knew not this to be an iland till morning, but were devided in their

Miles Standish's rapier

An early printed picture of an ear of corn

minds; some would keepe the boate for fear they might be amongst the Indians; others were so weake and could [cold], they could not endure, but got a shore, and with much adoe got fire, (all things being so wett,) and the rest were glad to come to them; for after midnight the wind shifted to the north-west, and it frose hard. But though this had been a day and night of much trouble and danger unto them, yet God gave them a morning of comforte and refreshing (as usually he doth to his children), for the next day was a faire sunshining day, and they found them sellvs to be on an iland secure from the Indeans, wher they might drie their stufe, fixe their peeces, and rest them selves, and gave God thanks for his mercies, in their manifould deliverances. And this being the last day of the weeke, they prepared ther to keepe the Sabath. On Munday they sounded the harbor, and founde it fitt for shipping; and marched into the land, and found diverse cornfeilds, and litle runing brooks, a place (as they supposed) fitt for situation; at least it was the best they could find, and the season, and their presente necessitie, made them glad to accepte of it. So they returned to their shipp againe with this news to the rest of their people which did much comforte their harts.

On the 15. of Desem^r: they wayed anchor to goe to the place they had discovered, and came within 2. leagues of it, but were faine to bear up againe; but the 16. day the winde came faire, and they arrived safe in this harbor [Plymouth]. And after wards tooke better view of the place, and resolved wher to pitch their dwelling; and the 25. day begane to erecte the first house for commone use to receive them and their goods.

William Bradford
Of Plimouth Plantation, 1606–46

Isaack de Rasieres came to New Netherland in 1626 as secretary of the colony but was sent home within the next two or three years when he became involved in a factional dispute. On arriving home, sometime between 1626 and 1630, he wrote to a friend describing New Netherland; it is the earliest picture we have of the colony.

The island of the Manhatas extends two leagues in length along the Mauritse River [Hudson River], from the point where the Fort "New Amsterdam" is building. It is about seven leagues in circumference, full of trees, and in the middle rocky to the extent of about two leagues in circuit. The north side has good land in two places, where two farmers, each with four horses, would have enough to do without much clearing at first. The grass is good in the forest and valleys, but when made into hay is not so nutritious for the cattle as here [in Holland], in consequence of its wild state, but it yearly improves by cultivation. On the east side there rises a large level field, of from 70 to 80 morgens of land [about 150 acres], through which runs a very fine fresh stream; so that that land can be ploughed without much clearing. It appears to be good. The six farms, four of which lie along the River Hellgate [East River], stretching to the south side of the island, have at least 60 morgens of land ready to be sown with winter seed, which at the most will have been ploughed eight times. But as the greater part must have some manure, inasmuch as it is so exhausted by the wild herbage, I am afraid that all will not be sown; and the more so, as the managers of the farms are hired men. . . .

The small fort, New Amsterdam, commenced to be built, is situated on a point opposite to Noten Island [Nut Island, now Governors Island]; [the channel between] is a gun-shot wide, and is full six or seven fathoms deep in the middle. This point might, with little trouble, be made a small island, by cutting a canal through Blommaert's valley, so as to afford a haven winter and summer, for sloops and ships; and the whole of this little island ought, from its nature, to be made a superb fort, to be approached by land only on one side (since it is a triangle), thus protecting them both. The river marks out, naturally, three angles; the most northern faces and commands, within the range of a cannon shot, the great Mauritse River and the land; the southernmost commands, on the water level, the channel between Noten Island and the fort, together with the Hellegat; the third point, opposite to Blommaert's valley, commands the lowland; the middle part, which ought to be left as a marketplace, is a hillock, higher than the surrounding land, and should always serve as a battery, which might command the three points, if the streets should be arranged accordingly.

Letter of Isaack de Rasieres to Samuel Blommaert, 1628 (?)

The travels of David De Vries took him to four continents, including many parts of the New World. In 1631 he and others established a settlement on a Dutch grant on the Delaware River, but it was destroyed by Indians. Later attempts—ending in 1644 —to begin settlements on Staten Island and up the Hudson River at Tappan were halted by the Indian war that broke out following Governor Willem Kieft's savage massacre of a sleeping village on Staten Island.

David De Vries used both words (right) and pictures (above) to describe the New World natives.

As I have related the manner of living, and the appearance, of the savages at Fort Orange [Albany], I will state something of the nations about Fort Amsterdam; as the Hackinsack, Tapaen, and Wicquas-geck Indians [Hackensacks, Tappans, and Wecquasgeeks, Algonquin bands living along the lower Hudson]; and these are located at some two, three, or four leagues from the entrance of the river. Their manner of living is for the most part like that of those at Fort Orange; who, however, are a stronger, and a more martial nation of Indians—especially the Maquas [Mohawks], as before mentioned, who hold most of the others along the river to Fort Amsterdam under tribute. The Indians below here are also tolerably stout, have black hair, with a long lock, which they braid and let hang on one side of the head. The hair is shorn on the top of the head like a cock's-comb. . . . Their disposition is bad. They are very revengeful; resembling the Italians. Their clothing is a coat of beaver-skins over the body, with the fur inside in winter, and outside in summer; they have, also, sometimes a bear's hide, or a coat of the skins of wild cats, or *hesspanen* [raccoons], which is an animal almost as hairy as a wild cat, and is also very good to eat. I have frequently eaten it, and found it very tender. They also wear coats of turkey's feathers, which they know how to plait together; but since our Netherland nation has traded here, they trade their beavers for duffels cloth, which we give for them, and which they find more suitable than the beavers, as they consider it better for the rain; and take two and a half in length of duffels, which is nine and a half quarters wide. Their pride is to paint their faces strangely with red or black lead, so that they look like fiends. They are then valiant; yea, they say they are *Mannette*, the Devil himself. Some of the women are very well-featured, and of tall stature. . . . they are very foul and dirty. . . .

David De Vries
Short Historical Notes, 1655

ELIZABETH REGINA. IACOB REX. CAROLVS PRINCEPS

Ould Virginia. C. Henry. Renolds. I. New England.

Fear. C. Charels. B. la Ware. C. Anne. C. Elizabeth.

Hatorask. C. Iames. C. Richmond.

Willowby Ils.

Pembroks CB.

THE
GENERALL HISTORIE
OF
Virginia, New-England, and the Summer
Isles: with the names of the Adventurers,
Planters, and Governours from their
first beginning An: 1584. to this
present 1624.

*With the Procedings of those severall Colonies
and the Accidents that befell them in all their
Journyes and Discoveries.*

Also the Maps and Descriptions of all those
Countryes, their Commodities, people,
Government, Customes, and Religion
yet knowne.

DIVIDED INTO SIXE BOOKES.

*By Captaine IOHN SMITH sometymes Governour
in those Countryes & Admirall
of New England.*

LONDON.
Printed by I.D. and
I.H. for Michael
Sparkes.
1624.

VIRGINIA. EN DAT QUINTVM.

COGNITA MIHI. GENS IN SERVIET.

QUO FATA FERUNT.

Atlantic Foothold

The later years of Elizabeth's reign saw an acceleration of mercantile activity in London and the outports, with renewed efforts to extend English trade to the distant parts of the earth. The merchants of London, Bristol, Southampton, Exeter, Norwich, and other towns had grown rich from trade across the English Channel, and with increasing prosperity came a further demand for an extension of trade to a wider world. The Muscovy Company, which even before the accession of Elizabeth had opened an avenue of commerce with Russia, had continued to explore the possibilities of trade with Eastern countries beyond the confines of Muscovy. In 1592 the Levant Company received a charter to trade with countries of the eastern Mediterranean and established its main base at Aleppo in northern Syria. Using Aleppo as a jumping-off point, the Levant merchants penetrated Persia and brought home the fabulous products of the East, all manner of goods from raisins to rugs. On December 31, 1600, the British East India Company, most famous of all the trading ventures, received its charter and began operations that were to influence the course of British expansion for more than two and a half centuries.

America seemed another logical area for the trading companies to extend their activities. The merchants were eager and enterprising, and they had money to invest. Although they were not always quite certain what opportunities America had to present, Hakluyt, Hariot, and others had indicated that a fruitful and unexploited land awaited conquest by English masters, and they were convinced that products of value would be found, products that they had previously obtained from what Richard Hakluyt the elder called their "doubtful friends." Particularly, they hoped to obtain commodities that normally came from the Mediterranean basin and the East: olive oil, dates, raisins, dyestuffs, silks, drugs, and spices. England also needed naval stores—timber, masts, rosin, turpentine, and pitch—items that she had customarily traded for in the Baltic region. And always there remained the lure of gold, silver, copper, and pearls, for the hope of finding rich mines never completely died. Gradually, however, hardheaded merchants came to realize that fish from the waters of the New World

John Smith's Generall Historie—*the title page of the first edition is reproduced—remains a primary source of information on early English colonization. The portraits are those of the monarchs Smith served: Queen Elizabeth, James I, and Charles I.*

might be much more profitable than elusive gold mines.

In the last decade of the sixteenth century, London and Bristol shipmasters were competing with French, Spanish, and Portuguese skippers for fish and whales in the waters off Nova Scotia and in the Gulf of St. Lawrence. Whale oil and oil and ivory from walruses were in demand, and furs obtained from the Indians opened up new possibilities for trade. In 1591 Thomas James, a Bristol captain, reported the discovery off southern Newfoundland of a small island, which he named "Ramea." Six years later a group of Dissenters proposed to establish a colony there, but apparently French opposition proved discouraging, and nothing came of it.

Although the lure of privateering continued to excite English seamen, they were learning that America offered other and more reliable sources of profit. Even Raleigh had discovered that importing sassafras and sarsaparilla, believed to have wondrous curative powers, could be highly profitable. During the last years of Queen Elizabeth's reign, Raleigh was not the only explorer to send trading expeditions to North America. In 1602 Bartholomew Gosnold led an expedition that sailed from Falmouth in the *Concord*, a vessel of about thirty tons. Gosnold explored the coast from southern Maine to Martha's Vineyard and built a fort on nearby Cuttyhunk Island (which they named Elizabeth's Isle).

Gosnold's voyage was something more than a simple trading venture, for he intended to leave twenty men to garrison the post on Cuttyhunk and trade with the Indians. With him he had Bartholomew Gilbert as sailing master and John Brereton, a preacher who wrote a narrative of the voyage. They traded for skins and furs, established friendly relations with the Indians, loaded a ton of sassafras roots and a quantity of cedar logs, and observed the vast schools of fish. However, because of the shortage of supplies and the objections of Gosnold's intended colonists to being left on Cuttyhunk, his plan to garrison the fort failed. The expedition returned to England in July, after a voyage of seventeen weeks.

Whether this expedition had Raleigh's permission to make the voyage is a moot point, for Raleigh, who still held a patent that gave him the right to license voyages to North America, made an effort to have all the *Concord*'s cargo of sassafras impounded lest it glut the market. One of Raleigh's own vessels had made port shortly before the *Concord* with a valuable cargo of sassafras, and he was interested in maintaining a high price. Some amicable agreement apparently was worked out, for Brereton a little later dedicated to Raleigh his report on the expedition—the *Briefe and True Relation of the Discoverie of the North Part of Virginia in 1602*.

Although Gosnold failed to make a settlement, his expedition helped to support the argument for colonies, since it brought back proof of the fertility of New England and of the value of commodities to be obtained there; and Brereton's description of the voyage induced other venturers to attempt trading expeditions to the North Atlantic coast. Gosnold himself was later to be one of the first settlers in Virginia.

In the spring of 1603, a group of Bristol merchants organized an expedition to the northern coast of America. After obtaining Raleigh's permission, the merchants fitted out two small vessels, the *Speedwell* of fifty tons, under Martin Pring, the over-all commander; and the *Discoverer*, a bark of twenty-six tons, with William Browne as captain. They went supplied with a varied lot of trading goods, enumerated in an account printed by Samuel Purchas, a compiler of travel books: "slight Merchandizes thought fit to trade with the people of the Countrey, as Hats of divers colours, greene, blue and yellow, apparell of coarse Kersie and Canvasse readie made, Stockings and Shooes, Sawes, Pick-axes, Spades and Shovels, Axes, Hatchets, Hookes, Knives, Sizzers, Hammers, Nailes, Chissels, Fish-hookes, Bels, Beades, Bugles, Looking-glasses, Thimbles, Pinnes, Needles, Threed, and such like." Leaving Milford Haven on April 10, they made a quick crossing directly to the coast of Maine. They explored the coastline to the south, entered Massachusetts Bay (which Gosnold had overshot), and anchored in Plymouth harbor.

Like Gosnold, they were looking for sassafras, which they found in sufficient quantity to load their vessels. All along the coast they noted the fish, "better than those of New-found-land," and they observed that the rocky coast made a good place to dry their catch. They also could "see no reason to the contrary, but that Salt may bee made in these parts, a matter of no small importance." The mainland of what we call Massachusetts they thought a promising country. "The Land is full of Gods good blessings," they reported, and "so is the Sea replenished with great abundance of excellent fish, as Cods sufficient to lade many ships, which we found upon the Coast in the moneth of June, Seales to make Oile withall, Mullets, Turbuts, Mackerels, Herrings, Crabs, Lobsters, Crevises, and Muscels with ragged Pearles in them."

Although the Indians were eager to trade, they proved treacherous. Fortunately, Pring's sassafras gatherers suffered no attacks, partly because they had two English mastiffs named Fool and Gallant, who terrified the Indians (one of the dogs was trained to carry a half-pike in his mouth, to the astonishment of the natives). Having loaded the *Discoverer* with sassafras and furs, Pring dispatched the bark in late July "to give some speedie contentment to the Adventurers," and about two weeks later he departed in the *Speedwell*. The two vessels reached Bristol after absences of five and a half and six months respectively, and their cargoes were easily sold.

An expedition in 1605, commanded by George Waymouth in the *Archangel*, was sponsored by the Earl of Southampton and his Roman Catholic son-in-law, Thomas Arundell. This too was a trading venture, but Arundell was also anxious to find a suitable site for a Catholic colony. Waymouth sailed at the end of March and on May 14 made a landfall on an island off the Maine coast, probably Monhegan. The ship's company marveled at the ease with which they caught fish of many sorts, all fat and tasty, and James Rosier, who wrote an account of the voyage, enumerated many varieties of sea life that he considered commercially valuable, including whales, seals, and porpoises.

Waymouth explored the coast and found a great river (not definitely identified, but either the Penobscot or the Kennebec), which excited his interest. He thought there might be mines of precious metals on its shores, and he examined enough mussels to convince him that they produced valuable pearls. The summer climate pleased the explorers; and tall evergreens, magnificent oaks, and other trees held a promise for shipbuilding.

Leaving the American coast on June 16, Waymouth made the return trip to Dartmouth in one month and two days, a quick crossing. Besides a profitable cargo of furs obtained in trade, Waymouth brought back five Indians whom he had kidnapped. They proved not unwilling captives and were a sensation in England. Sir Ferdinando Gorges, the military governor of Plymouth and Dartmouth, who was already nursing a scheme for colonizing in America, commandeered the Indians, kept three of them, and sent the other two to a friend, Sir John Popham, the Lord Chief Justice. Gorges and Popham saw to it that the Indians were taught English (the Indians also adopted English habits and developed a taste for beer). What made them particularly valuable was their willingness to learn and recite speeches pro-

Identified only as Mme. Penobscot (the name of her tribe), the above lady in Elizabethan ruff and farthingale was one of five Indians brought back from Maine in 1605 by George Waymouth, taught to speak English, and used very effectively to promote subsequent colonizing projects.

OVERLEAF: *Broad quay on the Bristol waterfront. Beginning with Cabot in 1497 and continuing into the 1600's, a large number of exploring and colonizing expeditions to America set out from this English port.*

moting their native land as a veritable paradise for English settlers. Gorges and Popham had found a way of dramatizing the propaganda that Richard Hakluyt and his expansionist colleagues had been disseminating for nearly a generation, and the land boom was on. All over England, especially in London and in the port towns of the West Country and East Anglia, men were talking about the possibilities of trade in North America.

King James's accession in 1603 gave this movement further stimulus. The years of uncertainty about the succession were over. Businessmen could breathe easier now that the threat of civil disturbance had passed. But more than that, James, a man of peace, set about ending the long conflict with Spain, which he accomplished in 1604. No longer were Englishmen privileged to capture Spanish and Portuguese vessels on the high seas; they would have to look elsewhere for quick riches. Although Spain did not formally admit England's right to colo-

nize lands in America, no overt action was taken against English trading expeditions to unsettled regions of the North, and it was tacitly understood that settlements might be made there.

The increased concern over colonization came to a head with the issuance of a charter on April 10, 1606, providing for two colonies in North America between the thirty-fourth and forty-fifth parallels of latitude. The charter, issued on petition of Sir Thomas Gates, Sir George Somers, Richard Hakluyt, Edward Maria Wingfield, Thomas Hanham, Raleigh Gilbert, William Parker, George Popham, and others, established a royal Council of Virginia that would have over-all supervision of the colonial activities. The charter granted the petitioners rights to establish "two several colonies and companies; the one consisting of certain Knights, gentlemen, merchants, and adventurers, of our city of London and elsewhere" who would settle anywhere between the

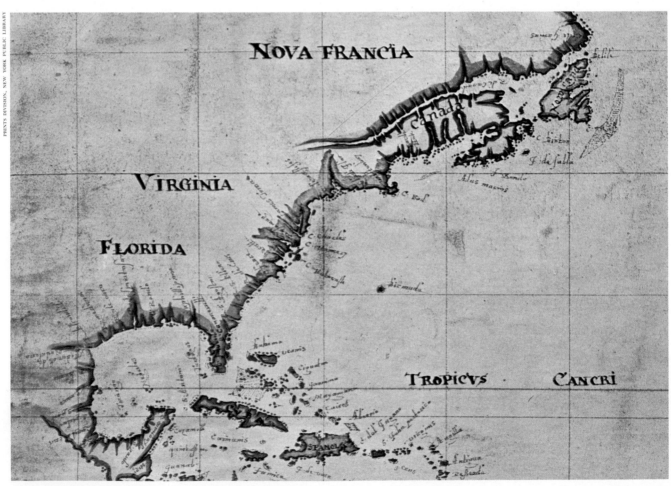

When this Virginia Company map was drawn about 1607, North America already showed the three-way division that would prevail during a century and a half of colonial rivalry: France was in Canada, Spain held Florida, and the land between was English.

thirty-fourth and the forty-first parallel, and "the other consisting of sundry Knights, gentlemen, merchants, and other adventurers of our cities of Bristol and Exeter, and of our town of Plimouth, and of other places" who were permitted to settle between the thirty-eighth and the forty-fifth parallel, providing that the last colony to plant itself should not choose a location within one hundred English miles of the first.

The colonies were to be established by two stock companies, which came to be known as the Virginia Company of London, or simply the London Company, and the Plymouth Company. On November 20, 1606, the king issued "Articles, Instructions, and Orders" that included the names of fourteen individuals who "shall be our councel for all matters which shall happen in Virginia or any [of] the territories of America." The royal Council of Virginia was empowered to appoint for each of the separate colonies resident councils that would elect one of their number to be president for a term of one year. These resident councils would govern the colonies "as neer to the common lawes of England, and the equity thereof, as may be."

With a charter and a plan of government, albeit a plan that proved almost unworkable, the next problem was to raise capital and find willing settlers. By December, 1606, something over a hundred potential settlers were enlisted and embarked in three vessels, the *Susan Constant*, the *Godspeed*, and the *Discovery*. Under the command of Captain Christopher Newport, an experienced officer who had served in the Muscovy Company and had led privateering expeditions to the West Indies, the three vessels sailed from their Thames dock at Blackwall on December 19, 1606; but the weather proved fickle, and they had to anchor in the Downs for more than a month and did not clear the coast of England until January 29, 1607.

Following a southerly route, they sailed for the West Indies and made their first landfall at Martinique on March 23. Slowly they proceeded northward until on April 26 they reached the entrance to Chesapeake Bay, where they went ashore at what is now Old Point Comfort and at an Indian settlement called Kecoughtan. After a fortnight's exploration that took them up a great river, which they named the James, they chose a peninsula far enough inland to be out of danger from sea marauders. In water deep enough to moor their vessels to the trees, they tied up on May 13 and began unloading supplies. This site, named Jamestown in honor of

their sovereign, was destined at last to become the first permanent English settlement in North America.

But for several years to come, the survival of Jamestown would be in doubt, for rarely had so incompetent a lot of colonists arrived in a foreign land. Even before their arrival, the leaders were quarreling, and the rank and file were sea-weary and discouraged. On the way over, enemies of Captain John Smith, one of seven named to the council in Virginia, had him "restrained" —a form of arrest—on the ground that he planned to murder the rest of the council and make himself king in Virginia. The charge was without foundation, but Smith was not released until they landed and was not admitted to the council until June 10.

Edward Maria Wingfield, who was chosen first president of the council, developed a profound dislike for Smith, and the feeling was mutual. Wingfield, an Elizabethan "gentleman" aware of all of the prerogatives of his class, looked down upon Smith, who was of less imposing social rank. On his part, Smith, who let nobody forget that he had been a captain in the armies of the Holy Roman Empire, was not beyond showing his contempt for some of his colleagues, including Wingfield.

Discipline was almost totally lacking in the colony, and nobody was keen about work. Of ninety-three men whose names are known, fifty-nine were classified as gentlemen, and they regarded the manual labor of digging, cutting trees, and planting crops as beneath their dignity, if indeed these labors were not beyond their skills. They had come to fight the heathen, to search for mines, and hopefully to get rich as the Spanish conquistadors had got rich. The class consciousness of these early gentlemen-adventurers is considered one of the primary reasons for the incompetence of the Jamestown settlers. After two months, the hundred men had planted hardly anything and had built no houses or permanent shelters of any kind.

Though Smith blamed Wingfield for lack of adequate leadership, the whole group must share the blame for indolence and even stupidity. In addition, the settlers had no incentive to work for themselves. A few were shareholders, but most were merely employees of the Virginia Company of London—and poorly paid employees at that. Since individual initiative was lacking, only a firm disciplinarian with the authority to enforce his commands could have driven these ill-fed, dispirited, inexperienced, and lazy colonists to do an honest day's work. But the gentlemen would not even turn a hand to the building of houses for themselves; they were waiting for Captain Newport to go back to England for laborers and carpenters to do this work.

Although the glowing accounts of the fruitfulness of the country published by propagandists convinced many adventurers to the New World that they could live off the land, the Jamestown colonists were too inexperienced and lacking in enterprise for that. The James River swarmed with edible fish of many varieties. A few years later a parson, the Reverend Alexander Whitaker, wrote in his *Good News from Virginia* (1613) about the abundance of fish, many of which he had caught with his own hook and line. But the first settlers had neither the gear nor the skill to catch fish. In the surrounding woods, deer, bears, squirrels, turkeys, and wild fowl abounded, but the Jamestown colonists had little or no knowledge of how to take them. Furthermore, they were terrified of the Indians who roamed the same woods. Hence the settlers huddled together on their peninsula and consumed the peas, meal, and ships' biscuits that Captain Newport spared from his stores. They supplemented this fare with game and corn bartered from the Indians. Indeed, they soon came to depend upon the Indians for their subsistence. But before the first summer was over, poor diet, contaminated water, mosquitoes, and the hot climate had taken their toll, and Jamestown's graveyard was growing.

The truth is that the gentlemen still hoped to find gold and other valuable minerals. Newport, who sailed for England on June 22, had explored as far as the falls of the James, the present site of Richmond, and was convinced that the country thereabouts contained mineral wealth. He had picked up a few pieces of "ore" that looked promising. Much more certain that he had found gold-bearing earth was Captain John Martin, a member of the Jamestown council and the son of a London goldsmith, who had some of his ore loaded on Newport's vessel. When Newport returned to Plymouth, England, in late July, he sent a letter to Robert Cecil, Earl of Salisbury, to tell him, "The contrie is excellent and very rich in gold and Copper. Of the gould we have brought a say [an assay] and hope to be with your Lordship shortlie to show it to his Majesty and the rest of the Lords." Fortunately, Newport also brought back a cargo of timber and sassafras that helped to pay the expense of the voyage, for the ore proved to be only dirt containing mica.

Newport returned to the colony in January, 1608,

This page from John Smith's Generall Historie of Virginia is unabashed boasting about Smith's own feats. Smith is pictured, among other things, being tied up to be killed with arrows, slaying Indians, capturing two towering chiefs, and, of course, being rescued by Pocahontas. Many historians think that most of these adventures—allowing for exaggeration—really befell Smith.

bringing the first supply of recruits, including two refiners and two goldsmiths, competent, presumably, to examine ore and evaluate its mineral contents. Later, in *The Generall Historie of Virginia* (1624), John Smith complained that there was "no talke, no hope, nor worke, but dig gold, wash gold, refine gold, load gold" —all to no avail, for glittering earth and ore were worthless. Quick wealth was not destined to come to the Virginia Company of London and the gallants whom it sent to Virginia in the guise of settlers.

In the meantime, the colony had gone from bad to worse. Soon after Newport's return, most of the shacks that the colonists had put together were destroyed by fire. The winter was bitter cold, the Indians were chary of trading, food was scarce, and sickness and death stalked the colony. Although Newport's sailors set to work to erect shelters for the men and their meager supplies, the outlook was dismal.

Before Newport's return from England, Smith, on an exploring and trading expedition, had been captured by tribesmen of Powhatan, the overlord of several Indian tribes in the back country from Jamestown. On this occasion, according to Smith's account, Powhatan's daughter Pocahontas, a girl of eleven or twelve years of age, had saved his life by placing her head next to his when Powhatan's warriors had him stretched on the ground with his head between two stones, ready to bash out his brains. Powhatan released Smith, who came back to Jamestown with a tale of some kind of alliance with this Indian potentate, who was described as "king" or "emperor" of the Indians of the region.

Perhaps, as one historian suggests, this celebrated experience, later embellished by Smith, was a form of ritual, and his reprieve was a symbol of his acceptance into the tribe. At any rate, Powhatan declared Smith a werowance, or chief, and the curious and fickle friendship established between Powhatan and Smith enabled the English to barter with the Indians for corn. And without corn and occasional deer and turkeys obtained from the natives, the colonists would have perished.

In season and out, the leaders of the colony quarreled. In September, 1607, only a few months after the colonists had established themselves, the council preferred absurd charges against Wingfield (one accusation was that he was conspiring with the Spaniards to destroy the colony). Robert Hunt, the parson, tried earnestly to make peace between the squabbling factions, but his efforts were of no avail. The council arrested and deposed Wingfield and put in his place as president Captain John Ratcliffe, as vain as he was incompetent. For his aggrandizement he ordered a presidential palace constructed, a folly never completed.

While Ratcliffe was finding ways to satisfy his vanity at Jamestown, Smith took a barge and a party of men and again went exploring. He found the entrance to the broad Potomac and conceived the notion that it might lead to the Great South Sea, the eternal dream of seventeenth-century explorers. In July, 1608, Smith and his party pushed their barge through marshes that one day would be the site of the State Department in Washington. A little later they reached the Potomac rapids above Georgetown—a sure sign that the Potomac would not lead to the South Sea. Smith sorrowfully turned back and made his way to Jamestown. There he found the colonists in rebellion against Ratcliffe, and in September, 1608, he was installed as president of the Virginia council.

Smith realized that food, substantial quarters, and security from Indian attack were more important than the vain search for gold, and he immediately set about putting his views into practice. The grim facts were that death had removed some of the more obstreperous and indolent of the gentlemen-adventurers, and the rest had learned an object lesson. Smith put everybody to work. Gentlemen whose hands were so soft that they blistered swore at their pain, but Smith kept them busy cutting timber, sawing boards, ditching drains, preparing the soil for crops, and improving their buildings. Furthermore, lest their oaths should offend the Almighty, whose presence Smith felt acutely, he ordered a penalty of a cup of cold water per oath poured down the sleeve of each profane swearer. For the first time since the settlers landed at Jamestown, a constructive disciplinarian was in charge.

In October, 1608, Newport again sailed into the James River with the second supply of recruits, seventy in number, including the first women to arrive, a Mistress Forrest and her maid, Ann Burras. In this group were four "Dutchmen" (probably meaning Germans), one Swiss, and three Poles who were to teach the colonists various industrial skills, including the manufacture of glass, the making of pitch, and the smelting of iron and other ores. The Virginia Council back in London was determined to find a profitable source of wealth in America. Smith got a glassworks started and some building construction under way, but the "Dutchmen"

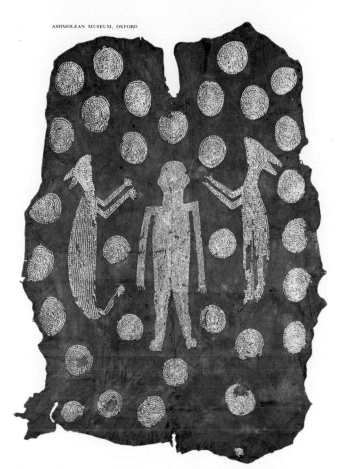

This shell-decorated deerskin, which was brought to England from Jamestown in the early 1600's, is believed to have been the cloak of the powerful chief Powhatan.

defected to Powhatan. They plotted to lure other dissidents from Jamestown and with the help of the Indians to take over the colony. The plot failed, but Smith was unable to recapture them for punishment.

A report of Powhatan's importance in Virginia, given by Newport to the Virginia Council in London, had induced those diplomatic planners to devise a ceremony to draw Powhatan to the English cause and make him a staunch liege lord of King James. They would have him solemnly crowned as emperor of the Indians, with all the trappings of royalty. Newport had brought the regalia. The only problem was to get Powhatan to submit to the ceremony.

Smith undertook this task and sought to persuade Powhatan to come to Jamestown to be crowned. Powhatan, asserting his royal prerogatives, replied that if he was a great king, then let the English come and

crown him in his own territory. Thus it was that Captain Newport set out on one of the most bizarre expeditions of his varied career. Dressed in his best uniform as the captain of the king's ship, with an appropriate retinue, he journeyed to Powhatan's village in what is now Gloucester County with the imperial regalia, consisting of a gilt crown, a bowl and pitcher, an English bed, some other pieces of furniture and knickknacks, and a marvelous scarlet cloak.

Powhatan was ready enough to receive the gifts, but he was uncertain about a few elements in the coronation ritual. Kneeling was new to him, even to be crowned, and it took physical force to complete this portion of the ceremony. "He, neither knowing the majesty nor meaning of a Crowne," Smith later wrote, "nor bending of the knee, indured so many perswasions, examples, and instructions as tired them all. At last, by leaning hard on his shoulders, he a little stooped, and *Newport* put the Crowne on his head; when, by the warning of a pistoll, the boates were prepared with such a volly of shot, that the king start[ed] up in a horrible feare till he saw all was well. Then remembering himselfe, to congratulate their kindnesse, he gave his old shoes and his mantle to Captain *Newport*." But crowning Powhatan a king in the service of King James brought little change in his relations with the settlers. From time to time he continued to withhold supplies of corn and to devise other stratagems to discourage them.

If the colony did not flourish under Smith, it at least survived, and Smith's gentlemen-axemen cut enough timber and made enough clapboard to give Newport a comfortable cargo for his return trip to London. During Smith's presidency, in 1609, the London merchants and investors procured another charter that gave direct control of the Jamestown colony to the Virginia Company of London instead of vesting control in the royal Council of Virginia. Under this second charter, the London Company was empowered to select a governor and give him administrative power. Although Smith was doing all he could to save the colony from disaster, the history of bickering and near-mutiny was such that the authorities in London appointed Lord De La Warr, a man of unimpeachable character, to go out as lord governor and captain general. Since he could not leave at once, the company chose Sir Thomas Gates to be deputy governor pending De La Warr's arrival. Gates sailed in June, 1609, in the largest expedition yet organized for Virginia—seven stout ships and two small pinnaces

Cal Sacks

Jamestown
1614

No one can know, except in a general way, what Jamestown looked like in 1614—or any other year. To make reconstruction even more difficult, the James River has washed away the site of the old fort. However, this panoramic view of Jamestown in 1614 is not mere conjecture but is based on considerable evidence, especially contemporary descriptions.

The old triangular fort, a structure of which good descriptions remain, was showing its age, and some of the small houses within its cramped acre had probably been abandoned, but artillery was still emplaced in the round bastions. In 1614 there were "two faire rowes of howses" outside the fort, protected by a new palisade, and a few farmers had built outside this pale. Most new houses were two-and-a-half stories high, and all buildings were either clapboard or wattle-and-daub construction. Two blockhouses kept watch on the Back River against crossings by Indians. Within a few years the fort's disappearance and the settlement's growth due to the new tobacco prosperity would completely change Jamestown.

under the command of Sir George Somers, bearing some six hundred men, women and children.

The fleet ran into a hurricane, and on July 25 the *Sea Venture*, commanded by Captain Newport and bearing Gates and Somers, foundered on a reef off the Bermudas. Fortunately, she wedged on the reef, and the ship's company with their supplies and tools got ashore. There they remained for eleven months while they constructed two pinnaces that eventually carried them safely to Virginia. Accounts of this shipwreck furnished Shakespeare with details used in *The Tempest*.

Seven of the vessels rode out the hurricane and in early August limped into the James River. Shortly afterward, Captain John Smith was badly burned in a powder explosion and embarked for England on one of the returning vessels. Pending the arrival of the new deputy governor, George Percy, brother of the Earl of Northumberland, was named president of the council.

The winter that followed Smith's departure was the worst that the miserable colony had yet endured. Percy was less than competent and showed little of Smith's capacity for making the colonists work and trade with the Indians. Disease and malnutrition took their toll. During this "starving time," the settlers devoured every living animal they had brought with them, even their dogs and cats, and such rats and mice as they could catch. Reduced to cannibalism, one man murdered his wife and salted her down for food. Despite their fear of the savages, some men, crazed for food, ran away to the Indians and were never seen again. When spring came, some sixty survivors remained of nearly five hundred.

At length, on May 23, 1610, Gates, Somers, and Newport arrived from Bermuda in their two pinnaces, bringing just enough food for their own crews and passengers. Discouraged at the state of the colony and thinking it a hopeless cause, Gates agreed to embark the survivors in his two pinnaces and two possessed by the colony. He planned to make for Newfoundland, where they might find passage back to England in the fishing fleet. Accordingly, they abandoned Jamestown on June 7 and set sail. The next morning, while lying off Mulberry Island, they saw a longboat approaching and were told that Lord De La Warr had arrived in the mouth of Chesapeake Bay with three ships, three hundred men, and a "great store of provisions." On hearing these joyful tidings, Gates returned to Jamestown and put his ragged band of disconsolate settlers ashore again.

De La Warr's ships arrived at Jamestown on June 10,

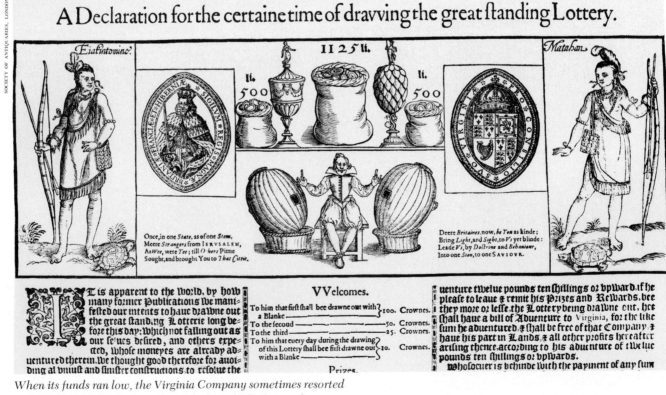

When its funds ran low, the Virginia Company sometimes resorted to lotteries to replenish its coffers. The broadside shown above announced a lottery in London in 1615, a year when news from Jamestown had been bad and investments in England were lagging.

and his Lordship came ashore and took possession with considerable pomp and circumstance. After a sermon by the minister, De La Warr had his commission read and made a stern speech warning the colonists of their vanities and idleness, which might cause him to "draw the sword of justice." Finding the town a "very noisome and unwholesome place," he set his sailors to cleaning it up. He also restored the palisades around the fort and rebuilt the church, where he went in great state each Sunday to worship, accompanied by a guard of halberdiers in red cloaks. The Jamestown populace was given to understand that they had a governor who knew his dignity and would brook no idleness or mutiny.

But not even the vigorous rule of De La Warr could stop the inroads of disease or keep the Indians from picking off the colonists when they strayed beyond the palisade. Death from malaria and typhoid fever and from the arrows and tomahawks of the Indians took a disastrous toll of the colonists. De La Warr himself came down with a fever and eventually had to return to England, leaving George Percy in charge as deputy governor. The population had been reduced to less than one hundred and fifty.

The investors in the Virginia Company of London had reason to be discouraged over the failure of the colony to show a profit. Some were in favor of taking their losses and abandoning the colony once and for all, but the leadership in the company refused to admit defeat. Pamphlets and sermons inspired by the company praised Virginia and its products and held out the promise of unbounded prosperity just around the corner. A few realists, however, privately gave the company some sound advice. De La Warr reported that a better quality of colonist was needed, and John Smith had made similar recommendations. The Virginia Company began a more careful system of recruiting, but for years governors complained about unruly, indolent, and licentious rogues who came to Virginia as colonists. Later, when the English government sent over convicts, the quality of immigrants further deteriorated.

But if stern rule could whip the Jamestown colonists into anything resembling a civilized society, the governors who came after De La Warr were determined to provide it. Two veteran soldiers, Sir Thomas Dale (deputy governor on two occasions, from May to August, 1611, and from March, 1614, to April, 1616) and Sir Thomas Gates (lieutenant governor from August, 1611, to March, 1614), did their best to give the colony

The plant above is the species of mild tobacco (Nicotiana tabacum) *that John Rolfe introduced into Virginia. Below is a woodcut from a 1622 work on silkworm culture, an industry that, despite several attempts, never succeeded in the colonies.*

were imported throughout the seventeenth century. In time, African slave-labor became the mainstay of tobacco production. During most of the seventeenth century, however, white indentured servants—those who signed a bond to pay their passage over by working from four to seven years—provided most of the labor.

Small as the colony was, its government remained a vexatious problem to the Virginia Company and to the inhabitants as well. Governors might be good or bad, and no one in the colony had much to say about it. But in November, 1618, the company drew up another charter—the fourth—known as the Great Charter, which established a number of reforms, including a more liberal provision for land grants and a commission for setting up a legislative assembly. To carry out these provisions, the company in April, 1619, sent out Sir George Yeardley as governor. Sir Edwin Sandys, who succeeded Sir Thomas Smythe as treasurer of the company, began a vigorous effort to improve matters in the colony. For example, lands were set aside for the establishment of a university in Virginia at Henrico, and funds were collected for the purpose.

The legislative assembly, the first held in English America, met on July 30, 1619, in the church at Jamestown. Twenty-two burgesses, two each elected by popular vote of the citizens of the eleven districts, met with the governor and the council to consider the whole problem of the colony's government. The assembly lasted for a week or two and broke up on account of the intemperate heat and the illness of several of its members. But in that time it had enacted a number of new laws, recommended changes in the laws sent over by the company, and acted on several judicial matters.

Popular government in the English colonies had made a start. It is true that the Virginia Company could veto any laws passed in Virginia, but the first assembly began a procedure that would be followed in the future: laws enacted would become operative at once; if later they were vetoed, they could be modified and sent back for approval. Thus, owing to the time required for communication, it was possible to enact and retain a law that might eventually receive a veto.

By 1622 Virginia seemed to be on the way to a prosperous future. During the three preceding years, forty-two ships had brought in more than thirty-five hundred settlers. The Virginia Company, out of its care for the lonely men in the colony, had sent over godly and virtuous maids to be their wives. The settlers had lost their fear of the Indians and no longer carried weapons except when hunting. Throughout the colony peace prevailed. But the Indians secretly resented the continuing expansion of the white population.

Powhatan, who had died in 1618, had been succeeded by his half brother Opechancanough, who kept up a show of friendship with the English while plotting their destruction. In March, 1622, on Good Friday, he gave the signal for an attack. In all the outlying settlements in Virginia, the Indians fell on the whites and slaughtered men, women, and children. A warning from a Christian Indian saved Jamestown and a few other communities, but before the day was over, between three and four hundred settlers were dead. The others rallied and fought off the Indians. Quickly the news was carried to London, with a request for old armor and weapons in the Tower, which were sent. In time the colonists wreaked such vengeance on the Indians that they made only one other disastrous attack, that of 1644. But the massacre of 1622 forever ended any peaceful relations between the Virginians and the red men of the forest. Henceforth the colonists were determined to annihilate such Indians as threatened their expansion.

The Virginia Company of London, despite Herculean efforts, had not made a success of its stock-company venture in colonization. Political factions inside the company created dissension. Finally, in 1624, King James intervened, dissolved the company, and transformed Virginia into a crown colony. Henceforth it would be a royal province ruled by a governor appointed by the king. But the king allowed the continuance of the general assembly, which ensured some local autonomy.

Virginia was now firmly established under the royal authority. Since land was available to emigrants in fee simple, younger sons, men with a little capital and ambition, could come to Virginia and be sure of founding landed estates for themselves and their heirs. No longer were the dwellers in Jamestown and subsidiary settlements merely laborers working for a stock company. They were free citizens in a venture that promised great personal rewards. Furthermore, a commodity had been found that ensured a ready source of money. Tobacco continued to increase in economic importance.

If in 1624 Virginia had much to accomplish, it was well on its way to a creative and prosperous existence. Years of tribulation had at last brought forth a permanent colony. The English were in North America to stay.

Pocahontas, renamed Rebecca and married to Virginia planter John Rolfe, was visiting in London in 1616 when this portrait was made. The next year, while preparing to return home, she died of smallpox, at the age of twenty-two.

NATIONAL PORTRAIT GALLERY, WASHINGTON

Ætatis suæ 21. A°. 1616.
Matoaks als Rebecka daughter to the mighty Prince
Powhatan Emperour of Attanoughkomouck als Virginia
converted and baptized in the Christian faith, and
Wife to the Wor.ll Mr Tho: Rolff.

RETORICA SEER AERDICH „ WORT DOOR BACCHVS WEER ONWAERDICH

Religious Havens

While the Virginia Company of London was struggling to settle a colony in the southern part of "Virginia," as the great sweep of the Atlantic coast between the Cape Fear River and Bangor, Maine, was then called, the Plymouth Company and other venturers were making tentative efforts to exploit the northern portion of this territory. Sir Ferdinando Gorges and Chief Justice Sir John Popham, both of whom were representative of the land-hungry Englishmen of the day, became prominent in the Plymouth Company. Popham already had interested himself in Irish colonization and in draining the fens in East Anglia. North America now offered greater prospects for the acquisition of land and bases for trade.

After sending two exploratory voyages to the New England coast, the Plymouth Company embarked some ninety colonists in two ships, the *Gift of God*, commanded by George Popham, a nephew of the chief justice, and the *Mary and John*, under Raleigh Gilbert, son of Sir Humphrey Gilbert. Sailing separately on May 1 and June 1, 1607, they reached the Kennebec River, then called the Sagadahoc, in early August and chose a site for settlement not far from the mouth. At the end of two months the colonists had built a fort and some houses inside the palisades.

The settlement at Sagadahoc was beset by the same troubles that had nearly destroyed Jamestown. George Popham, elected governor, was fifty-three years old, fat, timorous, and incompetent; Gilbert, twenty-four years old, was headstrong and arrogant. A clash between the two leaders and their partisans was inevitable. Furthermore, as in Jamestown, the colonists were undisciplined, lawless, lazy, and quarrelsome. Again, like the first Jamestown settlers, they were mere hirelings, without any personal stake in the success of the venture. Even so, the group contained a few skilled workers and at least enough shipwrights and carpenters to make a stout pinnace of thirty tons, named the *Virginia*, which later sailed to Jamestown and proved useful in that colony.

It was inevitable that the colony at Sagadahoc would fail. Half of the potential settlers went back in the returning ships. During the winter some of the buildings, with the colonists' essential supplies, burned. One piece of bad luck followed an-

Holland, refuge of the Pilgrims, was an island of tolerance in a Europe torn by religious dissension. In this 17th-century painting, the "Rhetoricians' Guild" of Haarlem harmoniously argues a point of theology. The debaters include such opposing types as a Calvinist, a Moslem, a Jew, and a libertine.

85

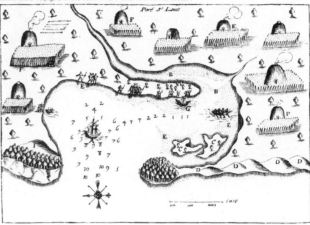

Sir John Popham (left) gained an unpleasant notoriety,
while acting in his capacity as Lord Chief Justice, by the
way he browbeat Sir Walter Raleigh during the latter's
trial in 1603. A short time later Popham was emulating
Raleigh as a promoter of American colonization, and in
1607 he and his colleague, Sir Ferdinando Gorges, sent the first
English colony to New England. The colony was the victim
of adversity—the Maine winter was bitter, the warehouse
burned, the leader died—and the settlers came home in
the fall of 1608, but a beginning had been made. The
colonists carried plans for a stout fort (below), but what
they actually built fell far short of the dream. The
chart of Plymouth harbor (above) was made by Samuel de
Champlain in 1605. John Smith was another noted explorer
who saw the harbor—in 1614—before the Pilgrims did.

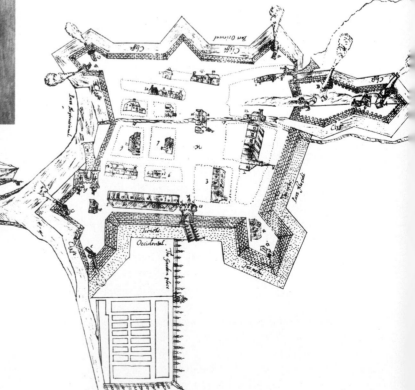

other. In England, Sir John Popham, who had dreamed of getting rich by settling Maine with England's surplus population, especially paupers, died suddenly. Before the winter was over, his nephew at Sagadahoc was also dead. Raleigh Gilbert received news of the death of his older brother and found it necessary to return to England to look after his inheritance. Since everybody at Sagadahoc was sick of Maine and eager to leave, the colonists abandoned the site as early in 1608 as they could get away. No further serious effort would be made to colonize New England for more than a decade.

But interest in the region did not die. Reports of its rich fisheries had long since reached Europe, and not only English fishermen but Spanish, Portuguese, and French frequented the coast and set up temporary bases where they could salt their catch and dry their nets. Sir Francis Popham, another son of the chief justice, sent several expeditions to fish and trade for furs. In 1614 Captain John Smith led an expedition, underwritten by certain London merchants, to the coast of Maine to hunt for gold and copper mines, catch whales, fish, and trade for furs. He was accompanied in a second ship by Captain Thomas Hunt. They made a landfall at Monhegan Island and tried their luck with whales, but to no avail—the finbacks were too elusive for their unskilled harpooners. The expedition could find no evidence of gold or copper mines, but fish were abundant, and Smith knew that the Indians would part with skins and furs for trinkets. Leaving Hunt and his own ship at anchor off Monhegan while their crews fished from small boats, Smith and a party of eight or nine set out in another boat to explore the coastline and to trade. Before he got back to the ship, he had visited the shores of Massachusetts Bay, including Plymouth harbor, skirted the whole of Cape Cod Bay, touched at Provincetown harbor, and rounded the cape before heading north again. Smith was carefully mapping the region as he went, and the details he wrote down were so exact that sites described can be recognized to this day. Smith returned to England with two firm convictions: that here was a region suitable for another English colony, and that fishing and fur trading would be more profitable than mining. Although he managed to interest Sir Ferdinando Gorges in an attempt at colonization, a series of mishaps frustrated their hopes.

One result of Smith's expedition of 1614 was the publication in 1616 of his *A Description of New England*, together with a map, dedicated to Prince Charles (later Charles I). At Smith's request the prince looked over the map and suggested names in place of those supplied by Smith, but the name "New England," first used by Smith, remained unchanged. "Of all the foure parts of the world that I have yet seene not inhabited," Smith declared in his *Description*, "could I have but meanes to transport a Colonie, I would rather live here then any where: and if it did not maintaine it selfe, were wee but once indifferently well fitted, let us starve." He emphasized the value of fish, which had made the Hollanders rich, the vast quantity of timber and naval stores, the profits from furs, and the fertility of the soil.

Thomas Hunt, who commanded the second ship in Smith's expedition of 1614, was a villainous fellow who not only tried to steal Smith's maps and data but, when left in New England to fish, kidnapped twenty-four Indians in the Cape Cod region with the intention of selling them as slaves in Spain. One of the Indians, named Tisquantum, or Squanto, eventually got back to New England, where he later befriended the Pilgrims.

John Smith's dreams of founding a prosperous and profitable colony in New England were never realized, but only a few years later, New England would become a refuge for groups who sought a haven from religious persecution as well as a means of livelihood.

As early as Sir Humphrey Gilbert's explorations of Newfoundland and Nova Scotia, a few Englishmen had thought of the New World as a place where those who dissented from the established religion might find a refuge. Later, Waymouth's voyage of exploration had as one of its objectives the search for a place where Catholics might settle. But the revelations of the 1605 Gunpowder Plot to blow up the Houses of Parliament for the time being halted plans of Catholics to emigrate to America with the blessing of the government.

In the early seventeenth century, others besides Catholics found it difficult to reconcile their beliefs with those of the established Anglican church. The term "Puritan" is generally used to describe a variety of dissenting sectarians who objected to the polity and ritualism of the English church as smacking too much of "popery." Great differences existed among the sects. Some merely wished to purify the ritual of elaborate ceremonies; others objected to bishops and hierarchical control; many found the use of the prayerbook distasteful; some grounded their objections on the wearing of surplices by the clergy, or on the requirement to kneel at the altar rails, or on some other detail of the service.

The more extreme dissenters objected to all these traditions and to others as well in their quest for complete simplicity. Although the majority of the Puritans at this time wanted to stay within the fabric of the established church if they could remodel or "purify" it to their taste, others gave up hope of improving it and sought to withdraw. They were the Separatists. The Protestant doctrine that every man had the right to read the Bible and interpret it according to his own lights held the potential for infinite fractionalization.

One group of Separatists from the neighborhood of Scrooby Manor in Nottinghamshire suffered so much persecution from church authorities, who were determined to force them to conformity in their worship, that they decided to emigrate to Holland, then the most tolerant country in Europe. A few slipped away secretly in 1607, and a larger group got away in 1608. The Scrooby Separatists, eventually to be known in American history as the Pilgrims, first settled in Amsterdam, but, disturbed by the quarrels of religious groups there and confused by so large a city, they decided to move to the university town of Leiden. There they established a church and found employment as weavers, clothworkers, tailors, bakers, and artisans of various sorts. Their pastor was John Robinson, and their lay leader, an elder in their church, was William Brewster, who, like his father of the same name, had been bailiff and postmaster at Scrooby Manor.

After a little more than a decade in Holland, some of the Separatists became restive. Their children were learning the Dutch language and customs; their labor was extremely hard; and many were worried lest war with Spain break out at the expiration of the truce made in 1609. They had heard of the opportunities in America, and some began to agitate to move to the New World. Although a majority voted to remain in Holland, something fewer than a hundred agreed to attempt the American venture and petitioned the Virginia Company of London in 1617 for permission to settle in Virginia. Negotiations dragged on for two years, until finally, in June, 1619, they received a patent for a plantation.

King James had been asked to give his royal approval to their request for freedom to worship according to the doctrine of the Leiden congregation. Although he refused them explicit approval, he promised that they would not be molested. In the meantime another group of Amsterdam Separatists under Francis Blackwell, who had received a patent and had sailed for Virginia in 1618, met with disaster. Of 180 who embarked, 131 died on the voyage. When the news of this calamity reached Leiden, it dampened enthusiasm for emigration, but a hardy few continued their plans.

The cost of outfitting a colonial expedition was greater than the Leiden Separatists had anticipated, and they at length fell in with a company of London promoters headed by Thomas Weston and known as John Peirce and his Associates, which also had a patent for a plantation in Virginia. The Pilgrims joined forces with Weston's fellow merchants and formed a stock company, under the terms of which each investor of ten pounds would have one share; an emigrant who contributed only his labor for seven years would also have one share. If an emigrant had capital enough to put up ten pounds and his labor, he would be entitled to two shares. All profits and capital would go into a common fund, and at the end of seven years the shareholders would divide everything in proportion to their investment. The control of the colony was to be shared by London and Virginia. Business affairs would be conducted from London by Weston and the associates. The government of the colony would be in the hands of the emigrants, who would choose a governor. This arrangement proved an unfortunate one, but at the time it seemed the best that the Pilgrims could make.

The Leiden emigrants sold enough possessions to enable them to buy a small craft of sixty tons called the *Speedwell*, a vessel that belied its name. It left Delfshaven on July 22, 1620, and was joined at Southampton near the end of July by the *Mayflower* from London, a ship of one hundred and eighty tons, with some eighty passengers, including Separatists, laborers, and others recruited by Weston in London. After clearing Southampton, the vessels got only a hundred leagues west of Land's End when the *Speedwell* proved so unseaworthy that they had to put into Plymouth. There the *Mayflower* took aboard as many of the *Speedwell*'s passengers as she could accommodate and finally set sail on September 16, 1620. Besides officers and crew, the emigrants numbered one hundred and one, only thirty-five of whom had come from Leiden. The other sixty-six were from London and its environs and from Southampton.

After a long and tedious voyage, they made a landfall on November 9 at Cape Cod, farther north than they intended. They considered sailing south but after some hesitation rounded Cape Cod and entered Provincetown harbor. There the *Mayflower* lay at anchor while men

The Anabaptist. **The Brownist.**

The Familist. **The Papist.**

An unknown 17th-century cartoonist satirizes (above) the many-sided quarreling in England in the name of Christianity; in the drawing, an Anabaptist, a Brownist, a Familist, and a Papist toss a Bible in a blanket. At left is a detail from a portrayal of the martyrdom of Bishop John Hooper, a Catholic turned Anglican who was executed in 1555 after Mary Tudor became queen and repealed the laws that had established Protestantism. Hooper's ideas had considerable influence on the development of Puritanism. After Mary's death the pendulum swung the other way, and it was Catholics who were persecuted. The men below are the conspirators who planned to blow up Parliament in 1605. Guy Fawkes, third from right, was seized in a gunpowder-filled chamber below Parliament and forced, under torture, to betray his fellow plotters.

Gunpowder Plot
See "Horizon" Winter 1975
P 58

in the ship's boat explored the coastline. On December 11 they discovered Plymouth harbor and decided that the land there appeared suitable for a settlement.

Although they did not have a patent for territory so far north, they were in no mood to risk their lives in a longer sea voyage. The weather was bitter cold (the explorers in the ship's boat had had the spray freeze on their coats), and it was imperative to find a haven where they could find shelter during the winter months. Returning to the *Mayflower*, the advance party reported that they had found a place with a good harbor, "divers cornfields" already cleared, and running brooks. This news, says William Bradford in *Of Plimouth Plantation*, "did much comfort their hearts," and the *Mayflower* was brought around to Plymouth.

Bleak though New England is in late December, the land they saw from the deck of the *Mayflower* looked inviting to voyagers who had been on shipboard more than four months. They placed their settlement on the site of an Indian village. Above the beach was a hill that they could fortify against Indian attack, and the cornfields waiting to be planted in the spring were an asset not to be overlooked. Although they did not know it at the time, the danger from attack was minimal, for a terrible plague had recently decimated the New England Indians. The emigrants waiting to go ashore numbered one hundred and two, one more than had sailed from Plymouth. On the voyage over, one of the emigrants had died, but a boy had been born at sea and christened Oceanus Hopkins. Another boy, Peregrine White, had been born while the *Mayflower* lay at anchor.

Before the emigrants landed, some decision on the government of the colony had to be made, for, says Bradford, some of the "strangers" among them (meaning the people recruited by Weston) were already uttering "discontented and mutinous speeches," claiming that since they had a patent for Virginia and not New England, nobody had any right now to exert authority over them. To anticipate such anarchy, on November 21, while the *Mayflower* was still off Cape Cod, forty-one men met in the main cabin and signed a compact calling for a "civil body politic" that would rule by "just and equal laws." The Mayflower Compact served as the Pilgrim platform of government. At the same time, it articulated the anxiety for self-government felt by all the emigrants to the New World.

Among the signers were some who were not Separatists, including Captain Miles Standish, who had been employed to serve as a military leader, and John Alden, hired at Southampton as a cooper to look after the barreled beer that they brought as safeguard against scurvy. Both Standish and Alden later elected to remain permanently with the Pilgrims. Alden married Priscilla Mullins and during a sixty-three-year marriage fathered a family of eleven children.

With the Mayflower Compact to serve as their constitution, the Pilgrims chose John Carver as governor for the coming year. Although in the ensuing months, Bradford reports, during "these hard and difficulte beginings they found some discontents and murmurings arise amongst some, and mutinous speeches and carriags in other[s]; but they were soone quelled and overcome by the wisdome, patience, and just and equall carrage of things by the Govr and better part, which clave faithfully togeather in the maine."

The winter was miserable, and before spring came, half of the settlers lay in the graveyard; disease and malnutrition were too much even for these stouthearted Saints. But the coming of warmer weather at last brought a renewal of hope. And about the middle of March an Indian turned up at Plymouth who could speak a little English. He was Samoset, from Pemaquid Point, Maine, where English fishermen had taught him their language. He told the Pilgrims of an Indian who had been in England. This was Squanto, one of those kidnapped by Hunt in 1614. Through Samoset's intervention, the Pilgrims received a visit from the great sachem of the Wampanoag tribe, which dominated the region, a chief named Massasoit, with whom they made a treaty of peace. With Massasoit came Squanto, who happily joined the Pilgrims because all his own tribe had died in the epidemic three or four years before.

From Squanto the Pilgrims received instruction in the ways of the country, and Bradford declares that he "was a spetiall instrument sent of God for ther good beyond their expectation. He directed them how to set their corne, wher to take fish, and to procure other comodities, and was also their chief pilott to bring them to unknowne places for their profitt, and never left them till he dyed." It was Squanto who taught them to plant a herring under each hill of corn for fertilizer and who assured them that by the middle of April enough herring would run up their brook to supply their needs.

When Governor Carver died of a stroke in April, the Pilgrims elected William Bradford governor. In his history, Bradford recounts this fact and remarks that he

This may be Dutch artist Van de Velde's concept of the Pilgrims' return to England from Holland. Despite its name, their ship, the Speedwell, *may have been a Dutch type.*

"by renewed election every year, continued sundry years togeather, which I here note once for all."

The Pilgrims, being artisans and farmers, put their first spring and summer to good use. Unlike the indolent gentry at Jamestown, they planted crops, fished, hunted, traded for furs, and improved their housing. When autumn came, they were prepared for their second winter with a comfortable store of supplies. Grateful for a good season, they declared a three-day period of thanksgiving. Massasoit came with ninety of his braves to take part in the festivities. As his contribution he brought game, including five deer, freshly killed. Bradford sent out four men to hunt enough turkeys, duck, and geese to last a week. With feasting, target shooting, and other sports and pastimes, the settlers passed this thanksgiving period right merrily.

Plymouth's legal status was at first precarious because it was on land to which the Pilgrims had no right. To rectify this situation, on June 1, 1621, the merchants in London who were joint stockholders with the emigrants in the venture obtained a patent from the Council for New England, which had succeeded to the privileges of the Plymouth Company. Another patent, known as "The Old Charter," obtained in 1630, more clearly defined the physical boundaries and confirmed the Pilgrims' title to their lands. But Plymouth was never able to obtain a royal charter to fix territorial boundaries and continued to have an unsanctioned existence in the eyes of the mother country until it was finally absorbed into the Massachusetts Bay colony in 1691.

The economic condition of Plymouth at first had been as precarious as its legal status, for under the conditions that the emigrants made with the London merchants who backed them, they had to pool all profits and assets for seven years, after which time everything would be divided among the shareholders. This arrangement was impractical and worked a hardship upon those Pilgrims who could not afford to wait that long. Early in the settlement, each householder had been given a garden plot, and in 1624 each received an acre of land on which he was supposed to raise enough corn for the use of his family. However, it was soon apparent that without the incentive of the ownership of farms, not even the pious and industrious Pilgrims would work as conscientiously as they ought, and by 1632 a division was made so that every householder could have his own arable land, pasturage, and meadow for hay.

In the meantime, the Pilgrims, unhappy with their deal with the London merchants, had arranged to buy them out, and eight of the most substantial of the settlers, including Governor Bradford, William Brewster, Miles Standish, and John Alden, formed a holding company to put up the money. With the buying up of the Londoners' shares, the Pilgrims became masters of their own economic fate, and they prospered modestly from farming, fishing, and the fur trade. Their friendly relations with the Indians gave them an opportunity to trade for beaver, marten, and other furs, which found a ready market in London.

Plymouth never became a large colony. By 1637 the population numbered only 549, but their numbers grad-

Plymouth
1627

Although a busy modern town now stands where the Pilgrims built their homes, it is possible to turn the calendar back and reconstruct the Plymouth of 1627 with some confidence. In that year a census was made that, together with other data, permits the drawing of a plan of the colony. While it is not possible to know what any particular house looked like, the

general architectural features are known. The lower story of the fort on the hill was the Pilgrims' meeting house; cannon for defense were mounted on the gun floor above. Four small cannon—called "patreros"—were mounted at the intersection of the settlement's two streets to sweep the roadways with fire in case of an Indian break-in. The house nearest the reader was that of Captain Miles Standish, and next to it was that of John Alden. Governor William Bradford lived in the fourth house with the big yard in the same row. Buildings were of plank, often faced with clapboard. Some roofs were shingled, some thatched. The first movement of Pilgrims beyond the walled town began in 1627, when outside land was divided for farms.

ually increased until the town of Plymouth was able to send out groups to settle outlying districts. By 1643 it had ten little satellite towns, including Duxbury, Scituate, Sandwich, Yarmouth, and Taunton. This growth required some elaboration in government, and the colony now had a governor, a deputy governor, and assistants. Each town sent two elected representatives to a general court that made the laws.

One of the more significant effects the Plymouth colony had on the course of English expansion in North America was the contribution it made to religious development. Its congregational system of church government became the characteristic form for the New England churches and ultimately for several large religious groups in the United States, including the Congregational and Baptist denominations. The compact made on the *Mayflower* for the political government of the colony was the logical forerunner of the covenant that members of each congregation made with one another for the government of their own church. Although kindred churches might have some loose association for mutual information and help, the individual congregation was autonomous and owed no allegiance to any other. No central organization, no bishop, no presbytery, nor anybody else had any authority over the covenanted group who made up the congregation, which chose its own pastor and went its own way. This plan opened the way for variations in belief, but in practice the congregations clung to a simple type of theology based on the Bible as the inspired word of God, which held all the answers to problems of morality, ethics, and the conduct of life.

In later American history, Plymouth has loomed much larger than its contemporary importance warrants, largely because it became a theme for poems, plays, and novels. Henry Wadsworth Longfellow's "The Courtship of Miles Standish," published in 1858, with its tale of the doughty captain's wooing of Priscilla Mullins by proxy and his loss of the maid to his emissary, John Alden, is only one of many literary treatments of early life at Plymouth. And the story of the first thanksgiving, with an infinite number of variations on the facts, has profoundly affected the American imagination. William Bradford's chronicle *Of Plimouth Plantation*, written in a style of biblical simplicity, is a legitimate classic of American literature. But Plymouth produced no body of learned men, founded no college, had no conscious men of letters, and developed no profound body of

theology. Its people for the most part were simple farmers, fishermen, traders, and artisans.

While the Pilgrims were creating a tiny commonwealth for themselves, other settlers were finding their way to the shores of New England. In 1620 Sir Ferdinando Gorges, who had been a moving spirit in the old Plymouth Company, had succeeded in obtaining a patent for a new group, a proprietary body called the Council for New England, which had among its members a distinguished list of peers and gentry from the west of England. It received proprietary rights to a vast domain between the fortieth and forty-eighth parallels of north latitude and extending from ocean to ocean. For the next fifteen years, until the charter was finally surrendered to the king in 1635, the Council for New England, a feudal body, tried vainly to stimulate colonial activity by issuing, for a fee, patents to lands within its jurisdiction. Unlike the Virginia Company, it was not a stock company financing and outfitting colonies, but was merely a lease-granting proprietor. Although several

The title page above is from William Bradford's Bible, which he and his descendants used in America. Presumably it is the one he brought to Plymouth with him in 1620.

venturers received grants from the council, most of the settlements made under its patents amounted to little.

In June, 1622, a company of "rude and profane fellows" (the Pilgrims thought) under the leadership of Andrew Weston landed at Plymouth on their way to the southern shore of Massachusetts Bay. After wearing out their welcome among the Pilgrims, they moved to Wessagusset (now Weymouth), where they set up a base for fishing and trading. Too late to plant corn, and too negligent to lay up supplies for the winter, they nearly starved during the ensuing cold months and scattered the next year.

A year after the collapse of the Wessagusset settlement, a certain Captain Wollaston brought over a large number of servants and established himself at a place that he called Mount Wollaston, within the area now embraced by Braintree. With him came Thomas Morton, one of Weston's associates at Weymouth, who is said to have left England "for his country's good." Wollaston soon tired of New England and betook himself with a

Edward Winslow, Mayflower passenger and three times the governor of Plymouth colony, was the only Pilgrim in America of whom any likeness is known to have been made.

number of his servants to Virginia. But Morton made some of the servants merry with wine and persuaded them to stay with him at Mount Wollaston, which became known as Merry Mount. Morton's "colony" soon became a scandal and a disgrace in the eyes of the Pilgrims, soberly watching from a distance of twenty-five miles, for, says Bradford, "they fell to great licenciousnes, and led a dissolute life, powering out them selves into all profanenes. And Morton became lord of misrule, and maintained (as it were) a schoole of Athism."

Morton's lack of Christian faith was not the least of his iniquities. After trading with the Indians, he and his crew invited them to join in drinking "both wine and strong waters in great exsess." One sin led to another, Bradford continues, until "they allso set up a May-pole, drinking and dancing aboute it many days togeather, inviting the Indean women, for their consorts, dancing and frisking togither (like so many fairies, or furies rather), and worse practises. . . ."

Such frivolity offended the Pilgrims, but even more serious was the sale to the Indians of guns, powder, and shot, followed by instruction in the use of these weapons. At least that was the charge made against Morton by the Pilgrims. At this point, Captain Miles Standish led a file of troops to Merry Mount to arrest Morton, who barricaded himself in his house with some of his cronies and threatened to shoot it out with the intruders. Morton and his friends were too far gone in drink to do much damage, Bradford asserts. Fearing that Standish would damage his house, Morton stumbled out "not to yeeld, but to shoote; but they were so steeld with drinke as their peeces were too heavie for them; him-selfe [Morton] with a carbine (over charged and allmost halfe fild with powder and shote, as was after found) had thought to have shot Captaine Standish; but he stept to him, and put by his peece, and tooke him. Neither was ther any hurte done to any of either side, save that one was so drunke that he rane his owne nose upon the pointe of a sword that one held before him as he entred the house; but he lost but litle of his hott blood."

The Pilgrims chopped down Morton's Maypole and shipped him off to England in June, 1628. (The main objection was perhaps less to Morton's frivolity than to his ability to win the friendship of the Indians and cut into the Pilgrims' trade in furs.) But by the summer of 1629 Morton was back at Merry Mount busily trading with his friends the Indians, to the distress of his pious competitors. This time settlers in Massachusetts Bay de-

10 of May the Boocke of Spartes vpon the Lords day was burnt by the Hangman in the place where the Crosse stoode, & at Exchange

To the Puritans, hard work and soberness were ends in themselves, and laughter was highly suspect. They were deeply offended when James I recommended Sunday games and sports and eventually had the royal declaration, called "the Book of Sports," publicly burned by the London hangman (above). However, this act of protest did not occur until 1643, during the civil wars in the reign of Charles I.
Below, in a 1653 cartoon, Father Christmas is being driven away by a Puritan, while an unidentified but friendlier individual bids him stay. The Puritans regarded Christmas as a pagan festival, and most refused to observe it.

cided to get rid of him for good. After putting him in the stocks and burning down his house, they once more shipped him to England. His account of life in New England, published in Amsterdam in 1637 with the title *The New English Canaan*, lightens the gloom of New England literature with flashes of humor.

While the Pilgrims were getting themselves established—and giving a little help to assorted adventurers who turned up at Plymouth—other plans were being made in England to exploit the resources of New England and its waters. A group of enterprising merchants and shipowners at Dorchester conceived the notion of a permanent fishing colony in New England where resident fishermen would catch and cure fish for the European market. This would avoid sending out fishermen each season from England and save money and time. In March, 1624, the Dorchester Company was organized, with shareholders not only from Dorchester but from the surrounding counties. One of the leading spirits in this organization was a Puritan preacher, the Reverend John White, who probably was the author of a persuasive paper entitled "General Observations for the Plantation of New England." Certainly White was already thinking of New England as a place where men who shared his religious beliefs might create a commonwealth of godly folk of their own persuasion. A practical man, White believed that a colony, established under a patent from the Council for New England, could further the work of the Lord at a profit. While these pious colonists went about their daily business of fishing and fur trading, they could set an example of righteous behavior, and their ministers could disseminate the word of God to both the Indians and itinerant fishermen who visited that coast. The scheme appeared divinely inspired in both its economic and religious prospects.

A tentative settlement was made at Cape Ann (near today's Gloucester, Massachusetts) by some of the Dorchester promoters in 1623. The next year another expedition went out and left thirty-two men, but unhappily the season was late when they reached Cape Ann, and the catch was small. A third expedition with three vessels in 1625 met with no better luck. At this stage the company found a fisherman living nearby, Roger Conant, who agreed to become resident manager at Cape Ann. Conant had joined the Plymouth colony two years before but left Plymouth for a nearby fishing island (now Hull) to which others discontented with Pilgrim rule had retreated. The Pilgrims made trouble for the Cape Ann fishermen, who, like Morton and his crew, were competitors. Captain Miles Standish marched to Cape Ann and, threatening fire and brimstone, ordered them off, claiming that the fishing wharf belonged to Plymouth. Conant managed to quiet the fiery little captain and persuaded the Plymouth settlers to move their fishing operations to the Kennebec. But the Cape Ann colonists continued to have bad luck. Fish deserted their immediate shore, and their trade with the Indians was insufficient to cover their losses. In 1626 the company, for all of Conant's high hopes, lost heart and abandoned the enterprise.

A few of the Cape Ann fishermen and traders decided to stay in New England, and under Conant's leadership they moved south to Naumkeag, soon to be called Salem. Conant wrote to John White of their resolve and received a promise of supplies and help. Even though White's colleagues in the Dorchester Company had lost their enthusiasm for a colony of religious fishermen and traders, he himself never wavered. Furthermore, he was soon in contact with Puritans in Lincolnshire and London who independently had begun to talk about a refuge in New England. The upshot was the organization of the New England Company, which was designed to take over the old Dorchester Company and to utilize Roger Conant's struggling little settlement at Salem as the nucleus for a colony of the faithful.

The negotiations of the New England Company with the Council for New England, or with individual members like the Earl of Warwick, are obscure, but by some means it obtained a patent for a grant of land reaching from three miles south of the Charles River to three miles north of the Merrimac and extending westward to the Pacific. That this grant overlapped territory claimed by Sir Ferdinando Gorges and his associates appears to have been overlooked or disregarded.

To begin the occupation, the New England Company in June, 1628, dispatched the ship *Abigail* with some forty emigrants under the leadership of John Endecott. They were destined for Conant's village of Salem, where Endecott was to take over as governor. This unsmiling zealot—he had chopped down a second Maypole put up by Morton's men in 1628—set to work diligently to prepare housing for other emigrants to come. Conant's individualistic fishermen might grumble, but Endecott ruthlessly drove them to complete their tasks while assuring them that they were about the Lord's work.

Some of the leaders in the New England Company, worried over the legality of their title to land claimed by members of the Gorges family and others, conceived the notion of petitioning Charles I for a royal charter to their territory, which they received on March 4, 1629. The charter absorbed the old New England Company into the Massachusetts Bay Company, which its letters of incorporation empowered to "govern and rule all His Majesty's subjects that reside within the limits of our plantation." This charter was to be one of the most important legal documents obtained by any colony, for, as it turned out, it made the incorporators self-governing and to all practical purposes virtually independent of the government in London. It also disregarded previous grants to the Council for New England and to others and thus was a fruitful source of future controversy.

The Massachusetts Bay Company immediately began plans to enlarge the colony under Endecott at Salem and in April, 1629, sent out a fleet of vessels with emigrants, supplies, tools, and livestock. With the passage of the years, the promoters of colonies had learned something about the kind of people and equipment required. This group made a quick crossing, and some of them wrote back enthusiastically about the outlook. One of their ministers, the Reverend Francis Higginson, declared in a pamphlet, *New-England's Plantation* (published in London in 1630), that "there is hardly a more healthful place to be found in the world that agreeth better with our English bodies," and "a sup of New England's air is better than a whole draft of old England's ale." A few months after this encomium, Higginson died, but most of the newcomers—hardy farmers and skilled artisans—survived and spread out from Salem to form other settlements nearby.

During the year 1629, a group of Puritans in Suffolk, Lincolnshire, and southern Yorkshire, some of them related by blood or marriage to the settlers in Massachusetts Bay, began to talk of emigrating to America. Among the leaders of this group were John Winthrop, a country gentleman from the manor Groton in Suffolk; Thomas Dudley, steward to the Earl of Lincoln (who was himself a Puritan and sympathetic with the prospective emigrants); Isaac Johnson, brother-in-law of the Earl of Lincoln; Emmanuel Downing, Winthrop's brother-in-law; John Humphrey, a son-in-law of Lincoln's and deputy governor; and Sir Richard Saltonstall.

At this time John Winthrop, like many of his fellow Puritans, was discouraged over the state of England, which he believed was ripe for destruction because of its corruption and its falling away from the true God. The ascendancy of the high Anglicans, led by William Laud, Bishop of London and later Archbishop of Canterbury, was a further cause of worry. Winthrop was also in debt, for he, like many other landowners, had been caught in a financial squeeze that was particularly hard on those who depended upon regular rents in a period of rising costs. He was looking for a way to recoup his fortune and to improve his estate. The prospect of land in New England, particularly land where the owners might establish a godly commonwealth uncontaminated by the corruptions of the Old World, was vastly appealing to Winthrop and others who were fearful of the political and religious trends in England.

Twelve of the leaders of this Puritan group met at Cambridge on August 26, 1629, and made an agreement to be ready to embark with their families by March 1, 1630, "provided, always that before the last of September next the whole government together with the Patent for the said plantacion bee first by an order of Court legally transferred and established to remayn with us and others which shall inhabite upon the said plantacion." This provision reveals the concern of the Puritans for making their position legally secure. At a meeting of the general court of the Massachusetts Bay

JOHN SMITH, Generall Historie, 1632

Company on August 29—a meeting packed with Puritans sympathetic to the proposal—the would-be emigrants managed to get their measure approved.

Until this time, the management of all companies supporting colonial ventures had been in the hands of individuals who themselves remained in England. Under the provision passed by the Massachusetts Bay Company's general court on August 29, the emigrants would take the charter with them and would assume the management and government of the colony. This was a radical departure and perhaps had not been contemplated by the stay-at-home members of the company.

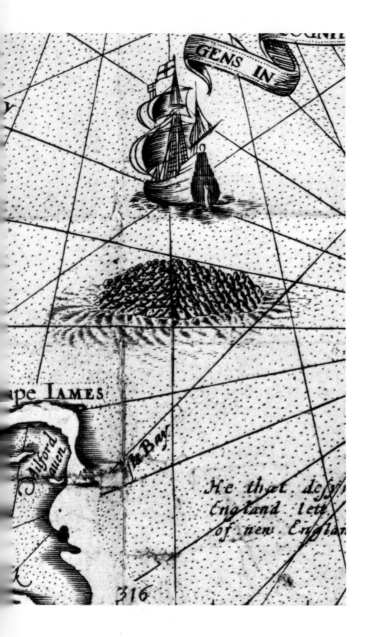

That careful observer, Captain John Smith, mapped the New England coast in 1614; in the next eighteen years his map was revised many times to keep up with growing knowledge and new settlements. This detail from the 1632 and ninth revision includes a number of towns—among them Plimouth, Salem, and Charles Towne—where Smith saw only wilderness.

The more than seven hundred men, women, and children comprising the body of emigrants represented a cross section of English society. Among them were a number of learned men, some from Emmanuel College, Cambridge, where Puritan preachers were trained (six years later Emmanuel provided the model for Harvard College); some belonged to the landed gentry; and others were members of substantial merchant families. Also included were many yeomen farmers, fishermen, craftsmen, and servants, not all of them Puritans. A noted Puritan preacher, John Cotton, vicar of St. Botolph's, Boston, in Lincolnshire, came to Southampton to see the first contingent off and to cheer them on with a sermon, "God's Promise to His Plantation." Three years later, Cotton himself emigrated to New England and became one of its most influential Puritan ministers.

After more than two months at sea, the vessels finally anchored at Salem, where Endecott had erected a few houses in anticipation of their arrival. Since Salem "pleased them not," they moved on to Charlestown, but, the water supply there proving inadequate, some crossed the river to Boston, while others settled at Medford, Watertown, Roxbury, and other nearby localities.

The region around what is now greater Boston was not totally unoccupied when the first Puritans arrived, for a number of stray settlers of the sort who would be called "squatters" in later frontier parlance were already established. Some of these were individualists who had fled from the regimen of the Pilgrims at Plymouth or the severity of Endecott at Salem. A few had come from England with the fishing fleets, and others were remnants of abortive colonies like Weston's and another settled a bit later by Robert Gorges at Weymouth. After nearly starving, Gorges and some of his colonists had gone back to England, but others scattered along the coast. Among those who had already settled in New England was the Reverend William Blaxton or Blackstone, an Anglican minister of Puritan leanings—but not so much a Puritan as the newcomers of 1629–30. He was living on what is now Beacon Hill, Boston, com-

The winter of 1629–30 was spent in orderly but excited preparation for the move to New England. By the end of March, eleven vessels were ready at Southampton. The fleet included the *Arbella*, named for Isaac Johnson's wife, sister of the Earl of Lincoln, and the *Mayflower*, already a veteran of several New England voyages. Four vessels, including the *Arbella*, in which Winthrop, who had been elected governor, embarked with the charter, sailed on March 29, 1630; the other seven vessels were delayed nearly a month loading equipment, supplies, and livestock—forty cows, sixty horses, goats, and poultry.

fortably surrounded by his garden, orchard, and fields when Winthrop's group settled around him. They proved too stern and intolerant for Parson Blaxton, who in 1635 left for Rhode Island with a parting declaration: "I came from England because I did not like the Lord Bishops, but I cannot join with you because I would not be under the Lord Brethren."

During the decade that followed the arrival of Winthrop and his group, a period known in New England history as that of the Great Migration, something like two hundred ships brought some twenty thousand settlers to Massachusetts Bay. They were not all Puritans, but the majority were nonconformists of some persuasion. These people funneled through the port of Boston and spread out through New England to form the characteristic towns of the region. Boston and the area around it was a hive from which Puritan groups swarmed from time to time, usually under the leadership of their minister, who led them as a church unit to some fresh settlement on the frontier. Heavy emigration continued until 1641, when the Puritan Revolution in

Puritan migration to New England greatly increased when William Laud (above) became Archbishop of Canterbury in 1633 and tried to impose a highly ritualistic Church of England on all Scotland and England. His rigid policy incited revolt, and in 1645 he was beheaded for treason.

England for a time caused a sharp drop in the movement of nonconformists to America. But the numbers who arrived in New England between 1629 and 1641 were so large that they created a problem in assimilation within the covenanted churches of the Puritans. The leaders were determined to retain strict control. They had come to New England to establish a commonwealth where Christians like themselves could remain unsoiled by the corruptions that, they fancied, plagued England and the English church. Consequently they directed their efforts toward establishing a form of government pleasing to the heads of each church, lay and clerical. What the Puritans of Massachusetts Bay achieved was part oligarchy and part theocracy.

The charter provided that the government of the colony should be in the hands of a governor, a deputy governor, and eighteen assistants, also called magistrates. In the future, the freemen (members) of the company were to fill these offices by election at meetings of the General Court, which also would make the laws in conformity with the laws of England, or as nearly so as conditions would warrant. The charter provided for four meetings of the General Court each year. But John Winthrop was governor, and Winthrop's ideas about the unreliability of the people were as dogmatic as those of Alexander Hamilton in a later period.

Though he had fled an England ruled by Stuarts who were convinced of the divine right of kings, Winthrop was a firm believer in the divine right of the inspired leaders of New England to rule the multitude. He had searched the Scriptures and could find nothing to condone "democracy." In 1645, after serving many times as governor, he expressed in his *Journal* his skepticism of "liberty" that the people insistently demanded, a liberty "incompatible and inconsistent with authority. . . . The exercise and maintaining of this liberty makes men grow more evil and in time to be worse than brute beasts: *omnes sumus licentia deteriores* [we are all worse for liberty]," he wrote. ". . . But if you will be satisfied to enjoy such civil and lawful liberties as Christ allows you, then will you quietly and cheerfully submit unto that authority which is set over you, in all the administrations of it, for your good." Convinced of his own rightness and his wisdom to govern, Winthrop was loath to delegate authority to the less able.

Nevertheless, the charter decreed a certain amount of popular government in that the freemen could hold elections. The problem of the Puritan leaders was to see that the freemen were themselves a carefully picked body. At a meeting of the freemen, therefore, on May 18, 1631, at which Winthrop was re-elected governor, it was voted that henceforth "noe man shal be admitted to the freedom of this body politicke, but such as are members of some of the churches within the limitts of the same." This was obviously a violation of the charter, but the Puritans were ever ready to justify the means by the ends, and they asserted that the provision was necessary in order to insure a franchised electorate of "honest and good men."

It was not easy to become a church member. One had to testify in open meeting to a conviction that he was divinely elected for salvation and submit to interrogation by the minister or the elders before being admitted. In this fashion, for many years in the Massachusetts Bay colony a body of church members retained complete political control and managed to suppress or drive out those who would not conform to their views. Tolerance, in their view, was unchristian, and religious liberty for the individual was unthinkable.

Yet conformity in matters of belief posed many problems, because the creed of the Puritans was based on the Bible as the ultimate authority, and the Bible was sometimes ambiguous. Moreover, not even all the preachers agreed on interpretations of certain important passages of Scripture. In this dilemma the best the Puritans could do was to pin their faith on the wisdom of the most respected of their ministers. The Reverend John Cotton exerted tremendous power for many years after his arrival in 1633. What he uttered in the pulpit, it was said, soon was enacted into law. In fact, the clergy of Massachusetts Bay during the first two generations after the settlement served as advisers to the magistrates and exercised almost supreme political influence.

Even so, conformity was hard to enforce. New England was settled by a varied lot of men and women, many of them strongly individualistic, a trait bequeathed to later generations. From the first, the authorities were faced with schism and the threat of political as well as ecclesiastical disintegration. The earliest Puritans in Massachusetts Bay had come not as Separatists but as

Above is the first of the four pages of the royal charter of 1629, confirming to the Massachusetts Bay Company the patent it had received the year before from the Council for New England. The document is beautifully engrossed on parchment and bears a picture of Charles I, the grantor, in the upper left corner.

101

John Winthrop was the first governor of Massachusetts Bay colony. Although a friendly and outgoing person by nature, he was said to have deliberately trained himself from youth to show the reserve and sobriety considered proper in a Puritan.

members of the Church of England. They denied that they wished to separate from the mother church; instead they hoped to establish a purer and more ideal version of the church that in England was being transformed by Archbishop Laud and his clergy into an image of Rome.

But once in New England, the Puritans had to decide upon a form of church polity, and they chose that of the Plymouth church. In fact many of them had come with the notion that bishops were bad and that some nonepiscopal form of church government must be found. They quickly adopted the covenant type of rule, in which the individual congregations agreed or covenanted together to form a church and call a minister. This decentralized form of church government was in contrast to Winthrop's notion of a strongly centralized civil government, but the Puritans managed to reconcile this inconsistency. What they could not reconcile were conflicts within church groups, which led to secessions, withdrawals, and sometimes to what the Puritans considered heresy. Many New England towns owed their establishment to discontented groups who withdrew from one church and, under the leadership of a minister, migrated in a body to another locality.

Typical was the case of the Reverend Thomas Hooker, who was pastor of the congregation at Newtown (Cambridge) in 1633. He objected to the way in which Cotton manipulated control, dictated decisions of the magistrates, and insisted upon the clergy's right to advise the civil authorities in matters of law and justice—justice interpreted according to the Mosaic code. In Hooker's opinion, this assumption of clerical authority was dangerously close to tyranny. His congregation was also dissatisfied with the land available to them. Hearing about the fertile land of the Connecticut Valley, they determined to move and petitioned the General Court for permission. Somewhat grudgingly this was granted, and in 1636 Hooker followed the example of other dissenters and led his congregation to Connecticut. Like the Israelites leaving Egypt, they marched through the wilderness with their cattle and all of their possessions in search of a better land where they would have greater liberty than under the theocratic oligarchy of Massachusetts.

Hooker's congregation settled at Hartford, and two other congregations joined settlements at Windsor and Wethersfield. In 1637 these three towns elected deputies who met at Hartford as a general court to establish a government separate and distinct from the control of Massachusetts Bay. Two years later they adopted a platform of government that they called "the Fundamental Orders of Connecticut." Although the government established in Connecticut was a far cry from a democracy, it was slightly less oligarchic than that of Massachusetts. In Massachusetts, for instance, John Cotton had insisted that magistrates ought to hold office for life; in effect he would have had them a self-perpetuating body. Connecticut took care to prevent this. Yet Connecticut, like Massachusetts, condemned toleration, and Connecticut's chief contribution to liberality in government—if liberality is not too strong a word—was to give more authority to the body of orthodox church members instead of letting the clergy and the magistrates monopolize power. In both colonies, only the godly according to the Puritan prescription were permitted a voice in the government.

A separate colony, later absorbed into Connecticut, was New Haven, established in 1638 by the Reverend John Davenport and Theophilus Eaton, a London merchant of strict Puritan beliefs. Davenport and Eaton permitted no democratic ideas to invade their borders and peopled their colony with devout believers, chiefly from London, who were willing to live under the laws of Moses. Eaton, the first governor, remained in office for twenty years and ruled with the advice of the clergy and the magistrates, who drew their wisdom from the Scriptures. Because the Bible did not describe any trials by jury, New Haven found no reason to extend this right to its citizens, who had to depend upon the magistrates, advised by the clergy, for justice.

The situation in Rhode Island, where Roger Williams had fled in 1635 after he was convicted of holding unsound beliefs, was very different. As pastor of the congregation at Salem, Williams had preached doctrines abhorrent to the authorities: the magistrates, he declared, had no right to direct a man's conscience; and the New England church should make a formal declaration of separation from the Church of England, for in claiming to remain within the fabric of the English church, it was guilty of pollution. But worst of all, perhaps, Williams questioned the validity of the charter of Massachusetts Bay and the colonists' right to Indian lands.

John Cotton and his fellow clergymen were scandalized. Since heresy of this sort struck at the very fundamentals of the Puritan commonwealth, it could not be tolerated. Williams was driven from his pulpit, and the court ordered his banishment from Massachusetts Bay.

In Rhode Island, Williams bargained with the Indians for sufficient land to make a settlement for people unhappy under the grim rule of the Puritans and founded a community that he called Providence Plantation. There he and his followers agreed that the civil authorities would have no power over any man's conscience and that church and state would be separate. For the first time in America, this fundamental doctrine was clearly enunciated. Tolerance was a new idea in New England, but Williams steadfastly maintained its principles. For example, he condemned the Quakers for refusing to bear arms or to pay taxes, but, unlike the authorities in Massachusetts Bay, he defended them from persecution and let them settle in Providence.

Williams's colony at Providence prospered as a farming community. Land in Rhode Island was more fertile than the uplands of Massachusetts Bay, and the colonists made abundant crops of corn, grain, hay, and tobacco. Their livestock multiplied, and they were soon able to export foodstuffs, cattle, horses, and hogs. Rhode Island in time achieved an economic and political freedom that was the envy of less well governed colonists.

Other refugees from Massachusetts Bay filtered into Rhode Island, sometimes individually, sometimes in small groups. The efforts of the Puritan clergy to maintain their type of orthodoxy benefited regions over the Massachusetts border, for many able men and women either found it expedient to migrate or were banished.

The trial of Anne Hutchinson at Cambridge in 1637 ultimately resulted in more than one settlement in Rhode Island. In the eyes of the Puritan hierarchy, Mrs. Hutchinson's sins were multiple: first, she was a woman with unorthodox ideas that she insisted upon expressing; second, she declared a belief in divine love, somewhat akin to Quaker doctrines that were repugnant to Calvinists, a belief that the individual by contemplation and illumination could come into direct contact with the divine; third, despite the duties that bore down upon a mother of fourteen children, she found time to hold meetings in her home to analyze the sermons that the ministers preached on Sundays and lecture days. Much that she believed and said contradicted the legalistic doctrines of the Puritans. Inevitably she was brought to trial, convicted of heresy, and sentenced to banishment. When she inquired the reason for her punishment, all John Winthrop could respond was, "Say no more, the court knows wherefore and is satisfied."

In his "Thomas Hooker's Party Coming to Hartford," artist
Frederick E. Church presents an idyllic picture of the
emigrants from Massachusetts Bay colony going into camp
in the woods at their new home. The setting is undoubtedly
quite accurate, for Church lived and painted in Hartford.

Anne Hutchinson had many friends and followers, whom the authorities called Antinomian heretics. One of these was William Coddington, who had made a strong plea for her defense. Unable any longer to live in peace in Massachusetts, Coddington, with Roger Williams's help, bought land from the Indians in Rhode Island and settled at Portsmouth in 1639. His group included Anne Hutchinson and her family. But the settlement had a surfeit of argumentative and independent philosophers, and its members were soon at such cross-purposes that some began to move out to establish new settlements. Coddington himself left to found Newport. Another member of the group, Samuel Gorton, lost faith in the strong convictions of the Hutchinsons and departed. He became the founder of Warwick. Although the religious views of dwellers in the four Rhode Island communities varied, they all were staunch defenders of freedom of conscience, and ultimately, in 1644, they came together in a sort of federated body under a charter obtained by Williams. Controversial and argumentative as the Rhode Islanders were, they managed to create the most democratic commonwealth in British America. Individual liberty was respected and protected under the colony's enlightened laws, which were ahead of their time in many respects. In 1647, for instance, witchcraft was outlawed and imprisonment for debt was forbidden.

Another fugitive from Massachusetts' persecution of the Antinomians, John Wheelright, led a small group of dissenters to New Hampshire and in 1638 founded the town of Exeter. New Hampshire, outside the jurisdiction of Massachusetts Bay, already had a few towns inhabited by fishermen and farmers. To them the Bay authorities complained that they should not have permitted Wheelright to commit so "unneighborly" an act as to settle in their midst. Since many of the earlier inhabitants of New Hampshire were Anglicans, this complaint had no effect.

Despite the flight of occasional heretics, however, the Massachusetts Bay colony prospered. In fact, no other colony in British America displayed greater dynamic energy in the first half of the seventeenth century. Her citizens, confident that they were the chosen of the Almighty, were determined to make Massachusetts Bay a garden of the Lord where righteous men might prosper and where the wicked would sin not only at the peril of their souls but also at the risk of incurring the wrath of the magistrates, a much more tangible threat. To these people, work was an end in itself, for they feared idleness as they feared the devil. They cultivated diligence, thrift, and sobriety as cardinal virtues, and so great was their application to their vocations that material success could hardly elude them.

As John Smith had predicted, the sea proved a source of wealth. As the Virginians discovered in tobacco a staple to provide economic security, so the New Englanders found in fish a resource that never failed. Dried codfish became an article of international commerce, eagerly bought in the Catholic lands of the Mediterranean. If any New Englander ever stopped to think that he was supporting heresy by supplying food for popish fish days, he never let that trouble his conscience or curtail his profitable labor.

Fishing, however, which King James had commended as being the vocation of the Holy Apostles, was only one of the profitable operations of Massachusetts Bay. The forest provided white oak for barrel staves and ships' timbers, spruce and pine for spars, and turpentine, rosin, and tar for ships' stores. Shipbuilders in New England were soon supplying vessels for both colonial and English commerce. Massachusetts farms existed primarily for the subsistence of the owners, but they also produced a surplus of foodstuffs for shipment to the West Indies and other markets. Through a combination of farming, fishing, industry, and sea-borne commerce, the vision of the New World as a garden of the Lord where the faithful could prosper through their own diligence and thrift was proving a reality.

The example that New England set as a haven for religious refugees was not lost upon other persecuted groups in England and elsewhere. The fact that thousands of Englishmen had actually made satisfactory homes for themselves in New England, where they had established a virtually independent government, gave encouragement to others who looked across the Atlantic for similar opportunities. But the search for religious and political freedom would not be the dominant motive in the settlement of the colonies. Most settlers in British North America—whatever additional motivations they may have had—would come primarily to improve their economic conditions. The eagerness to possess land was always the strongest impulse influencing the majority of emigrants. They believed that opportunities in America were unlimited. And they thought that if they could obtain land along with freedom from religious or other persecution, that would be little short of reaching the earthly paradise.

The People Who Came

The colonial ancestor above, peering dourly from his gravestone niche, is the same man who settled and civilized the early wilderness. In 1660 only seventy-five thousand settlers were spread thinly from Maine to Virginia. By the outbreak of the Revolution in 1775 there were more than two and a half million. America was the land of bright promise and new beginnings. Its expanse seemed endless, its soil was wonderfully fertile, and it held hope and opportunity for men who had none. For persecuted Quaker and proscribed Catholic it offered freedom of worship. To the plowman living the meager life of a tenant farmer, the colonies meant land and independence. In their eagerness to come, great numbers indentured themselves to work for years to repay their ocean passage. Besides bringing their varied dreams, they came from different soils to make the colonies a melting pot. There were Scotch, Irish, Welsh, Scotch-Irish, and the varied dialects of England. There were the Dutch in the Hudson River Valley, many Huguenots, and a sprinkling from other European nations. And there were those immigrants by compulsion, the Negroes, who had no hope of better days. By 1775 one colonist in five was black. On the following pages are pictured a very few of those who came.

OVERLEAF: *Persecuted Lutherans in Salzburg province of Austria depart to make homes in Georgia; a 1732 engraving.*

"DIE FREUNDLICHE BEWILLKOMMUNG DER SALZBURGISCHEN," BROADSIDE, 1732

Die ankunfft 13. u. 14. Jun

Sub umbris

Der abzug 16. u. 17. Jun.

Pioneer Puritan, sire of noted progeny: Sir Richard Saltonstall

Man of peace, devout in faith, industrious colonizer: a typical Quaker

Some convicts and riffraff were forcibly sent to America; above, "Gin Lane" by Hogarth. Right, many European peasants became frontier settlers; detail from a Bruegel canvas.

OVERLEAF: *The dream attained—New York merchant William Denning and family*

Competition for Colonies

The ultimate success of the English in establishing themselves in North America was so complete that one forgets the early years when the great powers of Spain and France held the little English settlements in a vast pincers threatening to close upon them from both the south and the north. Even the Dutch for a time held a domain in the Hudson Valley that split the English colonies into two segments; but as it turned out, the Dutch served as a useful buffer at a time when the French might have occupied this region to the destruction of English power in the North Atlantic region. Only fate—and the vagaries of European politics—can explain the survival of the British colonies during this period.

After the failure of Cartier and Roberval to establish a base in the St. Lawrence Valley in the 1540's, France frittered away her opportunities to seize Canada, although her kings made sporadic efforts to reinforce settlements in Canada, and French fishermen made yearly voyages to the Newfoundland banks and sometimes to the St. Lawrence and the coast of Nova Scotia to fish and trade for furs. Then, in 1603, Samuel de Champlain sailed to Canada with a trading, exploring, and colonizing expedition. Like Captain John Smith, he became an ardent advocate of settlement in America and a leader in colonial enterprises.

Many French seamen who sailed the Atlantic had been corsairs more intent upon taking treasure ships than upon exploring or trading, but conditions had altered in the more than sixty years since Cartier had embarked from St-Malo on his Canadian expeditions. Henri IV, now king of France, had made peace with the Spaniards in 1598 and was trying to unite his own countrymen. Frenchmen had turned from piracy to trade, and Champlain represented the new type of French seaman-adventurer. He himself had gone in the service of Spain to the West Indies and on his return had published an account of his observations of Spain's successful exploitation of a rich American empire. Among other shrewd observations he made was that a canal across the Isthmus of Panama would be a sensible means of reaching the South Sea.

In 1603 the Sieur de Chastes, governor of Dieppe, persuaded Henri IV to give him

The coats of arms at left are those used by the colonial rivals of the 1600's. Clockwise from top: Great Britain, simply the arms of the Stuarts; France, combining the national fleur-de-lis with the bearings of Navarre, Louis XIII's family line; Sweden, in which Charles X's bearings are superimposed on the national shield; the arms of the Netherlands.

117

a monopoly of the fur trade in Canada on condition that he establish there the Cross of Christ and the flag of France. Allied with De Chastes were several prominent merchants, the best known being Du Pont Gravé of St-Malo, who commanded one of the two vessels that sailed for the St. Lawrence in 1603. To bring back exact information about the country, the king appointed Champlain as geographer royal. From this time on, Champlain was to devote all his energies to colonization.

The expedition of 1603 explored the St. Lawrence as far as the site of Montreal (along the route that Cartier had followed in 1535) and proved to the satisfaction of the *voyageurs* that trade with the Indians would be profitable. Champlain mapped both sides of the river and made notes on the Indians, the flora and fauna of the country, and other details that might be useful. The traders returned to Le Havre in September, 1603, with a cargo of furs sufficient to arouse the interest and cupidity of other merchants. Champlain hastened to complete his report for the king and printed it the next year with the title *Des Sauvages: ou Voyage de Samuel Champlain, de Brouage, faict en la France Nouvelle l'an mil six cens trois.* With the great north country christened New France, Champlain was ready to guide his countrymen to that land of promise.

Unhappily, the Sieur de Chastes had died, and the merchants of St-Malo, who were the principal investors in the voyage, found themselves without a patron at court. The king transferred the monopoly of the fur trade to a friend of Champlain's, a Huguenot nobleman, the Sieur de Monts, with the understanding that De Monts should admit to his company any merchants and others who wished to invest in the enterprise. To make clear that the king contemplated something more than a trading post, the grant to De Monts stipulated that the company must send out each year not less than a hundred settlers.

Bearing the high-sounding title of "Lieutenant General in Acadia," De Monts sailed in April, 1604, from Le Havre with two ships. His principal associates on the voyage were Champlain, the merchant-trader Du Pont Gravé, and Baron Jean de Poutrincourt, who came along for adventure and in the end became an ardent colonist. The nobleman was the exception in this expedition, for, unlike the first groups who went out to Virginia, the Frenchmen in De Monts's ships for the most part were skilled artisans and farmers who had the capacity for hard work. After touching the coast of

Nova Scotia, De Monts sailed around into the Bay of Fundy and, on Champlain's unfortunate advice, chose a site for their habitation on St. Croix Island in Passamaquoddy Bay. There they erected houses and laid out gardens, but no sooner had seed sprouted in the sandy soil than the sun burned the young plants to a crisp. In his choice of the island, Champlain was thinking more of defense than of farming. The soil on the mainland was suitable for grain and garden crops, but fear of the Indians, as at Jamestown, confined the settlers to their island.

De Poutrincourt returned to France in one of the two vessels, while the remaining colonists prepared for the winter, which came sooner than they expected. They had not made sufficient preparations against cold more severe than any of them had known in France. Without adequate cellars to protect their supplies, all of their cider and wine, except some Spanish sherry, froze. Lacking fresh food of any kind, living exclusively on bread and salt meat, all except eleven of the colonists had scurvy before the winter was over. Drifting ice kept them from attempting to go to the mainland for game. The frozen beaches did not offer even so much as a clam, and no fish could be caught. The scurvy, which Champlain described in graphic detail, left those who survived weak and nearly helpless, their mouths swollen and their teeth falling out.

Despite the terrible winter, which, Champlain observed in a notable understatement, "produced discontent in Sieur de Monts and others of the settlement," the colonists were not ready to desert. But they were eager to find a better place of settlement. When a rescue vessel arrived in the middle of June, De Monts organized an exploring party that went south as far as Boston harbor and returned in early August. After due consideration of available sites, De Monts moved his colony across the bay to the north side of what is now Annapolis Basin, the present site of Lower Granville, in the harbor that the French called Port Royal in the land of Acadia. The colonists transported timbers and clapboards from their buildings at St. Croix and erected new houses with better protection against the cold. They had learned from experience to lay in supplies to ensure a variety in their diet and passed the winter of 1605–6 in relative comfort. In the spring, De Monts, who had returned to France on business of the colony, dispatched De Poutrincourt with a cargo of supplies and fresh recruits. In this company came Marc Lescarbot, an adventurous lawyer from Paris, who lived to write an entertaining history of New France. Thanks to the writings of Lescarbot and of Champlain himself, French efforts to establish settlements in Canada are well and wittily documented.

The prospects for a permanent French settlement now looked promising. The farmers in the little colony at Port Royal were pleased with the fertility of soil that had produced good crops in the summer of 1606. The Indians were not unfriendly and were eager to trade beaver, mink, and marten skins for knives and trinkets. But the settlers' success induced envy among French Catholics, and De Monts, a Huguenot, found himself beset on all sides by enemies who had gained the ear of the king. De Monts's monopoly was canceled, and the company was obliged to go out of business. Since no further support could be expected from France, the colony at Port Royal had to be abandoned.

Champlain, however, was not easily discouraged. The very next year he persuaded De Monts to try a trading and colonizing expedition in the St. Lawrence Valley. In the spring of 1608, with a commission from the king giving him a monopoly for one year, De Monts sent out two ships to Canada under the command of Du Pont Gravé, who was to trade with the Indians and return in the autumn, leaving Champlain in charge of the settlement. They sailed up the St. Lawrence, and Champlain picked a spot for his colony at the foot of the Quebec cliffs. There they erected houses on the shore and spent a winter so dreadful that it would have discouraged a man of less determination. Of the twenty-eight men who began the winter, only eight survived the scurvy and were alive in the spring. Nevertheless, in June, 1609, when a rescue ship came with additional settlers, Champlain was ready for further exploration and adventures.

The Huron and Algonquin tribes in the vicinity of Quebec were at war with the Iroquois who lived further south. In order to gain a knowledge of the country, Champlain and several other Frenchmen agreed to join a war party against the Iroquois. This venture took them across a large lake that Champlain named after himself and as far south as the site of Ticonderoga, where the Algonquins, with the help of Champlain's muskets, routed a party of Iroquois and took a number of prisoners. From this time onward, the French were identified as allies of the Algonquins, while the Iroquois were usually on the side of the English. The expedition

CHAMPLAIN, *Voyages*, 1613

The musket shots of Champlain and his two companions at Ticonderoga were a fateful volley in colonial history, for thereafter the powerful Iroquois tribes usually fought the French and supported the British. The above is a detail from a picture of Algonquins and Iroquois in battle array.

also gave Champlain some knowledge of the waterways leading to the interior regions and paved the way for expansion westward.

Champlain provided one of the earliest descriptions of the cruelty of the Indians toward their captives. One victim was ordered to sing his death song while the savages danced about, burning him slowly with brands from a fire, tearing out his nails and tendons, scalping him, and piercing him with sharp sticks, until finally they allowed Champlain to put him out of his misery with a musket shot.

A few years later, Champlain himself was to lead expeditions to explore the western region. Shortly after his return from the foray against the Iroquois, he made a visit to France and had an audience with the king, to whom he showed a girdle of porcupine quills, two birds of the country (scarlet tanagers), and the head of a curious long-snouted fish, all of which caused the king to wonder at the marvels of New France. Of more interest to the sponsors of the colony were the furs that the ships brought home, enough to show a profit and to excite the greed of other investors.

The fur trade was the immediate objective of the French, for it was clear that in barter with the Indians they had found a profitable source of revenue. Consequently, investors in colonial enterprises were more concerned with establishing trading posts than with developing the country for French inhabitants. Champlain, however, through his writings and by his personal efforts, labored unceasingly to stimulate interest in colonizing New France, to which he returned after his audience with Henri IV. He led small parties of Frenchmen into the interior to bolster the strength of warring groups of Algonquins, thus strengthening the alliance of the French with the Indians, to whom they looked for continuing trade. In 1615–16 he made his most extensive exploration of the interior in a journey with eleven Frenchmen that gave him a view of the Great Lakes and the vision of a vast inland empire that might one day belong to France.

But the political situation in France at the time was not conducive to colonization in America. Henri IV had been assassinated in 1610, and his widow, Marie de Medici, fat and stupid, ruled as regent with the aid of an Italian adventurer named Concini. No longer could De Monts, or any other Huguenot, expect favors at court. Various merchants and noblemen received concessions for trade in New France, but little was done to promote colonization. At Quebec, however, Champlain held on with grim determination, although less than fifty Frenchmen were to be found in all of New France. Finally, in 1627, after the rise of Cardinal Richelieu as the power behind Louis XIII, the future of New France began to look up.

Richelieu reorganized a group of investors into the Company of New France, sometimes called the Company of the Hundred Associates, which excited the greed of speculators to such a degree that noblemen, bishops, courtesans, and merchants competed for the privilege of buying stock at three thousand livres per share. In effect, the company was to be proprietor of New France and have a perpetual monopoly of the fur

Cardinal Richelieu, despite major accomplishments in revitalizing French foreign policy, had meager success in making France stronger in Canada. At right is Catherine Tekakwitha, an Iroquois girl who died in 1680, steadfastly Catholic despite persecution by her own people.

trade. But to retain this monopoly it had to send out not less than two hundred Frenchmen each year to occupy the country, and it was enjoined to encourage missionaries to convert the heathen. Since Richelieu was determined to break the power of the Huguenots, he decreed that no Protestant colonists should be allowed to settle in New France, lest heretics gain a foothold abroad. New France was to be solidly Catholic. To carry on the work of evangelizing the Indians, the Society of Jesus obtained a monopoly of this pious enterprise and established missions that exerted a tremendous influence on Canada for the next century.

To give an immediate stimulus to the colony, the new company sent a fleet of eighteen vessels loaded with supplies and colonists to the St. Lawrence in the spring of 1628. At that time, however, the English were trying to aid the Huguenots in their struggle against the forces of Louis XIII, and English privateers were free to seek French prizes. An English corsair named David Kirke heard of the rich prizes headed for the St. Lawrence and cornered the whole fleet there. Only his desire to make off with his prizes—combined with the stubborn refusal of Champlain to surrender Quebec—saved the French colony from annihilation. A year later, however, Kirke returned and forced Champlain to capitulate. Not until the Treaty of St-Germain-en-Laye in 1632 was Canada restored to France and Champlain permitted to return to Quebec, where a few Frenchmen had held the post intact during his absence.

Until his death in 1635, Champlain busied himself in furthering the cause of French settlements in Canada. He dreamed of pushing westward and creating a French domain in the region of the Great Lakes; and although that development did not come until later, Champlain paved the way. To him more than to any other individual, France owed its foothold in North America.

For three decades after Champlain's death, the development of the French settlements in Canada was slow. In 1642 Montreal was founded and became an important trading post, but Canada remained for many years little more than an outpost for the fur trade. Despite all the fine words about colonization, not much was done to establish French residents and to develop agriculture and industries. In 1663 the total French population, including missionaries and itinerant fur traders, hardly numbered twenty-five hundred.

In that year, Louis XIV dissolved the old Company of New France and declared the country a royal colony, with a sovereign council to rule it. The council was eventually composed of a governor, a bishop, an intendant, and twelve other members. Already the Jesuit missionaries and the secular authorities were competing for power, and for many years they were in constant disagreement. The missionaries, for example, wanted to bar the sale of brandy to the Indians, while the traders insisted upon swapping brandy for beaver pelts. This tug of war between religion and trade became one of the facts of provincial life in French Canada.

The transformation of Canada into a royal province did not immediately increase emigration from France, but gradually *habitants* settled farm lands and developed a self-sufficient agriculture. One of the inheritances

OVERLEAF: *Ships of the Dutch West India Company attack Salvador (Bahia), Brazil, in 1624. The company, which was engaged in such operations before it founded New Netherland, retained possession of Salvador for a year.*

Cal Sacks

New Amsterdam
1664

New Amsterdam on the lower tip of Manhattan Island looked, on the eve of its capture by the British in 1664, much like this view, which was developed from a survey made shortly before that time. Each house and other structure is placed just as in the old town; each appeared much as it does here. Most of the streets shown survive in modern New York, but

filling has since added much land beyond the shorelines of the Dutch town. The wide road leading north beyond the wall, then De Heere Straet (Men's Street), is now named Broadway. Parallel to it is the road now called Broad Street; the canal down its center was filled in 1676. Extending from Broadway to the East River (at right) just inside the defense wall at the north edge of town is a lane later named, for obvious reasons, Wall Street. The large formal gardens at upper left on Broadway are those of the Dutch West India Company. The large house behind the gallows on the island's tip is that of Governor Peter Stuyvesant. When the British came, Fort Amsterdam (lower left) gave up without a shot.

preacher asserted, "are exceedingly addicted to whoring; they will lie with a man for the value of one, two, or three schillings [twelve cents] and our Dutchmen run after them very much."

Although Kiliaen Van Rensselaer was eager for profits from trade, he was also anxious to develop a farming economy in his American barony. The emigrants that he sent over were for the most part farmers, who cleared land and planted grain and tobacco on farms that they held as tenants of Van Rensselaer. Taught by the example set by the farmers of Rensselaerswyck, other colonists found in agriculture prosperity greater than they had dreamed of when they first had faced the task of clearing the forests. Cattle throve on the grass and wild forage, and hogs roamed the woods and fattened on acorns and other food they found for themselves. The rich soil produced heavy crops of wheat, rye, barley, Indian corn, and tobacco. Farmers could hardly have found a more favored place than the river valleys of New Netherland.

Two flaws, however, prevented the rapid development of the land. Unfriendly Indian tribes were a constant hazard that every settler had to take into account, and the West India Company at first did not make it easy for small farmers to acquire land in their own right. Since most emigrants came to the New World in search of land of their own, the company at length had to make it possible for farmers to obtain land without becoming tenants of some great patroon.

The settlers around Fort Orange made a treaty of friendship with the Mohawks that enabled the farmers of Rensselaerswyck to live in relative peace, but further south the Dutch were not so farsighted. Although the Dutch made a habit of buying land from the Indians, they drove a hard bargain and habitually cheated the natives. During the regime of Wouter Van Twiller (a nephew of Kiliaen Van Rensselaer), who succeeded Sebastiaen Jansen Krol as director-general of New Netherland, the Dutch established an uneasy peace with the Indians on upper Manhattan and along the lower Hudson, but it was not destined to last. Van Twiller, who is remembered in legends of New York as a drunken incompetent, at least won the friendship of the Indians, partly by honest dealing, partly by providing them with liquor. When at last, in 1637, complaints against Van Twiller forced the West India Company to recall him, they sent out as director-general a more sober but harsher man named Willem Kieft. Believing that the

Cornelis Steenwyck held responsible civic positions in New Amsterdam, and then adjusted so well to the changed situation after the English take-over that he served as mayor of New York in 1668–70 and again in 1682–83.

only good Indian was a dead one, Kieft precipitated a war that brought ruin upon the colony and threatened to wipe out most of the settlements below Fort Orange.

During the years before Kieft took over, the colonists had made many scattered settlements that could not be easily defended. English settlers had filtered into Dutch territory from Massachusetts Bay and other English colonies. For example, Anne Hutchinson, who had stirred a religious controversy in Boston, ultimately moved with her family and a few friends from Rhode Island to Long Island, where the Dutch let her preach as she pleased. Other nationalities carved out farms for themselves in Dutch territory. A Dane named Jonas Bronck settled a spot that eventually took its name from him and became the Bronx. A Dutch gentleman who insisted on his title of *jonker* had an estate north of the Harlem River that today is called Yonkers. Many isolated farms were being cultivated on upper Manhattan, on Long Island, and along the Hudson River. Their prosperity and indeed their very existence depended upon peace with the Indians. If Kieft understood this fact, he showed no capacity to ensure peace, and the measures he took brought disaster.

Kieft accused Indians of many crimes committed by Dutchmen, and his soldiers shot down the natives with little thought of the revenge that their tribesmen might exact. When a Dutch wheelwright on Manhattan was killed by Indians, Kieft planned their extermination. In February, 1643, he sent a troop of his henchmen to Staten Island, where they slaughtered at least eighty harmless Indians, men, women, and children, and in another place forty more, deeds that prompted a critic of Kieft's, David De Vries, to ask: "Did the Duke of Alva in the Netherlands ever do anything more cruel?" If Kieft's cruelty had brought the Indians into subjection, he might have argued that his warfare was justified by the dangers to his people. But on the contrary, his wanton slaughter merely aroused the tribesmen to a general attack on outlying farms. Anne Hutchinson, her family, and many other settlers on Long Island, Manhattan, and elsewhere in New Netherland were killed.

To protect lower Manhattan, Kieft had to build a palisade of heavy timbers (the line of his fortified barricade against raiding Indians became Wall Street). Had it not been for English volunteers, recruited by Isaac Allerton, one of the Mayflower company who had moved from Plymouth to New Netherland, the outlying Dutch around Manhattan might have been exterminated. But Allerton persuaded Captain John Underhill, a soldier of fortune who had been banished from Massachusetts Bay for heresy, to organize a company of English settlers for war against the Indians of the lower Hudson Valley. In February, 1644, Underhill joined with the Dutch in an attack on an encampment of Indians in Westchester that left between five and seven hundred dead Indians on the field. The war dragged on, however, with recurrent slaughter until finally, in August, 1645, the Mohawks helped patch up a treaty of peace with the Indians to the south. The importance of the consistent friendship of the Mohawks cannot be overestimated. Had the Dutch not maintained their alliance with the Mohawks, the French, with their Algonquin allies, might have occupied the Hudson Valley and

thrust a wedge between the English colonies on the Atlantic seaboard. Thus in 1645 the Mohawks helped the Dutch end a destructive war that threatened the very life of the colony.

Isaac Allerton, Captain Underhill, and the English militia who aided the Dutch against the Indians had a stake in the welfare of New Netherland. Englishmen had infiltrated Dutch territory on Long Island and disputed territory in the Connecticut and Delaware valleys. Some had settled legally, but others had simply moved in as squatters. They were a potential danger to Dutch sovereignty in case of a conflict with the English, who had never conceded Dutch rights to territory in North America.

Kieft's rule over New Netherland proved as unpopular as it was incompetent. To placate his own people, he was forced to permit the election of a body of twelve counselors, called simply "the Twelve," who were later replaced by a smaller body called "the Eight." The complaints of these counselors to the West India Company resulted in Kieft's replacement by a picturesque soldier, Petrus (or Peter) Stuyvesant.

Stuyvesant had a long experience as a soldier and administrator. He had served the West India Company in Brazil and in 1643 was governor of Curaçao. On a military expedition against a French fort on the island of St. Martin the next year, he lost a leg and thereafter stumped about on a peg leg. But his was no ordinary wooden leg; to call attention to his loss in the service of his country, Stuyvesant had the wooden leg decorated with silver bands, and he was sometimes referred to as "Old Silver-Leg." In 1646 he received a commission as director-general of New Netherland. When he reached New Amsterdam in May, 1647, the citizens of that town, eager to give him a royal welcome, were taken aback at his arrogance, which, someone observed, was as great as if he had been the czar of Muscovy.

Stuyvesant, the son of an orthodox minister of the Dutch Reformed Church, was possessed of a Calvinistic assurance of his own right to prescribe law and justice for the colonists, and he showed no inclination to encourage any religions other than that of the Reformed Church. Dissenters might worship in secret, but no other church would be openly approved. If the mother country had more liberal views, that fact did not bother Stuyvesant. In New Netherland he was the law.

Yet despite his arbitrary and often tyrannical rule, Stuyvesant was New Netherland's most competent director-general. He brought some order out of administrative chaos, imposed discipline on an unruly citizenry, curbed the sale of liquor in New Amsterdam, and restricted the use of brandy and guns in trade with the Indians. He was determined to make a successful colony of New Netherland in spite of its citizens.

When Stuyvesant began his rule, New Amsterdam woefully lacked schools. A church started earlier was still unfinished. One fourth of all the buildings in the town were taphouses, and loafing and drunkenness in these taverns created a public scandal. Stuyvesant set about remedying these defects with a Calvinistic zeal.

But though his motives were often good, he was a dictator at heart and antagonized the populace. Realizing that he must give the people some voice in the government, he accordingly appointed a board called "the Nine" from a list of eighteen men elected by the inhabitants. The Nine quickly exerted pressure to modify the dictatorial rule of the director by sending to the States-General a *Remonstrance of New Netherland*, drawn up by Adriaen Van der Donck. This document asked for a reduction in taxes and port duties, a reduction in the number of traders licensed for business in New Netherland, and an increase in the number of farmers sent to colonize. It also requested schoolmasters for the children, adequate public buildings including a schoolhouse, and rulers "not too covetous." The document included an appeal to the States-General to take the colony under its own authority and thus end the monopoly of the West India Company. Just as a joint stock company in control at Jamestown had proved inadequate for the larger purposes of colonial development, so the West India Company, intent upon profits for the shareholders, had proved inadequate in the New Netherland colony.

The West India Company, however, was not ready to surrender to the States-General. To prevent assumption of control by the government, the company made some concessions, including the establishment of a town government for New Amsterdam paralleling the type of town government in Holland. A municipal charter created two classes of citizens, greater burghers and lesser burghers. One could become a greater burgher by purchasing the right for fifty guilders; thus the rank was ensured to the well to do, although military officers, preachers, and government officials enjoyed the rank without payment of a fee. Although this effort to establish class distinctions by law was abandoned after the

English took over New Netherland, the notion of a mercantile aristocracy was prophetic of a social evolution that eventually occurred in America.

A development on the Delaware River threatened Dutch claims in that area and provided Stuyvesant with an opportunity for vigorous action that pleased the veteran of wars against the Portuguese. This time the enemy was Swedish. Stuyvesant disliked the Swedes on two counts—they were interlopers, and they were Lutherans—and he endeavored to exclude them from the territories of New Netherland.

Ironically, the Swedes had first entered the Delaware Valley under the leadership of the same Peter Minuit who had purchased Manhattan Island for the Dutch. In the 1630's, Sweden, then leading a crusade against the Hapsburgs and the power of Catholic Spain, determined to create a base for attacking Spanish possessions in the New World. At the same time, she hoped to reap some of the profits of colonial trade. To that end, Sweden chartered in 1637 the New Sweden Company, modeled after the Dutch West India Company, and sent Minuit with a party of Swedes and Dutchmen to make a settlement on the Delaware. Minuit selected a spot where the city of Wilmington now stands and called it Fort

Johan Printz (left), marvelously profane and said to have weighed four hundred pounds, gave New Sweden ten years of prosperity, 1643–53, but he was so excessively severe that the colonists' complaints brought about his return to Sweden. Above is a map of the Delaware River and New Sweden, showing the location of the settlers' homes. To avoid friction, the Swedes were careful to settle on land beyond the limits of that claimed by the Dutch, and they purchased their region from the Indians, but that did not prevent increasing Dutch and English encroachments. Some Dutch and Finns were among the New Sweden settlers.

Christina after the Swedish princess and later queen.

Sweden, like Holland, had no surplus population or dissident groups of citizens who wished to emigrate, and enlisting settlers for New Sweden was difficult. Since the Finns, a minority group in Sweden, were skilled in forest crafts, the New Sweden Company induced a few to settle on the Delaware to help clear the forests. But try as she might, Sweden could not arouse any enthusiasm for emigration to America. The New Sweden Company found the fur trade sufficiently profitable to maintain its bases on the lower Delaware, but it could not develop the back country. So the Dutch retained a tenuous hold on the upper Delaware with a few soldiers at Fort Nassau and watched with misgivings as the Swedes established themselves lower on the river. Since both were threatened by the infiltration of English settlers from neighboring colonies, they made common cause against the English invaders and in 1642 burned one of their villages on the Schuylkill.

In the same year, the New Sweden Company sent Johan Printz to be director of the colony. Printz, like Stuyvesant a veteran soldier, had fought for King Gustavus Adolphus and was a man of courage and competence (because of his huge girth, the Indians called him "Big Guts"). For the ten years from 1643 until 1653, Printz labored to make something of the Swedish colony. By fair dealings with the Indians, he kept the peace and increased the profits from the fur trade. His continued efforts induced the company to send over a few more farmers and artisans. So impressed were some of the English who had become squatters in the valley that they swore allegiance to Sweden in order to live under Printz's rule in the Delaware Valley. As the little colony grew to something approaching two hundred inhabitants, Printz moved a few settlers up the river and built two forts there.

So long as the Swedish colony was merely a small trading post with little prospect of growing, Stuyvesant tolerated it, but when Printz established additional bases on the Delaware and began to recruit colonists, the Dutch director-general acted. Moving two hundred men to the Delaware, he established Fort Casimir between Printz's new fortresses and Fort Christina, thus dividing and neutralizing the Swedish strength, all too little in any case.

Stuyvesant had served notice that he would not permit Swedish expansion. Although Printz strove to recruit fresh settlers and to induce the New Sweden Company to send aid, little was forthcoming. An insurrection among his own people so discouraged him that he left the colony to settle its own quarrels and went to New Amsterdam to await a ship bound for Europe. With Printz's departure, the best days of New Sweden ended. Though the Swedes in 1654 sent over another vigorous director, Johan Rising, with additional settlers, he made the fatal mistake of taking Fort Casimir from the Dutch, an affront that Stuyvesant would not tolerate. Consequently, in the summer of 1655, Stuyvesant sent to the Delaware troops who forced the capitulation of the Swedes and thus ended any effective development of a rival colony.

Although the Swedish population was never greater than two hundred, the Swedes helped establish the Lutheran Church in America. They also contributed a technique of building that became enormously useful on the frontier, the use of notched logs to make cabins. Only the Swedes—and later the Germans—originally used this type of construction, which their example taught other frontiersmen to adopt.

The days of Dutch rule in New Netherland were also numbered. After the Restoration of Charles II as king of England, his courtiers began a systematic search for means of recouping losses they had suffered during the long years of Puritan domination. One source of wealth lay in lands across the seas and in trade with the colonies already established there. Charles was ready to make grants of vaguely defined territory in America, grants that required merely a stroke of the king's pen, for neither he nor his counselors knew or cared much about existing boundaries. If these grants stored up trouble for the future, the Merry Monarch showed very little concern about it.

One vast territory known to English traders was the region claimed by the Dutch between the Hudson and the Delaware, and it was this region that the king's own brother, James, Duke of York, fancied. The Duke of York was head of the Royal African Company, which was intent upon monopolizing the slave trade with the New World, and their most energetic rival was the Dutch West India Company. As it happened, the Duke of York was also Lord High Admiral in command of Charles II's navy.

The upshot of all this was that the Duke of York in 1664 dispatched a fleet to American waters to protect English interests against violations of the Navigation Acts and to assert English authority over trespassers on English territory. The worst offender, it turned out, was the West India Company, and at the end of August the English fleet anchored off New Amsterdam and summoned Peter Stuyvesant to surrender. This was not an act of war against a friendly nation, the duke made clear, but merely a police action to clear trespassers from land rightfully English.

Stuyvesant's rage knew no bounds. He mounted the ramparts of the fort and threatened to open fire upon the enemy, but his chief gunner informed him that the powder was so scanty and damp that no proper defense was possible. Stuyvesant then offered to lead his men, in spite of his peg leg, in an assault upon the English. The parson pleaded with him to be calm, and a petition from the women and children of New Amsterdam begged him to surrender without exposing them to destruction. Though the old director declared that he himself would rather be carried out dead, he agreed to capitulate. The English commander, Colonel Richard Nicolls, who had been named deputy governor, promised to respect all property rights of the Dutch inhabitants and to give them a voice in the government. The prospects for the average citizen looked better under Nicolls than under Stuyvesant. Although old Peter Stuyvesant was bitter at having to surrender to the English, he was not so heartbroken that he could not return to New York and live out his days there. He had a farm in the Bowery and a fine house near the site of St. Mark's Episcopal Church. There he died in 1672 and was buried in a chapel on his farm.

With the exception of a period from July 30, 1673, until November 10, 1674, when the Dutch temporarily regained control, the English henceforth occupied the former Dutch territory and consolidated their possession of the Atlantic seaboard from Maine to Florida. Thereafter, the city on the Hudson and the province would be called New York. The Dutch left their mark, however, on the architecture, on customs, on business habits, on the language, and on the legendary history of New York. Perhaps the most pervasive commercial contribution they made was to introduce Santa Claus to the American people.

The greatest benefit to the English of the Dutch occupation of the Hudson Valley was a gift of time. The Dutch and their Indian allies served as a shield against the French until the English themselves were strong enough to resist French attempts to seize this vital and strategic territory.

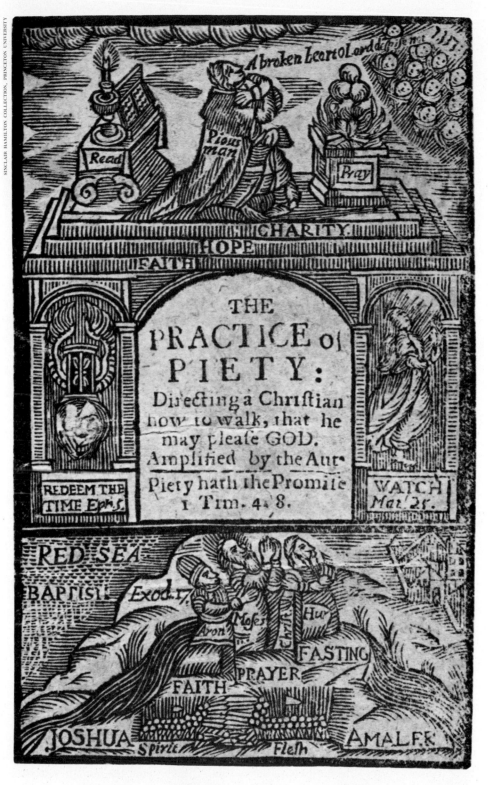

In Their Words...

Burdens and Blessings

At Jamestown the waters abounded with fish and the land with game, but the colony nearly perished from starvation in its first winter. By 1610, however, as this account indicates, the Virginia settlers already were concerned with problems of a more sophisticated nature, including air and water pollution.

There shall no man or woman, Launderer or Launderesse, dare to wash any uncleane Linnen, drive bucks [wash clothes], or throw out the water or suds of fowle cloathes, in the open streete, within the Pallizadoes, or within forty foote of the same, nor rench, and make cleane, any kettle, pot, or pan, or such like vessell within twenty foote of the olde well, or new Pumpe: nor shall any one aforesaid, within lesse then a quarter of one mile from the Pallizadoes, dare to doe the necessities of nature, since by these unmanly, slothfull, and loathsome immodesties, the whole Fort may bee choaked, and poisoned with ill aires, and so corrupt (as in all reason cannot but much infect the same) and this shall they take notice of, and avoide, upon paine of whipping and further punishment, as shall be thought meete, by the censure of a martiall Court.

For the Colony in Virginea Britannia.
Lawes Divine, Morall and Martiall, &tc., 1612

John Winthrop, the first governor of the Massachusetts Bay colony, was a meticulous recorder of colonial life, as the following entries from his Journal *indicate.*

[October 11, 1631] The governor, being at his farm house at Mistick, walked out after supper, and took a piece in his hand supposing he might see a wolf, (for they came daily about the house, and killed swine and calves, etc.;) and, being about half a mile off, it grew suddenly dark, so as, in coming home, he mistook his path, and went till he came to a little house of Sagamore John, which stood empty. There he stayed, and having a piece of match in his pocket, (for he always carried about him match and a compass, and in summer time snake-weed,) he made a good fire near the house, and lay down upon some old mats, which he found there, and so spent the night, sometimes walking by the fire, sometimes singing psalms, and sometimes getting wood, but could not sleep. It was (through God's mercy) a warm night; but a little before day it began to rain, and, having no cloak, he made shift by a long pole to climb up into the house. In the morning, there came thither an Indian squaw, but perceiving her before she had opened the door, he barred her out; yet she stayed there a great while essaying to get in, and at last she went away, and he returned safe home, his servants having been much perplexed for him, and having walked about, and shot off pieces, and hallooed in the night, but he heard them not. . . .

[August 14, 1632] This summer was very wet and cold, (except now and then a hot day or two,) which caused great store of musketoes and rattle-snakes. The corn, in the dry, sandy grounds, was much better than other years, but in the fatter grounds much worse, and in Boston, etc., much shorn down close by the ground with worms.

The windmill was brought down to Boston, because, where it stood near Newtown, it would not grind but with a westerly wind.

Mr. Oldham had a small house near the wear at Watertown, made all of clapboards, burnt down by making a fire in it when it had no chimney. . . .

Great store of eels and lobsters in the bay. Two or three boys have brought in a bushel of great eels at a time, and sixty great lobsters. . . .

[February 26, 1633] Two little girls of the governor's family were sitting under a great heap of logs, plucking of birds, and the wind driving the feathers into the house, the governor's wife caused them to remove away. They were no sooner gone, but the whole heap of logs fell down in the place, and had crushed them to death, if the Lord, in his special providence, had not delivered them. . . .

[November, 1633] The scarcity of workmen had caused them to raise their wages to an excessive rate, so as a carpenter would have three shillings the day, a laborer two shillings and sixpence, etc.; and accordingly those who had commodities to sell advanced their prices sometime double to that they cost in England, so as it grew to a general complaint, which the court, taking knowledge of, as also of some further evils, which were springing out of the excessive rates of wages, they made an order, that carpenters, masons, etc., should take but two shillings the day, and laborers but eighteen pence, and that no commodity should be sold at above four pence in the shilling more than it cost for ready money in England; oil, wine, etc., and cheese, in regard of the hazard of bringing, etc., [excepted]. . . .

[January-February, 1642] The frost was so great and continual this winter, that all the bay was frozen over, so much and so long, as the like, by the Indians' relation, had not been these 40 years, and it continued from the 18th of [January] to the 21st of the 12th month [February]; so as horses and carts went . . . where ships have sailed. . . .

There was great fear lest much hurt might have been done upon the breaking up of the frost, (men and beasts were grown so bold,) but by the good providence of God, not one person miscarried, save one Warde of Salem, an honest young man, who going to show a traveller the safest passage over the river, as he thought, by the salt-house, fell in, and, though he had a pitchfork in his hand, yet was presently carried under the ice by the tide. The traveller fell in with one leg while he went to help the other, but God preserved him. . . . .

John Winthrop
Journal, 1630–49

A New England preacher, from an early gravestone

he Puritans made such rapid progress that in 1636 they were able to found an institution of higher learning, mainly to ensure a supply of ministers. Two years later John Harvard, a church elder who had been in Massachusetts only about a year when he died, left the college half of his estate, his entire library—and his name.

After God had carried us safe to *New-England*, and wee had builded our houses, provided necessaries for our liveli-hood, rear'd convenient places for Gods worship, and setled the Civill Government: One of the next things we longed for, and looked after was to advance *Learning*, and perpetuate it to Posterity; dreading to leave an illiterate Ministery to the Churches, when our present Ministers shall lie in the Dust. And as wee were thinking and consulting how to effect this great Work; it pleased God to stir up the heart of one Mr. *Harvard* (a godly Gentlemen and a lover of Learning, there living amongst us) to give the one halfe of his Estate (it being in all about 1700. l.) towards the erecting of a Colledge, and all his Library: after him another gave 300. l. others after them cast in more, and the publique hand of the State added the rest: the Colledge was, by common consent, appointed to be at *Cambridge*, (a place very pleasant and accommodate) and is called (according to the name of the first founder) *Harvard Colledge.*

New England's First Fruits, 1643

℘he prosperity of Virginia was assured when John Rolfe planted the colony's first tobacco in 1612. The crop took hold, found an immediate market in England, and brought this tribute to Rolfe from one of the Jamestown settlers.

. . . the valuable commoditie of Tobacco of such esteeme in England (if there were nothing else) which every man may plant, and with the least part of his labour, tend and care will returne him both cloathes and other necessaries. For the goodnesse whereof, answerable to *west-Indie Trinidado* or *Cracus* (admit there hath no such bin returned) let no man doubt. Into the discourse whereof, since I am obviously enterd, I may not forget the gentleman, worthie of much commendations, which first tooke the pains to make triall thereof, his name Mr. John Rolfe, *Anno Domini* 1612, partly for the love he hath a long time borne unto it, and partly to raise commodity to the adventurers, in whose behalfe I witnesse and vouchsafe to holde my testimony in beleefe, that during the time of his aboade there, which draweth neere upon sixe yeeres, no man hath laboured to his power, by good example there and worthy incouragement into England by his letters, then he hath done, witnes his mariage with *Powhatans* daughter [Pocahontas]. . . .

Ralph Hamor
A True Discourse of the Present Estate of Virginia, 1615

Slave labor became vital to the cultivation of tobacco and other crops. Here John Rolfe reports to London on the arrival of the first Negroes to be brought to Virginia.

About the letter end of August, a Dutch man of Warr of the burden of a 160 tunnes arrived at Point-Comfort, the Comandors name Capt Jope, his Pilott for the West Indies one Mr Marmaduke an Englishman. They mett with the Trēr [treasurer] in the West Indyes, and determyned to hold consort shipp hetherward, but in their passage lost one the other. He brought not any thing but 20. and odd Negroes, which the Governor and Cape Marchant bought for victualles (whereof he was in greate need as he pretended) at the best and easyest rates they could. He hadd a lardge . . . Commyssion from his Excellency to range and to take purchase in the West Indyes.

Letter to Sir Edwin Sandys, January, 1620

Slaves on way to be sold wear a heavy yoke to prevent escape.

The greatest lure of the New World was the land, and on the whole the settlers found American soil to be rich and bountiful. In 1621 the Pilgrims took a three-day holiday—a period now celebrated as Thanksgiving Day.

Our corne did prouve well and God be praysed we had a good increase of Indian corne, and our Barly indifferent good, but our Pease not worth the gathering. . . . Our harvest being gotten in, our Governor [William Bradford] sent foure men on fowling that so we might after a more speciall manner rejoice together, after we had gathered the fruit of our labours; they foure in one day killed as much fowle, as with little helpe beside served the Company almost a weeke, at which time amongst other Recreations, we exercised our Armes, many of the Indians coming amongst us, and among the rest their greatest King Massasoit, with some ninetie men whom for three days we entertained and feasted and they went out and killed five Deere, which they brought to the Plantation and bestowed on our Governour, and upon the Captain Miles [Standish] and others. And although it be not alwayes so plentifull, as it was at this time with us, yet be the goodnesse of God, we are so farre from want that we often wish you partakers of our plentie.

Edward Winslow
Letter to a friend in England, 1623

Wearing deerskin disguise, Florida Indians stalk deer.

Once land was obtained, the settler's first concern was to clear it. As the following accounts indicate, it was no easy job, and the farmer soon looked to the interior lands, where he found rich soil that did not require clearing.

[Newcomers] must immediately set about preparing the soil, so as to be able, if possible to plant some winter grain, and to proceed the next winter to cut and clear the timber. The trees are usually felled from the stump, cut up and burnt in the field, unless such as are suitable for building, for palisades, posts and rails, which must be prepared during the winter, so as to be set up in the spring on the new made land which is intended to be sown, in order that the cattle may not in any wise injure the crops. In most lands is found a certain root, called red Wortel, which must before ploughing, be extirpated with a hoe, expressly made for that purpose. This being done in the winter, some plough right around the stumps, should time or circumstances not allow these to be removed; others plant tobacco, maize and beans, at first. The soil even thus becomes very mellow, and they sow winter grain the next fall. From tobacco, can be realized some of the expenses incurred in clearing the land. The maize and beans help to support both men and cattle. The farmer having thus begun, must endeavor, every year, to clear as much new land as he possibly can, and sow it with such seed as he considers most suitable.

Cornelius Van Tienhoven
Report on agriculture in New Netherland, 1650

The Land is generally good and yet there is some but ordinary and barren ground. Here are Swamps which the Sweads prize much, and many people will want: And one thing more I shall tell you, I know a man together with two or three more, that have happened upon a piece of Land of some Hundred Acres, that is all cleare, without Trees, Bushes, stumps, that may be Plowed without let, the farther a man goes in the Country the more such Land they find. There is also good Land, full of Large and small Trees, and some good Land, but few Trees on it. The Winter is sharp and the Cattel are hard to keep. The people that come must work and know Country affairs; They must be provided with some provisions for some time in the Country, and also some to help along on Board the Ship. I have more to write, but am shortned in time. *Vale.*

Thomas Paskell
Letter from Philadelphia, January, 1683

In 1635 a pamphlet written in Maryland and published in London gave sound advice to potential emigrants: "Treat the People of the Countrey well."

Experience hath taught us, that by kind and faire usage, the Natives are not onely become peaceable, but also friendly, and have upon all occasions performed as many friendly Offices to the English in Maryland, and New-England, as any neighbour or friend uses to doe in the most Civill parts of Christendome: Therefore any wise man will hold it a far more just and reasonable way to treat the People of the Countrey well, thereby to induce them to civility, and to teach them the use of husbandry, and Mechanick trades, whereof they are capable, which may in time be very usefull to the English; and the Planters to keepe themselves strong, and united in Townes, at least for a competent number, and then noe man can reasonably doubt, either surprise, or any other ill dealing from them.

A Relation of Maryland, 1635

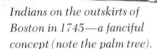

Indians on the outskirts of Boston in 1745—a fanciful concept (note the palm tree).

In 1643 Willem Kieft, director-general of New Netherland, ordered a pointless raid on an Indian village on Staten Island. In the war that followed, a combined Dutch-English force attacked a large encampment of Indians in Westchester.

[1644] In the evening about eight o'clock they came within a league of the Indians, and inasmuch as they should have arrived too early and had to cross two rivers, one of two hundred feet wide and three deep, and that the men could not afterwards rest in consequence of the cold, it was determined to remain there until about ten o'clock. The order was given as to the mode to be observed in attacking the Indians—they marched forward towards the houses, the latter being set up in three rows, street fashion, each row eighty paces long, in a low recess protected by the hills, affording much shelter from the northwest wind. The moon was then at the full, and threw a strong light against the hills so that many winter days were not brighter than it then was. On arriving there the Indians were wide awake, and on their guard, so that ours determined to charge and surround the houses, sword in hand. They demeaned themselves as soldiers and deployed in small bands, so that we got in a short time one dead and twelve wounded. They were also so hard pressed that it was impossible for one to escape. In a brief space of time there were counted one hundred and eighty dead outside the houses. Presently none durst come forth, keeping within the houses, discharging arrows through the holes. The general perceived that nothing else was to be done, and resolved with Sergeant Major Van der Hil, to set the huts on fire, whereupon the Indians tried every means to escape, not succeeding in which they returned back to the flames preferring to perish by the fire than to die by our hands. What was most wonderful is, that among this vast collection of men, women and children not one was heard to cry or to scream. According to the report of the Indians themselves the number then destroyed exceeded five hundred. Some say, full seven hundred, among whom were also twenty-five Wappingers, our God having collected together there the greater number of our enemies, to celebrate one of their festivals in their manner, from which escaped no more than eight men in all, and three of them were severely wounded.

Journal of New Netherland, 1647

In Virginia an effort was made to weaken the Indians by keeping them away from tidal rivers with their rich protein resources. By 1662 the Virginia council felt secure enough to relax this policy, at the same time prohibiting unlicensed Indian trading and the imprisonment of an Indian chief without a warrant.

And be it further enacted that for the better releife of the poore Indians whome the seating of the English hath forced from their wonted conveniencies of oystering [and] fishing . . . Be it therefore granted, enacted and confirmed that the said Indians upon addresse made to two of the justices of that county they desire to oyster . . . they the said justices shall grant a lycense to the said Indians to oyster . . . *provided* the said justices lymitt the time the Indians are to stay, and the Indians bring not with them any guns or ammunition or any other offensive weapon but only such tooles or implements as serve for the end of their comeing; and if any Englishman shall presume to take from the Indians soe comeing in any of their goods, or shall kill, wound or maime any indian, he shall suffer as if he had done the same to an Englishman, and be fined for his contempt.

And because many underhand and unlicensed traders doe truck and trade with the Indians, contrary to the act of assembly, and to the greate prejudice of all such as legally procure comissions from the governor, under pretence that the things trucked for be given them by the Indians, *Be it therefore enacted* that what person soever shall upon any pretence whatsoever buy, take, or receive any thing or comodity from any Indian shall upon proofe thereof at any court be ordered to pay treble the value of the thing received to the person injured thereby.

And because sometimes differences may arise between the Indians and those they trade with . . . *Be it therefore enacted* that any . . . trader haveing a difference with any Indian king . . . shall repaire to the governor . . . to determine the matter. . . .

And because the imprisonment of an Indian may bring a warre upon the country, and consequently the making of peace and warre wrested out of those hands it is by his majestys comission intrusted into the power of every individuall in the country, *Be it therefore enacted* that noe person of what quality soever presume to imprison any Indian King without spetaill warrant from the governor and two of the councell as they will answer the contrary at their utmost perill.

Virginia Statutes, Act CXXXVIII, March, 1661/62

Iroquois musket and ceremonial pipe

In 1675 the harsh Indian policy of the Puritans precipitated King Philip's War, a full-scale rebellion involving most of the tribes in New England. This excerpt from a letter to London, probably by Nathaniel Saltonstall, a Boston merchant, conveys the fierce nature of the conflict.

There were also among these Men, about Ten or Twelve Privateers, that had been there sometime before: They carried with them several Dogs, that proved serviceable to them, in finding out the Enemy in their Swamps; one whereof, would for several Days together, go out and bring to them six, eight, or ten young Pigs of King Philip's Herds. There went out also amongst these Men, one Cornellis a Dutchman, who had lately been Condemned to die for Piracy, but afterwards received a Pardon; he willing to shew his Gratitude therefore, went out and did several good Services abroad against the Enemy.

Plimouth also sent out several Men at the same Time, both Horse and Foot: Also most Towns in all the United Colonies thereabout sent out some more, some less, as they were in Number. By this Time the Indians have killed several of our Men, but the first that was killed was June 23, a Man at Swansey, that he and his Family had left his House amongst the Rest of the Inhabitants; and adventuring with his wife and Son, (about twenty Years old) to go to his House to fetch them Corn, and such like Things: He having just before sent his Wife and Son away, as he was going out of the House, was set on and shot by Indians; his Wife being not far off, heard the Guns go off, went back: They took her, first defiled her, then skinned her Head, as also the Son, and dismist them both, who immediately died. They also the next Day killed six or seven Men at Swansey, and two more at one of the Garrisons; and as two Men that went out of one of the Garrisons to draw a Bucket of Water, were shot and carried away, and afterwards found with their Fingers and Feet cut off, and the Skin of their Heads flayed off.

The Present State of New England, 1675

Under Cardinal Richelieu's aggressive foreign policy, France moved to expand her bases in the New World while the English watched apprehensively. In this excerpt John Winthrop, governor of the Massachusetts Bay colony, records his concern over the "papist" purchase of a fort at Cape Sable in Nova Scotia.

[January 17, 1633] The governor, having intelligence from the east, that the French had bought the Scottish plantation near Cape Sable, and that the fort and all the ammunition were delivered to them, and that the cardinal [Richelieu], having the managing thereof, had sent some companies already, and preparation was made to send many more the next year, and divers priests and Jesuits among them,—called the assistants to Boston, and the ministers and captains, and some other chief men, to advise what was fit to be done for our safety, in regard the French were like to prove ill neighbors (being Papists;) at which meeting it was agreed, that a plantation and a fort should forthwith be begun at Natascott, partly to be some block in an enemy's way, (though it could not bar his entrance,) and especially to prevent an enemy from taking that passage from us; and also, that the fort begun at Boston should be finished—also, that a plantation should be begun at Agawam, (being the best place in the land for tillage and cattle,) least an enemy, finding it void, should possess and take it from us. The governor's son [John Winthrop, Jr.] . . . was to undertake this, and to take no more out of the bay than twelve men; the rest to be supplied at the coming of the next ships.

John Winthrop
Journal, 1630–49

Perhaps no one upset the sober Pilgrims more than Thomas Morton, the jocular squire of Merry Mount, whose frivolity proved more than the Saints could bear. Twice they stormed Morton's house, tore down his Maypole, and shipped him off to England. Apparently undaunted, Morton published an account of what happened at Merry Mount in 1637. This excerpt from New English Canaan *relates Morton's temporary escape from Miles Standish—"Captain Shrimp" to Morton—in 1628.*

The Inhabitants of Pasonagessit [now Quincy], (having translated the name of their habitation from that ancient Salvage name to Ma-re Mount, and being resolved to have the new name confirmed for a memorial to after ages,) did devise amongst themselves to have it performed in a solemne manner, with Revels and merriment after the old English custome; [they] prepared to sett up a Maypole upon the festivall day of Philip and Jacob, and therefore brewed a barrell of excellent beare and provided a case of bottles, to be spent, with other good cheare, for all commers of that day. And because they would have it in a compleat forme, they had prepared a song fitting to the time and present occasion. And upon Mayday they brought the Maypole to the place appointed, with drumes, gunnes, pistols, and other fitting instruments, for that purpose; and there erected it with the help of Salvages, that came thether of purpose to see the manner of our Revels. A goodly pine tree of 80. foote longe was reared up, with a peare of buckshorns nayled one somewhat neare unto the top of it: where it stood, as a faire sea marke for directions how to finde out the way to mine Hoste of Ma-re Mount. . . .

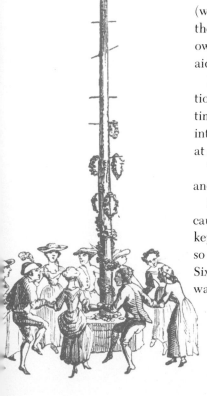

The Seperatists, envying the prosperity and hope of the Plantation at Ma-re Mount, (which they perceaved beganne to come forward, and to be in a good way for gaine in the Beaver trade,) conspired together against mine Host especially, (who was the owner of that Plantation,) and made up a party against him; and mustred up what aide they could, accounting of him as of a great Monster.

Many threatening speeches were given out both against his person and his Habitation, which they divulged should be consumed with fire: And taking advantage of the time when his company, (which seemed little to regard theire threats,) were gone up into the Inlands to trade with the Salvages for Beaver, they set upon my honest host at a place called Wessaguscus [Wessagusset], where, by accident, they found him. . . .

The Conspirators sported themselves at my honest host, that meant them no hurt, and were so joccund that they feasted their bodies, and fell to tippeling. . . .

Mine host fained greefe, and could not be perswaded either to eate or drinke; because hee knew emptines would be a meanes to make him as watchfull as the Geese kept in the Roman Cappitall: whereon, the contrary part, the conspirators would be so drowsy that hee might have an opportunity to give them a slip instead of a tester. Six persons of the conspiracy were set to watch him at Wessaguscus: But hee kept waking; and in the dead of night, (one lying on the bed for further suerty,) up gets

Dancing around a Maypole

mine Host and got to the second dore that hee was to passe, which, notwithstanding the lock, hee got open, and shut it after him with such violence that it affrighted some of the conspirators.

The word, which was given with an alarme, was ô he's gon, he's gon, what shall wee doe, he's gon! The rest (halfe a sleepe,) start up in a maze, and, like rames, ran theire heads one at another full butt in the darke.

Theire grande leader, Captaine Shrimp [Miles Standish] tooke on most furiously and tore his clothes for anger, to see the empty nest and their bird gone.

The rest were eager to have torne theire haire from theire heads; but it was so short that it would give them no hold. Now Captaine Shrimp thought in the losse of this prize, (which hee accoumpted his Master peece,) all his honor would be lost for ever.

Thomas Morton
New English Canaan, 1637

Matthew Hopkins, an
English Puritan, was
a noted witch-finder.

When the Puritan minister Roger Williams articulated the doctrine of the separation of church and state powers from his pulpit, he struck at the very foundation of the Massachusetts theocracy. For this and other "strange opinions," Governor Bradford banished him from the colony—but asked the Lord to show him mercy.

Mr. Roger Williams (a man godly and zealous, having many precious parts, but very unsettled in judgmente) came over first to the Massachusets, but upon some discontente left that place, and came hither, (wher he was friendly entertained, according to their poore abilitie,) and exercised his gifts amongst them, and after some time was admitted a member of the church; and his teaching well approved, for the benefite whereof I still blese God, and am thankfull to him, even for his sharpest admonitions and reproufs, so farr as they agreed with truth. He this year begane to fall into some strang[e] oppinions, and from opinion to practise; which caused some controversie betweene the church and him, and in the end some discontente on his parte, by occasion wherof he left them some thing abruptly. Yet after wards sued for his dismission to the church of Salem, which was granted, with some caution to them concerning him, and what care they ought to have of him. But he soone fell into more things ther, both to their and the governments troble and disturbance. I shall not need to name perticulers, they are too well knowen now to all, though for a time the church here wente under some hard censure by his occasion, from some that afterwards smarted them selves. But he is to be pitied, and prayed for, and so I shall leave the matter, and desire the Lord to shew him his errors, and reduse him into the way of truth . . . for I hope he belongs to the Lord, and that he will shew him mercie.

William Bradford
Of Plimouth Plantation, 1606–46

Johan Printz, the 400-pound governor of New Sweden, ran his colony like a military garrison and well deserved his reputation as a martinet. The domain of "Big Tub," as the Indians called him, was large, but the number of his colonists never numbered over 200, and his reports to Sweden emphasized the need for additional settlers.

The Fort in Skylenkÿll, called Kårsholm is pretty nearly ready. We are filling and working at it every day. So that, if we had people, ammunition, and other necessary resources, we should certainly not only be in a position to maintain ourselves in the said places, but also be enabled to settle and fortify other fine sites. Again, 28 freemen are settled, and part of them provided with oxen and cows, so that they already begin to prosper; but women are wanting. Many more people are willing to settle, but we cannot spare them on account of the places wanting them. The country is very well suited for all sorts of cultivation; also for whale fishery and wine, if some one was here who understood the business. Mines of silver and gold may possibly be discovered, but nobody here has any knowledge about such things. The Hollanders boast that three years ago they found a gold mine between Manathans and here, not in any place purchased by us, but nearer to New Sweden than to New Netherland. Hitherto, however, they have not got any gold out of it. There is no appearance here of salt, or of silkworms, because the winter is sometimes so sharp, that I never felt it more severe in the northern parts of Sweden.

The people have all the time been in good health; only two men and two small children have died. The reason that so many people died in the year 1643 was that they had then to begin to work, and but little to eat. But afterward we gave them, besides their regular rations, board to apply on their wages, and they have done well from it. Still, all of them wish to be released, except the freemen. And it cannot be otherwise. If the people willingly emigrating should be compelled to stay against their will, no others would desire to come here. The whole number of men, women, boys, girls, and children now living here is 183 souls, according to the annexed roll.

Report of Governor Johan Printz, 1647

Tohn Hammond claimed to have received no pay for writing a glowing account of life in Virginia and Maryland. The objectivity of his pamphlet is open to question, but there is no doubt that it helped to promote emigration to the colonies.

*English debtors' prison—
detail from a Hogarth print*

And therefore those that shall blemish Virginia any more, do but like the Dog bark against the Moon, untill they be blind and weary; and Virginia is now in that secure growing condition, that like the Moon so barked at, she will passe on her course, maugre [in spite of] all detractors, and a few years will bring it to that glorious happinesse, that many of her calumniators will intercede to procure admittance thither, when it will be hard to be attained to; for in smal time, little land will be to be taken up; and after a while none at all; and as the Mulberry Trees grows up, which are by every one planted, Tobacco will be laid by, and we shall wholly fall to making of Silk (a Sample of 400*l*. hath already been sent for England, and approved of) which will require little labour; and therefore shall have little use of Servants; besides, Children increase and thrive so well there, that they themselves will sufficiently supply the defect of Servants: And in small time become a Nation of themselves sufficient to people the Country. . . .

And therefore I cannot but admire, and indeed much pitty the dull stupidity of people necessitated in England, who rather then they will remove themselves, live here a base, slavish, penurious life; as if there were a necessity to live and to live so, choosing rather then they will forsake England to stuff New-Gate, Bridewell, and other Jayles

147

with their carkessies, nay cleave to tyburne [a well-known London place of execution]
it selfe, and so bring confusion to their souls, horror and infamie to their kindred or
posteritie, others itch out their wearisom lives in reliance of other mens charities, an
uncertaine and unmanly expectation; some more abhorring such courses betake them-
selve to almost perpetuall and restlesse toyle and druggeries out of which (whilst their
strength lasteth) they (observing hard diets, earlie and late houres) make hard shift to
subsist from hand to mouth, untill age or sicknesse takes them off from labour and
directs them the way to beggerie, and such indeed are to be pittied, relieved and
provided for.

John Hammond
Leah and Rachel, 1656

*M*any settlers worked for years to obtain clear title to land, but the Reverend
Jonas Michaëlius came to New Netherland armed with the Dutch West India Com-
pany's promise that he would have acreage. In this letter home, however, the disap-
pointed minister expresses a yearning for dairy products and reports the land useless
in the absence of cattle and of farm laborers.

The promise which the Honorable Directors of the [Dutch West India] Company had
made me of some morgens or acres of land for me to sustain myself, instead of a free
table which otherwise belonged to me, is void and useless. For their Honors well knew
that there are no horses, cows, or laborers to be obtained here for money. Every one
is short in these particulars and wants more. I should not mind the expense if the opportunity only offered, for the sake of our own comfort, although there were no profit
in it (the Honorable Directors nevertheless remaining indebted to me for as much as
the value of a free table), for refreshment of butter, milk, etc., cannot be here obtained; though some is indeed sold at a very high price, for those who bring it in or
bespeak it are jealous of each other. So I shall be compelled to pass through the winter
without butter and other necessities, which the ships do not bring with them to be
sold here. The rations, which are given out here, and charged for high enough, are all
hard stale food, such as men are used to on board ship, and frequently not very good,
and even so one cannot obtain as much as he desires. I began to get considerable
strength, by the grace of the Lord, but in consequence of this hard fare of beans and
gray peas, which are hard enough, barley, stockfish, etc., without much change, I cannot fully recuperate as I otherwise would. The summer yields something, but what is
that for anyone who does not feel well? The savages also bring some things, but one
who has no wares, such as knives, beads, and the like, or *seewan*, cannot come to any
terms with them. Though the people trade such things for proper wares, I know not
whether it is permitted by the laws of the Company. I have now ordered from Holland
almost all necessaries; and I hope to pass through the winter, with . . . scanty food.

   The country yields many good things for the support of life, but they are all too
unfit and wild to be gathered. Better regulations should be established, and people
brought here who have the knowledge and implements for seeking out all kinds of
things in their season and for securing and gathering them. . . . For as long as there is
no more accommodation to be obtained here from the country people, and I shall be
compelled to order everything from the Fatherland at great expense and with much

English farm laborer,
a type who often became
an indentured servant

risk and trouble, or else live here upon these poor and hard rations alone, it will badly suit me and my children. We want ten or twelve more farmers with horses, cows and laborers in proportion, to furnish us with bread, milk products, and suitable fruits. . . .

Letter from the Reverend Jonas Michaëlius, 1628

George Alsop came to Maryland as an indentured servant but soon earned his free-dom. In this excerpt from a letter to his brother in England he remarks that liberty has its drawbacks and ends with a lecture on the ills of tobacco.

To my Brother P. A.

Brother,

I have made a shift to unloose my self from my Collar now as well as you, but I see at present either small pleasure or profit in it: What the futurality of my dayes will bring forth, I know not; For while I was linckt with the Chain of a restraining Servitude, I had all things cared for, and now I have all things to care for my self, which makes me almost wish my self in for the other four years.

Liberty without money, is like a man opprest with the Gout, every step he puts forward puts him in pain; when on the other side, he that has Coyn with his Liberty, is like the swift Post-Messenger of the Gods, that wears wings at his heels, his motion being swift or slow, as he pleaseth. . . .

You writ to me this year to send you some Smoak; at that instant it made me wonder that a man of a rational Soul, having both his eyes (blessed be God) should make so unreasonable a demand, when he that has but one eye, nay he which has never a one, and is fain to make use of an Animal conductive for his optick guidance, cannot endure the prejudice that Smoak brings with it: But since you are resolv'd upon it, I'le dispute it no further.

I have sent you that which will make Smoak, (namely Tobacco) though the Funk it self is so slippery that I could not send it, yet I have sent you the Substance from whence the Smoak derives: What use you imploy it to I know not, nor will I be too importunate to know; yet let me tell you this, That if you burn it in a room to affright the Devil from the house, you need not fear but it will work the same effect, as Tobycs galls did upon the leacherous Fiend. No more at present.

George Alsop
A Character of the Province of Maryland, 1666

John Josselyn, an English writer who for a time lived in America, found much in the colonies to interest his English readers. As the following excerpt indicates, his account of life in New England also contained helpful hints for the settlers.

The Diseases that the *English* are afflicted with, are the same that they have in *England*, with some proper to *New-England*, griping of the belly (accompanied with Feaver and Ague) which turns to the bloudy-flux, a common disease in the Countrey, which together with the small pox hath carried away abundance of their children, for this the common medicines amongst the poorer sort are Pills of Cotton swallowed, or

Sugar and Sallet-oyl boiled thick and made into Pills, Alloes pulverized and taken in the pap of an Apple. I helped many of them with a sweating medicine only.

Also they are troubled with a disease in the mouth or throat which hath proved mortal to some in a very short time, Quinsies, and Imposthumations of the Almonds, with great distempers of cold. Some of our *New-England* writers affirm that the *English* are never or very rarely heard to sneeze or cough, as ordinarily they do in *England*, which is not true. For a cough or stitch upon cold, Wormwood, Sage, Mary-golds, and Crabs-claws boiled in posset-drink and drunk off very warm, is a soveraign medicine. . . .

Men and Women keep their complexions, but lose their Teeth: the Women are pittifully Toothshaken; whether through the coldness of the climate, or by sweet-meats of which they have store, I am not able to affirm, for the Toothach I have found the following medicine very available, Brimstone and Gunpowder compounded with butter, rub the mandible with it, the outside being first warm'd.

For falling off of the hair occasioned by the coldness of the climate, and to make it curl, take of the strong water called Rhum and wash or bath your head therewith. . . .

For frozen limbs, a plaister framed with Soap, Bay-salt, and Molosses is sure, or Cow-dung boiled in milk and applyed.

For Warts and Corns, bathe them with Seawater.

John Josselyn
An Account of Two Voyages to New-England, 1674

Sage, used in medicine and in cookery—from a 1719 herbal

*A*nyone familiar with the slums of London and the condition of the lower classes in 17th-century England was impressed by the way William Penn organized his colony. Here one of the first settlers to arrive comments on the advantages of Pennsylvania.

. . . Because the Countrey at the first laying out, was void of Inhabitants (except the Heathens, or very few Christians not worth naming) and not many People caring to abandon a quiet and easie (at least tolerable) Life in their Native Countrey (usually the most agreeable to all Mankind) to seek out a new hazardous, and careful one in a Foreign Wilderness or Desart Countrey, wholly destitute of Christian Inhabitants, and even to arrive at which, they must pass over a vast Ocean, expos'd to some Dangers, and not a few Inconveniencies: But now all those Cares, Fears and Hazards are vanished, for the Countrey is pretty well Peopled, and very much Improv'd. . . .

I must needs say, even the present Encouragements are very great and inviting, for Poor People (both Men and Women) of all kinds, can here get three times the Wages for their Labour they can in England or Wales. . . .

Reader, what I have here written, is not a Fiction, Flam, Whim, or any sinister Design, either to impose upon the Ignorant, or Credulous, or to curry Favour with the Rich and Mighty, but in meer Pity and pure Compassion to the Numbers of Poor Labouring Men, Women, and Children in England, half starv'd, visible in their meagre looks, that are continually wandering up and down looking for Employment without finding any, who here need not lie idle a moment, nor want due Encouragement or Reward for their Work, much less Vagabond or Drone it about. Here are no Beggars to be seen (it is a Shame and Disgrace to the State that there are so many in England) nor indeed have any here the least . . . Temptation to take up that Scandalous Lazy Life.

Jealousie among Men is here very rare, and Barrenness among Women hardly to be heard of, nor are old Maids to be met with; for all commonly Marry before they are Twenty Years of Age, and seldom any young Married Woman but hath a Child in her Belly, or one upon her Lap.

What I have deliver'd concerning this Province, is indisputably true, I was an Eye-Witness to it all, for I went in the first Ship that was bound from England for that Countrey, since it received the Name of Pensilvania, which was in the Year 1681.

Gabriel Thomas
An Historical and Geographical Account of Pensilvania and of West-New-Jersey, 1698

Prosperity could hardly elude the industrious Puritans and was considered one of God's blessings, but with it came materialistic notions that the Saints found incompatible with their concept of a religious colony. In 1663 John Higginson, a pastor at Salem, reminded his flock of the idea behind the founding of New England.

Accordingly when the Lord stirred up the spirits of so many of his people to come over into this wilderness, it was not for worldly wealth, or a better livelyhood here for the outward man: the generallity of the people that came over professed the contrary: nor had we any rationall grounds to expect such a thing in such a wilderness as this.

And though God hath blessed his poor people here with an addition of many earthly comforts, and there are [those] that have encreased here from small beginnings to great estates, that the Lord may call this whole generation to witness and say, *O generation see the word of the Lord, have I been a wilderness unto you?* . . . *O generation see!* look upon your townes & fields, look upon your habitations & shops and ships, and behold your numerous posterity, and great encrease in the blessings of the Land & Sea, *have I been a wilderness unto you?* we must needs answer, *No Lord, thou hast been a gracious God, and exceeding good unto thy Servants, ever since we came into this wilderness, even in these earthly blessings, we live in a more plentifull & comfortable manner then ever we did expect,* But these are but additions, they are but additionall mercies, it was another thing and a better thing that we followed the Lord into the wilderness for.

My Fathers and Brethren, this is never to be forgotten, that *New-England is originally a plantation of Religion, not a plantation of Trade.*

Let Merchants and such as are increasing *Cent per Cent* remember this, Let others that have come over since at several times understand this, that worldly gain was not the end designe of the people of *New-England,* but *Religion.* And if any man amongst us make Religion as *twelve,* and the world as *thirteen,* let such an one know he hath neither the spirit of a *true New-England man,* nor yet of a *sincere Christian.*

John Higginson
The Cause of God and His People in New England, 1663

Decorative border from a table of values of coins in use in the colonies

The Settlers Prosper

In the seventy years between 1630 and 1700, English colonists succeeded in establishing an unbroken chain of settlements that pre-empted for England the whole Atlantic seaboard from northern Maine to the Savannah River. The French held Canada and would continue to penetrate the western lake country and the interior river systems to the south. The Spaniards still clung to Florida and were a danger on the southern flank of the colonies, not yet protected by friendly settlements in Georgia. But during these seventy years, the English made themselves masters of the intervening coastal regions, consolidated their gains, and gradually began to push inland Spain and France might threaten, and the English would have to struggle to retain their possessions, but England in the seventeenth century gained the strategic bases that enabled her to hold what she had seized.

In the North, New England, dominated by the Massachusetts Bay colony, made a phenomenal development, both economically and culturally. The Puritans who settled Massachusetts Bay had a purposefulness, an energy, and a dynamic sense of their own destiny. Convinced that they were chosen of God to create a commonwealth of his saints in America, they were determined to allow neither the forces of nature nor the hostility of the aboriginal inhabitants to deter them from their manifest destiny. Equipped with blunderbuss and Bible, supported by the tables of the law, and reinforced with a theology congenial to their spirit, they moved relentlessly into the wilderness and conquered it for themselves and the Lord.

Early in the development of Massachusetts Bay, the colonists realized that they must be assured of a supply of learned ministers, and to that end in 1636 they established a college in Cambridge, named Harvard after its first benefactor, John Harvard. Many learned men had emigrated to Massachusetts in the period before the outbreak of the Puritan Revolution in 1640, and the colony had a nucleus of scholars and teachers. During the middle years of the seventeenth century, Harvard College earned such a reputation for the purity of its orthodox teaching that some of the stricter Puritans in England sent their sons to Harvard rather than risk their

*This detail is from a 1728 plan of Boston; the town then had
something over 10,000 people. Boston's place as the colonies'
chief port is intimated here by the large number of wharfs.*

153

imbibing heresy at Oxford and Cambridge. Not all these youths from the mother country were models of behavior. The evidence indicates that some parents looked to Harvard and the rigors of the New World to work a reformation in their errant sons.

Three years after the founding of Harvard College, Stephen Daye began operating a printing press in Cambridge, and in 1640 he brought out the first important work published in English in the New World, *The Whole Book of Psalms*, edited by Richard Mather. Known to us as the *Bay Psalm Book*, this work was the precursor of a flood of books published in Massachusetts Bay. That most of these publications were works of piety or of religious controversy goes without saying, but they were indicative of the intellectual caliber of a highly literate citizenry. Massachusetts Bay was the first colony to have a printing press, and Boston eventually became an important publishing center. It was from Boston that printers went out to the other colonies to establish presses and newspapers.

The printing press in Massachusetts Bay in the seventeenth century was an important instrument for disseminating and propagating the religious and secular ideas of the dominant Puritan group. The Mathers alone, Increase and his son Cotton, printed more than four hundred titles. Cotton Mather, a zealous propagandist, supplied peddlers with tracts for distribution and even sent printed sermons to a group of Puritan settlers in South Carolina to keep them from falling into the heresy of Anglicanism.

The main concern of the ruling class in Massachusetts Bay in the seventeenth century was to maintain their commonwealth of God's saints uncorrupted by outside influences. At all costs they felt obliged to prevent schisms in the religious community and to exclude heretics from their garden of the Lord. To accomplish this, they had to retain control of the machinery of government. But the retention of control by orthodox leaders and the maintenance of strict conformity proved harder to achieve than Winthrop and his colleagues in the Great Migration would have believed.

By a curious irony, God's blessings upon Massachusetts Bay helped to disrupt the neat patterns of orthodoxy. The Puritan emphasis upon diligence, thrift, sobriety, and all the prudential virtues, to the exclusion of every wasteful activity, made prosperity almost inevitable. Since it was sinful to waste God's precious time, and since extravagance and wasteful expenditure were forbidden, a strict Puritan could hardly do otherwise than prosper materially. So the citizens of Massachusetts Bay increased in wealth and praised God for his blessings. They little realized that prosperity would bring with it the seeds of corruption.

A thrifty population had developed a diversity of trades and industries. Hundreds of farmers combined agricultural pursuits with a variety of home industries: the making of wooden utensils and barrel staves, weaving, tanning, leatherworking, shoemaking, milling, and the manufacture of almost anything required by the demands of everyday life. Yankee ingenuity had become an accomplished fact.

The forests of New England supported a thriving shipbuilding industry and also supplied material for the cooper's trade. During the long winters, farmers would make barrel staves and hoops for casks required for wine, oil, and fish—the waters of New England supplied an infinite quantity of cod, mackerel, and other seafood for the European market. Thousands of casks of salt mackerel were also shipped to the West Indies to be used as cheap protein in the diet of slaves employed in growing and processing sugar cane.

From the West Indies New Englanders imported molasses and sugar and soon learned the art of distilling rum from West Indian molasses. The rum distilleries of Boston, Newport, and other New England towns provided an invaluable commodity in international trade.

Early in the history of Massachusetts Bay, shipbuilding became an important industry. In 1631 John Winthrop built a thirty-ton vessel, the *Blessing of the Bay*, whose launching was prophetic of an industry that developed rapidly. Eleven years later a much larger vessel, the two-hundred-ton *Trial*, launched in Boston with a sermon by John Cotton to give it an auspicious start, made a voyage to the Canary Islands with a cargo of fish and barrel staves and returned via the West Indies with wine and sugar.

The enterprising skipper of the *Trial*, aware that anchors and other hardware for ships were in great demand in Boston, acquired a cargo of these commodities in the West Indies by salvaging them from sunken ships by means of an ingenious "diving tub." From the sea he obtained fifty guns, a supply of anchors, hardware of sundry sorts, and a quantity of hawsers. He also traded some of his wine for cotton and molasses and reached Boston with a mixed cargo of highly profitable wares. The maiden voyage of the *Trial* was an omen of future

154

trade with the Wine Islands and of the development of one element of the famous triangular trading ventures that proved so profitable to New England skippers in the years to come. On her second voyage, the *Trial* went to Spain with fish and barrel staves and returned with wine, oil, fruit, iron, and wool.

The method of trade established by the *Trial* was soon followed by other vessels, though individual skippers made many variations upon the triangular pattern. Before the end of the century, ship captains from Massachusetts and Rhode Island discovered the profits to be made in taking rum, distilled from West Indian molasses, to the coast of Africa, where they used it to barter for slaves. The Royal African Company had held a monopoly, at least in theory, of the Negro slave trade, but in 1698 Parliament legalized the slave trade for private individuals. A traffic in slaves that colonial shippers had conducted surreptitiously before 1698 now lured many New England captains to the African coast.

Slavery was accepted as a benefit to mankind—Puritan slaveowners justified the practice from Scripture (as southern slaveowners in the nineteenth century continued to do). Had not William Perkins, a famous English preacher and Puritan casuist, shown that slavery was not against "the law of corrupted nature since the fall [of Adam]"? Were not Christian captains bringing these heathen souls to a land where they could exchange their labor for salvation? For generations to come, New Englanders engaged in the slave trade would thus salve their consciences. Before the development of the trade in Negro slaves, they had trafficked in Indian slaves whom they readily sold in the West Indies.

The Reverend Patrick Copland, a preacher in Bermuda, writing to John Winthrop in 1639, commented: "If you send us any more of your captive Indians, I will see them disposed of here to honest men; or if you send mee a couple, a boy and a girl for myselfe, I will pay for their passage, so they be hopefull."

Even so devout a Puritan as Cotton Mather owned both Indian and Negro slaves. In 1641 a pious citizen of Boston, Samuel Maverick, conceived a notion of making Noddle's Island, now East Boston, a breeding ground for Negro slaves. Wait Winthrop, writing from Boston on July 7, 1682, to Fitz-John Winthrop, commented that a slave named Black Tom threatened to kill himself, and though he thought he was bluffing, it might be well to sell him in Virginia or the West Indies.

Ships built in New England and sailed by New England crews multiplied rapidly in the seventeenth century. By 1676 more than two hundred and thirty vessels exceeding fifty tons burden claimed Boston as their home port. Other towns, especially Newport, had vessels engaged in international trade. Sometimes these ships were loaded with cargo and taken to England, where both cargo and craft were sold. The export of ships built in New England was an important item in the developing industry of that region.

Not only were New England sailors exposed to outside influences in foreign ports, but many vessels from England, Holland, and other countries brought to New England aliens with alien ways. Some ships, especially those from Holland, brought contraband articles that were delivered without the payment of duties, since New Englanders, for all their religion, were not immune to smuggling. Foreign sailors swaggering about Boston paid little attention to the sensibilities of disapproving Puritans and disregarded conventions in a way that Boston youths were ready to imitate. In 1699 Ned Ward observed that Lecture Days were "call'd by some amongst them Whore Fair," and that many young people after wanton pleasure "have recourse to the Ordinaries, where they plentifully wash away the remembrance of their Old Sins, and drink down the fear of a Fine or the dread of a Whipping-post."

Even Harvard College reflected the iniquity of the times, and the counterparts of modern long-haired youths were such a scandal that on May 5, 1672, a group of irate citizens presented a petition to the magistrates of Massachusetts Bay against the ungodliness of Harvard in permitting students to wear their hair

Puritan minister Richard Mather was the father of Increase and the grandfather of Cotton Mather. He was very influential in the formation of the Congregational system of church government in New England and, collaborating with Thomas Welde and John Eliot, produced the famous Bay Psalm Book.

The slave trade: a mutinous slave hangs alive from a hook in his ribs, and (small picture) a Negro slaver in the Cape Verde Islands bargains over slaves with a white man.

long. The petitioners desired "the removal of an evyl (as it appereth to us) in the educacion of youth at the Colledg. and that is, that they are brought up in such pride as doth no wayes become such as are brought up for the holy service of the lord, either in the Magistracy, or ministry especialy. and in perticular in their long haire, which last first tooke head, and broke out at the Colledg so far as we understand and remember. and now it is got into our pulpits, to the great greife and feare of many godly hearts in the Country." Pious citizens looked back to the earlier days of the colony with longing. Although virtue, even in the first years, had not always prevailed, conditions toward the end of the century were more distressing to the strict Puritans.

If worldliness and iniquity gradually undermined the authority and effectiveness of the agents of the Lord in Massachusetts Bay, these Christian warriors battled long and earnestly against the hosts of Satan. They used every weapon in their arsenal to eliminate nonconformity and heresy and to punish outright sinners. Wickedness they made as unprofitable and unpopular as possible, and they struggled hard to maintain the authority of the church by means of civil law. For many years only church members could vote, and only those persons who had experienced conversion were admitted to the church. But as Massachusetts Bay grew more populous, the proportion of church members diminished until even the ruling oligarchy was forced to consider broadening the franchise. They brought this about by a compromise known as the Halfway Covenant, adopted by the churches in 1662, which provided that children of church members, even though they themselves could not avow that they had experienced salvation, might be admitted to church membership and thus vote, though they could not take the sacrament of the Lord's Supper. This small crack in the monolithic authority of the church signified a gradual weakening of theocratic influence.

Try as the ruling groups might, they could not suppress all manifestations of independence. One institution that became famous a little later as the nursery of democratic institutions, the town meeting, provided a platform for the expression of opinions. Everyone, whether church member or otherwise, had a right to attend the town meeting, to present petitions, to complain, either verbally or in writing, against any injustice or inequity, and to express any opinion that seemed pertinent. The town meeting became the means of shaping public opinion, and not even the most fanatical members of the oligarchy could flout public opinion indefinitely. By degrees, often by slow degrees, democratic institutions and procedures were introduced.

Under the charter that John Winthrop and his colleagues brought with them to Massachusetts Bay, the colony was virtually independent, but the freedom of the Puritan commonwealth from interference depended upon the continuance of that charter. Naturally, the Puritans regarded the charter as their Magna Charta. So long as they were an obscure and distant group of dissidents, better forgotten than remembered, the home government left them undisturbed. But when Massachusetts Bay grew populous, wealthy, and capable of launching satellite settlements in adjacent regions, the authorities in London began to take a closer look at it, and what they saw did not always please them.

Under an economic theory generally described as "mercantilism," the English government regarded colonies as the source of raw materials needed by the mother country and as a market for manufactured products produced in England. Raw materials had to be processed in England and shipped to England in English or colonial vessels. The whole idea was to create a self-sufficient empire. Beginning in 1650, Parliament passed a series of laws, known as the Navigation Acts, to implement the mercantilist doctrine and to prevent outsiders, particularly the Dutch with their enterprising merchant marine, from usurping trade that the English claimed for themselves.

By the reign of Charles II colonial affairs had become of such importance that in 1675 he appointed a special committee from the Privy Council, known as the Lords of Trade, to deal with the colonies. In 1696, to further increase the surveillance of colonial affairs, William III reorganized the administrative control of the colonies by placing responsibility for them in a Board of Trade and Plantations, usually referred to simply as the Board of Trade.

The colonies had been doing business with the Dutch before the first of the Navigation Acts, and New England continued, more or less openly, to engage in trade forbidden by law. The laxity of enforcement of the laws of trade, particularly in Massachusetts Bay, was so displeasing to London that the Lords of Trade in 1676 sent over an inquisitive and disagreeable agent named Edward Randolph to investigate and make a report on the state of affairs in New England. Randolph, loyal to both

Charles II and the Church of England, could find little good to say about the Saints of New England. He described the harshness of their laws, their persecution of those who did not conform to their religion, their evasion of the Navigation Acts, and their arrogant and independent ways. Since Randolph's charges confirmed views already held by the Lords of Trade, they persuaded the king on October 23, 1684, to nullify the charter of Massachusetts Bay.

For a time the colony was without any legal government, for the governor, the magistrates, and the deputies who had been chosen by the electorate under the charter no longer had any official status. After a few years of a provisional government dictated by London, the Lords of Trade appointed Sir Edmund Andros to be governor general of New England. Rhode Island and Connecticut were required to surrender their charters and submit to Andros's rule. Connecticut made the rather futile gesture of hiding its charter in a tree instead of surrendering it, but that did not prevent Andros from extending his authority over that colony too.

In 1688, two years after Andros's arrival in New England, the London authorities commissioned him to extend his rule over New York and the Jerseys; but the overthrow of James II in the Glorious Revolution of 1688 gave the colonists an opportunity to rebel. They resumed their former status, and Massachusetts sent Increase Mather to London to plead for a renewal of their charter. Only partially successful, Mather managed in 1691 to procure a compromise charter, under which William III appointed the governor and the electorate chose a legislative assembly that in turn chose the governor's council. Under this charter, Massachusetts relinquished control over New Hampshire, which henceforth was an independent colony. Maine, however, remained under the jurisdiction of Massachusetts until the early years of the nineteenth century.

Another calamity that overtook the orthodox Puritans of the Bay colony, along with the loss of their charter, was the arrival in Boston in 1686 of the Reverend Robert Ratcliffe, an Anglican divine, who organized the first congregation of the Church of England in Boston. To the scandal of Puritan conservatives, he also obtained permission to hold service in Old South Meetinghouse before the regular Congregational service on Sunday.

If the Saints had failed to keep Boston pure and virtuous, it was not for lack of diligence in wrestling with heresy and in casting out nonconforming intruders.

*A contemporary artist, Egbert van Heemskerk, recorded the
furor in the Oxford town hall when certain officials were
removed from the town council on orders from James II.
Such arbitrary acts to stifle local democracy were
being reflected in New England, where James's appointee,
Governor Andros, had limited town meetings to once a year.*

Many a settler in Rhode Island, New Hampshire, and even Connecticut had shaken the dust of Massachusetts from his feet after being reminded of his obligation to conform. A few had not been lucky enough to escape and had suffered for their unorthodoxy.

Particularly obnoxious to the Puritans of Massachusetts Bay were the Quakers, who persisted in coming to Boston even in the face of death. In 1658 two ministers of Boston, the Reverend John Norton and the Reverend Charles Chauncy, persuaded the General Court that it was imperative to make death the penalty for Quakers who insisted upon returning after banishment. Otherwise, they pointed out, Boston would be forever plagued with these pests. Two years before, in 1656, Mary Fisher and Ann Austin, Quakeresses from Barbados, had suffered for five weeks in a cell without light after being stripped naked and searched for signs that might identify them as witches and provide a legal reason for hanging them. At the time, the authorities had just hanged a witch by the name of Ann Hibben.

The two parsons assured the General Court that the laws against Quakers were too lenient, for they permitted only torture, imprisonment, mutilation, and banishment. For example, the authorities had been obliged to let off an old man named William Brend with only torture: he had his heels and his neck locked together for sixteen hours and was then beaten into unconsciousness by one hundred and seventeen lashes applied with a tarred rope that cut the flesh from his back. The populace of Boston had not seen the justice of this punishment and had made a disturbance, but Parson Norton set them straight with a sermon defending the sentence and the jailer who carried it out.

After 1658 the law was clear. Quakers could be legally hanged for returning after banishment, and in October, 1659, John Endecott and his fellow judges sent to the gallows William Robinson and Marmaduke Stevenson. A third member of the group, Mary Dyer, was also sentenced to hang but was reprieved at the place of execution and banished. When she insisted upon returning the next year, she was immediately hanged.

The religious Bostonians were understandably annoyed by the Quakers, who were then more assertive than they later became. For example, a Quaker had gone to Rome to convert the pope. Another had journeyed to Constantinople and had endeavored to convert a somewhat puzzled sultan. Others had made disturbances in church and had interrupted the sermons of the most respected ministers. They refused to pay certain taxes or to take oaths. In short, they were a trial to orderly and godly folk, and the orthodox people of Massachusetts Bay saw no reason why they should endure them.

Traditionally, saints suffer many temptations to test their virtue and try their patience, and the founding fathers of New England were obsessed by the notion that the old deluder, Satan, had singled them out for his principal attack. For this reason they felt that they had to be particularly alert to foil the wiles of the devil and stamp out Satanic influences as fast as they could be discovered. One of Satan's most effective agencies for evil, the Puritans believed, was witchcraft. And although the belief in witchcraft was not confined to the Puritans, they were the most vigorous witch-hunters in the seventeenth century.

From 1647 until the end of the century, Massachusetts Bay and Connecticut, which were particularly concerned about witches, sought zealously to root them out. The most energetic campaign took place between the years 1688 and 1693. To help justify witch-hunting, Increase and Cotton Mather lent the weight of their learning. In 1684 Increase Mather published *An Essay for the Recording of Illustrious Providences*, which was eagerly read by a populace already excited over supernatural appearances. Mather quoted from the church fathers, classical writers, and learned theologians to prove the existence of black and white witches, and he called down the wrath of God upon both. "They that do hurt to others by the devil's help are called 'black witches,'" he explained, "but there are a sort of persons in the world that will never hurt any; but only by the power of the infernal spirits will un-bewitch those that seek unto them for relief. I know that by Constantius his law, black witches were to be punished, and white ones indulged; but M. Perkins saith, that the good witch is a more horrible and detestable monster than the bad one."

Five years later, when the children of a Boston brickmason named Goodwin claimed they were bewitched, Cotton Mather undertook a careful examination of the case and wrote an electrifying analysis, *Memorable Providences Relating to Witchcrafts and Possessions* (1689), which helped to confirm the fears that were tormenting the community. Between 1689 and 1692 more than two hundred persons in Massachusetts and Connecticut were accused of witchcraft, and more than

Cotton Mather helped create the witchcraft hysteria and aided at the Salem trials, but though he failed to protest the hangings, he did not believe in harsh punishment for witches. The creatures surrounding him are some of the scores of forms a demon assumed in the "documented" case of an English family that was besieged by witches in 1621.

twenty were hanged. An old man, Giles Corey, confused and perplexed by the charges of witchcraft, refused to plead either guilty or not guilty. For this offense he suffered the penalty prescribed by English common law, that of being pressed to death under heavy weights.

Although the hysteria was confined to no single community, it was more intense in Salem than elsewhere, for there witches were believed to have congregated—and the imaginations of the residents of Salem were inflamed. Cotton Mather lent his help to the judges and offered expert testimony, which was received with the respect accorded that of psychiatrists in the present day. The hysteria reached its height in 1692, and the next year Mather published his *Wonders of the Invisible World* (1693), which defended the wisdom of the hanging judges of Salem. The clergy, or the dominant members of it, had staked their prestige on the trials.

At last the orgy of persecution of wretched old women and men or of deluded eccentrics came to an end when a few men of common sense raised their voices in protest. At the height of the furor, Thomas Brattle, a merchant of Boston, castigated the prosecutors of witches as ignoramuses. In 1700 another merchant, Robert Calef, published a satirical attack on the credulity of the Mathers in a pamphlet entitled *More Wonders of the Invisible World*. Yet the prestige of the Mathers was such that no Boston printer would publish Calef's pamphlet, which had to be printed in London. Finally good sense asserted itself, and many New Englanders, including Judge Samuel Sewall of Boston, expressed regret over the excesses of the witchcraft trials. The part that the clergy had played in the trials added no luster to their reputations and helped to weaken clerical influence in Massachusetts Bay.

While the witchcraft fury was raging, a colorful figure arrived in Boston to serve as royal governor. He was Sir William Phips, erstwhile ship's carpenter and contractor of Boston, who had done what thousands had dreamed of: discovered a sunken Spanish treasure ship off Haiti and succeeded in recovering from the wreck gold, silver, and jewels amounting in value to more than three hundred thousand pounds sterling. For this exploit, King James II in 1687 dubbed him knight. Although Increase Mather was unable to persuade King William III to restore Massachusetts' old charter, he did manage to gain the king's promise to make Phips the first royal governor of Massachusetts, for Mather

saw in Phips a tool that he might use. One of Phips's first duties on arriving in Boston in May, 1692, was to appoint William Stoughton, a fanatical bigot, to serve as the judge in the witch trials at Salem. Later, when even Phips came to believe the prosecution of witches had gone too far, he contrived to lay the blame for the excess on Stoughton.

The companion of dubious waterfront characters in the days before the discovery of the Spanish treasure, Phips as governor was not above winking at piracy and smuggling. Purse-proud and arrogant, he once publicly caned the captain of an English man-of-war. On another occasion he shoved a customs officer off a wharf. At length, in 1694, Phips was summoned to England to account for his shortcomings as governor; but he died before his case was heard.

West of the coastal regions, the back country was also developing. Settlers penetrated the rich Connecti-

Ninigret, sachem (chief) of the Niantic Indians of Rhode Island, was also made sachem of the related Narragansets by the English as a reward for keeping the Niantics out of King Philip's War in 1675. Ninigret refused to the end of a long life to become a Christian, telling the missionaries to "go and make the English good first."

cut River Valley as far as Deerfield and beyond. Farms dotted the other river valleys, and farmers on these frontiers frequently engaged in fur trade with the Indians, who in general kept the peace. For the most part, New England had been lucky in her Indian relations. The first settlers found the coastal tribes so decimated by an epidemic that they made little resistance to the white invaders. Occasional quarrels between white traders and Indians caused trouble to outlying settlements. A series of murders and punitive measures by the whites led in 1637 to an outbreak of war with the Pequot Indians in the lower Connecticut Valley in which that tribe was virtually annihilated. Captain John Mason led an expedition that surrounded more than four hundred of the Pequots in a palisaded fort on the Mystic River. Setting fire to the fort in the night, Mason's men burned all but seven of the occupants to death. William Bradford, describing this episode, commented: "It was conceived they thus destroyed about 400 at this time. It was a fearfull sight to see them thus frying in the fyer, and the streams of blood quenching the same, and horrible was the stinck and sente ther of; but the victory seemed a sweete sacrifice, and they gave the prays thereof to God, who had wrought so wonderfuly for them, thus to inclose their enimise in their hands, and give them so speedy a victory over so proud and insulting an enimie."

Before the campaign against the Pequots was over, militiamen had killed or captured more than seven hundred Indians. Indian captives were highly prized, for they could be sold as slaves in the West Indies or traded for more tractable Negro slaves. The Reverend Hugh Peter wrote to Governor Winthrop requesting a few slaves for himself: "Sir, Mr. Endecot and myself salute you in the Lord Jesus. Wee have heard of a dividence of women and children in the bay and would bee glad of a share viz: a young woman or girle and a boy if you thinke good. I wrote to you for some boyes for Bermudas, which I thinke is considerable." They got seventeen Indian slaves—fifteen boys and two women.

Save for sporadic and localized trouble, the New England Indians remained relatively peaceful for nearly forty years after the subjugation of the Pequots. White settlers pushed farther and farther into the interior and acquired more and more land once used by the Indians. Some of this land came by treaty and purchase; other territory came into official possession of the colonies of Plymouth, Connecticut, or Massachusetts Bay as compensation for alleged wrongs committed by the Indians. It became an easy matter to find a reason for imposing fines on the Indians, who could pay only through the forfeit of tribal lands.

During this period of peace, some headway was made by missionaries in converting Indians to Christianity, especially among those tribes too weak to retain their independence from stronger tribes. The Reverend John Eliot of Roxbury, who labored earnestly to gather the heathen into the Christian fold, conceived the notion of settling the "praying Indians" into towns, which by 1674 numbered fourteen. Daniel Gookin, a devout Puritan who formerly had lived in Virginia and Maryland, moved to Roxbury in 1644 and collaborated with Eliot in proselytizing the Indians. Eliot's most remarkable feat was the translation of the Bible into the Indian language. The New Testament was printed in 1661 and the Old Testament in 1663, the first complete Bible to be printed in British America.

In 1675 the land hunger of the colonies and the efforts of the Puritans to force the Indians into obedience to their laws at last precipitated a rebellion that involved most of the coastal Indians of New England. The conflict is known as "King Philip's War," for Metacom, whom the English called King Philip, the son of Massasoit, sachem of the Wampanoag tribe. Philip and his tribe were bitter over their treatment by Plymouth colony. Particularly unjust, the Indians felt, was the colony's demand that they turn in guns they had bought legally at great cost from Plymouth traders. Philip also was obliged to pay fines for tribal misdemeanors, sign away land, and declare himself the subject of the governor of Plymouth and the king of England.

Humiliated by continued indignities, he at last revolted. Other tribes, also seething with animosity toward the whites, followed Philip's example, and the outlying districts of New England rang with the war cry of marauding Indians who burned isolated farmhouses and villages and slaughtered men, women, and children. In September a band of Philip's warriors attacked Deerfield and a little later fell on a troop of colonial soldiers and killed sixty-four of them at a stream that ever since has been called "Bloody Brook." (Deerfield, for a time abandoned, was resettled in time for a second Indian massacre, in 1704, in another war on the frontier.)

The flames of war enveloped the whole frontier from Maine to New York. Before it was over, the Indians had killed one man out of every sixteen able to bear arms. In

Massachusetts alone the Indians had destroyed sixteen towns. But eventually the colonists gained the upper hand. Philip, not a very competent leader of his people, was killed in a swamp in August, 1676, by an Indian friendly to the whites. After almost two more years of frontier conflict, a treaty brought an uneasy peace. Many Indian captives, including Philip's wife and son, were sold as slaves in the West Indies. Some whites taken into captivity by the Indians never returned. One who did, Mrs. Mary Rowlandson, has left a vivid account of her sufferings, first printed in 1682 as *A Narrative of the Captivity and Restauration of Mrs. Mary Rowlandson.* The cruelty of the Indians described by Mrs. Rowlandson helps to explain the vindictiveness of the whites, which led even to the persecution of the Christian Indians, who had remained loyal to the settlers, and to threats of violence against John Eliot and Daniel Gookin, who befriended them. After King Philip's War, missionary activity on the frontier virtually ceased, despite John Eliot's continued efforts. The savagery of King Philip's War was merely a prelude to the fierce conflicts of the eighteenth century, when French Canada and English America involved the Indians in the dynastic wars of Europe.

While enterprising New Englanders were probing the river valleys, penetrating the back country, and displacing the Indians, colonists in New York and New Jersey were extending the settled areas of those regions.

The Duke of York, who took over the proprietorship of New York after the displacement of the Dutch West India Company, had as his administrator Colonel Richard Nicolls, one of the few good colonial governors that New York could boast. In 1665 Nicolls put into effect a code known as the Duke's Laws, which proved useful in welding the Dutch and English elements together. However, the Duke of York was opposed to popular government and for several years refused to authorize a legislative assembly, which he suspected of "dangerous consequence, nothing being more known than the aptness of such bodies to assume to themselves many privileges which prove destructive to, or very oft disturb, the peace of the government wherein they are allowed." In 1683, however, continued pressure from the English settlements, particularly those on Long Island, induced the duke to call an assembly representing the landed property holders. They drew up a Charter of Liberties and Privileges, which the duke approved, but before it became the operating constitution for the col-

The above water color of an Irish peasant woman was painted during the early colonial period; she is typical of the Irish who were among the colonizers of New Jersey and New York during the 1600's. At the right is the elaborate initial "J" on the royal commission that appointed Sir Edmund Andros governor of New England in 1686. The portrait is that of James II, who granted the commission.

164

ony, the duke had ascended the throne as James II and at once set about trying to change the governments of New York and New England.

Shortly after the Duke of York had taken over New York, his brother, Charles II, with careless generosity and an indifference to precise geography, had awarded him not only New York but much of what we now call New Jersey. In turn the Duke of York transferred his right to the territory between the Hudson and the Delaware rivers to two courtiers, John Lord Berkeley and Sir George Carteret, who had defended the island of Jersey off the English coast against the Puritan troops. As a compliment to Carteret, the territory was given the name of New Jersey. These two proprietors divided the grant between them, Berkeley taking West Jersey and Carteret East Jersey. Berkeley soon sold his portion to two Quakers, John Fenwick and Edward Byllinge, who quarreled so bitterly over the division of the land that they had to call in William Penn to mediate between them, a move that resulted in exciting Penn's interest in American land.

Both Quakers eventually sold their proprietary rights to others. Thus the problem of land tenure in West Jer-

sey almost immediately became immensely complicated. When Carteret died, his widow sold his rights to East Jersey to a syndicate of twelve men, who later added twelve more. As they bequeathed their proprietary rights to numerous heirs, the problem of land tenure in East Jersey became as complicated as that in West Jersey. To this day, proprietary boards are necessary in New Jersey to untangle the titles to landed property.

The two Jerseys gained settlers of all kinds. Persecuted Quakers from England flocked to West Jersey and established prosperous communities at Burlington, Salem, and Greenwich. They combined trade, farming, and industry. Like the New Englanders, they became shipbuilders. Some developed plantations, and if they had any original distaste for slavery, it was overcome by the need for servants to work their farms. Since the proprietors of the two Jerseys and of New York were eager for immigrants willing to pay quitrents or to purchase land outright, they showed little concern about the religious or political beliefs of potential settlers. As a result, these colonies developed a more polyglot population than existed in New England. Quakers, Catholics, French Huguenots, Germans from the Palatinate, disgruntled Scots, some Irish, a few Jews, and an occasional adventurer from other countries of western Europe found a welcome and an opportunity to acquire land in the Jerseys and New York.

In the second half of the seventeenth century, the province of New York was already developing social qualities that would be characteristic of its later history. Merchants, who had gained wealth in trade carried on through the growing port of New York, eagerly sought land in the interior, and many of them put together vast baronial estates. Toward the end of the century, the royal governors designated some of these estates as manors and invested the owners with the privileges accorded lords of manors in England. These great landowners constituted an aristocracy that monopolized both power and privilege in the province. The names of many of them are written large in the history of New York.

In 1693, for example, Frederick Philipse, a merchant-trader who shrewdly managed to stay in favor with the ruling power, whether it was Dutch or English, and whose ships traded with the pirates off the Madagascar coast, consolidated large blocks of land into the manor of Philipsburgh and built Castle Philipse in Sleepy Hollow and the Manor Hall in Yonkers, landmarks of early

New York. In 1686 Robert Livingston, a refugee Scot, got a patent for the manor of Livingston, which consisted of at least one hundred and sixty thousand acres in Dutchess and Columbia counties. As secretary of the board of commissioners for Indian affairs, Livingston had opportunities that he did not overlook to obtain concessions for himself from the Indians. In 1697 Stephanus Van Cortlandt obtained a patent for the manor of Van Cortlandt, comprising some eighty-five thousand acres in the Hudson highlands. He wielded great power over the lower Hudson Valley. Peter Schuyler, made mayor of Albany when that town was incorporated in 1686, owned enormous holdings of land on the upper Hudson. He gained the friendship of the Iroquois Indians with whom he traded and was one of several successive landowners in upper New York who helped to maintain the alliance with the Iroquois against the Algonquins and the French. All these magnates exerted an enormous influence upon the provincial government. The power that the merchant-landowners gained in New York in the seventeenth century was challenged but never broken during the colonial period.

Since manorial estates had to be populated and worked, the proprietors did their best to attract tenants by offering land on easy terms. Some land they leased for quitrents; other tracts they sold outright. Small traders could also buy land from the Indians, and in time many yeoman farmers obtained holdings of their own

in the province of New York, as they had in New Jersey. As these small farmers grew more numerous, they became increasingly restive under the domination of the land barons, who continued to hold advantages in the assessment of taxes and to monopolize emoluments from public offices and opportunities for adding still more land to their holdings.

Discontent over the power and arrogance of the wealthy aristocracy came to a head in 1689, in a conflict known as the Leisler Rebellion, a movement so confused by prejudice and personal animosities that a clear understanding of all the issues is difficult to arrive at.

When James II named Sir Edmund Andros governor general of New York, he appointed Francis Nicholson lieutenant governor. A few months later, James himself was deposed and was succeeded by William of Orange and Mary (daughter of James II). Andros, who had been the ruler of New England since 1686, incurred so much hostility that the New Englanders rose against him in April, 1689, immediately after they heard news of James II's deposition, and threw him in jail. That left Nicholson, his lieutenant, as acting governor of New York; but public opinion and a man named Jacob Leisler were to unseat him.

Leisler, a soldier who had come to the New World as an employee of the Dutch West India Company, married the rich widow of Pieter Van der Veen and grew wealthy in his own right in the fur, tobacco, and wine

This picture by an unknown country artist of a New York farm in the early 1700's once hung over the mantel of the house it depicts. Besides painting the farm with its animals and people, the artist has put owner and wife in front watching a passing scene that includes a farm wagon, a man thrown by his horse, and trudging Indians. The Catskill Mountains form the backdrop.

trade. A devout member of the Dutch Reformed Church, he bitterly resented the appointment of an Anglican parson to serve as pastor of his church and became convinced that Anglicans and Catholics were about to make common cause to restore the authority of King James in the province. Nicholson was accused of being in the conspiracy. Wild rumors circulated that the papists were also plotting with the French to invade the colony from Canada and to slaughter and pillage the Protestants. At this juncture Leisler, a militia officer, came forward with the announced intention of saving New York for William and Mary. He made himself commander of the militia, seized the fort, and assumed the title of lieutenant governor. Then, in 1690, a legislature called by Leisler enacted a law that abolished special privileges enjoyed by the merchants of New York City and declared that all towns in the province should have equal rights to sell and distribute their manufactures and produce where they wished. In the meantime, Nicholson escaped to England.

Leisler, an obstinate, bigoted man, had never been popular with the other merchants of New York, and he was now opposed by the magnates, who looked upon him as a rabble-rouser. On the other hand, the small tradesmen and yeoman farmers flocked to his support, and the disturbance took on all the appearances of a class struggle.

At this point William and Mary commissioned a royal governor, Colonel Henry Sloughter, and sent with him two companies of troops, commanded by Major Richard Ingoldesby, to pacify the troublemakers. When the troops arrived in January, 1691, ahead of the governor, Leisler refused to surrender to Ingoldesby and on March 17 fired on the royal troops, killing two men. This act sealed his own fate. When Governor Sloughter arrived and received Leisler's submission, the governor placed him, his son-in-law, Jacob Milborne, and eight others under arrest, charged with treason. Tried before judges already convinced of their subversiveness, Leisler and Milborne were condemned to death and eventually hanged. (It was reported that the executioners obtained Sloughter's signature to the death warrant while the governor was drunk, a condition that official attained with some frequency.) Thus ended Leisler's Rebellion— but not the underlying discontent against aristocratic monopolists in the province of New York. Class feeling and the bitterness engendered by Leisler's execution long plagued New York politics.

Despite Indian wars, the growing threat of French intervention, and occasional periods—typified by Leisler's Rebellion—when home rule was interrupted, the colonies in the North prospered. By the latter years of the seventeenth century, New England was a populous region with growing towns stretching from Maine to New York, and England had established her claim to a valuable portion of the New World.

Years of Expansion

The rapid growth of Pennsylvania in the last two decades of the seventeenth century was the result to a large degree of William Penn's skill as a real-estate salesman and advertiser. Along with an altruistic vision of a domain where his fellow Quakers and other oppressed peoples might find peace and prosperity, Penn also had a dream of a land where his own family would prosper. When Charles II confirmed to him the proprietary grant of the territory of Pennsylvania in 1681, he eagerly set out to achieve both goals.

To excite the interest of prospective colonists, Penn published his first promotion piece in July, 1681, with the title *Some account of the province of Pennsilvania in America; Lately Granted under the Great Seal of England to William Penn, etc. Together with Priviledges and Powers necessary to the well-governing thereof. Made publick for the Information of such as are or may be disposed to Transport themselves or Servants into those Parts.* Penn tried to be scrupulously accurate in his description of the land that he wished to settle, but he showed a shrewd understanding of the points that would appeal to the persecuted and landless people of Europe. He emphasized that the "Rights and Freedoms of England (the best and largest in Europe) shall be in force there," and he stressed the ultimate freedom, economic as well as personal, that a colonist might expect. The conditions that he outlined were clearly and simply expressed, and he provided information that any prospective emigrant would need: the cost of land, the cost of passage, the equipment needed, and the procedure that a settler might expect to follow on first arrival. Land could be either purchased or rented. Buyers might procure land at the rate of one hundred pounds for five thousand acres plus an annual quitrent of one English shilling per hundred acres. Renters could obtain land for an annual rental of a penny an acre. In addition, anyone who brought over servants would be allowed fifty acres for each servant, and the servant, at the expiration of his contracted period of service, would be allowed fifty acres for himself.

To the land-hungry people of Great Britain and the Continent, these terms must

In this detail of a canvas by Charles II's court painter, Cecil Calvert grasps a chart of Maryland held by his grandfather, Lord Baltimore, who organized the colony.

169

have read like a promise of prosperity. No one was so poor that he could not look forward to being a land-owner. Even though he came as a bond servant committed to serve from four to seven years, he could expect to own land when his contract expired.

In 1683, after a visit to his domain, Penn wrote another even more appealing tract bearing the title *A Letter from William Penn . . . to the Committee of the Free Society of Traders of that Province, residing in London*, which provided a matter-of-fact description that nevertheless managed to convey the notion that here indeed was the earthly paradise. It was a land where "the Air is sweet and clear, the Heavens serene, like the South-parts of France, rarely Overcast." The fertility of the varied soils, Penn pointed out, would simplify the growing of the crops, vegetables, fruits, herbs, and trees needed by man. "Of Fowl of the Land," he wrote, "there is Turkey (Forty and Fifty Pound weight) which is very great; Phesants, Heath-Birds, Pidgeons and Partridges in abundance." The duck and teal, Penn maintained, were better than any one could "ever eat in other Countries."

Of the origin of the Indians, Penn observed: "I am ready to believe them of the Jewish Race, I mean, of the stock of the Ten Tribes" (a misconception that has produced a considerable literature). Although he thought that the Indians were "under a dark Night in things relating to Religion," Penn wrote of them in a way to fascinate rather than frighten his readers, describing them as people in a golden age: "They care for little, because they want but little, and the Reason is, a little contents them. . . . if they are ignorant of our Pleasures, they are also free from our Pains. They are not disquieted with Bills of Lading and Exchange, nor perplexed with Chancery-Suits and Exchequer-Reckonings. We sweat and toil to live; their pleasure feeds them, I mean, their Hunting, Fishing, and Fowling."

Translated into Dutch, French, and German in 1684, this tract was widely circulated in areas where Penn believed he might recruit settlers. A year later he published *A Further Account of the Province of Pennsylvania* (1685), with a Dutch translation in the same year. This served as a sequel to his *Letter to the Free Society of Traders* and pointed out the improvements and developments already taking place in the province. The impact of these tracts and of other news of Pennsylvania that circulated in Great Britain and on the Continent was impressive. Ships loaded with immigrants were soon dropping anchor at Philadelphia, and a stream of hopeful settlers began making their way into the interior of the new colony.

Most of the early colonists were English and Welsh Quakers, along with some Welsh Baptists and a few Anglicans. The Welsh settled on what became known as "the Welsh Tract" west of the Schuylkill River. There they prospered, built fine homes, and bequeathed to their descendants what was to become the most aristocratic section of the Philadelphia region—the "Main Line" of the late nineteenth century, where Welsh names like Bryn Mawr, Merion, and Haverford, given by the early settlers, still survive.

Penn was scrupulously fair in all his dealings, and he was careful to compensate the Indians for land that he acquired from them. Word of a pact he made with the natives prompted Voltaire to observe that "this is the only treaty between those people and the Christians that was not ratified by an oath and was never infringed." Not until those firm believers in the Old Testament, the Presbyterians from Scotland, began to yearn for Indian land did Pennsylvania have trouble with the Indians. The Scots, with ample texts from Scripture, equated the Indians with the Canaanites and found reasons to take their land.

Philadelphia, which Penn's surveyor general, Thomas Holme, had laid out in broad squares, grew rapidly. The more prosperous Quakers bought town lots and erected comfortable houses on the tree-lined streets. Penn himself had a house there and another more imposing establishment at Pennsbury in Bucks County. Merchants built warehouses along the Delaware River, which was deep enough to allow ocean-going vessels to tie up at the wharves. Before the end of the century, Philadelphia was a busy port and trading center with the promise of further growth as immigrants arrived to push into the back country.

The promise of a peaceful land where they could worship as they pleased appealed particularly to German Mennonites living in the Rhine Valley who had been harried by warring armies through much of the seventeenth century. The Mennonites were pacifists with beliefs much like the Quakers, and they soon came in large numbers to Pennsylvania. In 1683 the first group, led by Francis Daniel Pastorius, a lawyer of Frankfurt, settled not far from Philadelphia in a community that soon came to be known as Germantown. Pastorius's group included other oppressed peoples in search of freedom and opportunity, making up a company of many trades and crafts. During the next forty years, several thousand German and Dutch sectarians (as the first wave of German immigrants were called) swarmed into Pennsylvania. A few found work around Germantown, but most moved on into the country and became farmers. They were followed early in the eighteenth century by thousands of other Germans, chiefly of Lutheran and Reformed faiths, many of them so poor that they had to mortgage their freedom for a period of years to pay for their passage. Hence they were called "redemptioners." The length of time they had to serve before they could redeem themselves and go free ranged from four years to ten years in the case

of children, who had to work until they came of age.

The sectarians were of infinite variety, for in their strongly individualistic society, anyone with even a slight difference of belief could start another sect. But while their beliefs differed in many important aspects, they all shared a common hatred of war and its associations (one sect refused to use buttons on their clothes because brass buttons, and hence all buttons, were associated in their minds with military uniforms). Though most of them were of German origin, they became known as "Pennsylvania Dutch."

The Germans were industrious, hard-working, and skillful as farmers and in a variety of trades. To their labor the province of Pennsylvania owed much of its

William Penn by tradition first met with the Indians in 1682 at Shackamaxon, a village of the Delawares, but the "Great Treaty" he is reputed to have made there is actually a time-blurred fusing of several agreements. A Quaker artist here idealizes the Shackamaxon meeting even more by adding nonexistent houses.

for English privateers was Jamaica, taken from Spain by forces dispatched by Oliver Cromwell in 1655 as part of his ill-conceived and poorly executed "Western Design" for taking Spain's Caribbean possessions. In spite of these British outposts in the Caribbean, Spain remained a potential threat to the more southerly of the British colonies, for there was always the danger of encirclement by a combination of Spanish and French forces. Hence the settlement of Carolina by Englishmen in the latter part of the seventeenth century was welcomed by the northern colonies, just as the occupation of Georgia in the eighteenth century gave South Carolina greater security against a Spanish attack.

After Raleigh's abortive efforts to establish a colony on the coast of North Carolina, no successful colonizing activities had taken place in this region for more than three quarters of a century. Charles I in 1629 had granted the territory, called in honor of himself "Carolina," to his attorney general, Sir Robert Heath, but Heath had failed to colonize it. Finally, in 1663, Charles II granted to eight proprietors land from Currituck Inlet to a line sixty-five miles south of St. Augustine, Florida, and extending from ocean to ocean. The eight who received this imperial domain were Edward Hyde, later Earl of Clarendon, George Monck, later Duke of Albemarle, William Lord Craven, John Lord Berkeley, Sir William Berkeley, Anthony Ashley Cooper, later Earl of Shaftesbury, Sir George Carteret, and Sir John Colleton. These men, backed by bankers and merchants of London, were the lords proprietors of Carolina, vested with the ownership of the land and the power to make the laws and administer justice.

To provide a legal instrument of government, the philosopher John Locke and the politician Anthony Ashley Cooper drew up the strangest platform that any British colony ever tried to put into practice. Called the Fundamental Constitutions, it set forth a plan for an aristocratic hierarchy. The lords proprietors, of course, stood at the apex, and each proprietor had an individual right to twelve thousand acres in each of Carolina's counties. Next to the lords proprietors stood the landgraves, with a right to not less than forty-eight thousand acres. The third and lowest rank of the nobility were the caciques, with twenty-four thousand acres. After them came gentlemen commoners, who were required to have not less than three thousand but not more than twelve thousand acres. They were to be appointed as lords of manors, with manorial rights similar to those in medieval England. At the bottom of the hierarchy of landowners were the yeomen, who had to possess not less than fifty acres in order to vote. The hierarchy, of course, envisaged a laboring class of landless workers composed of free laborers, indentured servants, and Negro slaves. This elaborate system, which could have emanated only from the brains of dreamers, never actually became a social reality that endured, but the proprietors did create a total of twenty-six landgraves and thirteen caciques.

The Fundamental Constitutions not only sought to create an aristocratic social system, but the document outlined an equally elaborate system of government that also proved completely impracticable. The proprietors would appoint a governor, but if any proprietor emigrated to Carolina, he would take precedence over the governor. In the absence of the proprietors, each would have a deputy resident in the colony. The government of the colony would be entrusted to a legislative assembly composed of the governor, the proprietary deputies, and the nobility, and elected representatives from the landholding commons. After 1693 the assembly became bicameral, with an upper and a lower house. Because the Fundamental Constitutions proved so unworkable, the proprietors constantly revised the document, but by the end of the century they tacitly abandoned it as a constitution of government because the legislative assembly would never accept its complicated provisions.

The London courtiers of Charles II who concocted unworkable schemes for enriching themselves from estates in Carolina did realize that it would take a host of settlers to make their dreams come true. To that end they set the mills of publicity turning in order to persuade potential colonists to emigrate. One influential tract, written by a Barbadian ship captain, William Hilton, was published in London in 1664 as *A Relation of a Discovery Lately Made on the Coast of Florida*. Hilton had been employed by a group of sugar planters in Barbados to search for land where they would have more opportunity for expansion than existed on their overcrowded island.

After two voyages of exploration, Hilton made such a favorable report of the Carolina coastal country that his Barbadian employers petitioned the lords proprietors for the privilege of settling in their domain, and an agreement was reached that ultimately led to the migration of many colonists from Barbados. So pleased were the proprietors with Hilton's report that they had it

Although Florida was Spanish, Charles II did not hesitate to include a big piece of it, including St. Augustine, in his grant to the proprietors of Carolina. At right is a section of a picture of what was labeled St. Augustine, but it is completely imaginative, for it was published in 1671, and the town's fort was not even begun until 1672.

published to stimulate further emigration. (Hilton had been careful to contradict unfavorable comment by a few New England cattle breeders, who for a time had settled in the Cape Fear region.) Other pamphleteers were soon extolling the Carolina country for its salubrious climate, its fertile soil, its valuable forests, and the prospects for getting rich from the natural products of the land. Thomas Ashe, for example, in a pamphlet published in 1682 called *Carolina, or a Description of the Present State of that Country, and the Natural Excellencies Thereof*, promised that a native herb, "the famous Cassiny," made into a tea, would "wonderfully enliven and envigorate the Heart . . . preserving the Mind free and serene, keeping the Body brisk, active, and lively." To anyone suffering from baldness, he also gave assurance that Carolina bear's grease had "great Vertue and Efficacy in causing the Hair to grow."

The publicity seemed to work, both in England and Barbados. In the summer of 1665 a contingent of some ninety Barbadian settlers, who had planned to land at Port Royal near the site of Jean Ribaut's ill-fated colony, were carried by adverse winds to the mouth of the Cape Fear River. There they built houses and named their village Charles Town. But the colony dispersed after two quarrelsome years, and the name of their settlement was left to another town that was settled in 1670 at Albemarle Point on the Ashley River by a party of Englishmen led by Joseph West. Ten years later the site was moved to the confluence of the Ashley and Cooper rivers, and much later the name of the settlement was altered to Charleston.

West brought his group of ninety-three English colonists to Carolina by way of Barbados. There Sir John Yeamans, the governor, had been instructed to fill in a blank commission with his own name for governor of Carolina, or with some other name if he chose. Yeamans decided to name an octogenarian former governor of Bermuda, William Sayle. On Sayle's death about a year later, West became governor.

Although Carolina's growth was slow at first, the colony did not suffer the hardships that were characteristic of some of the earlier settlements. West was a highly intelligent man and managed to supply, even before old William Sayle's death, the kind of leadership that the colony needed. In February, 1671, the first Barbadians arrived, and for many years the colony received a steady flow of settlers from that island.

The early colonists were convinced, probably from some of the enthusiastic tracts they had read, that they had reached a tropical paradise where oranges, lemons, dates, and other exotic products would grow. The first winter freeze discouraged them, but gradually they learned to grow other products—corn, grains, and other food crops. Cattle, hogs, and horses flourished, and, as in the other colonies, the forests provided naval stores. In 1685 a ship captain named John Thurber brought some rice seed from Madagascar, and the planters soon discovered in rice a crop that grew abundantly in the rich black soil of the swamplands. Within a few years, rice was one of the most important products in Carolina.

The early settlers brought in a few Negro slaves, and slavery quickly became an important factor in the colony's economy. Manual labor in the forests and swamps required little skill but much endurance, and the slaves admirably suited the planters' needs. Like the New Englanders, they felt no compunction about enslaving Africans, salving their consciences with the notion that they were the instruments for bringing these heathen to a land of Christian salvation. The Barbadians were accustomed to both Negro and Indian slavery, and in conflicts with the Carolina Indians they were quick to take prisoners whom they could sell into bondage. Since Indian slaves could easily slip away into the forests again, the Carolina Indian slave-traders found it expedient to ship such captives to the West Indies.

Trade with the Indians of the interior helped to increase the prosperity of the merchants who settled in Charles Town. They bartered for deerskins, mink pelts, and other furs—and also bought captives whom the Indians themselves had taken in their wars. The slave trade was not inconsequential in the commercial development of Charles Town.

Before the end of the seventeenth century many settlers were moving into Carolina, which was still one colony, for the division of North and South Carolina would not come until later. Huguenots came from Virginia, England, and later France. A considerable number of ne'er-do-wells slipped over the border of Virginia into northern Carolina, mostly runaway servants and others who wanted to escape the attention of Virginia authorities. Other settlers came all the way from the northern colonies. The climate and the lure of easy prosperity continued for many years to attract emigrants from Europe and from other British colonies. The great period for the development of Carolina, however, was to come in the eighteenth century.

Columbian Magazine, 1786

VENERATE THE PLOUGH

Making a Living

Contrary to a popular belief, most colonists were not seekers after religious freedom or refugees from political oppression. The overwhelming majority were driven by nothing more than a basic human yearning for more of the good things of the earth. Labor was scarce, and the newcomer with a skill or talent had little trouble making a living. But the greatest lure was cheap or free land, and it was the farmer, first to last, who dominated life in the colonies. Some 95 per cent of the colonists lived on farms, a term that encompassed everything from a frontier cabin with a corn patch in a stumpy clearing to a Virginia tidewater plantation. The soil was deep and productive, but with the supply seemingly inexhaustible, the colonist became a bad farmer. He wore out the soil, then moved on to virgin land—and this was true of the plantation owner as well as the log-cabin settler. Wasteful though it was, this type of agriculture nevertheless managed to be productive. The natural bounty of the region also provided other harvests: the lumberman, the fur trader, and the fisherman worked with resources almost unlimited. With such help from generous nature, the colonies developed a prosperous and sophisticated economy that could support without strain such luxuries as goldsmiths, wigmakers, and dancing masters.

183

Exemplifying the two principal cash crops of the colonies are the English tobacco merchant's label above advertising Virginia tobacco, and the idyllic wheat harvest scene at right from an 18th-century New England needlework picture. Though tobacco was always the more important, wheat very early became a source of cash for farmers in the Middle Colonies.

A fishing fleet, probably from New England, lies at anchor in a

Newfoundland harbor, about 1760, while its catch dries on shore.

Above: The wheelwright, an indispensable colonial artisan
Right: A section of an 18th-century Maryland shipyard

OVERLEAF: *A tinsmith's shop—colonial industry was largely handicraft.*

DIDEROT, *L'Encyclopédie*, IV, 1763

The Long Conflict Begins

The accession of William of Orange and Queen Mary to the English throne after the overthrow of James II in 1688 profoundly influenced the course of events both in England and in the most distant settlements of British America. As ruler of Holland as well as king of England, William III was committed to maintaining a balance of power in Europe, and to that end he had to curb the ambitions of Louis XIV. From 1689 until 1763, England was intermittently at war with France in an effort to prevent French domination of Europe, and the outcome was not finally settled until the defeat of Napoleon in 1815.

When William attacked France in 1689 in a conflict called in Europe the War of the League of Augsburg, he formalized a state of war in the colonies that was already endemic. The conflict in America came to be known as King William's War. Fighting between the French in Canada and the English to the south was inevitable, for the two were in competition for the profitable fur trade with the Indians. Each side had its own Indian allies. From the time of Champlain, the French had cemented their alliance with the Algonquin tribes. French Jesuits and other Catholic missionaries had carried the Cross to distant frontiers and had won the friendship of tribes in the interior. At the same time, the French had incurred the hostility of the Iroquois, traditional enemies of the Algonquins. The Iroquois confederation, known as the Five Nations (and after the Tuscaroras joined them in 1711, as the Six Nations), found it expedient to maintain a fairly consistent peace with the Dutch and the English. Their hunting grounds extended from Pennsylvania and New York to the Great Lakes and the upper reaches of the Ohio and Mississippi valleys. There the Iroquois came into conflict with hostile tribes under the influence of the French.

French traders, the *coureurs de bois*, showed great ingenuity and enterprise in winning the friendship of the Indians. They went into the back country, often took Indian squaws, and adapted themselves so completely to Indian life that they were frequently assimilated into the tribes with whom they traded. Only in rare cases were the English able to adapt to Indian life in this fashion. A few Englishmen, it is true, became friends

An artist of a later period has replaced frontier Schenectady's cabins with buildings of brick, but he has not exaggerated in portraying the terror and bloodshed of the massacre of 1690.

of the Indians, understood them, and took squaws for their bed companions, but they remained Englishmen among the Indians.

Although the Iroquois and allied tribes maintained a nominal peace with the English, they were not happy over the continued incursions of white settlers in the frontier areas where the settlements touched their hunting grounds. The wise men in their tribes could see that Englishmen were exerting pressure from the east and the south, just as the French and the Algonquins were pressing them from Canada, and they were troubled about the future as they saw the boundaries of their hunting grounds contracting. However, the Indians had acquired a taste for manufactured goods and had come to depend on the traders to supply guns, powder and shot, matchcoats, blankets, and particularly English rum. English blankets were better than those the French offered, and rum was cheaper and more to the Indians' taste than French brandy. (France had suppressed rum manufacture in her sugar islands of the West Indies lest it ruin the market for cognac, and this embargo on rum gave English traders an advantage in the Indian trade.) Yet despite the mutual interest of Indians and whites in maintaining smooth trading relations, tension always existed on the frontier, and localized violence might occur at any time.

A vast difference existed between the French settlements in Canada and those of the English to the south. Imperial France regarded the North American settlements merely as trading posts that would serve as outlets for French goods in exchange for furs. Some agriculture, it is true, was necessary to supply the traders, but only a few *habitants* thought of Canada as a place of permanent residence, and no Frenchman conceived of Canada as a self-sustaining or self-governing province. Control of French Canada was entirely in the hands of officials sent out from Paris. Furthermore, the French population of Canada was sparse. At the beginning of King William's War, Canada boasted only thirteen thousand French inhabitants, while the English colonies had two hundred thousand settlers. By 1715 the population of the English colonies had increased to four hundred thousand, while the French in Canada numbered a mere twenty-five thousand.

In effect, Canada served France not as an outlet for surplus population, as the English conceived of America, but as a place for garrisons to protect the lucrative fur trade. Regular troops from the king's armies came from France to protect the French trading posts. They made maximum use of their Indian allies, but the fighting strength of Canada depended upon professional soldiers, not upon a militia raised from the *habitants*.

Conditions were different in the British colonies. Although the fur trade was critically important there too, the English settlers planned to stay. They were ready to defend their own lines of communication with the trading posts on the frontier, but they were also fighting for homes in a land that they had seized for themselves. From time to time, the English sovereign had to send troops and naval vessels, and in the final battles with the French, regular troops were decisive, but much of the fighting in all the wars was done by colonial militia. Ill-trained and ill-disciplined, the militia was not always effective, but these troops constituted a force of citizen-soldiers who saved the colonies from devastation. Without them, English expansion along the frontiers would have been held in check.

When King William led England into a coalition at war with Louis XIV to prevent French aggression upon the Rhenish Palatinate (a part of the Holy Roman Empire), hostilities had already begun on the American frontier. English fur traders based at Albany had pushed westward in search of beaver pelts and were taking furs from areas on the Great Lakes that the French regarded as private preserves. Trouble was bound to ensue. In 1687 the Marquis de Denonville, governor of Canada, sent his troops into western New York to attack the Seneca Indians (one of the Five Nations), who were themselves warring against Algonquin tribes on the Great Lakes. Denonville ravaged the Senecas cornfields, captured some Indians and a few English traders, and built a fort on the eastern projection of land between the Niagara River and Lake Ontario. This campaign temporarily relieved the Iroquois pressure on Indian allies of the French, but Denonville had, as one Indian explained to him, knocked down a wasp's nest without killing the wasps. Furthermore, he stirred to action Governor Thomas Dongan of New York, who made an angry protest and called a council of the Iroquois at Albany. Dongan pointed out to the tribal representatives that they had invited trouble by attempting to trade with the perfidious French instead of bringing their beaver pelts to English traders. He recommended that the Five Nations unite with some of the western tribes and drive out the French. He also warned them against French Jesuit missionaries.

To Denonville, Dongan wrote demanding that English and Dutch captives be returned. "I hope, notwithstanding all your trained souldiers and greate Officers come from Europe, that our masters at home will suffer us to do ourselves justice on you for the injuries and spoyl you have committed on us," Dongan wrote, "and I assure you, Sir, if my Master gives me leave, I will be as soon at Quebeck as you shall be att Albany. . . . I advise you to send home all the Christian and Indian prisoners, the King of England's subjects, you unjustly do detein." Although Denonville wanted peace—and the opportunity to trade with the Iroquois—he could not return all the prisoners because some had been shipped to France to serve in the French galleys. Moreover, Denonville's Indian allies, who disliked the notion of the French trading with the Iroquois, contrived to sabotage peace negotiations.

Then, on the night of August 4, 1689, the Iroquois struck back at the French. A war party of fifteen hundred braves fell on the settlement at Lachine, eight miles from Montreal, massacred the inhabitants, and set fire to their houses. The French reported nearly two hundred slaughtered and one hundred and twenty taken prisoner, to be later tortured to death. The Iroquois continued for some weeks to range the countryside, burning and killing where they could. Denonville was forced to call in his garrisons at Fort Niagara and Fort Frontenac in the west to protect Montreal.

So serious was the crisis that Louis XIV chose an able veteran of New France, Comte de Frontenac, now a man of seventy, to return to command French forces. Frontenac arrived in October, 1689, with orders to capture New York, an assignment that proved impossible. But he did begin a campaign of revenge for the massacre at Lachine. Organizing three groups, he planned to attack Albany and the border outposts of Maine and New Hampshire. The first group to march was composed of a body of Indians and tough French *coureurs de bois*,

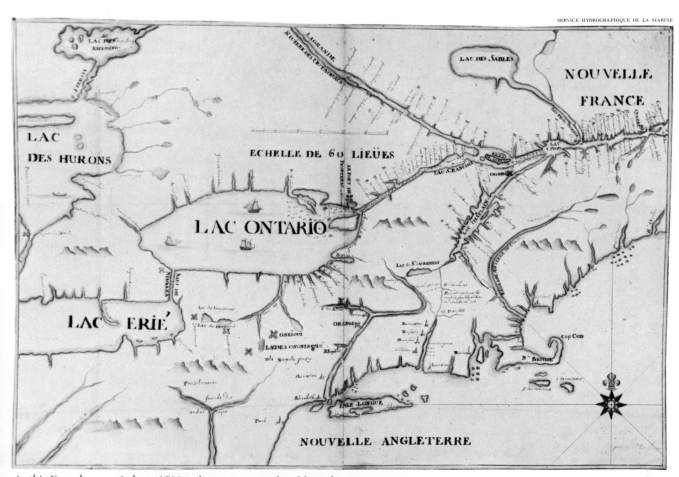

As this French map of about 1700 indicates, geographical knowledge of New England and New France was still sketchy. Though the general placement of principal lakes, rivers, and other features was known, there was ambiguity about size and shape.

195

with a handful of professional soldiers to lead them. In the dead of winter they set out for Albany across an endless white waste, moving silently on snowshoes. When the Indian allies grew sullen over the unending journey, the war party chose an easier objective, the outpost of Schenectady on the border of the Mohawk country. They approached the stockaded village during a blizzard on the night of February 8, 1690. Less than a dozen militiamen from Connecticut were stationed at Schenectady, and they were not on guard. Someone had set up two snowmen that stood as silent and futile sentinels in front of the two open gates of the stockade. No one dreamed of danger. Most of the inhabitants were Dutch farmers who went to bed with the coming of darkness. The French force waited until the village was asleep and then stealthily surrounded the houses. At a signal, they gave a war whoop and fell to the slaughter. Without discrimination they butchered men, women, and children alike. A few Mohawks sleeping in the village were spared so that they might carry a message of friendship to their tribesmen, whom the French hoped to keep neutral. Some sixty persons were killed, between eighty and ninety were taken prisoner, and a handful escaped and fled toward Albany. After burning and pillaging, the marauders made off for Canada with thirty or forty horse-drawn sledges loaded with booty.

The French gesture of friendship for the Mohawks did them no good. As soon as word of the foray reached these tribesmen, they set out in pursuit. One band of Mohawks clung tenaciously to the enemy's trail even to the outskirts of Montreal and at last killed or captured some fifteen men.

Frontenac's Indians and *coureurs de bois* harassed other frontier settlements. On the night of March 27, 1690, they fell upon the settlement of Salmon Falls on the Maine–New Hampshire border and butchered more than thirty of the inhabitants. Fifty-four others were carried off into captivity.

Late in May another of the three raiding groups organized by Frontenac attacked an English settlement at Casco Bay, now the site of Portland, Maine. Outnumbered and surrounded, the English surrendered after the French promised quarter and protection from the Indians. But no sooner had they laid down their arms than the French turned the captives over to their savage allies, who butchered many of them. The French excuse for this treachery was that the English in New York had persuaded the Iroquois to attack and torture

Frenchmen. The New England prisoners disclaimed responsibility for what New Yorkers had done, but it made little difference to the French what colony the British came from.

At this time both New York and the New England colonies were fighting under grave handicaps because of internal dissensions that followed the overthrow of James II. King James had organized the New England colonies, New York, and the two Jerseys into the Dominion of New England, with Edmund Andros as governor. But when news of the Glorious Revolution reached the colonies, they rebelled against Andros, the Dominion fell apart, and the colonies reverted to something approaching their previous status. New York, meanwhile, was rent by the revolt of Jacob Leisler. These quarrels and disruptions of orderly government at home made it difficult for the northern colonies to unite in their common defense.

None of the colonies had any really effective forces

came of it. New York, Connecticut, Massachusetts Bay, Plymouth, and Maryland promised small contingents for a campaign—less than a thousand altogether, and not all of them reported for duty. An expedition of sorts, under the command of Major Fitz-John Winthrop, finally set out at the end of July in the direction of Montreal. After waiting in vain on Lake Champlain for adequate supplies and for a force of Iroquois allies, they turned back to Albany. Governor Leisler of New York blamed Winthrop and threw him into jail, an action that immediately antagonized Winthrop's fellow militiamen from Connecticut.

Except for intensifying intercolonial animosities, the expedition accomplished virtually nothing. One small detachment led by Captain John Schuyler raided as far as La Prairie, on the St. Lawrence opposite Montreal. The party killed six men, burned outlying houses, captured nineteen prisoners, slaughtered a large number of cows, and returned.

Massachusetts Bay, which had furnished no men for Fitz John Winthrop's expedition, decided upon a campaign of its own. This would be a sea-borne expedition against Port Royal in Acadia, led by Sir William Phips, then a hero as the result of his success in recovering a vast treasure from a sunken Spanish hulk in the Bahamas. Phips was no great naval strategist, but in May, 1690, with a flotilla of fourteen assorted vessels manned by some seven hundred fishermen, sailors, and farmers, he managed to intimidate the French commander at Port Royal and persuade him to surrender. On the flimsy excuse that the French had violated terms of surrender, Phips and his men pillaged the shops at Port Royal, stole the communion plate from the church (an act of piety in the opinion of some of Phips's Puritan followers), and sailed back to Boston as conquering heroes. Shortly after Phips departed, Port Royal suffered again when English pirates fell on the town and burned a number of houses.

Encouraged by the success of Phips's expedition against Port Royal, Massachusetts Bay decided to make a grand attack on Quebec itself. In August, 1690, the colony collected thirty-four ships and two thousand

capable of sustained military action. Local militia, whose only training was an occasional drill on the village green, were woefully unprepared for war. Even on muster days, they usually spent more time guzzling beer in the taverns than practicing with their arms in the field. Although all able-bodied men were accustomed to firearms, their muzzle-loading muskets were not very effective except at close range; their sidearms were sometimes homemade; and powder and shot were often in short supply. Supplies usually consisted of what the men could carry on their backs, for lumbering carts had difficulty keeping up when the only road was a trail through the forest. A military force was better off when it could transport supplies by canoe.

Mutual suspicion and jealousy also helped to prevent any joint action by the colonies. Although several colonies sent representatives to a conference called by Jacob Leisler in New York in April, 1690, in an effort to plan collective action against the French, nothing much

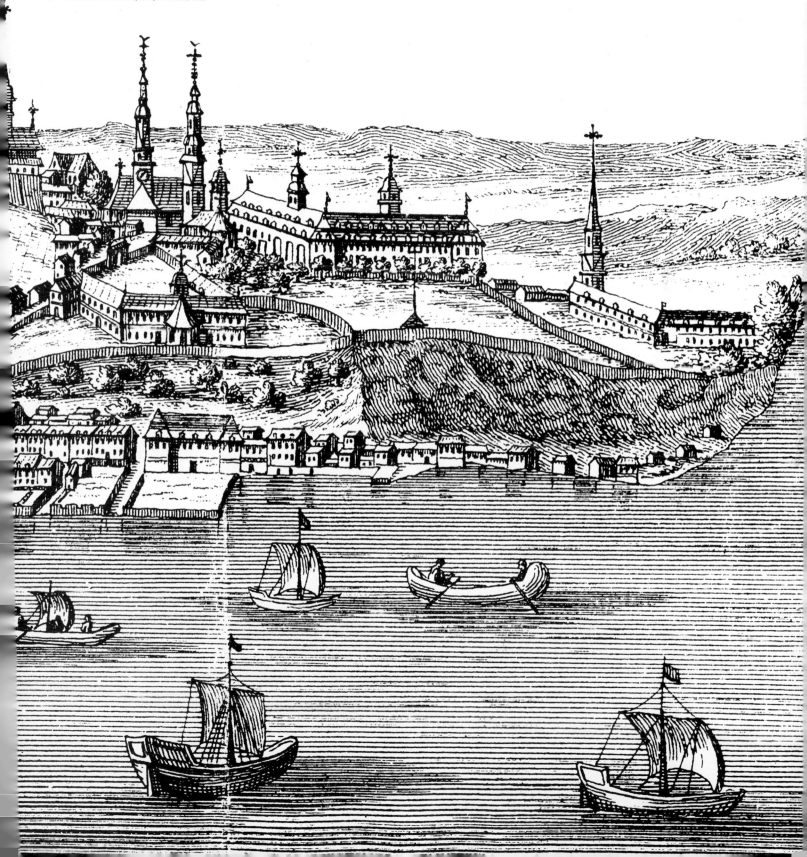

Quebec was the heart of France's Canadian empire: capital,
fur center, military stronghold. The engraving below is
of the city in 1722. At the extreme left on the hill is
the redoubt, but the fort itself lies below it to the right;
the two square blockhouses mark corners of the walls.
The engraver has undoubtedly tidied up things, for a
riverfront where trappers gather would hardly be so neat.

BACQUEVILLE, *Histoire de l'Amérique Septentrionale*, 1722

men, placed them under Phips's command, and dispatched the expedition against Quebec. Phips's ships did not arrive at the scene of action until October 17, when the weather was already turning cold. After a futile attack on the fortifications, led by Major John Walley, with the loss of thirty men, the survivors returned to the ships. After dallying in the St. Lawrence in an effort to repair two damaged ships, Phips sailed for home. He had failed to coordinate the naval bombardment of the town with the attempted assault, and the whole operation impressed the French regulars as an amateur performance (fortunately for Phips's reputation, the Puritans blamed his failure on God rather than on his own incompetence). So hard pressed was Massachusetts Bay to find money to pay the fifty-thousand-pound expense of the expedition that it decided to issue paper scrip, an innovation the colonies found expedient to follow in later times.

Frontenac, the shrewd French governor, now made it his goal to detach the Iroquois from their alliance with the English, and he very nearly succeeded. The Iroquois were disenchanted with the English because of their vacillation, their lack of force, and their disorganized efforts to meet the French invasions. If Frontenac had known how to compose the differences between the Algonquins and the Iroquois, he might have succeeded; but while the Iroquois were willing to bury the hatchet with the French, they would not agree to smoke the pipe of peace with the Algonquins. The hostility between some of the tribes, the Senecas and the Hurons, for example, was sealed in too much blood for them to be able to sit down together. Frontenac had to forego his cherished scheme of dividing the English and their Indian allies, for he would not make a unilateral treaty with the Iroquois.

For the next seven years, the war dragged on, with periodic forays on both sides. The conflict took on the characteristics of modern guerrilla warfare, and frontier settlements were never safe from hit-and-run attacks. The murder of settlers and the burning of cabins were common occurrences. Settlements in northern New York, western Massachusetts, New Hampshire, and particularly Maine suffered from frequent Indian raids, sometimes led by detachments of Frenchmen. Frontenac himself, though he had to be carried in a chair because of his age, led one of the heaviest raids into New York

The above fanciful scene of spirited trading between Indians of Mexico and Frenchmen at a nonexistent "Port of Mississippi" is from a 1717 promotion piece of the French Mississippi Company. Its text tells, among many things, how the Indians willingly traded gold and silver for knives or brandy. A port of Mississippi became reality in 1718 when New Orleans was platted.

in the summer of 1696, when he laid waste the country of the Onondagas.

Ferocity and cruelty were characteristic of both sides. When a raiding party of Indians from Maine fell on the settlement at Haverhill, Massachusetts, they carried off Mrs. Hannah Dustin, her infant child, and its nurse. Annoyed by the baby's crying, an Indian knocked out its brains. During the long trek back through northern Maine, Mrs. Dustin, a boy prisoner, and the nurse planned an escape. In the dead of night, they seized hatchets and silently slaughtered their ten captors, each of whom Mrs. Dustin carefully scalped. Hannah Dustin's ten scalps netted her a fifty-pound bounty from Massachusetts Bay when she eventually got back.

News that the war between Louis XIV and William III had ended finally reached the warring colonials at the end of 1697. The Treaty of Ryswick, signed on September 30, 1697, left Europe and the colonies of England and France much as they had been before the outbreak of hostilities. About all the war did in America was to sharpen the animosities between the English and the French and their respective Indian allies. The patterns established in King William's War would be followed in successive conflicts.

The first of the colonial wars with the French revealed the weakness of the English colonies, caused by their inability to unite either for common defense or for punitive campaigns against their enemies. Furthermore, the conflict showed that the colonies could expect little help from the mother country. Whereas Louis XIV, despite the pressures of his European campaigns, sent regular troops to defend Canada, William III gave almost no aid to his beleaguered colonies. Not until much later would British regulars fight effectively against the French in North America.

The Treaty of Ryswick may have ended the official war between France and England, but no document signed in Europe could make Indians in the forests of North America completely peaceful. Sporadic raids on the frontier continued despite the withdrawal of French regulars from the conflict. Even the relative calm would not last long, because the European powers were again jockeying for position in Europe, in America, and even in distant Asia.

Spain, which had a great empire stretching from Mexico south, exerted relentless pressure on the southern flank of the colonies. The little English settlement at Charles Town on the Carolina coast for many years

stood in peril from the Spanish in Florida. The Spaniards also had missions and trading settlements in the Southwest, and they hoped to consolidate their possessions on both sides of the Mississippi.

France, meanwhile, continued its efforts to encircle the colonies. In 1699 Pierre le Moyne, Sieur d'Iberville, landed a party at Biloxi on the Gulf of Mexico and took possession of the land in the name of the king of France. A few years later, in 1702, the French occupied Mobile. The French had also been pushing down the Mississippi and had made a settlement near the present site of St. Louis. Soon French forts would stretch from Detroit to the Gulf of Mexico, and the founding of New Orleans in 1718 by D'Iberville's brother, Jean Baptiste le Moyne, Sieur de Bienville, solidified French holdings in the interior of North America. An alliance between France and Spain after 1700 completed the encirclement of the British colonies by their traditional enemies.

Nevertheless, English and Scottish traders from South Carolina were beginning to compete with the Spaniards for the Indian trade—and ultimately for land—in the region that would one day become Georgia, Alabama, and Mississippi. This was the country of powerful Indian nations, the Creeks, Chickasaws, and Choctaws. In the northern part of Georgia and South Carolina lay the territory of another powerful Indian nation, the Cherokees. On the coast were many small tribes usually at war with one another. The Westos in the vicinity of Charles Town were the most warlike Indians at the time of the first white settlements; later the Yamasees, pushed north by the Spaniards, created a problem for the English settlers on the coast.

But at the end of King William's War, the South Carolinians were not in serious danger from Indian attack. Indeed, their traders were moving westward and making friends with Indians of the interior, whom they hoped to wean away from the Spaniards. Before 1700, traders from Charles Town had made alliances with the Creeks, the Chickasaws, and the Cherokees. In 1698 an enterprising trader, Thomas Welch, led an expedition from Charles Town through northern Georgia, Alabama, and Mississippi to a point on the western bank of the Mississippi River below the mouth of the Arkansas River. In the course of time, Welch reached an understanding with the Chickasaws and managed to persuade them to make war on the Choctaws, whom French traders had already won over. Welch's contributions to English power politics on the frontier were not entirely patriotic in nature, for Indian wars meant captives whom he could sell as slaves to sugar planters in the West Indies. The trade in Indian slaves through the port of Charles Town would continue to grow in importance during the wars that began afresh in 1702.

That year marked the beginning of a new outbreak in Europe, the War of the Spanish Succession, in which England, Holland, Austria, Portugal, Prussia, and various other German states sought to curb the growing power of France. (The death of the king of Spain, Charles II, without an heir had given Louis XIV an opportunity to advance the candidacy of his grandson Philip, with the probability that eventually the crowns of Spain and France would be united.) Shortly after the conflict began, it spread to North America, where it was known as Queen Anne's War.

As usual, the outlying settlements bore the brunt of Indian attacks, but the theater of operations was far more extensive than in King William's War, for military activity extended from the Caribbean to Canada. New York suffered less than in the previous war, however, for the French had persuaded the Iroquois to maintain something approaching neutrality by promising them freedom from raids by France's Indian allies.

In 1702 James Moore, governor of South Carolina, organized an expedition against the Spanish base at St. Augustine, which he hoped to destroy before the French could come to its aid. Moore was an Indian trader who was trying to expand Charles Town's commerce with the Indian tribes of the interior, and he was vastly concerned at the threat to English trade with the Creeks and the Chickasaws in the Southwest by French occupation of the Gulf Coast. Not all the English settlers in South Carolina were so farsighted, however, and Moore found himself the leader of an unpopular war party. (His enemies claimed that he wanted to invade Florida merely to catch hostile Indians to sell into slavery.) What popular support Moore commanded was further diminished when he failed to capture the Spanish fortress at St. Augustine and had to content himself with burning houses outside the fort, stealing the church plate, and marching away. When two Spanish warships bottled up his small vessels in the harbor, he had to burn them and retire overland until he could collect enough dugout canoes to take his men to the Carolina coast. The reluctant South Carolinians found themselves saddled with a debt of over eight thousand pounds, which they sought to liquidate by issuing paper money.

But lack of success at St. Augustine did not deter Moore from planning another expedition to thwart the French and Spanish allies in the Southwest. A century before Thomas Jefferson urged the purchase of Louisiana, Moore used the same arguments for the seizure of that territory. In a letter to the English admiral commanding in the Caribbean, Moore declared that if the English could capture Pensacola, Biloxi, and Mobile, it would "make Her Majestie Absolute and Soveraigne Lady of all the Maine as farr as the River Mischisipi, which if effected the Colony of Carolina will be of the Greatest vallue to the Crown of England of any of Her Majesties Plantations on the Maine except Virginia by ading a Great revenue to the Crown, for one halfe of all the Canadian Trade for furrs and Skinns must necessarily come this way, besides a vast Trade of Furrs and Skinns extended as far as the above mentioned River, Mischisipi, which is now interrupted by these Two little Towns [Biloxi and Mobile]."

When the colony of South Carolina would not finance a new expedition, Moore organized a private army of fifty Englishmen and a thousand Indians at his own expense. In 1704–6 he laid waste the Spanish missions in southern Alabama and northern Florida and devastated the country of the Apalachee Indians in the Tallahassee region. Moore captured hundreds of Indians for slaves and relocated more than a thousand on the South Carolina border near modern Augusta, Georgia, to serve as a bulwark against Spanish attacks on that frontier. The plunder of the Spanish missions and the profit from the sale of Indian slaves were sufficient for Moore to boast that the expedition had not cost the colony a penny. He had also virtually neutralized the Spanish Indians on the southern frontier.

The Spanish and the French attempted to avenge the Carolinians' invasion of territory that they regarded as their own with an attack by sea upon Charles Town in the late summer of 1706. Spanish troops from Cuba were aided by five French privateers, but they failed to take the town and lost some two hundred and thirty prisoners. The English, warned by this action, strengthened their defenses, improved their alliances with the Indians, and managed to withstand attacks from the south in the succeeding years of the war. In 1707 the English and their Indian allies again took the offensive, burning houses outside the fort at Pensacola and threatening Mobile. But Bienville, the French governor at Mobile, retained enough Indian support to prevent the

Queen Anne, though a dull woman of limited ability, was a good
queen. A colonial war was named for her, yet she opposed the
conflict with Spain and France and worked to bring it to an end.
This needlework portrait of Anne was done in the early 1700's.

When Indian chiefs friendly to the British visited England in 1710, an artist, probably Bernard Lens, dressed them in court costume of the period and painted their portraits. They are, from left: the chief of the River Nation (Mohegans) of eastern Connecticut; "King" Hendrick, Mohawk chief who was killed in 1755 fighting with the English against the French; the chief of Canajoharie village of the Mohawks; and a Mohawk chief not otherwise identified.

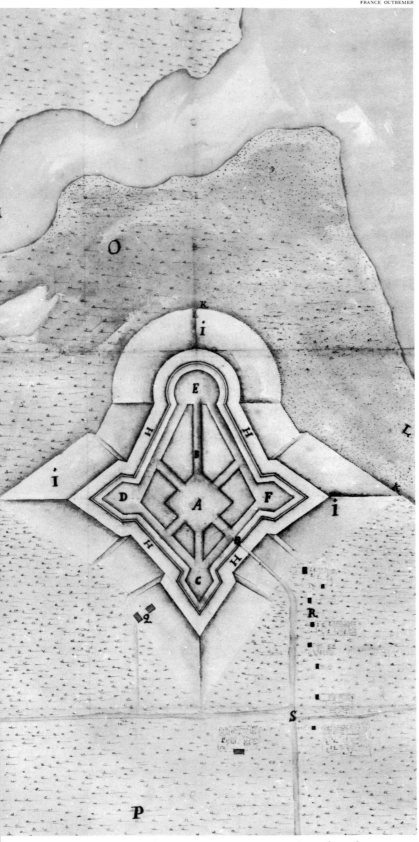

*This drawing of the fort of Port Royal, made in 1701, is
undoubtedly an idealized one, for it was a sodded
structure, and a governor of Acadia found it in poor
repair in 1702. However, it was put in better order, and
its fall in 1710 was the result of its being undermanned.*

the rabble of militia and sailors to return to Port Royal.
Once again they landed, skirmished a bit with the enemy, killed a few Frenchmen in an orchard, and sailed
away for Boston. Thus ended the effort to take the
French bastion in the North.

Frustration and disappointment at the conduct of the
war were general throughout New England at the end
of the year 1707. All efforts to avenge frontier raids had
failed, and attempts to ensure unity of action by the
several colonies had come to nought. Many settlers were
bitter because they believed, with some justification,
that rich merchants in Albany and Boston, finding trade
with Montreal and Quebec profitable, hoped to maintain a nominal peace with the French. It was a time of
dread and uneasiness all along the border, and no effective relief appeared to be forthcoming.

The fears of the frontiersmen were justified in the
summer of 1708, when Hertel de Rouville again led a
war party of Indians and Frenchmen into English territory. This time he struck into northeastern Massachusetts, at Haverhill. As at Deerfield four years before, the
marauders surprised the village at night and concentrated their attack upon the church. They killed forty-
eight villagers, including the minister, his wife, and one
child (his slave girl saved two other children by hiding
them under tubs in the cellar while the Indians plundered the house). During the summer and autumn, raiding French and Indians continued to slaughter isolated
settlers in eastern Massachusetts and New Hampshire.

In this dark hour, one of the very traders who had
profited from illegal trade with the enemy conceived a
plan to expel the French from North America. His motives were something less than altruistic, for the expul-
sion of the French would give the British a monopoly
of the rich fur trade with Canada and the back country,
which the French had already developed. This would-be
savior was Samuel Vetch, a Scot who had combined sol-
diering with commerce and had once been a member of
a short-lived Scottish colony on the Isthmus of Panama.

Vetch had come to New York in 1699 after the failure
of that venture and had married the daughter of Robert
Livingston, the secretary of Indian affairs. Soon Vetch
was involved in illicit trade with Canada. In 1702 he
moved to Boston, where he expanded his trade with
Acadia. At one point the British authorities seized and
condemned Vetch's sloop *Mary*, but this only temporarily halted Vetch's trade.

Because of Vetch's connections with the French, Governor Dudley, who himself was believed to have an interest in the French trade, sent Vetch to Quebec in 1705 to negotiate a truce with the French and to arrange for an exchange of prisoners. Improving his opportunity, Vetch made deals of his own with the French. Finally his open flouting of the law could not be overlooked, and in 1706 he and five others were tried and fined by the General Court of Massachusetts. Appealing the case to the Privy Council, Vetch and his companions had their sentences annulled on the ground that the General Court was not competent to try them.

This bout with the law did nothing to curb Vetch's interest in Canada or his influence with Dudley, who sent him to London with an address to the queen from the General Court begging for military aid against the French. Vetch proved such a persuasive emissary that early in 1709 the authorities in London sent him back with a promise of help—five regiments with naval support—and a commission to raise troops in the colonies north of Maryland. Colonel Francis Nicholson, the colonial expert, came along as a volunteer.

Vetch was to raise all the troops he could muster. The combined English-colonial force was to attack Montreal by way of Lake Champlain, and Quebec by sea. This pincers movement would force the French to surrender all Canada. The plan was excellent; the execution was faulty.

By summer Vetch had raised three regiments, though Pennsylvania and New Jersey refused to send troops. Colonel Nicholson was placed in command of the troops to attack Montreal. All through the summer the colonials waited for the arrival of British ships and the promised five regiments. Nothing happened, and the morale of the volunteers deteriorated. Finally, on October 11, Governor Dudley received a letter from the British ministry that the promised aid had been diverted to Portugal to meet an emergency. Vetch and others proposed that they make an attack on Canada anyway with such British shipping as they could commandeer in New England ports, but the British captains refused to cooperate.

The colonial leaders once more appealed to London. The General Court of Massachusetts sent Nicholson with a petition to the queen, requesting help in launching an attack on Port Royal. Peter Schuyler took five Mohawk chiefs to London (one of the five died before reaching England) to plead the cause. The Mohawks proved to be a sensation. Dressed in exotic apparel sup-

plied by a theatrical costumer, the Indians were presented to Queen Anne, one as an emperor and the others as kings. Members of the nobility competed for the privilege of entertaining the noble savages from America, and Schuyler's showmanship probably did more than Nicholson's petition to focus the attention of the government on North America. At any rate, in 1710 the government authorized an attack on Port Royal, commissioned Nicholson as commander, and promised five hundred marines with supporting naval vessels.

Although the colonial authorities had requested shipping by March, the British vessels did not arrive until July, and the expedition was not ready to sail until September. In the meantime, volunteers had been slow to leave their labors for military ventures; they remembered the long and fruitless wait of the previous year. But Massachusetts encouraged enlistment by promising a month's pay in advance, a coat worth thirty shillings, and the right to keep the queen's musket after the return from Port Royal.

On September 24 the expedition arrived off Port Royal, and the attack began the next day. The garrison was too weak to withstand a long siege, and the French capitulated on October 2. The surrender was conducted with much ceremony and punctilio. The French troops, marching out with drums beating and colors flying, passed between the ranks of the British and colonials and saluted. Nicholson, now a brigadier general, Vetch, already commissioned as military governor, and Sir Charles Hobby, the naval commander, marched into the fort after accepting the keys from Daniel d'Auger de Subercase, the governor of Acadia. As a mark of their respect for the French ladies, conquering officers gave a breakfast for them. It was all quite different from what took place when frontier villages were captured.

In honor of Queen Anne, Nicholson changed the name of the settlement to Annapolis Royal. Its capture gave the British command of all Acadia. But the French remained entrenched in the St. Lawrence Valley, and Samuel Vetch's plan for the complete elimination of the French in Canada still awaited fulfillment. Nicholson appealed to London for sufficient troops and ships to conquer Quebec and, surprisingly, gained the promise of adequate military and financial support.

The new expedition got under way in June, 1711, with the arrival in Boston harbor of nearly seventy naval vessels under the command of Admiral Sir Hovenden Walker, with more than five thousand regular troops commanded by General John Hill. This imposing expeditionary force was enough to satisfy the wildest dreams of the colonial governors, but they little knew the character of the expedition's leaders. Hill, known about the court as "Jolly Jack Hill," had no visible qualifications as an officer. He had received his appointment because he was a brother of Mrs. Masham, Queen Anne's favorite of the moment. Walker, equally incompetent, was timid and vacillating.

Although the Bostonians did their best to entertain the British officers with proper ceremony, they made no favorable impression upon the arrogant visitors. The British regarded the colonials as ill-trained yokels and made no effort to hide their feelings. One artillery officer wrote in his journal that he found the New Englanders intolerable because of their "ill Nature, and sowerness," their "Government, Doctrine, and Manners," their "hypocracy and canting." And he added that until the government canceled their charters, they would "grow more stiff and disobedient every Day." Many colonials were just as critical of the English troops. The stricter Puritans particularly disliked soldiers and sailors roistering upon the common and swaggering in the streets on the Sabbath.

On July 30, augmented by New England militia, the expeditionary force set sail for Canada. Counting soldiers, sailors, marines, and provincial militia, the force numbered some twelve thousand men. Never before had such a large force been assembled in North America.

Lacking pilots for the St. Lawrence, they captured a French vessel and bribed the pilot to guide them. On the night of August 22 the fleet was near Anticosti Island, in fog with a stiff east wind blowing. Walker, confused and ignorant of his course, led his ships onto reefs off the Isle aux Oeufs, where eight transports, a store ship, and a sloop were wrecked, with the loss of seven hundred and forty lives, thirty-five of them women whom Walker, as was the custom of the time, had brought along.

In the face of this disaster, Admiral Walker and General Hill held a council of war and decided that without pilots they could never find Quebec. They sailed away to Spanish River (now Sydney Harbour), Cape Breton Island, where they held another council of war over whether to attack the little town of Placentia on Newfoundland. When they convinced themselves that this also was too fearful an undertaking, Walker sailed for England; New England transports took the militia home;

and the vast show of might vanished into the mists.

In the meanwhile, Francis Nicholson was holding an army in camp on Lake Champlain ready to march on Montreal. When news reached him of Walker's failure, his rage knew no bounds. Stamping on his wig and crying "Roguery! Treachery!" he damned Walker, Hill, and all their works. Nicholson then destroyed his own fortifications and disbanded his volunteers except for a small detachment to guard the frontier.

The war in Europe was about to end. After a truce in August, 1712, Louis XIV sent his envoys to Utrecht to negotiate a peace, which was signed the next year. By the terms of the Treaty of Utrecht, Louis had to agree that the thrones of France and Spain would never be united under one head. Acadia, Newfoundland, Hudson Bay, and St. Christopher and Nevis Islands in the Caribbean were to be surrendered to the English; and Louis had further to acknowledge that the Iroquois were subjects of Great Britain. France retained Cape Breton Island, the St. Lawrence Valley, and territories beyond. No borders were clearly established, and no man knew where French possessions ended and British began. This failure to establish definite boundaries would inevitably lead to further conflict.

Spain, the almost forgotten ally of France, ceded to Great Britain Gibraltar and the island of Minorca and transferred from France the Asiento, a monopoly for thirty-three years of the African slave trade. Under this monopoly, the South Sea Company had the right to sell each year to the Spanish colonies in America forty-eight hundred Negro slaves, obtained first from the Royal African Company and later from Jamaica. The Asiento also provided that British merchants could send one ship each year to trade with the Spanish possessions.

The end of Queen Anne's War brought a measure of security to settlers on the frontiers of British North America, but the French did not suddenly disappear. In fact, they remained a hazard to British expansion. They also continued to intrigue with the Indians and to stir them up against the British. France hoped to regain Acadia and the rest of her lost territories in Canada. To that end she began building a great fortification at Louisbourg on Cape Breton Island, a fortress that would enable her to command the approaches to the St. Lawrence, the gateway to Canada. The next thirty years would be relatively peaceful for the colonies; but French power in the New World was by no means at an end.

French fascination with fortifications is caricatured in this German engraving of 1700. It was the era of Vauban, the great French military engineer, and fortbuilding in America reflected the French passion for defense works.

Peace and War

$\mathcal{T}$he Treaty of Utrecht in 1713, followed by the death of Louis XIV in 1715, brought a promise of peace to Europe and the colonies. No longer was France governed by a king obsessed with notions of military grandeur. Louis XIV had outlived his son and his grandson, and the new king, Louis XV, the Sun King's great-grandson, was a child of five.

England also had a new ruler. Queen Anne had died on August 1, 1714, without a direct heir. Her nearest of kin was a Stuart and a Catholic and therefore unacceptable, but she had a more distant relative who was a Protestant. He was a German princeling, George, elector of Hanover, the great-grandson of James I of England through the union of James's daughter Elizabeth with Frederick, the elector of the Palatinate. Although George could speak no English, he was invited to take the throne. His accession introduced a system of rule by prime minister and cabinet that has persisted to the present day. The English people acquiesced in the accession of a German king, but they showed little enthusiasm for the new monarch. They took offense at his two German mistresses, not on moral but on patriotic and aesthetic grounds. The German favorites were so fat and ugly that they were an embarrassment to the English. At length, however, King George made amends by taking an English mistress too.

The formal treaty of peace in 1713 did not end all warfare on the American frontiers. Although delegates to the peace conference in Utrecht might sign an infinite number of papers, they could not control the forces that had been unleashed in the North American wilderness. The English, the French, and the Spaniards actually resident in the colonies continued to eye each other warily, and they often incited their Indian allies to depredations on the others' territory. High stakes were involved, not only in the great territorial gamble of empire, but in the countinghouses of merchants and traders in America. By 1713, trading centers existed in all the colonies, and in some an urban life had already developed, with rich merchants eager to expand their commercial interests in the back country and overseas.

The eighteenth century is sometimes described as the Age of Enlightenment because

Admiral Vernon's English fleet takes Puerto Bello in Panama during the War of Jenkins's Ear. Lawrence Washington, half brother to George, served under Vernon and named his home for the admiral.

213

*An outstanding feature of this water color of Boston in 1764 is
the great number of ships in the city's harbor, convincing
evidence of the high level of colonial prosperity at that period,*

of its achievements in science, letters, and philosophy,
but it might also be called the Age of Trade. The explorations of the sixteenth and seventeenth centuries
were now bearing fruit. All the great maritime powers
—England, France, Spain, Portugal, and Holland—had
established overseas bases and were eagerly exploiting
territories in Asia, Africa, and America. Although the
wars that ravaged Europe—and the colonies overseas—
through much of the eighteenth century were frequently
dynastic in origin, the struggle for power to control
commercial development and exploitation lay behind
political rivalries. Commerce was to the eighteenth century what the Crusades were to the Middle Ages, an
enterprise that absorbed the energies and aspirations of
alert and ambitious members of society.

In the British colonies of North America, the greatest
urban development occurred in New England, which
by the first quarter of the eighteenth century had a large
number of towns depending upon commerce with the
outer world. New York and Pennsylvania were also becoming trading areas with a profitable hinterland that

was a source of agricultural products for export. In the
far South, Charles Town grew rapidly into an important
center for the export of furs and deerskins, rice, indigo,
and forest products.

The provisions of the English Navigation Acts were
designed to give the mother country a monopoly of colonial trade. Nevertheless, the colonies profited from
many of the restrictions, particularly one requiring commodities to be shipped in English or colonial vessels.
Shipbuilding and shipping became an important source
of profit for New Englanders.

Colonial affairs and the overseas trade had become
so important by the closing years of the seventeenth
century that in 1696 King William III created a Board
of Trade and Plantations. This group replaced the old
Privy Council committee known as the Lords of Trade
with an enlarged committee composed of privy coun-
cilors and eight paid members who were presumed to
be specialists in various phases of activity such as fisheries and commerce, colonial legislation, and the appointment of personnel to serve in colonial administra-

214

tions. The Board of Trade was an advisory body that made recommendations to the Privy Council and the sovereign. Until the end of the colonial period, it exerted varying degrees of influence. At times it virtually controlled colonial affairs; at other times the Privy Council or the secretary of state took direct action with little regard for the Board of Trade's recommendations, particularly in the appointment of colonial officials. The Board of Trade could rarely be held responsible for the poor quality of many colonial governors.

The English colonial structure, unlike that of Spain or even of France, was a ramshackle affair, with wide variations in the several colonies in the forms of government, the nature of land tenure, the quality of the inhabitants, religion, and the economic bases of development. Some colonies were virtually self-governing; others were under the jurisdiction of proprietors; and still others were crown colonies with governors appointed from London. But no two colonies in any of these categories were precisely alike. For example, Pennsylvania and Maryland were both proprietary colonies, but they differed widely in economic and political characteristics. Communication between the colonies through much of the early period was slow and difficult. South Carolina had more direct and quicker communications with England than with Massachusetts Bay, and the same was true of other widely separated colonies. The disparate nature of the colonies and the lack of an effective communications system prevented unity of action—even for the purpose of common defense—until late in the eighteenth century.

The need for union, however, was recognized by colonials as well as by government officials in London, and from time to time someone made a proposal to bring the colonies together. In 1697, for example, William Penn had submitted a plan to the Board of Trade calling for a congress that would meet in New York with equal representation from all the colonies. Four years later an anonymous Virginian published a pamphlet in London entitled *An Essay upon the Government of the English Plantations on the Continent of America.* It advocated, among other things, a union of the colonies with a scheme of representation more nearly proportionate to the population. The author asserted that it would be fairer to apportion the delegates so as to allow "Virginia four, Mary-Land three, New-York two, Boston three, Connecticut two, Rhode Island two, Pennsylvania one, the two Carolina's one, each of the two Jersey's one."

His intention was to give the crown colonies the dominant voice in the congress, which would meet in rotation in each of five districts into which the colonies would be divided.

This *Essay* is a revealing document, for in addition to calling attention to the need for a union of the British colonies, it maintained that colonials were as much British subjects as if they lived in England itself, and that they should have all the rights and liberties that other British subjects enjoyed. It also called upon the authorities in London to send honest officials overseas, to provide the colonies with competent administrators, and to reform the laws so that all colonies could enjoy the same justice. Significantly, the *Essay* did not object to the Navigation Acts nor plead for a relaxation of the control of trade by the mother country. But it did ask for equity of treatment in the several colonies. Although Virginia and Maryland were two of the most profitable colonies to England, the author maintained, they suffered from a heavy and unfair tax on their tobacco. He also objected to the way New York and Philadelphia pampered pirates and privateers.

Similar ideas were being expressed on both sides of the Atlantic, but the practical problems of union were too much for the ineffectual government in London and the recalcitrant colonies in America to overcome. The New England colonies, for example, had always been virtually independent, and it was for this reason that the government of James II had canceled their charters and placed them under the Crown. Although the Dominion of New England under its royal governor, Edmund Andros, collapsed after the Glorious Revolution of 1688, and although the New England colonies under William and Mary regained modified versions of their charters, they never recovered the freedom from interference that they had previously enjoyed.

Indeed, it had also been the policy of William and Mary to bring the colonies under the authority of the Crown. Massachusetts Bay, for all the efforts made by Increase Mather to regain its charter, became a royal colony, as did New Hampshire. Henceforth Whitehall appointed royal governors, who constantly squabbled with the legislative assemblies over royal prerogatives. Connecticut and Rhode Island managed to retain the right to elect their governors and thus escaped some of the controversy that kept the colonies of Massachusetts and New Hampshire in turmoil throughout most of the eighteenth century.

Incompetent or corrupt governors, sent out from London to improve their fortunes, were an affliction that plagued many of the colonies. "The chief End of many Governours coming to the Plantations, having been to get Estates for themselves," the author of the *Essay* complained, "very unwarrantable Methods have sometimes been made use of to compass those Ends, as by engrossing several Offices into their own Hands, selling them or letting them out at a yearly Rent of such part of the Profits, and also by Extortion and Presents, (or Bribery) these things have been [done] heretofore, and in ill Times may be done again."

Few colonies were more unfortunate in their royal governors than New York. The last decade of the seventeenth century had brought the administrations of a drunken profligate in the person of Henry Sloughter, a friend of pirates and rogues in Benjamin Fletcher, and an ornamental but incompetent dandy in Richard Coote, Earl of Bellomont. The eighteenth century began even less auspiciously with the appointment in 1702 of Edward Hyde, Lord Cornbury, as governor of New York and New Jersey. Avaricious, arrogant, and dissolute, Cornbury delighted in dressing in women's apparel and visiting the lowest taverns in New York. He squandered money stolen from the public treasury and borrowed from anyone foolish enough to offer him credit. He was at last arrested for debt but managed to return to England to inherit the title of the Earl of Clarendon. Not until 1710 did New York receive a royal governor who

combined honesty and competence. In that year Queen Anne appointed Robert Hunter, a Scot, who labored earnestly to bring some order into the administrative chaos of New York's royal government as well as that of New Jersey. Nevertheless, New York remained split between factions: rich merchants and great landowners monopolized power, while farmers, craftsmen, tradesmen, and lesser merchants complained about taxes and inequities in the government.

The proprietary colony of Pennsylvania proved a difficult problem for the London authorities, who had frequent cause to regret its virtual independence. Penn's charter made the proprietor and his heirs the owners of the land in Pennsylvania; the proprietor was also supreme head and governor, though he could appoint a deputy to serve in his place. Penn had set forth his plan for ruling the colony in a document that he called his first "Frame of Government," under which a popular assembly was called on December 4, 1682. Under Penn's Frame of Government the colony had a council (ultimately composed of eighteen members), elected by the freeholders. Together with the governor, the council initiated laws and submitted them for approval to the popular assembly. Laws made by the Pennsylvania assembly had to be approved by the Privy Council in London, and appeals could be taken from decisions of the Pennsylvania courts to the English courts. Both the people and the proprietor were unwilling to see the colony come under the rule of the Crown, but for a brief

Lord Cornbury
See "American Heritage"
April 1976 pg 60

time after 1688, William III managed to convert Pennsylvania into a royal colony with Benjamin Fletcher as governor. This experiment did not work well, and in 1694 the king restored Pennsylvania to the proprietor. At the beginning of the eighteenth century, in 1701, the proprietor granted a new charter of privileges that made a unicameral assembly the supreme lawmaking authority in the colony. The Quakers who controlled the assembly were unwilling to cooperate with the other colonies and were opposed to participation in the various wars that swept North America during the eighteenth century. Furthermore, the Quaker merchants of Philadelphia showed a persistent distaste for the acts of trade, and many a smuggler had his home port on the Delaware River. Orders from Whitehall often fell on deaf ears in Philadelphia, and London found Pennsylvania more often recalcitrant than obedient.

The religious tolerance guaranteed settlers in Pennsylvania, the ease with which land could be had, the fertility of the soil, and the opportunities for trade all combined to increase the flow of immigrants into Pennsylvania in the early years of the eighteenth century. Germans—Mennonites and related sectarians, as well as Lutherans—took up farmlands in what is now Lancaster County and the neighboring regions. French Huguenots, many of them skilled craftsmen, settled in Philadelphia. Scottish immigrants from Ulster in Ireland, unhappy over their treatment at the hands of the English, poured through the port of Philadelphia into the

back country, beyond the German settlements. Hardy and tough, they shared none of the pacifist notions of the Quakers and the sectarians; consequently, they made ideal frontiersmen and Indian fighters. Although the Pennsylvania government officially might follow a pacifist line, the Scottish frontiersmen were always ready to shoulder a musket in defense of hearth and home.

Maryland, like Pennsylvania a proprietary colony, underwent a political upheaval after the revolution of 1688 and the flight of James II. Because the proprietary family, the Calverts, the Lords Baltimore, were Catholics and Maryland had many Catholic settlers, William III's new government reasoned that they would support the deposed king. Protestant dissidents in Maryland spread rumors of a Catholic uprising and petitioned William to take over the proprietary government, which he did in August, 1691, with the appointment of Sir Lionel Copley as the first royal governor. Lord Baltimore was permitted to retain his rights in the lands of Maryland and to collect his quitrents, but he no longer had any say in the government.

During the early years of the eighteenth century, Benedict Calvert, the son and heir of Charles Calvert, third Lord Baltimore, publicly renounced the Catholic faith and became a communicant of the Church of England. Benedict was careful to bring this fact to the notice of the new sovereign, George I, in a petition to have the proprietary government restored. King George looked with favor upon the petition and in 1715 rein-

This early engraving is entitled "American Friends Going to Meeting in a Settled Frost." Ever since colonial times the distinctive customs of the Friends (Quakers) have intrigued their neighbors.

SUTCLIFF, *Travels in Some Parts of North America*, 1815

stated the proprietary government. Unhappily, Benedict Calvert did not live to enjoy it, but his minor son, Charles, fifth Lord Baltimore, became the fourth proprietor. (Although the colony was again a proprietary government, the influence of the royal authority remained an important factor, and the proprietors were careful not to risk another suspension of their charter.) Before handing Maryland over to the proprietor, the royal government began a revision of the laws of Maryland to bring them into closer conformity with the common law of England, and in 1715 the legislative assembly adopted a code of laws that remained in effect with little alteration throughout the colonial period.

The two Carolinas, which had started as a single colony under eight proprietors, from the beginning found the rule of a conglomerate body of absentee landlords unsatisfactory. The unwieldy Fundamental Constitutions, spun from the fertile brains of John Locke and Anthony Ashley Cooper, proved a totally impractical instrument of government. Proprietary governors were incompetent or corrupt, and sometimes both. During the late seventeenth and early eighteenth centuries, friction was constant between the settlers and the governing body of the aristocratic establishment, which had to be modified and eventually abandoned. In 1710 the proprietors sent out Edward Hyde, a cousin of Queen Anne's, to be governor of North Carolina and to be independent of the governor of South Carolina, a date that marks the division of the two Carolinas into separate jurisdictions. The Board of Trade was eager to cancel the charters of the proprietors, but they were both numerous and influential, and it was not until 1719 that an opportunity came. In November of that year the inhabitants of South Carolina rebelled against the proprietors, called a convention, and asked to be taken over by the Crown. On May 29, 1721, Francis Nicholson, by now a sort of professional colonial governor, arrived in Charles Town as the first royal governor of the province.

For eight years longer, North Carolina endured proprietary government, but in 1729 the king finally canceled the proprietary charters and made North Carolina a crown colony too. George Burrington, appointed royal governor in 1731, was the first of a line of governors who sought to strengthen the Crown's authority in North Carolina and to bring order out of the chaos that had previously existed under the proprietary government. North Carolina had already acquired a population of diverse peoples, many of them seeking freedom from persecution. Quakers from colonies to the north, French Huguenots from Virginia and from overseas, Palatine Germans and Swiss brought to New Bern by two promoters, Christopher de Graffenried and Franz Louis Michel, native English of various religious beliefs, malcontents and refugees from Virginia justice— all found their way into North Carolina. The total population of North Carolina in 1715 has been estimated at 11,200 people, of whom 3,700 were Negro slaves, held for the most part by the great landowners on the coast. A few years after the establishment of the royal government, Scots in large numbers began coming to North Carolina. The older settlements on the coast developed an aristocratic plantation society, but in the back country, small farmers made up a large part of the population.

Religious controversies racked both the Carolinas. The more well-to-do settlers who had come early to the coastal regions had been English and predominantly Anglican in religion. But in North Carolina, where Quakers and dissenters were numerous, the Anglicans had difficulty maintaining an established church, and it was not until 1715 that they managed to get a law enacted that provided for the support of an established church by taxation. Even so, recalcitrant Quakers, Presbyterians, and other nonconformists contrived whenever possible to evade the provisions of the law. Anglican partisans regarded the state of the church in North Carolina as deplorable. William Byrd of Virginia, a biased and critical commentator on North Carolina society, remarked in his *History of the Dividing Line* (1728) that "this [Edenton] is the only Metropolis in the Christian or Mahometan World, where there is neither Church, Chappel, Mosque, Synagogue, or any other Place of Publick Worship of any Sect or Religion whatsoever. What little Devotion there may happen to be is much more private than their vices. The People seem easy without a Minister, as long as they are exempted from paying Him. Sometimes the Society for propagating the Gospel has had the Charity to send over Missionaries to this Country; but unfortunately the Priest has been too Lewd for the people, or, which oftener happens, they too lewd for the Priest. For these Reasons these Reverend Gentlemen have always left their Flocks as arrant Heathen as they found them."

In 1706 South Carolina, where the Anglicans made up approximately half of the population, enacted a law

Though useless as a guide to the geography of the region, this map of "The English Empire in America," published in 1728, is interesting for the small sketches of Indians and animals of the colonies that embellish the work.

making the Church of England the official church of the colony. The Huguenots, who might have been expected to resist the establishment, saw the wisdom of joining the tax-supported state church. But, as in North Carolina, many nonconformists objected to paying taxes to support a state church and evaded the law. The established church, here as elsewhere in the colonies, also suffered from a dearth of worthy candidates for the pulpit. In some instances, clergymen disgraced their callings and brought scandal to the church by keeping concubines or being drunk in public.

Yet despite constant political bickering and religious controversy, both of the Carolina colonies made rapid progress in the first two decades of the eighteenth century. They had important natural resources: fertile soil, great rivers, good harbors, vast forests, and a hinterland occupied by Indians with whom they developed a profitable trade. By 1720 South Carolina had a white population of about nine thousand and Negro slaves estimated at twelve thousand. The influx of slaves from Africa was the result of the Asiento, the monopoly of the slave trade granted to Great Britain by the Treaty of Utrecht. Because of the great profits from this nefarious traffic, English slave traders pushed their human cargoes upon the West Indies and the southern colonies. In the Carolinas, untrained slaves fresh from Africa could be used in the pine forests to produce naval stores. After the turn of the century, rice, first grown in South Carolina about 1685, rapidly became a profitable crop for export, and Negro slaves proved useful in the steaming swamps where rice was grown. Customs records for 1718 show that South Carolina shipped to England in that year 6,773 barrels of rice, 18,414 barrels of pitch, and 27,660 barrels of tar, besides lumber, spars, and deerskins. Large quantities of these products were also shipped to other colonies.

During the first third of the eighteenth century, the two Carolinas were outpost colonies standing as a bulwark against Spanish penetration from the south and French infiltration from the lower Mississippi Valley. On their frontiers were powerful Indian nations who constituted a persistent and troublesome problem. Populous and powerful, the Cherokees, the Creeks, the Chickasaws, and the Choctaws were a barrier to indefinite expansion westward. These Indian nations had conflicting interests, and it was not always easy to keep peace with one nation without antagonizing another. Furthermore, as in the case of the Choctaws, the Indians were shrewd enough to play off the French (or the Spaniards) against the English colonists. In addition to these great Indian nations, other tribes from time to time caused trouble.

In 1711, for example, North Carolina suffered a devastating attack from an Iroquoian tribe, the Tuscaroras. These tribesmen, who had established themselves along the coastal rivers, were alarmed at the incursion of white settlers into their territories. The settlement of De Graffenried's colonists at New Bern in 1710 posed a threat to the Tuscaroras' continued occupancy of land along the Neuse River, and they had other grievances. Traders, they claimed, had cheated them of their goods, abused their wives, stolen their children to be sold into slavery, and committed other depredations. On September 22, 1711, the Tuscaroras made a concerted attack on settlements on the peninsula between the Neuse River and Pamlico Sound, slaughtering a large proportion of the settlers in this area. At the head of the Neuse River alone they killed more than one hundred and thirty persons. The Indians scalped men, women, and children, mutilated their bodies, set fire to houses and barns, and even killed livestock. The area was depopu-

lated; among the slain were more than eighty children.

At this juncture Governor Hyde called upon South Carolina and Virginia for help. Governor Spotswood of Virginia used the emergency to try to force North Carolina to cede disputed territory on the border as the price of assistance; when North Carolina refused, he ordered his militia not to go beyond the Virginia boundary. South Carolina, on the other hand, sent a force of thirty whites and five hundred Indians under Colonel John Barnwell (who earned the sobriquet of "Tuscarora Jack") to aid the beleaguered North Carolinians. They were short of ammunition and other supplies, and the

Charles Town (later Charleston), South Carolina, seen across the Cooper River, was painted probably in 1737 or 1738. The flag at far left flies from Granville's Bastion, one of the city's defenses. The three landward sides of the fort were demolished to enlarge the town after the defeat of the Indians in 1717.

Quakers, who were a numerous group in the population, refused to fight or to furnish food or horses. Nevertheless, Barnwell and a force of North Carolina militia won two battles with the Tuscaroras in January, 1712, and made a hasty peace. Before the end of the ensuing summer, however, the truce was broken and the war resumed. This time South Carolina sent a hard-bitten Indian fighter in the person of Colonel James Moore, who joined with the North Carolinians to wreak vengeance on the Indians and to defeat them decisively on March 20, 1713. He killed several hundred and captured nearly four hundred more to be sold into slavery at ten pounds each, a way of paying part of the cost of the expedition. After this defeat, the surviving Tuscaroras began a slow retreat to the North, where they eventually joined their Iroquoian brethren as one of the Six Nations.

Two years after the defeat of the Tuscaroras, South Carolina saw the beginning of a disastrous war with the Yamasees, a Muskhogean tribe that had moved from Georgia into territory north of the Savannah River. Like the Tuscaroras, they bore grudges against white traders who cheated them and against settlers who were moving into their hunting grounds. Early in the spring of

221

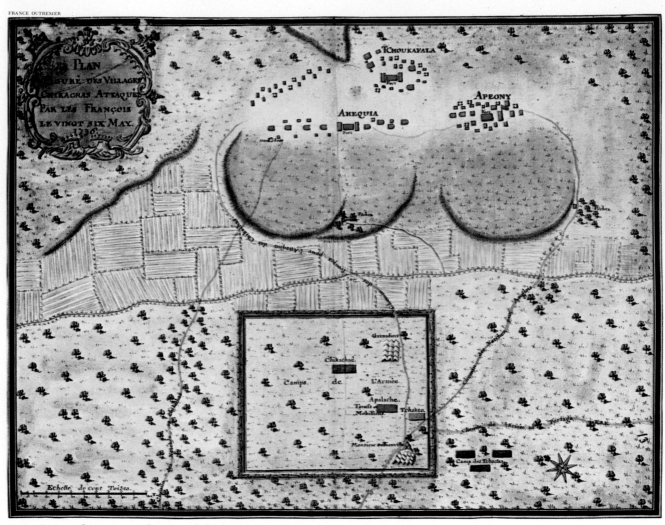

*From Paris archives comes this map of the situation as Governor
Bienville of Louisiana prepared to attack Chickasaw Indians
near their village of Amalahta in Mississippi on May 26, 1736.
Chickasaw bands are at top; Bienville and his Apalachee,
Mobile, and Choctaw allies are in and beside the square camp
below. Bienville was roundly defeated in the ensuing battle.*

1715, rumors of an Indian conspiracy reached Charles
Town, and on April 15 the Yamasees slaughtered the
members of a mission sent from Charles Town to negotiate their grievances. The Indians' objective was nothing less than the total annihilation of the South Carolinians, whom they hoped to drive from their lands
forever. The Yamasees had planned shrewdly and had
won the promise of aid from the Indians in South Carolina and its adjacent territories, except for the Cherokees and the Chickasaws. The settlers in South Carolina, on the other hand, were ill-prepared for war. Such

militiamen as the colony was able to muster were poorly
trained, undisciplined, and badly equipped. In the
emergency, the legislative assembly authorized an
"army" consisting of six hundred white South Carolinians, one hundred Virginians sent by Governor Spotswood, four hundred Negro slaves, who were armed during the crisis with great misgivings, and one hundred
friendly Indians.

Governor Charles Craven led a small force against
the Yamasees on the Combahee River, and by early
June, 1715, he had stemmed the first onslaught upon

222

the colony. Other Indian tribes, however, were already on the warpath. In midsummer, while Craven, reinforced by a small body of North Carolinians, was advancing against Cheraw Indians north of the Santee, the Creeks and other tribes fell on the settlements south of Charles Town. Beset on all sides, Craven sought aid from the other colonies. Governor Robert Hunter of New York responded by trying to persuade Indians in his jurisdiction to help the colonists in the South (the restlessness of the Indians in all the colonies was a cause of anxiety, for the threat of a general Indian war hung over the whole frontier). At this critical juncture the Cherokees, who had been neutral, attacked the Creeks. Their support was decisive, and by the summer of 1717 the Yamasees and their allies, the Creeks, were ready to make peace.

The Cherokees, a shrewd and intelligent people, knew that South Carolina owed its survival to their intervention, and they made the most of their position. In January, 1717, they demanded and received privileges that the traders thought "insulting." Indeed, some of the South Carolinians asserted that the Cherokees treated them as a tributary nation. Certainly the Cherokees had no love for the colonists and used the opportunity to drive a hard bargain in their own interest.

But the Cherokees were scarcely more influenced by self-interest than the Virginians. Although Governor Spotswood had sent only a few militiamen to the aid of the South Carolinians, he attempted to use the emergency to increase the prestige of Virginia with the Indians. Other Virginians were actually glad to see the discomfiture of their rivals in the Indian trade and, the South Carolinians charged, sold guns and powder to the warring Indians. These Virginians were bitter against the South Carolinians, who had tried to keep them out of the trading areas in their territory and had even appealed to the Board of Trade in London to forbid the incursion of other colonials into the Carolina back country. Intercolonial rivalry for the lucrative Indian trade helps to explain why the colonies found it hard to unite in a common cause.

During the early years of the eighteenth century the South Carolina coast was prey to pirates, who had their bases in the Bahamas or on islands farther south in the Caribbean. The coves and inlets on the North Carolina coast also proved to be convenient hideouts for these marauders, who attacked ships of all nations. Many of the pirates had been legitimate privateers during Queen Anne's War, but after the Treaty of Utrecht they refused to give up an occupation that had proved so profitable. Henceforth a ship's flag made little difference to them if the vessel carried a rich cargo. The Carolinians did not invariably regard English pirates as pests. Some argued that they served a useful purpose in fending off Spanish and French ships, which even in times of peace were not averse to acts of pillage. Other Carolinians saw a chance to line their pockets with pirate gold, as New Yorkers were accused of doing. In fact, the pirate Edward Teach (or Thatch), known as Blackbeard, found a haven at Bath, North Carolina, and made a friend of Governor Charles Eden's secretary, Tobias Knight, who allowed him to use his barn as warehouse. Governor Eden himself was openly accused of being friendly to pirates. Stede Bonnet, a pirate even more notorious in his day than Blackbeard, would raid shipping headed for Charles Town from a base on the lower Cape Fear River. These and other pirates became such a hazard to commerce that in 1718 Governor Robert Johnson of South Carolina ordered Colonel William Rhett to sea in command of an expedition bent upon ridding the coast of pirates. Rhett cornered Bonnet in Cape Fear River and after a six-hour battle captured him and his crew. Bonnet, a gentleman of wealth with a fine house on Barbados, had friends in Charles Town, and there is evidence of an attempt to set him free. But on December 10, 1718, he and twenty-nine members of his crew were hanged.

In May, 1717, Blackbeard captured eight or nine ships off Charles Town and then had the effrontery to sail into the harbor and demand a chest of medicine. Unless the town supplied the medicine, he threatened to burn shipping in the harbor, kill his prisoners, and devastate the town. He got his chest of drugs. But Blackbeard's days were numbered. In the autumn of 1718, Governor Spotswood of Virginia heard that the pirate was cruising off the North Carolina coast. He recruited sailors from the tobacco fleet and sent two armed sloops commanded by an officer of the Royal Navy, Lieutenant Robert Maynard, in pursuit of Blackbeard. Maynard encountered Blackbeard off Ocracoke Island. The pirates boarded Maynard's sloop, but the British lieutenant rallied his men and defeated the pirates. Maynard himself killed Blackbeard, cut off his head, lashed it to his bowsprit, and set sail for Virginia, taking along the surviving members of the pirate crew, who were duly tried, convicted, and hanged.

Before the end of 1718, South Carolina alone listed forty-nine pirates hanged in Charles Town, and the combined efforts of the Virginians and Carolinians had forced most of the pirates who survived to move to less hostile waters. Pirates continued to be a menace off the coasts of the northern colonies, but they developed a healthy respect for colonial justice in the South.

The end of the Yamasee War and the suppression of pirates increased the opportunities for trade and commerce in the southern colonies, but the region was still a frontier in danger of attack, not only from the unpredictable Indians, but also from the Spaniards and French. The founding of New Orleans in 1718 gave France a bastion in the lower Mississippi Valley that increased the danger of encirclement from the rear. The Spaniards strengthened their base at St. Augustine and were ever ready to infiltrate disputed territory in what is now Georgia and Alabama. All three competed vigorously for the Indian trade and sought to lure the border tribes into their respective orbits. The English settlers on the southern frontier were acutely aware of the three-cornered contest for imperial domination of the disputed territories, and colonial officials were constantly writing to the Board of Trade about the problem.

All the British colonies realized that France was an ever present threat to their existence, for France occupied strategic positions in their rear and had powerful Indian allies. Spain was also an inveterate enemy and from the base at St. Augustine could dispute any British expansion to the south, although Spanish strength, with less than two thousand white Spaniards in all Florida, was limited. Nevertheless, Spain had troops and ships in Cuba and elsewhere in her American empire that were a potential menace. Furthermore, Spanish Indian traders were competing actively with both the English and the French in the lower Mississippi Valley.

The keenness of the competition for this Indian trade was productive of much bitterness between all the groups involved. The activity of the French soon brought them into conflict with the Spaniards as well as the English. In 1717 the French Crown granted a monopoly of the Indian trade in Louisiana to the Compagnie des Indes, and Bienville, now governor, set about strengthening French bases in the South. In addition to the base at New Orleans, which he made the capital of Louisiana, he moved east into what was clearly Spanish territory. By 1719 the French and the Spaniards were in open conflict, fighting for the posses-

sion of the Spanish fort at Pensacola. On their part, the Spaniards moved into Louisiana from New Mexico and attempted to establish themselves at the forks of the Platte River, in what is now Nebraska. A combined force of Indians and French traders drove them back to New Mexico. The conflict between the erstwhile allies finally ended in 1721, and the French and Spanish returned to the territories that they previously had claimed or occupied. The intensity of their hostility was a measure of their greed for the profits of the lucrative Indian trade.

To the British colonists, the contention between Spanish and French colonials brought little comfort, for it meant that each would try to strengthen its position in the disputed territory. It also meant continued confusion and disturbance among the Indians. From Maine to South Carolina, the British colonists braced themselves for further trouble and took such steps as seemed expedient to them. In London the Board of Trade listened with more attention to reports from overseas and urged action upon the Privy Council and the king himself.

The authorities in London at last were beginning to realize the need to develop an imperial policy to checkmate France and, less importantly, Spain. Acting on pleas from South Carolina, the royal government in 1721 dispatched a company of regular soldiers to occupy a fort at the mouth of the Altamaha River, south of Savannah, in territory claimed by Spain. Although these troops were riddled with disease and proved worse than useless, they at least symbolized Whitehall's awareness of the colonial problem of defense against common enemies. The fort on the Altamaha was christened Fort King George.

The South Carolinians had already taken measures to guard their Indian trade in the interior by establishing fortified trading posts along the Savannah River, much like the later trading posts in the West. One of the most important of these posts was Fort Moore, at approximately the site of Augusta, Georgia. Other fortified posts were established along the Savannah and on the Congaree River, near the site of Columbia, South Carolina. To protect the south coast, a base was maintained at Port Royal with two scouting craft—the total "navy" that South Carolina could support. From the interior bases, rangers recruited from the militia patrolled the back country to keep the Indians in subjection and to intercept French and Spanish emissaries and traders.

Three of the pirates who terrorized the Atlantic coast are pictured in old prints: at top left is the depraved Captain Teach ("Blackbeard"); at top right, Stede Bonnet pays the penalty clutching flowers handed him by an admirer; right, Captain Worley refuses quarter till all his crew are slain.

ABOVE LEFT: JOHNSON, *Lives of Highwaymen and Pirates*, 1736; ABOVE RIGHT: HARRY ELKINS WIDENER COLLECTION, HARVARD COLLEGE LIBRARY; BELOW. *History and Lives of the Most Notorious Pirates*, 182?

In the eyes of these rangers—and of the merchants of Charles Town—traders from Virginia were almost as unwelcome as those from foreign countries.

Governor Spotswood of Virginia was eager to demonstrate to London and to the other colonies that he was a leader in the efforts to curb their common enemies on the frontiers. (His own reports and recommendations to the Board of Trade, however, simply echo those sent by Governor Nicholson of South Carolina.) So concerned was Spotswood over the danger from French infiltration of the back country that, with a fine disregard of logistics and distance, he proposed to the Board of Trade that Virginia use funds from customs and other fees to build a fortress on Lake Erie to serve as an outpost of English power and help stop the French advance into the Ohio and Mississippi valleys. Spotswood's intentions were sounder than his knowledge of geography, but his concern about the French presence in the upper Mississippi basin and the increasing thrust of the French from New Orleans helped to alert the authorities in London to the importance of devising a consistent western policy, one designed to contain both the French and the Spaniards.

By the beginning of the second quarter of the eight-

eenth century, English colonies all along the seaboard were pushing their trade with the Indians of the interior and doing their best to counter French efforts to restrict the English to the coastal region. A map of Louisiana, made by the royal cartographer, Guillaume Delisle, and issued in Paris in 1718, had plainly indicated that the French intended to deny all the interior of the continent to the English. Throughout the colonies the fear persisted that, unless the English took preventive measures, the French might ultimately push them into the sea. The forts erected on the Altamaha in 1721 and at Oswego in 1727 showed the beginning of an understanding of the nature of the impending conflict. London was coming to realize that the defense of the colonies required a chain of forts on the frontier and imperial troops to man them.

The southern frontier remained a problem. South Carolina traders, expanding their business with the Cherokee and Creek Indians, were in direct competition with French *coureurs de bois* pushing eastward, and the Carolinians were keenly aware of the seriousness of the French threat. Indeed, so great was their realization of danger that fear overcame greed, and the Carolinians welcomed the establishment of a buffer colony to the

MARTYN, *Reasons for Establishing the Colony of Georgia*, 1733

Although it purports to be a picture of the founding of Georgia, the above engraving is based principally on imagination. It was an illustration in a book, first published in 1733, whose purpose was to promote interest in the colonization of Georgia.

south in 1732, to relieve pressure on that frontier.

The settlement of Georgia was not the first attempt by British promoters to found a colony between Florida and South Carolina. The most curious plan was one devised by a Scot, Sir Robert Montgomery of Skelmorly, who dreamed of a feudal dominion in the New World that he would rule from a great palace in the center of his possessions. From the proprietors of South Carolina, who laid claim to the territory, Montgomery and two partners, Aaron Hill, a dramatic poet, and Amos Kettleby, a merchant of London, obtained a grant of all the land between the Altamaha and Savannah rivers extending west to the Pacific Ocean. This land the partners named Azilia, and they presently published one of the most extravagant pieces of promotion to appear in the colonial period, a tract entitled *Discourse concerning the Design'd Establishment of a New Colony to the South of Carolina in the most delightful Country of the Universe* (1717). The tract described the land as "our future Eden" and asserted that English writers "universally agree that Carolina, and especially its Southern Bounds, is the most amiable Country in the Universe: that Nature has not bless'd the World with any Tract, which can be preferable to it, that Paradise, with all her Virgin Beauties, may be modestly suppos'd at most but equal to its Native Excellencies." The pamphlet further pointed out that Azilia "lies in the same Latitude with Palestine Herself, That promis'd Canaan, which was pointed out by God's own Choice, to bless the Labours of a favourite People. It abounds with Rivers, Woods, and Meadows. Its gentle Hills are full of Mines, Lead, Copper, Iron, and even some of Silver. . . . Vines, naturally flourishing upon the Hills, bear Grapes in most luxuriant Plenty. They have every Growth which we possess in England, and almost every Thing that England wants besides. The Orange and the Limon thrive in the same common Orchard with the Apple, and the Pear-Tree, Plumbs, Peaches, Apricots, and Nectarins bear from Stones in three years growing. The Planters raise large Orchards . . . to feed their Hogs with."

Azilia, its promoters maintained, would supply England with all those commodities that she lacked: silk, cochineal, coffee, tea, raisins, olives, currants, almonds, wine, and, in fact, practically every good thing of the earth. Unhappily, the heady schemes of Montgomery, Hill, and Kettleby came to naught. The crash of the South Sea Company in 1720 swept Azilia into oblivion.

A few years later, a project even more fantastic than Azilia was concocted by another Scottish baronet, Sir Alexander Cuming of Coulter, who proposed to create a refuge for three hundred thousand Jews on the tribal lands of the Cherokees. This colony would serve as a bulwark against aggression by Indians or French from the west. What the Cherokees thought of the proposed Zion on their lands is not recorded, but Sir Alexander made a visit that created a lasting impression upon the Indians. Looking like a counterpart of Don Quixote, the Scottish baronet appeared among the Cherokees in the spring of 1730. Armed to the teeth and boasting of the power of King George II, he persuaded them that he represented a king whose power reached even to their hill towns. At a tribal council he persuaded the chiefs to kneel and swear allegiance to King George and had himself acclaimed the king's viceroy. With some persuasion, he induced six Cherokees, a minor chief and five warriors, to set out for London and the court of King George. Near Charles Town, they picked up another stray Indian. When they finally reached England, the chief was a king, and the other Indians were chiefs or generals. On June 18, 1730, King George received this strange delegation, and during the next three months the Cherokee "king" and his fellows were the sensation of London. They were entertained, feted, and taught English vices. On September 28 the play of *Orinoco* was performed at Lincoln's Inn Fields, and so great was the press of people who came to see the Indians that the theater's receipts trebled for that night. At length the Cherokees returned to their own people with tales of the power of the English sovereign and the wonders of his court and country. Their report of the strength of the English undoubtedly helped persuade the Cherokees to remain loyal to England during the French wars.

The public excitement created by the schemes of Montgomery and Cuming focused attention upon the southern frontier. Another plan for a colony, more practical than the others, was developed in the summer of 1730 by General James Oglethorpe and a group of associates who conceived the notion of a refuge in the New World for indigent debtors. Oglethorpe, a distinguished soldier and a member of Parliament, had served as chairman of a committee to look into the condition of debtors' prisons. What he discovered stirred a philanthropic impulse, and he persuaded twenty like-minded Englishmen, prominent in the government, to join him in petitioning for a grant of land to the south of Carolina (the very area that Montgomery had called Azilia) to be settled by debtors who would rehabilitate themselves by honest labor. Two years after the project was first started, the government, on June 9, 1732, granted a charter to the twenty-one trustees for a period of twenty-one years, authorizing the colony of Georgia. At the expiration of the charter, the colony would revert to the Crown. Any rights that the lords proprietors of Carolina had to the land were ended when seven of the eight proprietors sold out to the king.

The British government was eager for the establishment of this colony, for it recognized its strategic values. Oglethorpe, a military man, had not failed to point this out in his petition. The trustees, however, were determined not to let the colony become merely a military outpost serving the interests of nascent imperialism. They were genuinely concerned about its philanthropic aims and drew up elaborate regulations to promote the cause. Because of the social prominence of the trustees, all England soon heard about Georgia, and pamphleteers outdid themselves in commending it. Money, commodities, and advice poured in from sympathetic contributors, and the trustees immediately set about processing applicants for settlement. By the late autumn of 1732, something over a hundred colonists had won the approval of the trustees, and they set sail in the ship *Anne*, accompanied by Oglethorpe himself. Arriving at Charles Town on January 13, 1733, they took on additional supplies and sailed for a haven in Georgia. Oglethorpe got his people ashore on February 12, at a spot about eighteen miles from the mouth of the Savannah River, and there he laid out a town that he named Savannah. Like William Penn in Philadelphia, Oglethorpe planned a town of orderly squares. He also required the planting of mulberry trees to feed silkworms, for silk was one of the products that the promoters hoped would bring prosperity to the colony.

Again like Penn, Oglethorpe sought to make Georgia a refuge for oppressed people everywhere. The propaganda of the trustees induced some twelve hundred Lutherans from Salzburg to settle in Georgia. Another group of Germans, a body of Moravians who came under the sponsorship of Count Nikolaus von Zinzendorf, received land on the border, where they were in constant danger from both Indians and Spaniards. Since they were pacifists and refused to serve in the militia, they soon decided that Georgia was no place for them and moved to Pennsylvania and other safer places in

the North. During the period of the trustees' jurisdiction, Georgia acquired a polyglot group of settlers who included Swiss, Italians, Germans, Scottish Highlanders, Welshmen, Englishmen, and Jews. The Jews were numerous enough to organize a congregation and establish a synagogue.

Oglethorpe had the imagination and the vision of an empire builder, and he was determined to make Georgia a significant element in the growing empire. In the spring of 1734 he returned to England to further his plans. With him he took a group of Creek Indians, including a chief, Tomo-Chi-Chi, from whom he had bought the site of Savannah and other land. These Creeks created an even greater sensation in London than the Cherokees who had accompanied Sir Alexander Cuming of Coulter. The king and the Archbishop of Canterbury received the Indians in formal ceremonies. The Creeks also visited Eton, where Tomo-Chi-Chi begged a holiday for the students. One Indian won favor by reciting the Lord's Prayer in both Creek and English. Crowds followed them wherever they went and at times rioted in an effort to see them. At last, after collecting many gifts, the Indians returned to Georgia and spread the word of the might and glory of England to such good effect that both the Creeks and the Cherokees made pacts of friendship with the new colony of Georgia. Tomo-Chi-Chi remained a true friend of the colony, and when he died at the age of one hundred, he was buried, at his own request, in Savannah.

So impressed was Parliament with the importance of Georgia that it appropriated twenty-six thousand pounds to further the cause of settlement, and from 1735 onward a rush of colonists sought land in Georgia. In 1736 Oglethorpe himself returned, accompanied by John and Charles Wesley, the founders of Methodism, and other zealous souls. A military man realizing the importance of fortifications and communications, Oglethorpe at once set about building forts and roads. On St. Simons Island, the fortified town of Frederica pleased him so well that he made it his headquarters. A fortified outpost far up the Savannah River at Augusta proved a useful center for frontier defense and served as a gateway to the Indian country, where Georgia traders competed with the Carolinians. On the Florida border Oglethorpe persuaded Scottish Highlanders to establish outposts. To connect the various fortified areas, he laid out connecting roads, and the road from Savannah to Augusta became an important trade route.

Tomo-Chi-Chi, Creek chief who sold land to James Oglethorpe, had his portrait painted with a nephew when they visited England in 1734. For a time exiled by his tribe, Tomo-Chi-Chi later led them into friendship with the Georgia settlers.

The development of Georgia turned out to be more expensive than either the promoters or Parliament had anticipated, but trouble brewing with Spain induced the home government to continue its support of the colony's defenses and to send a regiment of troops to supplement the militia. The troops came none too soon, for in 1739 England declared war on Spain, a conflict known to history as the War of Jenkins's Ear, and the border between Florida and Georgia was immediately involved. The war was precipitated by an episode concerning the smuggling activities of one Thomas Jenkins, a ship captain. He appeared in the House of Commons and reported that Spanish seamen had searched and pillaged his ship, cut off his ears, and told him to take them to his masters. To prove his contention, he took out his handkerchief and unwrapped a dried ear. In fact, Jenkins had been caught smuggling goods to the Spanish islands in violation of the provisions of the Asiento, but

British shipping interests were so angry over the Spaniards' assertion of the right of search and seizure at sea that they forced the government into a declaration of war. Most of the fighting took place at sea and eventually merged into the War of the Austrian Succession, known in the colonies as King George's War.

The Spaniards, believing that they could drive the English from Georgia and South Carolina, collected in Cuba an expedition of fifty ships, eighteen hundred troops, and one thousand seamen. In July, 1742, this force sailed for the coast of Georgia, but by bravery, stratagem, and the luck of the weather, Oglethorpe managed to repulse the attack and send them back to the Caribbean. The next year he turned the tables on the Spaniards and attacked St. Augustine. However, lacking artillery to breach the walls and unable to lure the Spaniards to a fight in the open, he marched back to Georgia. Thus ended the War of Jenkins's Ear on the southern frontier.

In March, 1744, after thirty-one years of nominal peace, France and England once more found themselves at war. Though the two nations had not been belligerents during this period, their subjects in the American forests from time to time had been at each other's throats, and the declaration of war in the spring of 1744 once more made the whole frontier a war zone.

The French opened the war on the colonials by sending an expedition from their fortified base of Louisbourg on Cape Breton Island to prey on the New England fishing fleet and to capture the fishing town of Canso, Nova Scotia. The French commander promised to send the prisoners taken at Canso to Boston but kept them temporarily at Louisbourg while he made an unsuccessful attempt to take Annapolis Royal. When at length the prisoners were shipped off to Boston, they took with them detailed plans of the French fortress of Louisbourg and a firm conviction that they could take it. The capture of Louisbourg henceforth was the objective of belligerent Bostonians, who regarded it as a menace to the peace and commerce of all New England.

The French believed Louisbourg, the anchor of their defenses in North America, to be impregnable. Built on plans made by the great engineer, Vauban, its massive stone walls mounted two hundred and fifty guns. But, as the English prisoners reported in Boston, the garrison was weak. Convinced that Louisbourg could and should be taken, Governor William Shirley of Massachusetts launched a crusade that for once enlisted the

229

Printed for John Bowles at the Black Horse in Cornhil &c

New England forces land during the expedition against Louisbourg

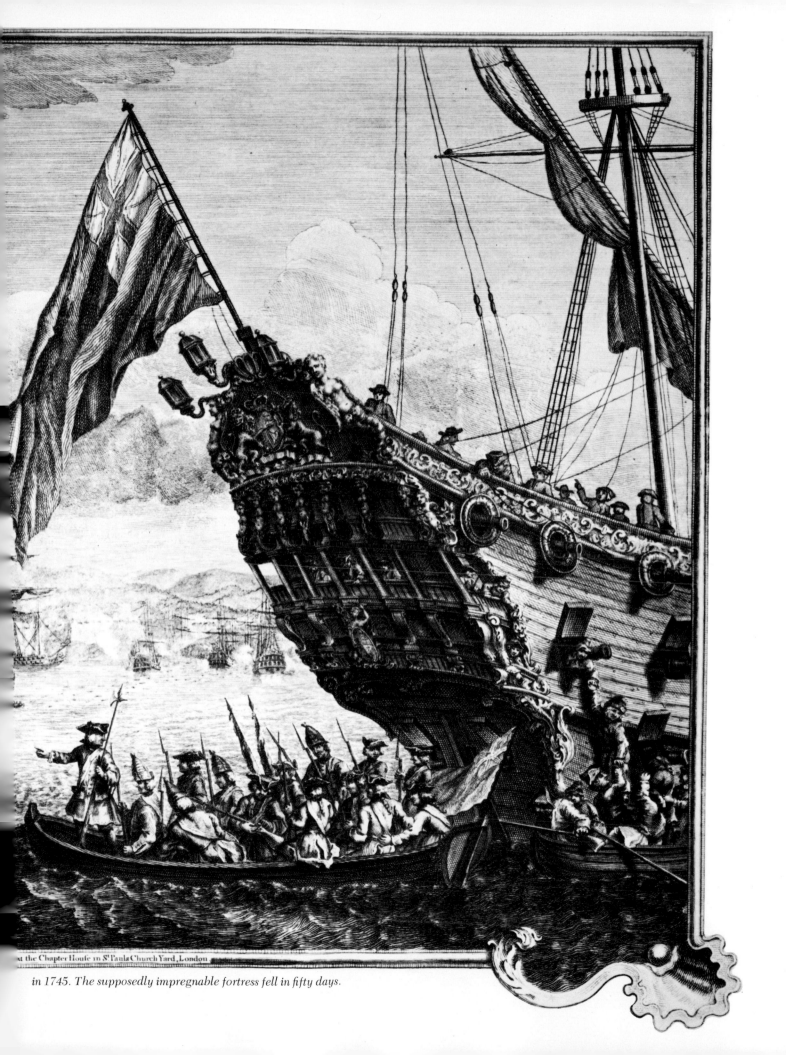

in 1745. *The supposedly impregnable fortress fell in fifty days.*

support of all New England and New York. He collected ships, troops, and supplies in Boston and received from London the promise of naval support.

The expedition embarked on March 24, 1745, with William Pepperrell, a fish merchant of Kittery, Maine, in command. On April 23 they made a rendezvous off Canso with Commodore Peter Warren in command of three ships of the Royal Navy. During the last two days of April the attackers began landing in preparation for an assault, but, to their surprise, on May 2 they found the Grand Battery abandoned and thirty of the great guns spiked—the garrison had decided that this outwork could not be held and had retired inside the fortress. In a short time blacksmiths removed the spikes from the touchholes, and the guns were turned against the fortress. Pepperrell decided to make an attack on the fort from the land side, where the fortifications were weakest, and dragged some of the captured guns around to bear on the walls. In the meantime, Warren was pounding the fort from the sea and preventing French supply ships from reaching the besieged garrison.

The siege continued through the month of May. Pepperrell had his troubles with undisciplined militia. A planned assault on May 23 had to be abandoned because most of the attacking force was drunk. Three days later, with enough sober troops to launch an attack, Pepperrell landed his men secretly at night at a point that he believed vulnerable, only to have a drunken soldier cheer and give away their position. The ensuing fire killed at least sixty men, and a French sortie captured one hundred and nineteen.

Despite the gloom caused by this miscarriage of plans, the attackers continued to pound the fortress with shot and shell. On June 15 they planned to make a joint land and sea assault, but a flag of truce sent by the French opened the way for negotiations that on June 17 ended in the surrender of the Louisbourg fortification. A motley army of militia and fishermen, sometimes drunk and sometimes sober, aided by three ships of the Royal Navy, had captured the strongest citadel in North America, and with it control of the St. Lawrence and the northern waters. No longer would French troops based at Louisbourg threaten the livelihood of New England fishermen.

To honor Pepperrell for his services, the British government created him a baronet. Governor Shirley was made the colonel of a regiment that was presently disbanded. Commodore Warren was promoted to admiral

and later knighted. He also obtained large grants of land in the back country of New York, and his nephew, William Johnson, came over from Ireland to look after his uncle's property. Johnson settled among the Mohawk Indians and in time became a powerful influence with the Iroquois.

In 1746 Governor Shirley, mindful of the great victory over the French at Louisbourg, proposed an expedition to capture Quebec. Acting on a promise of eight battalions of regular troops from England and British pay for the militia, he set about raising troops in New England. But the ministry in London decided to send the regulars to battlefields in France and failed to notify Shirley of a change in plans. Although reports of the expedition against Quebec frightened the French in Canada, nothing came of it. Some of Shirley's troops marched to join New York militia in a planned attack on Crown Point, but these were recalled to resist a rumored attack by a French fleet on Boston.

In the meantime the French had organized a great fleet to recapture Louisbourg. Rarely, however, has an expedition encountered worse misfortune. Hurricanes battered it; two of its commanding officers died in succession, one by suicide; a pestilence broke out that carried off hundreds of seamen and left the fleet barely enough men to work the ships. At last the fleet returned to France without having damaged a single hostile ship or fortress in America. Although Louis XV ordered another fleet to retake Louisbourg, it too met disaster, this time at the hands of a flotilla commanded by Admirals Warren and Anson.

The war at last dragged to a close in Europe and dwindled to a few scattered forays on the borders in America. The politicians sat down to work out terms for peace, and by October 18, 1748, they succeeded in completing the Treaty of Aix-la-Chapelle, which restored practically everything in colonial America to its status before the war. The greatest blow to the colonials was the return of Louisbourg to the French. With callous disdain for the welfare of New England, the British ministry relinquished Louisbourg to gain Madras in India. The victory that the New England militia had won turned to ashes, and they would not forget that London had let them down. The colonies had gained some military experience; they were beginning to perceive that they must stand together in the face of common enemies; and they were learning the bitter lesson of being pawns in the imperial game of chess.

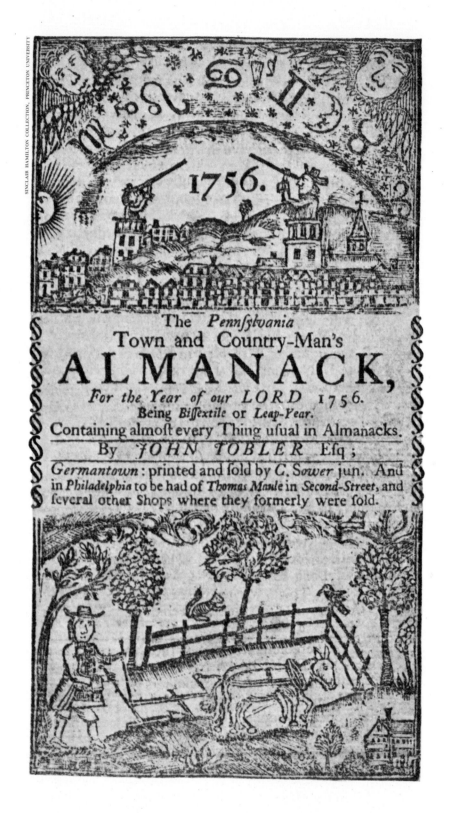

1756.

The *Pennsylvania*
Town and Country-Man's
ALMANACK,
For the Year of our LORD 1756.
Being *Biſſextile* or *Leap-Year*.
Containing almoſt every Thing uſual in Almanacks.
By *JOHN TOBLER* Eſq;

Germantown: printed and ſold by *C. Sower* jun. And
in *Philadelphia* to be had of *Thomas Maule* in *Second-Street*, and
ſeveral other Shops where they formerly were ſold.

In Their Words...

Colonial Life

The uprising of frontier farmers in Virginia known as Bacon's Rebellion was triggered, as the excerpt below relates, by a Nanticoke (Doeg) Indian attack on an outlying settlement. Later it took on many of the characteristics of a class struggle when Nathaniel Bacon, representing the farmers, put pressure on Governor William Berkeley and his council to institute social and political reforms.

About the year 1675 appear'd three Prodigies in that Country, which, from th' attending Disasters, were Look'd upon as Ominous Presages.

The One was a large Comet every Evening for a Week, or more at South-West; Thirty five Degrees high, Streaming like a horse Taile Westwards, untill it reach'd (almost) the Horrison, and Setting towards the Northwest.

Another was, Flights of Pigeons in breadth nigh a Quarter of the Mid-Hemisphere, and of their Length was no visible End; Whose Weights brake down the Limbs of Large Trees whereon these rested at Nights, of which the Fowlers Shot abundance and Eat 'em; This Sight put the old Planters under the more Portentous Apprehensions, because the like was Seen (as they said) in the year 1640 When th' Indians Committed the last Massacre, but not after, untill that present Year 1675.

The Third strange Appearance was Swarms of Flyes about an Inch long, and big as the Top of a Man's little finger, rising out of Spigot Holes in the Earth, which Eat the New Sprouted Leaves from the Tops of the Trees without other Harm, and in a Month left us.

My Dwelling was in Northumberland, the lowest County on Potomack River, Stafford being the upmost; where having also a Plantation, Servant's, Cattle, etc, My Overseer there had agreed with one Robt. Hen to come thither, and be my Herdsman, who then Lived Ten Miles above it; But on a Sabbath day Morning in the summer Anno 1675, People in their Way to Church, Saw this Hen lying th'wart his Threshold, and an Indian without the Door, both Chopt on their Heads, Arms and other Parts, as if done with Indian Hatchetts. Th' Indian was dead, but Hen when ask'd who did that? Answered "Doegs Doegs," and soon Died, then a Boy came out from under a Bed, where he had hid himself, and told them, Indians had come at break of day and done those Murders.

From this Englishman's bloud did (by Degrees) arise Bacons Rebellion . . . which Overspread all Virginia and twice endangerd Maryland. . . .

In these frightfull times the most Exposed small families withdrew into our houses of better Numbers, which we fortified with Pallisadoes and redoubts, Neighbours in Bodies Joined their Labours from each Plantation to others Alternately, taking their Arms into the Fields, and Setting Centinels; no Man Stirrd out of Door unarm'd. . . .

Frequent Complaints of Bloudsheds were sent to Sr. Wm. Berkeley (then Governour,) from the Heads of the Rivers, which were as often Answered, with Promises of Assistance.

These at the Heads of James and York Rivers (having now most People destroyed by the Indians Flight thither from Potomack) grew Impatient at the many Slaughters of their Neighbours and rose for their own Defence, who Chusing Mr. Bacon for their Leader Sent often times to the Governour, humbly Beseeching a commission to go against those Indians at their own Charge which his Honour as often promis'd but did not send; The Misteryes of these Delays, were Wondred at and which I ne're heard any coud Penetrate into, other than the Effects of his Passion, and a new (not to be mentioned) occasion of Avarice, to both which, he was (by the common Vogue) more than a little Addicted. . . .

"T.M."

The Beginning, Progress and Conclusion of Bacons Rebellion, 1705

Indian and captive white child, from an early book on "Indian barbarities"

*I*n 1675 Indians attacked and burned Lancaster, Massachusetts. Mary Rowlandson, the wife of the town's minister, was taken captive and later ransomed. Her vivid account of the experience became one of the most popular books in New England.

On the tenth of February 1675, Came the Indians with great numbers upon Lancaster: Their first coming was about Sun-rising; hearing the noise of some Guns, we looked out; several Houses were burning, and the Smoke ascending to Heaven. There were five persons taken in one house, the Father, and the Mother and a sucking Child, they knockt on the head; the other two they took and carried away alive. Their were two others, who being out of their Garison upon some occasion were set upon; one was knockt on the head, the other escaped: Another their was who running along was shot and wounded, and fell down; he begged of them his life, promising them Money (as they told me) but they would not hearken to him but knockt him in head, and stript him naked, and split open his Bowels. . . .

At length they came and beset our own house, and quickly it was the dolefullest day that ever mine eyes saw. The House stood upon the edg of a hill; some of the Indians got behind the hill, others into the Barn, and others behind any thing that could shelter them; from all which places they shot against the House, so that the Bullets seemed to fly like hail; and quickly they wounded one man among us, then another, and then a third, About two hours (according to my observation, in that amazing time) they had been about the house before they prevailed to fire it (which they did with Flax and Hemp, which they brought out of the Barn). . . . Then I took my Children (and one of my sisters, hers) to go forth and leave the house: but as soon as we came to the dore and appeared, the Indians shot so thick that the bulletts rattled against the House, as if one had taken an handfull of stones and threw them, so that we were fain to give back. We had six stout Dogs belonging to our Garrison, but none of them would stir, though another time, if any Indian had come to the door, they were ready to fly upon him and tear him down. The Lord hereby would make us the more to acknowledge his hand, and to see that our help is always in him. But out we must go, the fire increasing, and coming along behind us, roaring, and the Indians gaping before us with their Guns, Spears and Hatchets to devour us. No sooner were we out of the House, but my Brother in Law (being before wounded, in defending the house, in or near the throat) fell down dead, wherat the Indians scornfully shouted, and hallowed, and were presently upon him, stripping off his cloaths, the bulletts flying thick, one went through my side, and the same (as would seem) through the bowels and hand of my dear Child in my arms. One of my elder Sisters Children, named William, had then his Leg broken, which the Indians perceiving, they knockt him on head. Thus were we butchered by those merciless Heathen, standing amazed, with the blood running down to our heels. . . . The Indians laid hold of us, pulling me one way, and the Children another, and said, Come go along with us; I told them they would kill me: they answered, If I were willing to go along with them, they would not hurt me.

Oh the dolefull sight that now was to behold at this House! *Come, behold the works of the Lord, what dissolations he has made in the Earth*. . . . It is a solemn sight to see so many Christians lying in their blood, some here, and some there, like a company of Sheep torn by Wolves, All of them stript naked by a company of hell-hounds, roaring, singing, ranting and insulting, as if they would have torn our very hearts out; yet the Lord by his Almighty power preserved a number of us from death, for there were twenty-four of us taken alive and carried Captive.

I had often before this said, that if the Indians should come, I should chuse rather to be killed by them then taken alive but when it came to the tryal my mind changed; their glittering weapons so daunted my spirit, that I chose rather to go along with those (as I may say) ravenous Beasts, then that moment to end my dayes. . . .

A Narrative of the Captivity and Restauration of Mrs. Mary Rowlandson, 1682

In 1692 the witchcraft hysteria that raged through Massachusetts for nearly half a century reached its climax in Salem with the hanging of nineteen "witches." One of the victims, Mary Easty, might have saved herself by confessing; instead she protested her innocence and petitioned the court on behalf of those who would later be accused.

The humbl petition of Mary Eastick unto his Excellencyes Sir Wm Phipps and to the honourd Judge and Bench now s(i)tting In Judiacature in Salem and the Reverend ministers humbly sheweth

That wheras your poor and humble Petition[er] being condemned to die Doe humbly begg of you to take it into your Judicious and pious considerations that your poor and humble petitioner knowing my own Innocencye Blised be the Lord for it and seeing plainly the wiles and subtility of my accusers by my selfe can not but Judg charitably of Others that are going the same way of my selfe if the Lord stepps not mightily in i was confined a whole month upon the same account that I am condemned now for and then cleared by the afflicked persons as some of your honours know and in two dayes time I was cryed out upon by them and have been confined and now am condemned to die the Lord above knows my Innocencye then and likewise does now as att the great day will be known to men and Angells I petition to your honours not for my own life for I know I must die and my appointed time is sett but the Lord he knowes it is that if it be possible no more Innocent blood may be shed which undoubtidly cannot be Avoyd[e]d In the way and course you goe in I Question not but your honours does to the uttmost of your Powers in the discovery and detecting of witchcraft and witches and would not be guilty of Innocent blood for the world but by my own Innocencye I know you are in the wrong way the Lord in his infinite mercye direct you in this great work if it be his blessed will that no more innocent blood be shed I would humbly begg of you that your honours would be plesed to examine theis

A hanging in the 18th century

Aflicted persons strictly and keepe them apart some time and likewise to try some of these confesing wichis I being confident there is severall of them has belyed themselves . . . I know not the least thinge of witchcraft therfore I cannot I dare not belye my own soule I beg your honers not to deny this my humble petition from a poor dying Innocent person and I Question not but the Lord will give a blesing to yor endevers

Mary Easty
Petition of an Accused Witch, 1692

*U*rbane *Samuel Sewall of Boston was one of the presiding judges at the 1692 Salem witchcraft trials, but the spectacle of Gallows Hill haunted his conscience. On Fast Day, 1697, he had this notice read in the meetinghouse in which he worshiped.*

Samuel Sewall, sensible of the reiterated strokes of God upon himself and family; and being sensible, that as to the Guilt contracted . . . at Salem he is, upon many accounts, more concerned than any that he knows of, Desires to take the Blame and shame of it, asking pardon of men, And especially desiring prayers that God, who has an Unlimited Authority, would pardon that sin . . .

Samuel Sewall
Petition Put up on the Fast Day, January 14, 1697

Title page of a 1730 pamphlet on early antismallpox measures

*C*otton *Mather believed in witchcraft, and his scientific views included the notion that pigeons migrated to an ''undiscovered satellite'' in winter. Yet in many ways he was one of the most modern thinkers of his time. In 1721, when a smallpox epidemic hit Boston, Mather urged Boston physicians to employ the inoculation technique used by the Turks. In his diary he records the anguish he suffered for taking this stand.*

[May] 26. The grievous Calamity of the *Small-Pox* has now entered the Town. The Practice of conveying and suffering the *Small-pox* by *Inoculation,* has never been used in *America,* nor indeed in our Nation, But how many Lives might be saved by it, if it were practised? . . .

[June] 13. What shall I do? what shall I do, with regard unto *Sammy*? He comes home, when the Small-pox begins to spread in the Neighbourhood; and he is lothe to return unto *Cambridge.* I must earnestly look up to Heaven for Direction. . . .

[July] 16. At this Time, I enjoy an unspeakable Consolation. I have instructed our Physicians in the new Method used by the *Africans* and *Asiaticks,* to prevent and abate the Dangers of the *Small-Pox,* and infallibly to save the Lives of those that have it wisely managed upon them. The Destroyer, being enraged at the Proposal of any Thing, that may rescue the Lives of our poor People from him, has taken a strange Possession of the People on this Occasion. They rave, they rail, they blaspheme; they talk not only like Ideots but also like *Franticks,* And not only the Physician who began the Experiment, but I also am an Object of their Fury. . . .

[August] 1. Full of Distress about *Sammy*; He begs to have his Life saved, by receiving the *Small-Pox,* in the way of *Inoculation,* whereof our Neighbourhood has had no less than ten remarkable Experiments; and if he should after all dy by receiving it in the common Way, how can I answer it? On the other Side, our People, who have Satan remarkably filling their Hearts and their Tongues, will go on with infinite Prejudices against me and my Ministry, if I suffer this Operation upon the Child. . . .

15. My dear *Sammy*, is now under the Operation of receiving the *Small-Pox* in the way of *Transplantation*. The Success of the Experiment among my Neighbours, as well as abroad in the World . . . [has] made me think, that I could not answer it unto God, if I neglected it. . . .

25 *d. VI m.* Friday. It is a very critical Time with me, a Time of unspeakable Trouble and Anguish. My dear *Sammy*, has this Week had a dangerous and threatening Fever come upon him, which is beyond what the *Inoculation* for the *Small-Pox* has hitherto brought upon my Subjects of it. In this Distress, I have cried unto the Lord; and He has answered with a Measure of Restraint upon the Fever. The Eruption proceeds, and he proves pretty full, and has not the best sort, and some Degree of his Fever holds him. His Condition is very hazardous. . . .

[September] 5. *Sammy* recovering Strength, I must now earnestly putt him on considering, what he shall render to the Lord! Use exquisite Methods that he may come Gold out of the Fire. . . .

[November] 19. Certainly it becomes me and concerns me, to do something very considerable, in a way of Gratitude unto GOD my SAVIOUR, for the astonishing Deliverance, which He did the last Week bestow upon me, and upon what belong'd unto me.

Cotton Mather
Diary, 1721

Bad roads made horseback the one dependable mode of travel in the colonies.

In the fall of 1704 a Boston schoolmistress named Sarah Kemble Knight set out for New York through land inhabited by "the most salvage of all the salvages." This excerpt indicates why her frank account of the perils of the trip—including the food to be had at inns along the way—has survived to become a classic of colonial literature.

Tuesday, October the third,

about 8 in the morning, I with the Post proceeded forward . . . And about two, afternoon, Arrived at the Post's second stage, where the western Post mett him and exchanged Letters. Here, having called for something to eat, the woman bro't in a Twisted thing like a cable, but something lighter; and laying it on the bord, tugg'd for life to bring it into a capacity to spread; which having with great pains accomplished, she serv'd in a dish of Pork and Cabage, I suppose the remains of Dinner. The sause was of a deep Purple, which I tho't was boil'd in her dye Kettle; the bread was Indian, and every thing on the Table service Agreeable to these. I, being hungry, gott a little down; but my stomach was soon cloy'd, and what cabbage I swallowed serv'd me for a Cudd the whole day after.

Having here discharged the Ordnary for self and Guide (as I understood was the custom,) About Three, afternoon, went on with my Third Guide, who Rode very hard; and having crossed Providence Ferry, we come to a River which they Generally Ride thro'. But I dare not venture; so the Post got a Ladd and Cannoo to carry me to tother side, and hee rid thro' and Led my hors. The Cannoo was very small and shallow, so that when we were in she seem'd redy to take in water, which greatly terrified mee, and caused me to be very circumspect, sitting with my hands fast on each side, my eyes stedy, not daring so much as to lodg my tongue a hair's breadth more on one side of my mouth then tother, nor so much as think on Lott's wife, for a wry thought would have oversett our wherey: But was soon put out of this pain, by feeling the Cannoo on shore, which I as soon almost saluted with my feet; and Rewarding my sculler, again mounted and made the best of our way forwards. The rode here was very even and the day pleasant, it being now near Sunsett. But the Post told mee we had neer 14 miles to Ride to the next Stage, (where we were to lodg.) I askt him of the rest of the Rode, foreseeing wee must travail in the night. Hee told mee there was a bad River we were to Ride thro', which was so very firce a hors could sometimes hardly stem it. . . .

Now was the Glorious Luminary with his swift Coursers arrived at his Stage, leaving poor me wth the rest of this part of the lower world in darkness, with which *wee* were soon Surrounded. The only Glimering we now had was from the spangled Skies, Whose Imperfect Reflections rendered every Object formidable. Each lifeless Trunk, with its shatter'd Limbs, appear'd an Armed Enymie; and every little stump like a Ravenous devourer. Nor could I so much as discern my Guide, when at any distance, which added to the terror.

Thus, absolutely lost in Thought, and dying with the very thoughts of drowning, I come up with the Post, who I did not see till even with his Hors: he told mee he stopt for mee; and wee Rode on Very deliberatly a few paces, when we entred a Thickett of Trees and Shrubbs, and I perceived by the Hors's going, we were on the descent of a Hill, which, as wee come neerer the bottom, 'twas totaly dark with the Trees that surrounded it. But I knew by the Going of the Hors wee had entred the water, which my Guide told mee was the hazzardos River he had told me of; and hee, Riding up close to my Side, Bid me not fear—we should be over Imediatly. I now ralyed all the Courage I was mistriss of, Knowing that I must either Venture my fate of drowning, or be left like the Children in the wood. So, as the Post bid me, I gave Reins to my Nagg; and sitting as Stedy as Just before in the Cannoo, in a few minutes got safe to the other side, which hee told mee was the Narragansett country. . . .

Sarah Kemble Knight
Journal, 1704

*T*he diary of William Byrd of Westover paints an intimate portrait of life on a great Virginia plantation. In these excerpts Byrd remarks on the birth of a son, the "unusual" death of several of his slaves, and the servant problem in Williamsburg.

[September 6, 1709] About one o'clock this morning my wife was happily delivered of a son, thanks be to God Almighty. I was awake in a blink and rose and my cousin Harrison met me on the stairs and told me it was a boy. We drank some French wine and went to bed again and rose at 7 o'clock. I read a chapter in Hebrew and then drank chocolate with the women for breakfast. I returned God humble thanks for so great a blessing and recommended my young son to His divine protection. My cousin Harrison and Mrs. Hamlin went away about 9 o'clock and I made my [satisfaction] to them for that kindness. I sent Peter away who brought me a summons to the Council. I read some geometry. The Doctor brought me two letters from England from Captain Stith. I ate roast mutton for dinner. In the afternoon I wrote a letter to England and took a walk about the plantation. I said my prayers and had good health and good thoughts, thanks be to God Almighty. . . .

*Detail from a certificate
engraved by Paul Revere*

William Byrd's coat of arms

[December 31, 1710] . . . I dreamed that I saw a flaming sword in the sky and called some company to see it but before they could come it was disappeared, and about a week after my wife and I were walking and we discovered in the clouds a shining cloud exactly in the shape of a dart and seemed to be over my plantation but it soon disappeared likewise. Both these appearances seemed to foretell some misfortune to me which afterwards came to pass in the death of several of my negroes after a very unusual manner. My wife about two months since dreamed she saw an angel in the shape of a big woman who told her the time was altered and the seasons were changed and that several calamities would follow that confusion. God avert his judgment from this poor country. . . .

[February 7, 1711] I rose at 8 o'clock and found my cold continued. I said my prayers and ate boiled milk for breakfast. I went to see Mr. Clayton who lay sick of the gout. About 11 o'clock my wife and I went to wait on the Governor [Spotswood] in the President's coach. We went there to take our leave but were forced to stay all day. The Governor had made a bargain with his servants that if they would forbear to drink upon the Queen's birthday, they might be drunk this day. They observed their contract and did their business very well and got very drunk today, in such a manner that Mrs. Russell's maid was forced to lay the cloth, but the cook in that condition made a shift to send in a pretty little dinner. I ate some mutton cutlets. In the afternoon I persuaded my wife to stay all night in town and so it was resolved to spend the evening in cards. My cold was very bad and I lost my money. About 10 o'clock the Governor's coach carried us home to our lodgings where my wife was out of humor and I out of order. I said a short prayer and had good thoughts and good humor, thank God Almighty. . . .

Secret Diary of William Byrd of Westover, 1709–12

The New England town meeting gave free men a chance to vote on local problems. In 1721, in Providence, they passed legislation on stray geese and grey squirrels.

Att. a Towns Quarter meeteing held att Providence this 27th day of January anno Dom: 1720/21 . . .

It is voated and ordered that / from and after the first day of aprill next / Noo Geese shall be Lett goe upon the Common or in the highways nor in the water with in this Township of Providence or with in the Jurisdiction there of nor upon any other persons Land. Except those that one the Geese: on the pennilty of the forfiture of all such Geese that are so found—Past:

It is voated and ordered that Herndens Lane and the highway that Leads from thence to pautuckett may be fenced for the space of five years from hence next Comeing provided there be sufficiant Gates sett up and maintained in sd Lane and highway that may be Conveniant for both horse men and Cartes to pass through as well as foot men dureing all the said term . . .

It is also voated and ordered that Each free holder with in this Township of Providence shall from and after this day have two pence [per] head for every head of a Gray Squirrill that shall be by them brought before the Towns Treasuror: and to be payed out of the Townes Treasurrey: and this order to Continue dureing the Towns pleasure

And the s^d Treasuror shall be Carefull to accept of no squirrils heads but such as are killed within this Town ship

The meeteing is dissolved . . .

Town Meeting in Rhode Island, 1721

*D*espite all their problems, the colonists found ample time for sports and other amusements. These accounts relate three favorite pastimes—hunting, courting, and the pleasures connected with drinking.

They have another sort of Hunting, which is very diverting, and that they call Vermine Hunting; It is perform'd a Foot, with small Dogs in the Night, by the Light of the Moon or Stars. Thus in Summer-time they find abundance of Raccoons, Opossums, and Foxes in the Corn-Fields, and about their Plantations: but at other times, they must go into the Woods for them. The Method is to go out with three or four Dogs, and as soon as they come to the place, they bid the Dogs seek out, and all the Company follow immediately. Where-ever a Dog barks, you may depend upon finding the Game; and this Alarm, draws both Men and Dogs that way. If this Sport be in the Woods, the Game by that time you come near it, is perhaps mounted to the top of an high Tree, and then they detach a nimble Fellow up after it, who must have a scuffle with the Beast, before he can throw it down to the Dogs; and then the Sport increases, to see the Vermine encounter those little Currs. . . .

Robert Beverley
The History and Present State of Virginia, 1705

Sign from a tavern at the Rocky Hill, Connecticut, ferry landing

On Saturday last, a certain Gentleman, belonging to his Majesty's Ship the Aldborough, met a jolly Widow at a publick House In this Town, where after a Full Bowl or two, and a little Courtship in Form, they came to a Resolution to decide the Matter by a Game of All-Fours: Their Bodies and all their worldly Goods for Life, were the Stakes on each Side. Fortune favour'd the Fair, and she insisting on the Wager, nothing remained but for the Parson to tye the sacred Knot, which was accordingly done that very Afternoon.

South Carolina Gazette, January 15, 1732

. . . A very handsome Collation [was] spread on three Tables, in three different rooms, consisting of near 100 Dishes, after the most delicate Taste. There was also provided a great Variety of the choicest and best Liquors, in which the Healths of the King, the Prince and Princess of Wales, the Duke, and the rest of the Royal Family, the Governor, Success to His Majesty's Arms, Prosperity to this Colony, and many other Loyal Healths were cheerfully drank, and a Round of Cannon, which were reserv'd to the Capitol for this Purpose, was discharg'd at each Health, to the Number of 18 or 20 Rounds, which lasted 'til near 2 o'Clock. The whole Affair was conducted with great Decency and good Order, and an unaffected Cheerfulness appeared in the Countenances of the Company. All the Houses in the City were illuminated, and a very large Bonfire was made in the Market-Place, 3 Hogsheads of Punch given to the Populace; and the whole concluded with the greatest Demonstrations of Joy and Loyalty.

Virginia Gazette, July 18, 1746

As the colonies prospered and accumulated real wealth in the form of ships, farm surpluses, and other commodities, the need for specie increased, but the supply of precious metals for money failed to keep pace with demand. In this excerpt John Colman, a Boston merchant, calls attention to the shortage of coin and urges the governor of Massachusetts to issue paper money in the form of bills of credit.

Sir, Since you seem so much concerned about the Distresses of the Land, and want to know how *Boston* fares in this Day of Common Calamity; I could do no less than gratifie you, by giving you my Tho'ts, though I know the Theam will be as unpleasant to you to Read, as it is to me to Write. Truly Sir, This which was within these Ten years, one of the most Flourishing Towns in *America*, in the Opinion of all Strangers who came among us, will in less than half so many more years be the most *miserable Town therein*.

The Medium of Exchange, the only thing which gives life to Business, Employs the Poor, Feeds the Hungry, and Cloaths the Naked, is so Exhausted; that in a little time we shall not have wherewith to Buy our Daily Bread, much less to pay our Debts or Taxes. How happy are you in the Countrey, who have your Milk and Honey of your own, while we depend on the ready Penny from day to day; and there are so few Bills Circulating (for Silver there is not a Penny passing) that People are distressed to a very great degree, to get Bills to procure the Necessaries of Life; and that not the Poor only, but good substantial House-keepers, who have good real Estates in the Place. . . .

It is the Opinion of many, that within these Twenty Years, near a Million of Gold or Silver hath been exported hence, & I believe they are not much out in their Computation, yet I don't Remember in the best of Times I ever heard any complain that we abounded with Money, & now we are near double in Number and our Trade greatly Increased, and consequently it calls for a proportionable Cash to manage it. . . .

When People Complain and say there must be more Bills emitted on one foot or other; The cry is No? No more Bills, Silver will never come in while we have any Bills, when they are all in we shal have Silver; but I observe, the Gentlemen who talk at this Rate are only Usurers, and Men who Live on their Salaries, Officers of the Courts and Lawyers, who never Trade, and therefore we are sure no Silver nor any thing else will come in through their means; would these few Gentlemen (for there are not many of them) call in their Bonds and enter on Trade and cast their Bread upon the Waters with their Neighbours to employ the Poor, what fine Voyages they may Project to bring in Gold and Silver I know not, but I confess it is past my shallow capacity to Project any such. I believe Men never Traded with greater uncertainties then at this Day, no Man knows where to make an Adventure to see a new *Penny* for an old one, is the common Cry of the best Merchants in the Place.

. . . good Honest, Industrius, Modest People, are driven to such streights, as to Sell their Pewter and Brass out of their Houses, which is scarce worse for wearing, to Brasiers, at the price of Old Pewter and Brass to buy them food. . . .

It is a dark Day upon us, I pray GOD to Guide and Lead his Excellency [Samuel Shute] and his Council, and others concerned in the Government, into some Measures for the Relief of the People, that when ever his Excellency is called from us, he may (as I am perswaded is his desire) leave us in better ci[r]cumstances then he found us, which will endear his Memory to us, when he is gone from us.

John Colman
The Distressed State of the Town of Boston, &c., Considered, 1720

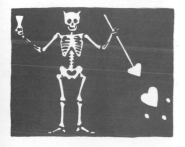

Famous pirate flags, from top:
Captain England, Bartholomew
Roberts, Thomas Tew, Black-
beard, Long Ben, Captain Wynne

The first part of the 18th century saw an increase in pirate activity along the American coast from Canada to South Carolina. The first two accounts below concern the notorious Edward Teach, or "Blackbeard." The third relates pirate Edward Low's capture of a fishing shallop in Nova Scotian waters.

1718. Rum all out. Our Company somewhat sober—A damn'd Confusion amongst us! Rogues a plotting—great Talk of Separation—so I look'd sharp for a Prize.

(Later) Took one with a great deal of Liquor on Board, so kept the Company hot, damned hot, then all things went well again.

Journal of Edward Teach, 1718

. . . our Heroe, Captain Thatch, assumed the Cognomen of *Black-beard*, from that large quantity of Hair, which like a frightful Meteor, covered his whole Face, and frightn'd *America*, more than any Comet that has appear'd there a long Time.

This Beard was black, which he suffered to grow of an extravagant Length; as to Breadth, it came up to his Eyes; he was accustomed to twist it with Ribbons, in small Tails, after the Manner of our Ramellies Wigs, and turn them about his Ears: In Time of Action, he wore a Sling over his Shoulders, with three brace of Pistols, hanging in Holsters like Bandoliers; he wore a Fur-Cap, and stuck a lighted Match on each side, under it, which appearing on each side his Face, his Eyes naturally looking Fierce and Wild, made him altogether such a Figure, that Imagination cannot form an Idea of a Fury, from Hell, to look more frightful.

Captain Charles Johnson
A Generall History of the Robberies and Murders of the most notorious Pyrates, 1724

Upon Friday, June 15th, 1722, After I had been out for some time in the Schooner Milton, upon the Fishing grounds, off Cape Sable Shoar, among others, I came to Sail in Company with Nicholas Merritt, in a Shallop, and stood in for Port-Rossaway, designing to Harbour there, till the Sabbath was over; where we Arrived about Four of the Clock in the Afternoon. When we came into the Harbour, where several of our Fishing Vessels had arrived before us, we spy'd among them a Brigantine, which we supposed to have been an Inward bound Vessel, from the West Indies, and had no apprehensions of any Danger from her; but by that time we had been at Anchor two or three Hours, a Boat from the Brigantine, with Four hands, came along side of us, and the Men Jumpt in upon our Deck, without our suspecting any thing but that they were Friends, come on board to visit, or inquire what News; till they drew their Cutlasses and Pistols from under their Clothes, and Cock'd the one and Brandish'd the other, and began to Curse & Swear at us, and demanded a Surrender of our Selves and Vessel to them. It was too late for us to rectify our Mistake, and . . . being in no Capacity to make any Resistance, were necessitated to submit our selves to their will. . . .

Low presently sent for me Aft, and according to the Pirates usual Custom, and in their proper Dialect, asked me, If I would sign their Articles, and go along with them. I told him, No; I could by no means consent to go with them, I should be glad if he would give me my Liberty, and put me on board any Vessel, or set me on shoar there. For indeed my dislike of their Company and Actions, my concern for my Parents, and my fears of being found in such bad Company, made me dread the thoughts of being carried away by them; so that I had not the least Inclination to continue with them.

Upon my utter Refusal to joyn and go . . . I was thrust down into the Hold. . . .

After this I was brought upon Deck again, and Low came up to me, with His Pistol Cock'd, and clap'd it to my Head, and said to me, You D—g you! if you will not Sign our Articles, and go along with me, I'll shoot you thro' the Head, and uttered his Threats with his utmost Fierceness, and with the usual Flashes of Swearing and Cursing. I told him, That I was in his hands, and he might do with me what he pleased, but I could not be willing to go with him: and then I earnestly beg'd of him, with many Tears, and used all the Arguments I could think of to perswade him, not to carry me away; but he was deaf to my Cryes . . . and there was no help for it, go with them I must, and as I understood, they set mine and my Townsmens Names down in their Book, tho' against our Consent. And I desire to mention it with due Acknowledgments to GOD, who withheld me, that neither their promises, nor their threatenings, nor blows could move me to a willingness to Joyn with them in their pernicious ways. . . .

John Barnard
Ashton's Memorial, 1725

*H*ugh Jones, *an Englishman who taught briefly at William and Mary, found Virginia to be the Crown's "most plentiful and flourishing" colony. Here he reports on the growing sophistication of the Virginians and reveals that the old dream of finding precious metals in the New World had not yet entirely faded.*

The *Habits*, *Life*, *Customs*, *Computations*, &c. of the *Virginians* are much the same as about *London*, which they esteem their *Home*; and for the most Part have contemptible Notions of *England*, and wrong Sentiments of *Bristol*, and the other *Out-Ports*, which they entertain from seeing and hearing the common Dealers, Sailors, and Servants that come from those Towns, and the Country Places in *England* and *Scotland*, whose Language and Manners are strange to them; for the *Planters*, and even the *Native* Negroes generally talk good *English* without *Idiom* or *Tone*, and can discourse handsomly upon *most* common Subjects; and conversing with Persons belonging to Trade and Navigation from *London*, for the most Part they are much civilized, and wear the best of Cloaths according to their Station; nay, sometimes too good for their Circumstances, being for the Generality comely handsom Persons, of good Features and fine Complexions (if they take Care) of good Manners and Address. The Climate makes them bright, and of excellent Sense, and sharp in Trade. . . .

As for Education several are sent to *England* for it; though the *Virginians* being naturally of good Parts, (as I have already hinted) neither require nor admire as much Learning, as we do in *Britain*. . . .

Moses's Words of Exhortation to the *Israelites* for Obedience to God's Laws, *Deut.* viii. 6, 7, 8, 9, may be applied to the *Virginians*; and particularly when he saith that God had brought them into a Land whose Stones are Iron; and for what we know the following Words may also be applied to them, when he saith out of the Hills of that Land might be digged *Brass*, for which there is no small Prospect and Expectation; and in all Probability there may be found the nobler Metals of *Gold* and *Silver*, if we did but search for them in the bowels of the earth, if we would but be at the expence and trouble to seek for them.

Hugh Jones
The Present State of Virginia, 1724

The College of William and Mary, about 1740

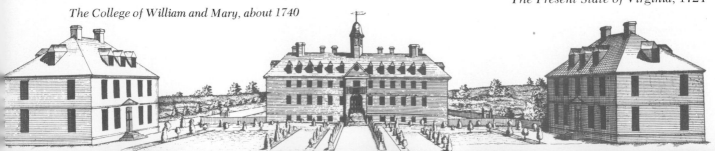

When these excerpts appeared in his journal, William Black was secretary of a Virginia commission that met with commissioners from Maryland and Pennsylvania to adjust certain land claims west of the Alleghenies. Here he takes a critical view of the Maryland assembly and records his approbation of the Philadelphia market place.

Woodcut from The Royal Primer, *published in Boston in 1770*

[Annapolis, *Saturday*, May 19th] About 4 in the afternoon, the Company . . . went to the Stadt-house, where the Assembly of that Province was then Sitting, and in a Debate on a Division of a County; but Order and Decorum, which Justly Regulated is always a great Addition to the Augustness, as well as Honour and Credit, of any Public Body, was not to be Observed in this House; Nothing but a Confus'd Multitude, and the Greater part of the meaner Sort, Such as make Patriotism their Plea, but Preferment their Design, and that not for the Honour but the Profit; nor is it to be so much Surprizing, as it ought to be Regreted of (to see a Country managed, and the Legislature in the Power of a party, the greater part of which having no more Regard to Law or Justice, but so far as it is productive of Good to themselves, most of them preferring a Private Advantage to a public Good) when the Method is Considered, which many of the Members of Assemblies take to make themselves popular, which puts it in the Power of Every Pretender that Enjoys Estate Enough to Enable him to make a few Entertainments or Barbecues, to be sent a Representative for his Country, without any other Motive on his Side, than what he can make it turn to his own Advantage, a little Self Interest and a Great deal of Ambition; while the true Patriot, a Lover of his Country, and a Real Honest man, is Rejected. . . .

[Philadelphia, June] The Sun had run his course . . . for the space of two hours, before the Leaden Scepter was removed from my Eye Lids, at last about a half an hour past 6, I had those Instruments of Sight and Doors of the Mind laid open, and Jump'd from my Bed in some haste, designing before that time to have been at the Market Place; the days of Market are Tuesday and Friday, when you may be Supply'd with every Necessary for the Support of Life thro'ut the whole year, both Extraordinary Good and reasonably Cheap, it is allow'd by Foreigners to be the best of its bigness in the known World, and undoubtedly the largest in America; I got to this place by 7; and had no small Satisfaction in seeing the pretty Creatures, the young Ladies, traversing the place from Stall to Stall where they cou'd make the best Market, some with their Maid behind them with a Basket to carry home the Purchase, Others that were designed to buy but trifles, as a little fresh Butter, a Dish of Green Peas, or the like, had Good Nature and Humility enough to be their own Porters; I have so much Regard for the fair Sex that I Imagin'd . . . some Charm in touching even the hem of their Garments; after I had made my Market, which was One penny worth of Whey and a Nose Gay, I Disengag'd myself from the Multitude. . . .

William Black
Journal, 1744

One class of immigrant to America could pursue liberty only by running away. These advertisements requesting information on runaway slaves in Pennsylvania are typical of many that appeared in newspapers throughout the colonies.

Run away, the 24th of last Month, from Bennet Bard, of Burlington, a Mulatto Spanish Slave, named George, aged about 24 Years about 5 Feet 10 Inches high, smooth-faced, well-set, and has his Hair lately cut off, speaks tolerable good English, born at the Havanna, says he was several Years with Don Blass, and is a good Shoemaker: Had on when he went away a corded Dimity Waistcoat, Ozenbrigs Shirt and Trowsers, no Stockings, old Shoes, and a new Hat. Whoever takes up and secures said Fellow, so that his Master may have him again, shall have Forty Shillings Reward, and reasonable Charges, paid by Bennet Bard.

The Pennsylvania Gazette, August 1, 1745

Run away from *Nicholas Bearcraft* of *Hunterdon County*, a Black Wench, named *Hecatissa* alias *Savina*, Country born, about 27 Years of Age, short Stature, gloomy down Look, often troubl'd with the Cholick, it is thought she may be gone towards Maryland. Whoever takes up and secures said Wench . . . shall have *Twenty Shillings* Reward, and reasonable Charges, paid by Nicholas Bearcraft.

The Pennsylvania Journal, June 8, 1749

Dockside activity; a decorative detail from a 1751 colonial map

*W**est Indies molasses made New England rum. Thomas Hancock, the uncle of John and a thriving Boston merchant involved in the triangular trade, here gives one of his captains considerable leeway as to the disposition of his ship and her cargo—even to the sale of the ship. But in the end he advises that "Molasses will be the best."*

Capt. Simon Gross

You having the Command of the *Charming Lydia* Brigantine and She in all Respects fitt for the Sea, My Order to you is that you take the first wind & weather for Sailing and proceed to the West Indies. You have Liberty to go to any of the English Islands, & if you think it Safe to any of the french Islands. But I advise you to proceed direct to St. Eustatia where you will hear how the Marketts Govern, & advise with Mr. Godet on your affairs, after which you will be able to form a better Judgement where will be the best place to make a voyage, & so proceed accordingly. You have Invoice & Bill of Lading Inclosed Consigned yourself, you are to procure a Load of Molasses & proceed back to Boston & if you have more cargo than Loads you, then Ship it on the best Terms you Can in Molasses or bring it in Indigo. I'd have you unload at Nantaskett if no man of War there. You are Interested One eighth in the Cargo & are to have one eighth of the neat proceeds of Returns, I doubt not of your making the best Sale of everything. . . . Make all possible Dispatch that you may be here early for the Land, See that your Casks be Good, & well Stow'd, bring me some fruit for the officers if any to be had, be prudent & saving of Expences—Should it happen that you Can get bills of Exchange on Holland or England for your Cargo at a good price & a good freight for Holland or England you may take it, advising me thereof that I may Insure, or if you have Oppertunity to Sell Vessell & Cargo for Bills on Holland or London at a price you think may answer you have my Liberty. You have Liberty also in every Respect to act as you think Shall be most for my Interests. But if you come back to this place a Load of Molasses will be the best Cargo you can bring here, write me by all Opportunitys. The Good Lord protect you & our Interests, from all Dangers & Enemies & Give you Conduct & prudence in all things to act for the Best, I wish you a Good Voyage & am your Owner.

Thomas Hancock to Captain Simon Gross, December 20, 1743

Dr. Alexander Hamilton of Annapolis suffered from a chronic illness, so in 1744 he made a tour of the northern colonies in the hope of improving his health. His Itinerarium *is one of the best travel accounts of the colonial period and, as these excerpts indicate, provides an incisive view of colonial people and places.*

[Philadelphia, Friday, June 8] I dined att a taveren with a very mixed company of different nations and religions. There were Scots, English, Dutch, Germans, and Irish; there were Roman Catholicks, Church men, Presbyterians, Quakers, Newlightmen, Methodists, Seventh day men, Moravians, Anabaptists, and one Jew. The whole company consisted of 25 planted round an oblong table in a great hall well stoked with flys. The company divided into committees in conversation; the prevailing topick was politicks and conjectures of a French war. A knott of Quakers there talked only about selling of flour and the low price it bore. The[y] touch a little upon religion, and high words arose among some of the sectaries, but their blood was not hot enough to quarrell, or, to speak in canting phraze, their zeal wanted fervency. A gentleman that sat next me proposed a number of questions concerning Maryland, understanding I had come from thence. In my replys I was reserved, pretending to know little of the matter as being a person whose business did not lye in the way of history and politicks. . . .

[Tuesday, June 12] I must make a few remarks. . . . The people in generall are inquisitive concerning strangers. If they find one comes there upon the account of trade or traffic, they are fond of dealing with him and cheating him if they can. If he comes for pleasure or curiosity, they take little or no notice of him unless he be a person of more than ordinary rank; then they know as well as others how to fawn and cringe. Some persons there were inquisitive about the state of religion in Maryland. My common reply to such questions was that I studied their constitutions more than their consciences so knew something of the first but nothing of the latter.

They have in generall a bad notion of their neighbouring province, Maryland, esteeming the people a sett of cunning sharpers; but my notion of the affair is that the Pennsylvanians are not a whit inferior to them in the science of chicane, only their method of tricking is different. A Pennsylvanian will tell a lye with a sanctified, solemn face; a Marylander, perhaps, will convey his fib in a volley of oaths; but the effect and point in view is the same tho' the manner of operating be different.

In this city one may live tollerably cheap as to the articles of eating and drinking, but European goods here are extravagantly dear. Even goods of their own manufacture such as linnen, woolen, and leather bear a high price. Their government is a kind of anarchy (or no government), there being perpetual jarrs betwixt the two parts of the legislature. But that is no strange thing, the ambition and avarice of a few men in both partys being the active springs in these dissentions and altercations, tho' a specious story about the good and interest of the country is trumpt up by both; yet I would not be so severe as to say so of all in generall.

Mr. T[homa]s, the present gov[erno]r, I believe is an upright man and has the interest of the province really att heart, having done more for the good of that obstinate generation, the Quakers, than any of his predecessours have done. Neither are they so blind as not to see it, for he shares more of their respect than any of their former governours were wont to do.

Dr. Alexander Hamilton
Itinerarium, 1744

A Quaker, by J. Grasset de St. Sauveur

Duel for Empire

In 1748 the Treaty of Aix-la-Chapelle ended the War of the Austrian Succession in Europe, but on the North American continent it brought only temporary peace. Englishmen and Frenchmen continued to try to outwit each other in the competition for lands in the West and for the profits of the Indian trade. Each side had its traditional Indian allies, and each side did its best to lure the other's away. In the mid-eighteenth century, through initiative and enterprise, English traders became vigorous competitors of the French on the frontiers across the Alleghenies—territory that the French claimed as their own. Since English colonies also claimed territory stretching across the American continent to the Pacific, no one could foresee any prospect of reconciling these conflicting interests. The two nations were on a collision course, and no treaties signed in Europe would have much influence upon French *coureurs de bois* or English traders.

Traders from both Pennsylvania and Virginia were finding their way across the mountains into the rich country beyond. Since they were eager to protect their discoveries from competitors, they did not boast of their exploits, and no one knows what Englishman first gazed upon the transmontane valleys. But English traders, hard-bitten frontiersmen like the "mountain men" who later explored the Rocky Mountain region, made their way along the creeks and rivers across the mountains to reach the Ohio and the Mississippi. Before 1750, traders from Pennsylvania had made a base as far west as Pickawillany, on the Miami River, near the present site of Piqua, Ohio. As many as fifty or more of these frontiersmen were accustomed to rendezvous there to traffic with the western Indians for beaver pelts and other furs. A famous Miami Indian chief, called "Old Briton" by the English because of his friendship for them, and "La Demoiselle" by the French, for what reason is not clear, was the dominant power at Pickawillany. The English set up a blacksmith shop where they sharpened iron tools for Old Briton's Indians; they brought in guns, powder, and lead for barter; and they maintained stores of blankets, rum, and other commodities desired by the Indians. In short, the Pennsylvania traders had a thriving market

An artist of a somewhat later date has aptly caught the mood of Braddock's army marching in full military pomp and panoply through the Pennsylvania wilderness in 1755 to defeat and death.

at Pickawillany that pleased both them and the Indians who flocked to it under the watchful eye of Old Briton.

Elsewhere in the western country, other traders were active. An important center for commerce with the Indians in the Ohio country was Logstown, on the north bank of the Ohio River, east of Beaver Creek and some twenty miles northwest of the present site of Pittsburgh. There Pennsylvanians and Virginians were accustomed to meet with the western Indians. The Pennsylvanians usually made their way into the back country by following the Susquehanna to its headwaters, while the Virginians proceeded up the Potomac and its tributaries. At Wills Creek, now Cumberland, Maryland, they had an important supply depot for their traders.

Officially Pennsylvania and Virginia were amicable and united in their efforts to counter the French and penetrate the West. Actually their traders were often hostile to each other and were not above sowing dissension among Indians who appeared to favor their competitors. Furthermore, since Virginia claimed all the land to the west of its dominions as far as the Pacific Ocean, Virginians regarded all outsiders who entered the lower Ohio Valley as trespassers. They were already infected with the virus of land speculation.

While the Virginians and Pennsylvanians were competing for trading posts in the West, the French were conniving with the Indians to circumvent their English rivals. On the basis of La Salle's discoveries, they claimed all the Ohio and Mississippi basin, in fact all the central area of the country south of the Great Lakes and west of the Alleghenies. In the summer of 1749, to reinforce their technical claim to the country, the French governor general, the Marquis de la Galissonière, ordered Captain Pierre-Joseph Céloron de Blainville (frequently called Bienville) to move down the Ohio River and to "repossess" the country. On June 15 Céloron set out from La Chine with a party variously estimated at from 156 to 246 men, counting French regulars, Canadians, and Indians, and including Lieutenant de Joncaire, a Seneca by adoption and a shrewd diplomat with the Indians.

The expedition made its way from Lake Erie, down Lake Chautauqua, and overland to the Allegheny River, whence Céloron proceeded downstream to its confluence with the Ohio and on down the latter stream. At various places he buried lead plates engraved with the date, location, and the statement that this action was "a token of renewal of possession heretofore taken of the aforesaid River Ohio, of all streams that fall into it, and all lands on both sides to the source of the aforesaid streams, as the preceding Kings of France have enjoyed, or ought to have enjoyed it, and which they have upheld by force of arms and by treaties, notably by those of Ryswick, Utrecht, and Aix-la-Chapelle."

Everywhere the French found evidence of the penetration of English traders, but they had to content themselves with warning the Englishmen they encountered. They continued to bury lead plates and to nail up tin plates claiming the country for France. On August 31, having made a long and circuitous journey along various Ohio rivers, Céloron buried his last plate at the mouth of the Miami River and headed back to Canada via Lake Erie. He had shown to the Indians and the English traders that France was determined to hold the disputed territory. He had also learned that France must act quickly or the land would be lost to invaders from the English colonies.

If the French needed any further evidence of the danger they ran of losing the West, it was provided by a significant episode at Pickawillany in the winter of 1751. George Croghan, Indian agent for Pennsylvania and a shrewd trader, came to Pickawillany with gifts from the government of Pennsylvania for the Miami Indians. Christopher Gist, an explorer and agent for the colony of Virginia, also came to invite the Indians of the Ohio region to come to Virginia to receive gifts sent by the king of England to his children in the wil-

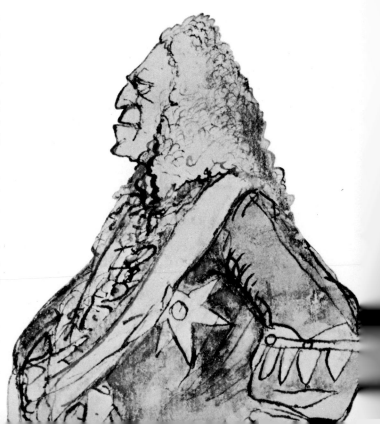

George II of Britain, here caricatured by an officer who fought at Quebec in 1759, was also elector of Hanover. Although successful in the colonial wars in America, his people disliked him for putting the interests of Hanover above those of England on the Continent of Europe.

derness. While Croghan and Gist were parleying with the Indians, four Frenchmen arrived on a similar mission. They brought some gifts and urged the Indians to trade with the French. The Indians received all these gifts and listened gravely to the speeches of the emissaries. During the council, while the speeches were being made, both English and French flags were flown. But when all had been heard, the Indians told the French to strike their colors.

What was more indicative, a delegation representing Indians in French territory on the Wabash came asking for an alliance with the English. For the time being, the English had won the day. Their secret lay in the abundance of their gifts and the strength they displayed.

The French, however, bided their time and planned the destruction of the English in the Ohio Valley. The first blow came on June 21, 1752, when a body of some two hundred and forty Chippewa and Ottawa warriors from Canada, led by two Frenchmen, swooped down on Pickawillany while most of the fighting men were off hunting. Only eight Englishmen were at the trading post. After a futile defense of the fort, the handful of defenders surrendered. Old Briton was killed, and in an orgy of exultation the victors made a great feast at which he was boiled and eaten. They cut the heart out of one of the English traders who had been wounded and boiled that too. The other Englishmen were carried off to Canada. The disaster at Pickawillany signaled the beginning of a renewed effort by the French to drive the English from the West.

In the meantime, however, a wave of land speculation was sweeping the colonies, and in Virginia particularly the fever of speculation was rising. Dozens of land companies were being organized to capitalize upon Virginia's claims to the territory across the mountains. The most famous of these was the Ohio Company, organized in 1747 by Thomas Lee and a group of associates. Unlike some of the other syndicates bent upon exploiting western land, the Ohio Company applied to the Privy Council through the Board of Trade for a grant of two hundred thousand acres on the Ohio River. This was given in 1749 with the proviso that the company should build a fort at the forks of the Ohio and settle a hundred families on the grant within the next seven years.

While the Ohio Company was attempting to stabilize its possessions by invoking the authority of the Privy Council in London, another syndicate, the Loyal Company, headed by John Robinson, obtained from the provincial government eight hundred thousand acres west of the Virginia–North Carolina border. Still other grants were made to promoters who promised to fortify and colonize territories to the west.

Few Virginians of property failed to be swept into the vortex of land speculation. All the great planters were dreaming of new estates in the West. Many of them had already taken up land in the Shenandoah Valley, which by the mid-century was attracting German and Scottish settlers from Pennsylvania and the Carolinas. Tobacco culture in the tidewater had exhausted the soil of the older farming areas, and planters were eager for fresh land for their sons and heirs. The drive for land, and the zest for speculation in a society in which gambling was common, help to explain the deep personal concern Virginians felt about the French threat to rob them of the Ohio Valley.

Governor Robert Dinwiddie of Virginia was determined to checkmate the French by diplomacy if possible or by force if necessary. Like all other prominent men of the colony, he was deeply involved in land speculations and did not propose to let the French ruin his investments. More than that, he realized that French domination of the Ohio and Mississippi river systems would mean ultimate disaster to all the English colonies, which would be forever confined to a narrow strip of the continent east of the mountains. Both a personal and an imperial destiny were at stake, and Dinwiddie, along with other colonial administrators, tried to wake London from its lethargy.

But stirring London out of its lethargy in the middle years of the reign of George II was no easy task. The North American continent was a long way from Whitehall and the clubs in St. James Street. The War of the Austrian Succession in 1740–48, the Jacobite Rebellion of 1745–46, and the pacification of the Scots had sapped the energies of politicians and left them with no enthusiasm for fresh problems. Let the judges send Scottish rebels to settle in America where they could do no harm, and let the colonists shift for themselves. A few old soldiers of the king might get lucrative appointments to colonial posts as a reward for their services, but in general, the less Whitehall heard about North America, the better the politicians liked it. They had difficulties closer at home, principally concerned with the struggle for place and preferment. Not much could be expected of men like Thomas Pelham-Holles, first Duke of Newcastle, the real head of the government, one of the most powerful politicians of the day—and one of the most ignorant. The cabinet officer charged with responsibility for the colonies was Sir Thomas Robinson, of whom a contemporary said that Newcastle had achieved the remarkable feat of finding a man for the post more incompetent than himself. It is not surprising that petitions to London from the colonies were disregarded. If the colonies were concerned about the French, they would do well to take action themselves.

This Governor Dinwiddie proposed to do. News filtered into Virginia that the French were planning to strengthen their outposts on Lake Erie and build forts in the Ohio country. In 1752 the Marquis Duquesne became governor general of Canada and submitted a plan to the ministry in Paris for garrisoning the country south of the Great Lakes. In February, 1753, Governor Dinwiddie heard reports that the French were building houses at Logstown and expressed the hope that these were only traders. The English realized that they ought to have forts in the region, but neither the Pennsylvania assembly nor the Virginia House of Burgesses would appropriate the necessary funds. Ohio Indians friendly to the English also realized their danger from the French and asked for guns and ammunition to defend themselves, which Dinwiddie promised and eventually sent. But while the English continued to talk about the need for a fort on the Ohio, the French erected and garrisoned forts: Fort Presqu'Isle on the present site of Erie, Pennsylvania; Fort Le Boeuf at the head of French Creek (the present site of Waterford, Pennsylvania); and Fort Venango, at the mouth of French Creek where it joins the Allegheny (Franklin, Pennsylvania covers the site today).

At this juncture, Dinwiddie decided to send a mission to the French in Ohio to warn them that they were trespassing on Virginia territory. To convey this message he chose a young man of twenty-one, commissioned a major for the task, named George Washington. Setting out from Williamsburg on October 31, 1753, Washington went to Fredericksburg to pick up a French interpreter, and thence to Wills Creek, where he enlisted frontiersman Christopher Gist. They recruited a small bodyguard and set forth into the wilderness to order the French out of land claimed by Virginia. It was not an imposing force for such a difficult mission, but Washington made no complaint.

Through winter woods and across icy streams, wet

with rain and powdered with snow, Washington's little party pushed on to the forks of the Allegheny and the Monongahela, a spot that Washington decided was much more suitable for a fort than the one selected by the Ohio Company a few miles down the river. In his *Journal* he gives his reasons, and his judgment was later confirmed by the French when they, too, decided that the site where the city of Pittsburgh now stands was the strategic place to fortify.

Twenty-five days after leaving Williamsburg, Washington arrived at Logstown, where he held a council with Indians presumed to be friendly to the English and informed them of his mission. While he was there, four French deserters turned up and gave him information about the disposition of French garrisons on the Mississippi. Washington also counseled with a Seneca Indian chief named Tanacharisson, called the Half-King by the English, who exercised a loose control over a miscellaneous group of Indians in the vicinity of Logstown. The Half-King, who professed an abiding friendship for the English, gave Washington a report

of his own speech to the French. He urged that both
the French and the English withdraw from the Ohio
and leave it to the Half-King's followers to maintain a
buffer between them.

As Washington reported the speech in his *Journal*,
the Half-King told the French: "Fathers, Both you and
the *English* are white, we live in a Country between;
therefore the Land belongs to neither one nor t'other:
But the Great Being above allow'd it to be a Place of
Residence for us; so Fathers, I desire you to withdraw,
as I have done our Brothers the *English*; for I will keep
you at Arms length: I lay this down as a Trial for both,
to see which will have the greatest Regard to it, and that
Side we will stand by. . . ." According to Washington,
the French commander replied sternly to this speech
that he would go down the river, even if it were blocked,
and would "tread under my Feet all that stand in Opposition, together with their Alliances; for my force is
as the Sand upon the Sea Shore."

The Indians were worried about the future, for they
did not want to be on the losing side, but for the time

being the Half-King, irritated by French arrogance,
favored the English. He promised to go with Washington on the remainder of his journey and to supply a
guard, which in the end amounted to no more than three
chiefs (including the Half-King himself) and a hunter.

By December 4 the party reached Venango, an old
Indian town and a former rendezvous of English traders
at the mouth of French Creek. To Washington's distress,
he found that French soldiers commanded by Captain
Joncaire were taking their ease in a house seized from
an English trader, John Frazier. Indeed, they made
Washington welcome, warmed their visitors and themselves with wine, and, Washington wrote, advised them
that "it was their absolute Design to take Possession of
the Ohio, and by G-- they would do it." Joncaire also
plied Washington's Indians with liquor and tried to win
them away from the English, but the Half-King remained sober enough to deliver a speech to Joncaire re-
nouncing any friendship for the invading French.

At last Washington reached Fort Le Boeuf. This was
his destination, and there he found the French commandant, Captain Le Gardeur de St. Pierre, "an elderly
Gentleman" with "much the Air of a Soldier." To him
Washington delivered Governor Dinwiddie's message.
While St. Pierre and his officers translated the governor's letter, Washington made a note of the fort's construction and armament and instructed his Indians to
count the canoes available for transport.

To Washington's verbal protests about the French
seizing English traders, St. Pierre replied that the country belonged to the French and that "no *Englishman*
had a Right to trade upon those Waters; and that he
had Orders to make every Person Prisoner that attempted
it on the *Ohio*, or the Waters of it." To Governor Dinwiddie, St. Pierre wrote that he should have sent his
protest to the governor general in Canada, but "as to
the . . . Summons you send me to retire, I do not think
myself obliged to obey it."

St. Pierre treated Washington courteously and provided him with a plentiful supply of provisions and

253

liquor for his return journey. On December 16, having already sent his horses back to Venango, Washington and his group launched a canoe and set out down the creek, which they found blocked in places with ice. Several times "we had like to have been staved against the Rocks, and many Times were obliged all Hands to get out and remain in the Water Half an Hour or more, getting over Shoals," Washington noted in his *Journal*. From Venango onward the going was even rougher. Their horses were too weak to ride or even to carry all the luggage. Washington, Gist, and the others in the party had to walk and carry part of their supplies in packs on their backs. To get across the Allegheny River, they had to chop down enough trees "with but one poor hatchet" to make a raft. The river was so choked with ice that their raft nearly floundered, and Washington was jerked into the water and almost drowned. Gist "had all his Fingers, and some of his Toes frozen."

Despite these hardships, they at length got back to Wills Creek, the outskirts of civilization, on January 7, 1754. On the day before, they had met "17 Horses loaded with Materials and Stores for a Fort at the Forks of Ohio, and the Day after some Families going out to settle." The Virginians were moving at long last to fortify the Ohio, but they were too late with too little. Washington arrived at Williamsburg on January 16 and reported the failure of his mission to the governor. He had made an arduous journey and his observations would be useful in the future, but if the English were to occupy the Ohio country and profit from its fertile lands, they would have to drive out the French by force.

This fact was now apparent to Governor Dinwiddie, who did his best to rally support among the other colonies and to induce the government in London to take action to protect His Majesty's dominions. But some of the colonies could not see why they should spend their treasure and risk their militia to secure land for Virginia land syndicates. Indeed, Dinwiddie's own legislative assembly balked at appropriating money for the defense of the Ohio. In February, 1754, however, it agreed to grant a sum of ten thousand pounds Virginia currency for the purpose. Although Pennsylvania was as deeply involved in the fate of the West as Virginia, Governor James Hamilton was unable to induce the Quaker pacifists who controlled the assembly to take action. Only North Carolina showed any alacrity in responding to Dinwiddie's request—her assembly voted money enough for three or four hundred men.

The government in London was also penurious. On June 15 the Duke of Newcastle wrote to Horace Walpole, auditor-general for the British Plantations, asking how to raise money for the defense of the colonies; six weeks earlier the Earl of Halifax had proposed the erection of a string of frontier forts from Nova Scotia to Florida, and Newcastle was concerned over the expense involved. Walpole could think of nothing better than a lottery to raise money, because the mother country was already loaded with debts "contracted for the good of all His Majesty's Dominions." He feared that "the Landed Gentlemen of this Country will be terribly alarmed with a notion that might prevayl that they are to be taxed on all occasions to defend our American Borders . . . as this Nation is at present at so great a charge in the settlement of Nova Scotia for the security of these very Colonys." The London government finally authorized the governor of New York to send to Virginia two companies of regulars stationed in his jurisdiction and ordered a company stationed in South Carolina to march to Virginia.

With only scanty supplies and an inadequate levy of men, Dinwiddie prepared for action. He appointed a surveyor and professor of mathematics at the College of William and Mary, Colonel Joshua Fry, to command the troops, with Washington, now promoted to lieutenant colonel, as second in command. Washington was already at Alexandria attempting to recruit a company. His success was less than he desired, for he described his troops, almost in Falstaff's words, as a parcel of "loose, idle Persons . . . quite destitute of House, and Home, and . . . many of them without Shoes, others want Stockings, some are without Shirts." Seventy-five men that he got together he further characterized as "self willed and ungovernable." Finally, on April 2, 1754, with a total of one hundred and twenty men formed into two companies, he set out from Alexandria for the wilderness. When he reached Wills Creek, he sent word ahead to the Indians that he was coming with an advance guard and that a large army with great guns would follow. He hoped for adequate Indian allies.

Washington's party was to provide protection for the building of an English fort at the forks where the Allegheny and Monongahela rivers join to form the Ohio, the site that Washington had selected as the best place for defense. A small detachment of some forty men under the command of William Trent was already at work there. While Washington was making his way west from

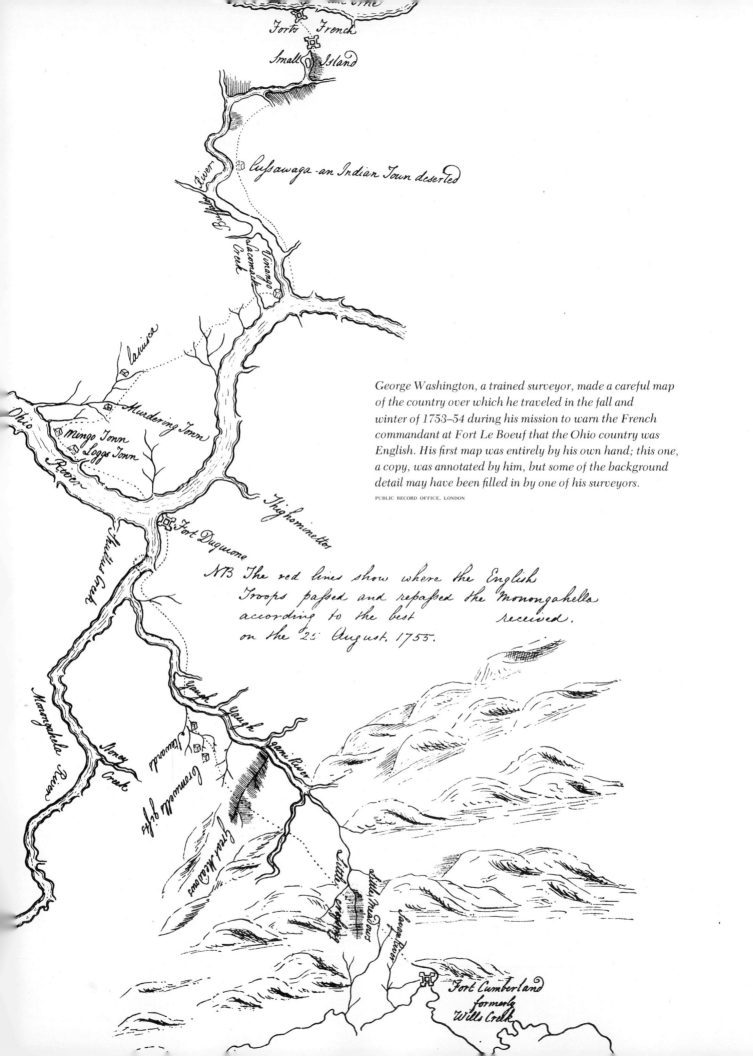

Forts French

Small Island

Cussawaga - an Indian Town deserted

George Washington, a trained surveyor, made a careful map
of the country over which he traveled in the fall and
winter of 1753–54 during his mission to warn the French
commandant at Fort Le Boeuf that the Ohio country was
English. His first map was entirely by his own hand; this one,
a copy, was annotated by him, but some of the background
detail may have been filled in by one of his surveyors.
PUBLIC RECORD OFFICE, LONDON

Caruca

Murdering Town

Mingo Town

Loggs Town

Ohio River

Highsminettos

Fort Duquesne

NB The red lines show where the English
Troops passed and repassed the Monongahela
according to the best   received.
on the 25 August. 1755.

Monongahela River

Sewickly Creek

Yough Yough

Gami River

Fort Cumberland
formerly
Wills Creek

Alexandria, Trent left the work at the forks in charge of Ensign Edward Ward and returned to Wills Creek. Ward urged his men to make haste. On April 17 he himself had just hung the gate to the stockade when his workmen were terrified to see coming down the river a great flotilla of canoes and bateaux loaded with Frenchmen and Indians, a host of a thousand, Ward thought, though actually they numbered only half that number. Forced to surrender, Ward and his men were allowed to depart with their tools and guns. Captain Pierre Claude de Contrecoeur, the officer in command, offered to buy their tools, which his men could use in completing the fort, but Ward refused. With food supplied by the French, Ward and his men made their way to Wills Creek, where he reported the bad news to Washington.

The seizure of the forks of the Ohio posed a new problem for the English. They were not strong enough to drive out the French, and yet if they remained inactive, they would lose all their Indian allies in the West. Since the Ohio Company had already built a storehouse at the mouth of Redstone Creek on the Monongahela, it was decided to fortify this place and make it a staging area for a future attack on the forks. Washington was to continue westward toward the Redstone.

He was about halfway between Wills Creek and the Redstone, at a place called Great Meadows, when he got word that a French force was nearby watching his movements. In a heavy rain on the night of May 27, Washington and about forty men set out to find the French scouting party, but it was not until the early morning of the next day that they surprised a patrol of Frenchmen in a rocky ravine. Both sides fired, and in the ensuing engagement the French lost ten men killed, including their commanding officer, Ensign Coulon de Jumonville. Twenty-one men surrendered, and one escaped to carry the news to Contrecoeur at the new fort,

named Duquesne by the French after the governor general. Washington lost one man killed and two or three wounded.

The French immediately claimed that Jumonville had been on a mission to warn the English, as Washington had warned the French a year earlier, and that he had been "assassinated" by the bloodthirsty Virginians. The French even made it appear that he was slaughtered while trying to read a communication to Washington. Although no credible evidence substantiates this view, the French employed the story for propaganda effect. England and France were nominally at peace, and France wanted to establish that the English had been the aggressors. As it turned out, Washington had fired the first shots in a new war.

The attack on Jumonville's scouting force would inevitably produce retaliation, and Washington was in a quandary as to the best method of meeting it. One thing was certain: he needed more men and supplies, and he sent a message to his commanding officer, Colonel Fry, asking for reinforcements. As it turned out, Fry had died at Wills Creek as the result of a fall from his horse. To succeed him, Governor Dinwiddie named an old friend, Colonel James Innes, and promoted Washington to full colonel. On June 9 some two hundred additional troops arrived at Great Meadows, followed three days later by a company of regulars from South Carolina under Captain James MacKay, who held his commission from the king and refused to take orders from, or even to recognize the rank of, a provincial officer. Washington wrote that MacKay's recall "would tend to the public advantage"; his regulars would not dig trenches, cut trees, nor do any of the work expected of frontier troops.

At Great Meadows, Washington's men had made a small palisaded fortification, later christened Fort Necessity, but Washington did not intend that to be his

From an 18th-century treatise on fortifications comes this detail of a trench typical of those used during the colonial wars. Basketwork woven from saplings was filled with dirt from the trench and topped with logs; the rest of the dirt dug from the trench was thrown in front of this structure. Such a work could stop almost any bullet.

main defense. He hoped to push on across the mountains and establish a base at the Redstone. With prodigious labor his men cut a road through the trees and vines across the mountains to a point now called Mount Braddock. Then, on June 28, Washington received a report that the French were advancing in strength, and after a council of war he decided to fall back, not merely to Great Meadows, but to Wills Creek. The expedition across the mountains already had exhausted Washington's troops and their horses, and the retreat took an even heavier toll. By July 1, when the troops regained Great Meadows, they were too worn and tired to go any farther. Washington, after consulting with Captain MacKay—by this time sufficiently reconciled to frontier conditions to communicate with a provincial—decided to make a stand.

The French, uncertain about the strength of the English facing them, were proceeding cautiously. Governor General Duquesne, having heard in Montreal that the English were sending five thousand troops to occupy the Ohio country, had dispatched a half brother of Jumonville, Captain Coulon de Villiers, to Fort Duquesne with orders to rally Indian allies. He also instructed Captain Contrecoeur to organize a force to march against Washington. Because De Villiers wished to avenge the death of his half brother, he received command of the expedition. Since France and England were not officially at war, Duquesne's instructions were that the expedition was to be merely one of retaliation for Jumonville's death. The English were to be chastised, even if the French had to pursue them to their settlements, which might be burned. After punishing the English and driving them from the Ohio, the French were to proclaim their desire for peace. When he left Fort Duquesne on June 28, De Villiers had under his command six hundred French soldiers and one hundred Indians. He expected to collect other Indians on the way and to receive further reinforcements of French troops.

Washington's force, reduced by desertion, amounted to approximately four hundred men, of whom at least one hundred were sick and unfit for duty. Nevertheless, he made such preparations as he could. Even MacKay's regulars, contemplating the fire of the French from the ominous woods on all sides, condescended to dig trenches. On July 3, with rifle pits dug in front of the stockade and platforms erected for six small swivel guns, Washington's men waited in the rain for the attack to begin.

That morning, during a continuous rainstorm, the French opened fire and kept up a fusillade till dusk. Both the English and the French had trouble keeping their powder dry and their guns in working order. By eight o'clock that night, the French, who were almost out of ammunition, offered to break off the fight if the English wanted to discuss a cease fire. With his powder wet, thirty men killed, seventy wounded, and no hope of rescue, Washington had no choice except surrender. He sent over a French-speaking Dutchman, Captain Jacob Van Braam, with his wounded adjutant, William Peyronie, to negotiate a capitulation. By the light of a flickering lantern, with rain dripping on the already damp paper, Van Braam and the French managed to work out articles of surrender (with an English translation), which Washington and MacKay signed. Unwittingly, Washington had permitted the French to slip into the articles of capitulation the word "assassinated" in referring to the death of Jumonville. That apparent admission of guilt was used by the French as proof of their former charges, and Washington's oversight was later criticized in Williamsburg and in London.

Washington and his men were permitted to depart with the honors of war, taking with them their belongings except artillery and munitions. They were even allowed to cache such stores as they could not carry away and return for them later with wagons. The next morning, with drums beating, the English marched out, leaving Fort Necessity to the French and the pillaging Indians, who paid no attention to the articles of capitulation. Washington, as he himself admitted, had been soundly beaten.

While Virginia was carrying on its private war with the French in an effort to save its western lands, the other colonies and the government in London were showing growing concern over the deterioration of English relations with the Indians. The great Iroquois confederation of the Six Nations, traditionally friendly to the English, showed signs of wavering. The French had sent missionaries among them and had lured away some groups. Now, with evidence of English weakness on the frontiers, many Iroquois might defect to France.

In New York William Johnson, who had settled on the Mohawk River and acquired vast holdings of land among the Mohawks, was a potent influence for the English cause. At Johnson's stone house on the Mohawk—"Fort Johnson" as it was called—Indians came and went in a feverish round of diplomacy as conditions became more acute in the 1750's. Johnson's own popularity with the Iroquois was secure. He himself was a sachem of the Mohawks; his wife was a niece of Chief Hendrick, a powerful Mohawk leader, and he had several Indian concubines, a situation that helped to cement his relations with the clan. His widespread trading ventures were carried on with scrupulous fairness, in contrast with those of other traders, and he was held in high respect by the Mohawks and other Iroquoian tribes.

Nevertheless, Johnson could not keep the Iroquois from listening to the French agents, and in 1753 there was grave danger that the powerful Six Nations might defect to France. If these Indians became the allies of France, not only would the West be lost, but all of New York and New England would be endangered. Indeed, the whole British colonial establishment from Maine to Georgia would be threatened with extinction.

Conditions had come to this parlous state for a number of reasons. The most deep-seated cause was the rivalry between the separate English colonies in dealing with the Indians and an inability to agree on a common Indian policy that made sense. The French, on the other hand, had a consistent policy that they pursued with remarkable persistence regardless of changes in administrations at Quebec. Moreover, they were helped by the missionary priests who also served as political agents. Finally, since French trade was carried on by a government-controlled monopoly, commercial activities and prices were regularized for all outposts. It was quite otherwise with the English. Individual English traders, responsible to no one and coming from various political jurisdictions that could enforce no effective laws in the frontier zone, were free to drive hard bargains and cheat the Indians when they could.

The threat of losing the support of the Iroquois confederation was so acute in 1753 that the Board of Trade in London wrote an urgent letter to the governor of New York instructing him to call a council of Iroquois leaders and of representatives from the colonies of New York, New Jersey, Massachusetts, New Hampshire, Pennsylvania, Maryland, and Virginia. Commissioners from the various colonies should work out a plan for "one general treaty" with the Six Nations instead of the separate treaties previously negotiated. Acting on these instructions, a congress was called at Albany for June 14, 1754. From this congress, designed to settle problems with the Indians, grew the famous Albany Plan of Union.

New Jersey refused to take part in the conference on the ground that she had never been a party to an Iro-

This cartouche with its scene of Anglo-Indian amity embellished certificates that Sir William Johnson gave to Indians of proved loyalty.

quoian treaty and the business did not therefore concern New Jersey. Since Governor Dinwiddie had called a meeting of his own with the Ohio Indians at Winchester, Virginia also was not represented at Albany. But the other colonies mentioned by the Board of Trade, plus Connecticut and Rhode Island, sent commissioners who met with spokesmen for the Six Nations.

The Indians made long speeches in which they told of their grievances. The English were taking over their land and were debauching their warriors with rum. Moreover, Chief Hendrick declared, "You have . . . thrown us behind your back, and disregarded us, whereas the French are a subtle and vigilant people, ever using their utmost endeavours to seduce and bring our people over to them." For several days the debate went on, the Indians stressing their grievances and the English defending their actions. During the conference some of the commissioners took advantage of the opportunity to purchase land from the Indians on terms that pleased the sellers. By July 9 the commissioners and the Indians had come to reasonably satisfactory agreements, including restrictions on the sale of rum, and the Iroquois departed with thirty wagons, lent by the governor of New York, to carry home presents from the colonial governments and from the king of England himself.

A by-product of the Albany Congress was a proposal that all the colonies should unite for concerted action against common enemies. Since New England had previously had some experience with efforts at union, the commissioners from Massachusetts came empowered to enter "into articles of union or confederation" with the other colonial governments. Other representatives also came with ideas about a union. Benjamin Franklin, one of the commissioners from Pennsylvania, had published in his *Pennsylvania Gazette* more than a month before the Albany Congress an article urging union. His essay was illustrated with the famous cartoon of a snake, cut in parts, with the motto, "Join or Die."

After much discussion the commissioners in Albany drew up for submission to the several colonies a "Plan of Union," which, if approved by the provincial governments, would be established by an act of Parliament. The plan provided for a governor general to be appointed by the king and paid by the English government. The governing body would be a grand council composed of members chosen for a term of three years by the legislative assemblies of the provincial governments. At the start, apportionment would be as follows: Massachusetts, seven; Virginia, seven; Pennsylvania, six; Connecticut, five; New York, Maryland, North Carolina, and South Carolina, four each; New Jersey, three; New Hampshire, two; Rhode Island, two. The two frontier provinces of Nova Scotia and Georgia would not at first be represented. After the first three years, representation would depend in some measure upon the amount paid into the union's treasury by each provincial government. Annual meetings of the grand council would be required, but the governor general could call emergency meetings with the consent of seven members.

The governor general and the grand council would be empowered to negotiate all treaties with the Indians, to purchase and administer all lands not within the boundaries of any provincial government, to defend the British possessions in America by erecting forts, raising armies, building ships, and levying taxes for these purposes. Under the proposed regulations, the Privy Council had to be informed of these actions, and it might disapprove within three years.

But the provincial governments were too concerned with their own affairs, and too jealous of their own prerogatives, even in the face of danger, to approve a plan that curtailed their powers. Without exception, they either disapproved of the Albany Plan of Union or ignored it. Nor did the home government find much good in it. The Board of Trade countered with a tentative plan of its own, but the Privy Council disallowed it.

If the colonies could not agree upon a confederation, at least they knew that Franklin's cartoon, "Join or Die," had in it something of truth, and as the French

threat to their security became more apparent in 1755, their governors showed a greater inclination to consult about defense—and offense. Governor William Shirley of Massachusetts, who had distinguished himself in 1745 in the War of Jenkins's Ear by engineering the capture of Louisbourg, was deeply concerned about the plans of the French to encircle the colonies. Although France and England were still nominally at peace, Shirley busied himself early in 1755 in an attempt to arouse the heads of other colonies to the realities of the impending conflict.

The government in London, finally aware that it must act in defense of the colonies, ordered two regiments of regular troops, adequately equipped with artillery and supplies, to proceed to Virginia. The commanding officer chosen was Major General Edward Braddock, an orthodox, unimaginative, stern disciplinarian, just the sort of officer that Whitehall believed would be able to whip untrained and unruly provincial militia into shape. Braddock arrived at Williamsburg on February 23, 1755, and late in March, after frequent conferences with Governor Dinwiddie, he proceeded to Alexandria, where his troops disembarked. There Braddock called a conference of colonial governors on April 14 to make plans for a broad attack on the French. Governor Shirley of Massachusetts proposed to the conference that he and Governor Charles Lawrence of Nova Scotia should attack the enemy at Fort Beauséjour at the tip of the Bay of Fundy. With help from all the New England colonies, Shirley also hoped to take Crown Point on Lake Champlain. With these two French bases secured, Shirley believed that the northern colonies might be safe from invasion. The next objective after Beauséjour and Crown Point recommended by Shirley was Niagara, the capture of which would cut off the French from their bases in Ohio.

Braddock's instructions called for him to proceed against Fort Duquesne. After driving the French from the forks of the Ohio, he was to fortify the site so that any French attempt to reoccupy the region would fail. His instructions also called for him to engage both northern and southern Indians in his operations against the French if he deemed it expedient. Governor James Glen of South Carolina had great influence with the Cherokees and other Indians in the South, but because Dinwiddie disliked Glen, he was not invited to the conference at Alexandria. Despite this slight, Glen persuaded the South Carolina assembly to appropriate six thousand pounds for the campaign. Braddock's aide-de-camp commented that this "was the only money raised by the provinces which ever passed through the General's hands." Braddock induced Shirley to take a commission as a colonel and to proceed against Niagara. To William Johnson he assigned the task of taking Crown Point. The reduction of Acadia to English authority was entrusted to Lieutenant Colonel Robert Monckton. Because all this action against the French was to take place during a period of nominal peace, the English were to claim that they were merely driving marauders off land that rightfully belonged to the king of England.

Braddock's regulars consisted of two regiments, one commanded by Sir Peter Halkett and the other by Colonel Thomas Dunbar. He had sent ahead of him Lieutenant Colonel Sir John St. Clair, quartermaster general, who was to arrange for supplies. The regiments were not up to full strength, but Braddock intended to recruit provincials to fill out their ranks. He also hoped to obtain grants from the provincial governments to pay the cost of maintaining his troops, but he had secret instructions authorizing him to proceed at the expense of the British government if the colonial governments proved recalcitrant, as they did. The Indian allies that Braddock had been assured would come to his aid never showed up, and in the end he had only eight Indians to serve as scouts. But by June 7 about twenty-five hundred men were ready to march from Wills Creek, now christened Fort Cumberland in honor of the Duke of Cumberland. Their progress was slow, sometimes only two miles per day, for the road in places had to be hewed out of the wilderness, and Braddock insisted upon dragging along heavy artillery with which he planned to pulverize Fort Duquesne.

Young George Washington accompanied Braddock as a civilian aide-de-camp. The British general had offered him a captaincy, but since Washington had recently resigned as a lieutenant colonel of the Virginia militia, he thought it beneath his dignity to accept a lower rank.

The march toward Fort Duquesne was slow and frustrating. Braddock and St. Clair were now both aware that the route chosen from Fort Cumberland by way of Great Meadows was the wrong approach and that they ought to have set out from Philadelphia across Pennsylvania. Furthermore, supplies, horses, and wagons promised by Virginia and Maryland had failed to arrive in sufficient quantity. Beef sent by Maryland contractors

spoiled before it reached camp and had to be buried. Contractors proved to be rogues and thieves. Because of improper food, men got sick and were hardly able to march. Washington himself was stricken with dysentery. The road was so rough that wagons shook to pieces and horses died in their traces from straining at the loads. Sailors assigned to the expedition hauled on the great guns with rope and tackle trying to get them over the mountains. After the army passed Great Meadows, Indians hiding in the woods occasionally picked off a soldier and vanished into the dark forest. The British officers were contemptuous of the provincial troops, and the provincials themselves had little respect for these arrogant martinets, whom they regarded as incompetent for the work in hand.

The army at last reached the Monongahela River and, because of the rough terrain, decided to cross to the left bank, march two miles down that side, and then cross back to the right bank near the mouth of Turtle Creek. This the army accomplished safely by the early afternoon of July 9. They were now nearing Fort Duquesne. Braddock ordered Lieutenant Colonel Thomas Gage to move forward with four hundred and fifty men to reconnoiter and lead the way to open ground where he proposed to make his last camp before attacking Fort Duquesne. A hill on the right commanded the route, but Gage failed to secure it. The narrow twelve-foot road passed between wooded ravines. Gage's scouts also failed to secure the wooded areas on his flanks.

In the meantime, a French officer, Captain Daniel Liénard de Beaujeu, was advancing to meet Gage with a troop of regulars, French provincials, and Indians. When Gage's advance scouts observed the attacking force coming down the trail, they fell back, and British grenadiers in the vanguard opened fire with their muskets and two six-pounders. Beaujeu was instantly killed and some of his provincials fled, but Captain Jean Dumas, the second-in-command, ordered his troops to divide and take to the woods on each side of the British and to occupy the commanding hill. From these vantage points they poured fire into Gage's troops. If Gage had pushed forward, he could have penetrated the thin line of the enemy and gained open ground. Instead, he ordered a retreat along the open road while the hidden enemy poured their fire into the milling redcoats.

At this juncture, Braddock ordered a force of eight hundred men under Lieutenant Colonel Ralph Burton to reinforce Gage. Burton's force met Gage's men, now

In this detail from a contemporary view explaining the 1755 Battle of Lake George (each element is tagged with a number), blue-coated French, flanked by Indian allies, attack colonials in red, behind felled trees and supported by artillery. The French were repulsed, their commander was taken, and that evening another American force routed them.

fleeing in panic, and blocked their further retreat. Worse still, the baggage train began to move up the narrow road, adding to the general confusion. Officers were unable to organize their men for an attack, and the invisible enemy from the woods on their flanks and from the hilltop continued to pour a devastating fire into the closely packed troops. As the firing continued, Braddock himself rode forward and tried to rally the troops. Five horses were shot from under him before he himself was finally wounded so desperately that he had to be carried from the field. After nearly three hours the British troops fled in panic to the rear. Of 1,373 privates and noncommissioned officers in the regular troops, all but 459 had been killed or wounded. Of 86 officers, all except 23 were killed or wounded.

Losses among the provincial forces were also heavy. Washington later commented: "Our poor Virginians behaved like men, and died like soldiers; for I believe that out of three companies that were there that day, scarce thirty were left alive." He attributed much of the slaughter to the panic of the regular troops: "In short the dastardly behavior of the English soldiers exposed all those who were inclined to do their duty to almost certain death. It is imagined (I believe with great justice, too) that two-thirds of both killed and wounded received their shots from our own cowardly dogs of soldiers, who gathered themselves in a body, contrary to orders, ten and twelve deep, would then level, fire, and shoot down the men before them."

Controversy over the causes of the defeat soon raged —and has continued to rage ever since—but there can be little question that the incompetence and ignorance of the British officers, including Braddock, must account in a large measure for the tactical predicament that the army got itself into and the panic that followed. It was a black day for the colonial and British cause. The French were left exulting over their victory, for British fire had done them little harm.

Braddock was mortally wounded. Washington managed to procure a cart in which he conveyed the dying general for fifty miles to a base camp not far from present-day Uniontown, where Colonel Thomas Dunbar was stalled with the supply train. There the refugee soldiers rendezvoused, and there Braddock died. Washington buried him in the roadway, which was churned into mud by the wagons, so that the Indians would not find his grave and mutilate the body.

The death of Braddock left Dunbar temporarily in

261

Fort Duquesne
1755

Fort Duquesne stood on the point where the Allegheny, then called the Ohio (foreground), joins the Monongahela (flowing from top right) to form the Ohio. It looked much like this view, which is based on French plans and on various sketches and descriptions, including those of two American prisoners. The fort was square with a bastion at each corner and was

entered over a drawbridge. Two sides were built of heavy timbers; palisades alone protected the river sides, whence attack was less likely. The outer line of defense was a palisade with an earthen platform enabling riflemen to fire over the top. The fort was so cramped that two of its buildings had to be built outside the walls, and most of the garrison and their Indian allies lived in cabins and wigwams beyond the palisade. Fort Duquesne was a poor stronghold. It was so small that it could have held no more than two hundred men during a siege. It flooded in high water. And it was so vulnerable to artillery that Contrecoeur, the commandant, was preparing to abandon it as Braddock approached.

command of the defeated army and Governor Shirley of Massachusetts the acknowledged commander in chief of all British forces in North America, a position to which he was formally appointed in August. Unless quick action could be taken to retrieve the losses incurred by Braddock's defeat, the whole frontier of Virginia and Pennsylvania would be left at the mercy of the French and the Indians. Alert to the danger, Governor Dinwiddie of Virginia sent an urgent message to Shirley offering four or five hundred men to reinforce Dunbar's decimated regiments if the British officer would renew the attack on Fort Duquesne. Shirley thereupon sent word to Dunbar to prepare for a second assault on Fort Duquesne unless he believed his force unequal to the task, in which case he should march his soldiers to Albany to help in the northern campaigns against the French. After consulting with his fellow British officers, Dunbar decided that he did not want to see any more fighting in the wilderness of Pennsylvania. In fact, he wanted to go into winter quarters in Philadelphia, though it was only late July, but reluctantly he set out for Albany, leaving the frontier open to attack.

The Indian allies of the French were already killing settlers and burning cabins in the outlying districts. To give some measure of protection, Dinwiddie procured a colonel's commission for George Washington from Shirley and ordered him to use such troops as he could raise for the protection of the border areas. It was a difficult assignment, but Washington accepted it. Dunbar's cowardice and refusal to use his regulars in making a second attempt on Fort Duquesne further embittered the Virginians against British officers sent to save them from the French and the Indians.

In the meantime, Governor Shirley was attempting to bring pressure on the French in the North. The plan to attack Fort Niagara, the French outlying fort on Lake Ontario, and Fort St-Frédéric, at Crown Point at the southern tip of Lake Champlain, occupied Shirley's mind during the summer of 1755. If the two attacks proved successful, Shirley planned to invade Canada and thus cut off the French from the Ohio Valley and relieve the pressure on the Virginia and Pennsylvania frontiers. Shirley himself intended to lead an expedition against Fort Niagara, and he appointed William Johnson a temporary major general and ordered him to move against Crown Point. The strategy was sound, but in the meantime the French were taking the offensive.

Late in May, Shirley sent Captain John Bradstreet with two hundred regulars and a crew of shipwrights to Oswego, the English trading center on Lake Ontario, to build four ships to transport troops down the lake to Fort Niagara. Shirley also commandeered all the bateaux in the region. Toward the end of July he began to transport additional troops up the Mohawk River and, with a long portage, into Lake Oneida and thence to Oswego. By mid-September he had assembled something over two thousand men at Oswego. With Indian support, he was preparing for a descent by water upon Fort Niagara when storms accompanied by torrential rains forced postponement of the expedition. News came of French reinforcements at Fort Frontenac on the other side of Lake Ontario and of additional strength at Fort Niagara. In the face of bad news and worse weather, Shirley decided that the onslaught on Fort Niagara would have to be delayed until spring. He had built a stockaded fort on a height outside Oswego to help protect it, and he left two regiments of regulars there as a garrison. The militia left.

William Johnson used the summer months to organize his attack on Crown Point. In June and early July he had called a ten-day council of Iroquois and three

The ingenious artist faced with depicting this round powder horn on flat paper did so by drawing it as though the horn's surface were peeled off. The horn was made about 1755 and carried, besides pictures and designs, a map of the Lake Ontario–Albany fur route.

other nations—over one thousand Indians—to gain their support for the campaign. He planned to advance up the Hudson and portage over to Lake George, where his men would go by bateaux and canoe to Lake Champlain. To secure his route, he planned to build forts at three strategic points.

With some thirty-five hundred militia raised in New England and New York, Johnson embarked in mid-July. Some four hundred Indians were recruited along the way, especially during the building of the first fort, named Fort Edward, which Johnson erected on an eminence overlooking the Hudson at a location known as the Great Carrying Place—a portage between the Hudson and Lake George. Leaving a small garrison at Fort Edward, he pushed on to Lake George, where he began work on another fort. Reports reached them of a large contingent of French troops advancing southward, and to meet the enemy, Johnson sent out a thousand men under Colonel Ephraim Williams, with a body of Indians under Chief Hendrick. The leader of the French was a German professional soldier, the Baron de Dieskau, who had been given command of French troops in North America.

On September 8 Dieskau's force of about fifteen hundred French and Indians set out to attack Fort Edward, which would have cut Johnson's line of communication, but the Indian allies of the French, hearing that Johnson was encamped on Lake George without a completed fort, urged Dieskau to attack that position first. When Dieskau was only two miles from Fort Edward, he held a council of war and decided to turn toward Johnson's camp. Shortly after the change in the route, Dieskau suddenly encountered Williams's force and opened a heavy fire. Williams's men turned and fled back to the main camp on Lake George. Both Williams and Chief Hendrick were killed.

Fortunately for the English, Johnson had taken pains to fortify his camp with felled trees, and the refugees streamed behind the barricade with the French and Indians hot in pursuit. But in pausing to regroup for the assault on the breastworks, the pursuers gave Johnson time to man his cannon and to prepare for the attack. In a successful sortie, Johnson's troops captured the wounded French commander, Baron de Dieskau.

The French then withdrew to the point where they had defeated Williams in the first encounter. There a force of two hundred men from Fort Edward struck them about eight o'clock in the evening and put them to rout after killing a considerable number and seizing their baggage. Thus the three battles of Lake George ended with an American victory, although Johnson himself was wounded and the Americans showed no disposition to pursue the French, who retired toward Crown Point. Although Shirley might later urge Johnson to get on with the campaign to take Crown Point, he had to be content with Johnson's building a fort on Lake George, which he named William Henry. It was too late to fortify the outlet of Lake George at Ticonderoga, as Johnson had planned, for the French had beaten him to it and were building their own stronghold, Fort Carillon. But the British government, grateful for one victory over the French, made Johnson a baronet.

When Shirley kept insisting that Johnson attack Crown Point, Johnson, who had been named superintendent of the Six Nations, resigned his commission with the excuse that his other duties required all his time. The truth was that Johnson disliked Shirley, and he was encouraged in his uncooperative attitude toward the New Englander by Lieutenant Governor James De Lancey of New York and others. De Lancey had no enthusiasm for Shirley's ambitious plans to invade Canada, for De Lancey and other New Yorkers were interested in contraband trade with Montreal and did not want to see it stopped. Furthermore, Massachusetts and New York were engaged in a bitter boundary dispute that did not improve the atmosphere for military cooperation. Intercolonial rivalries once again prevented effective unity in pursuit of a common goal.

The year 1755 saw small gains in Nova Scotia that lightened the general gloom. Governor Shirley recruited some two thousand volunteers in New England, who, with two hundred and fifty regulars, all commanded by Lieutenant Colonel Robert Monckton, undertook in June to capture Fort Beauséjour at the base of the Bay of Fundy. The French Acadians of that part of Nova Scotia, led by a fanatical fighting priest, the Abbé Jean Louis le Loutre, preferred to burn their houses and their church rather than let them fall into the hands of the English. Many of them took refuge in the fort, which held out against Monckton until his cannonading forced its surrender. A little later Monckton captured the remaining French point of defense in Acadia, Fort Gaspereau on Green Bay, opposite Prince Edward Island.

These two victories did not mean that French influence in the maritime regions of Canada was nullified, however, for the great fortress at Louisbourg, situated in his *Journal*: "Began to Embark the Inhabitants who went of [off] Very . . . unwillingly, the Women in Great destress Carrying off Their Children in their arms. Others Carrying Their decript [decrepit] Parents in their Carts and all their Goods. . . ."

The deportation of these Acadians was the theme of Henry Wadsworth Longfellow's "Evangeline":

Waste are those pleasant farms, and the farmers forever departed!
Scattered like dust and leaves, when the mighty
  blasts of October
Seize them, and whirl them aloft, and sprinkle them
  far o'er the ocean.
Naught but tradition remains of the beautiful village of Grand-Pré.

By October 13 Winslow had nine transports ready to sail, each with from one hundred and forty to one hundred and eighty-six deportees destined for Pennsylvania, Maryland, and Virginia. Additional *habitants* in the Minas Basin and other regions of Nova Scotia still remained to be loaded on transports for the Carolinas, Georgia, Massachusetts, and Connecticut.

By the time the removal of the Acadians was completed, some six thousand had been scattered through the English colonies. Besides those removed by the English, many more fled to French Canada, making a total dispersal of between twelve and fifteen thousand people. Their reception in the various colonies was anything but cordial. South Carolina, for example, which had a large group of Calvinist Huguenots, regarded the incoming Catholic French as potential enemies and took steps to prevent their departure to the interior, where they might stir up the Indians. The Huguenots were violently hostile to the newcomers and did all they could to prevent the captains of the transports from landing their human cargoes. The poor Acadians suffered great hardships, and many wandered like Ishmael with every man's hand against them. Some drifted back north to Canada. Many found an ultimate refuge in Louisiana, where their descendants to this day are called "Cajuns."

Despite the victory won by Johnson on Lake George and the English success in eliminating the Acadians, France still threatened the destruction of English trade in the Ohio Valley and the future safety of the colonies on the Atlantic coast. London decided that something must be done to check the French advance.

Although Governor Shirley of Massachusetts had shown himself a man of ingenuity and force, he had bitter enemies and could not unite the colonies behind him for effective military action. The authorities in Whitehall decided that he must be replaced as commander in chief of the armed forces in North America. Accordingly, in January, 1756, the Duke of Cumberland persuaded the Cabinet to appoint John Campbell, Earl of Loudoun, to the post of commander in chief in America. His commission was issued on March 17, and on July 22 Loudoun, with staff and mistress, landed in New York. Shirley, in the meantime, had been relieved and turned over his command, pending Loudoun's arrival, first to Major General Daniel Webb and then to Major General James Abercromby. Shirley was at length recalled to England in the autumn of 1756 after Loudoun complained that he had stirred up factions against him. Shirley, a competent official, was himself the victim of envious and hostile colleagues.

France had also appointed a new commander in chief for North America, Marquis Louis Joseph de Montcalm de Saint-Véran, an officer who was presently to show an ability that no British general in America displayed. Montcalm's first official duty was an inspection of the French forts on Lake Ontario, Lake Champlain, and Lake George. Learning that the English garrison at Oswego had been weakened by sickness and death during the winter, Montcalm sent a force from Fort Frontenac in August, 1756, and forced the English to surrender. The Earl of Loudoun did little except blame Shirley for not reinforcing the garrison at Oswego. The loss of this important trading post meant that henceforth the western Indians would side with the French.

Until 1755 England and France clung to the belief that they could fight an undeclared war in America and still keep the peace in Europe. But in the spring of ·1756, the French invaded Minorca, then held by England, and on May 18 England declared war on France. The Seven Years' War was now official. In America this conflict would be known as the French and Indian War, as if all previous wars of the eighteenth century had not deserved that title. A crisis was now impending, and much would depend upon the wisdom that the authorities in Whitehall would muster. In November the incompetent Duke of Newcastle resigned as prime minister. William Pitt succeeded to the power if not the title, and his authority would have vast implications for the American colonies.

The Sociable Colonist

Man is a social creature, and the colonist was no exception. However, in America there were obstacles to a full social life. Only a small fraction of the people lived in towns; the South was without even a pattern of small village life, while in New England, where villages did dot the countryside, the dour proscriptions of the Puritans were long laid against dancing, games, music, and almost everything else enjoyable. In this void, colonists devised their own pastimes. Neighbors joined to turn the work of a barn-raising or corn-husking into a "bee." In the South, planters entertained with an open hand to the extent that some posted a slave on the road to invite passing travelers to stop for food and lodging. This pathetic eagerness for company was the result of isolation and hunger for news of the outside world. There was little relation between social and cultural life, for the arts made slow headway. A man's worth was still measured in most places by his prowess with plow and axe rather than by his knowledge of literature and Greek.

ABOVE: *Dancing was a favorite pastime, whether it was the minuets of the gentry or country dances out in the open air. The picture is from a Pennsylvania German plate.*
RIGHT: *Although churchgoing tended to be an austere experience, especially in the unheated meetinghouses in winter, the church was the real heart of each colonial community. The scene is the center of an appliquéd quilt.*

OVERLEAF: *Southern planters tried to create a society like that of the English landowning class, but, as this 18th-century painting of a Virginia fox hunt indicates, the setting was considerably more primitive than England.*

BOTH ABOVE: *The Little Pretty Pocket Book*, 1787, ROSENBACH COLLECTION, FREE LIBRARY OF PHILADELPHIA; RIGHT: *The Juvenile Biographer*, 1787, ROSENBACH COLLECTION, FREE LIBRARY OF PHILADELPHIA

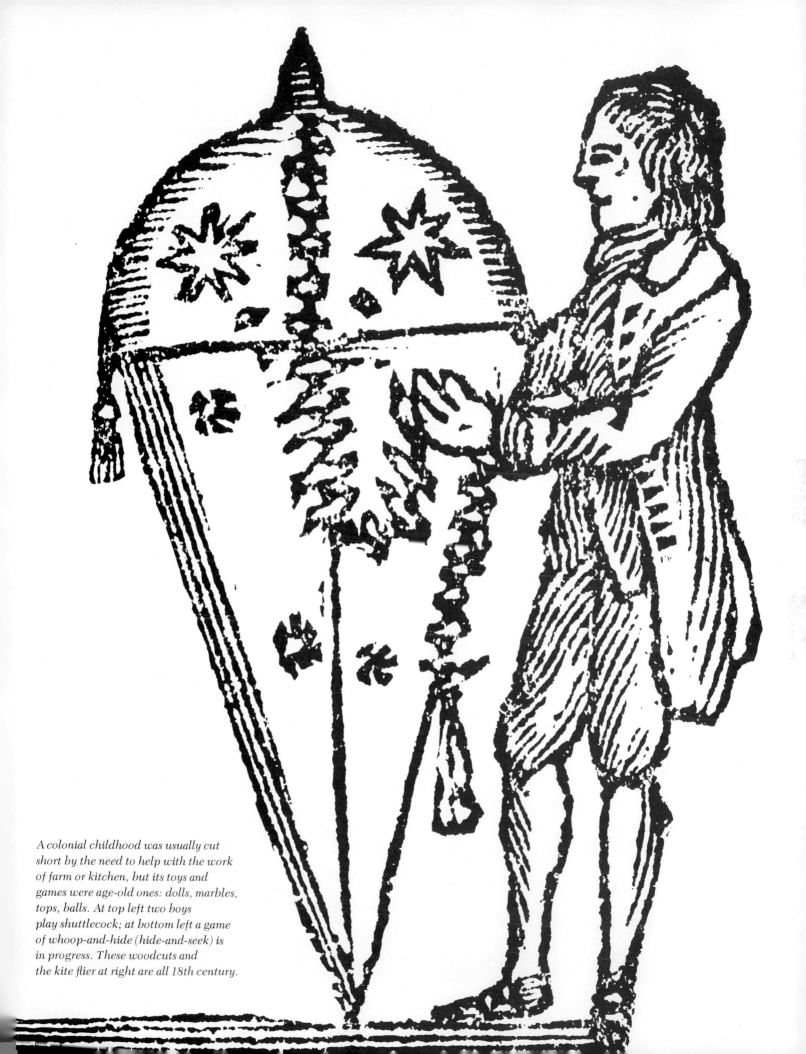

A colonial childhood was usually cut
short by the need to help with the work
of farm or kitchen, but its toys and
games were age-old ones: dolls, marbles,
tops, balls. At top left two boys
play shuttlecock; at bottom left a game
of whoop-and-hide (hide-and-seek) is
in progress. These woodcuts and
the kite flier at right are all 18th century.

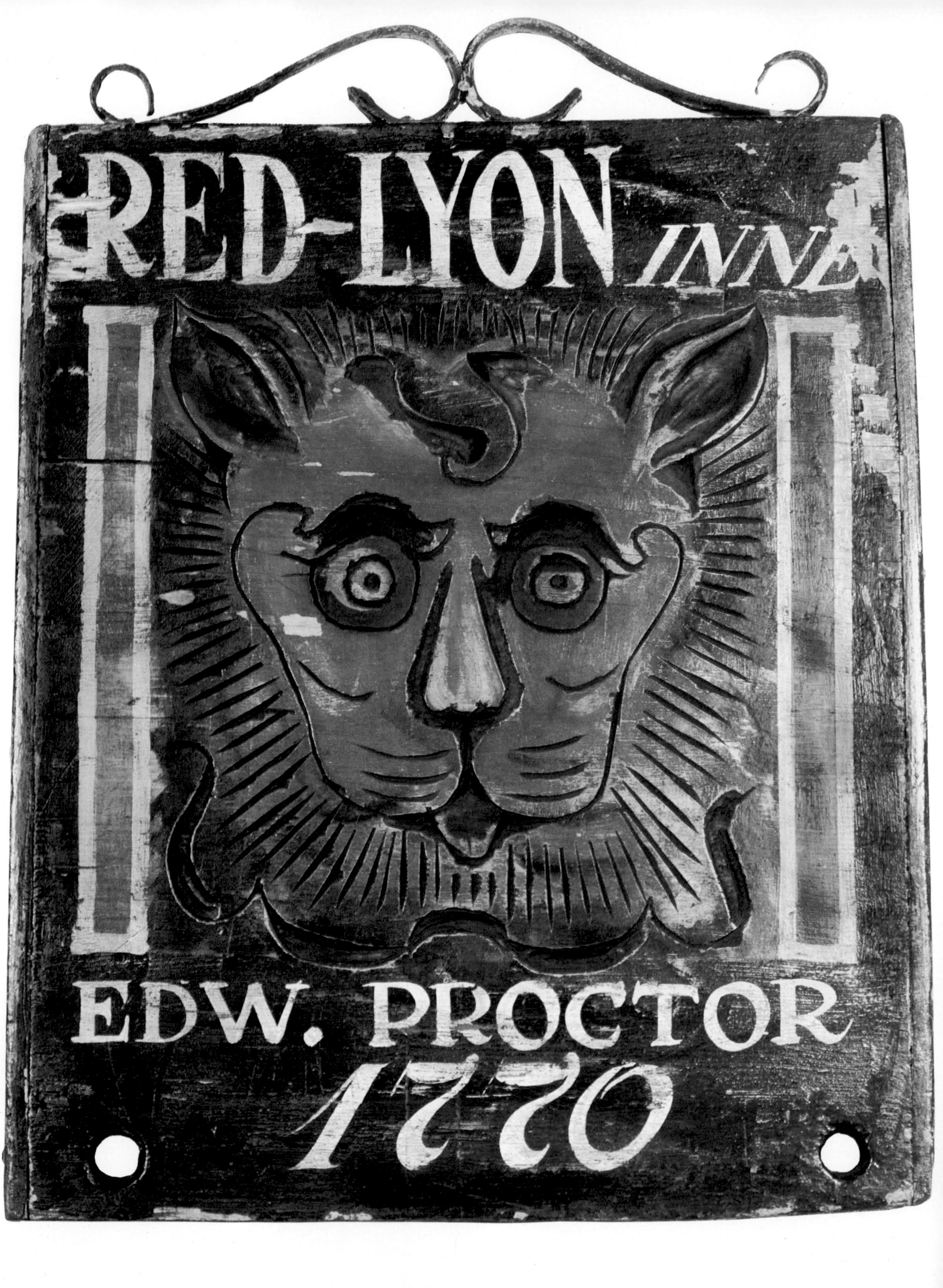
RED-LYON INN
EDW. PROCTOR
1770

LEFT: COLLECTION OF L. L. BEAN; RIGHT: ARENTS COLLECTION, NEW YORK PUBLIC LIBRARY

The tavern was the center at least of masculine social life in colonial cities. Each had its regular clientele and its own distinctive atmosphere. Men went to some to talk business, to others to read, to still others purely for conviviality. Though many were common grogshops, some catered solely to gentlemen. The sign at left once hung outside a Boston tavern. The overly jollified group above appear on a tobacco card of about 1750.

See here O fair Britania at thy Feet.
The Gallic Genius does her Keys submit.
The Standards too of her proud boasting bands.
She suppliant brings with her submissive hands.
When the brave Wolfe heroic, led the Way.
To Victory, and dying, won the Day;
Which brought them under George's milder sway.

Quebec no more is hers. Auspicious Heav'n!
Has that to Britains braver Genius given;
No more Acadian Swains, beneath the pow'r
Of Tyrants groan, but bless the happy Hour.

Britannia Rules

When thoughtful Englishmen sat down on New Year's Day, 1757, to take stock of the situation of the American colonies, they must have come to gloomy conclusions. Throughout the colonies, private interests, greed, envy, suspicion, and intercolonial rivalries prevented any effective action against the common enemy, France. When colonial troops were levied, they frequently were undisciplined, untrained, and ineffective. The British regulars had hardly proved any better, and the British officers sent over had failed because of lack of understanding, lack of energy, or gross incompetence.

To the French, the beginning of the year held out glittering promises of success in America. Their earlier victories had won over most of the western Indians and had raised the morale of the French provincials. The king of France had sent adequate reinforcements of regular troops and ample munitions. Further supplies were promised. Moreover, France had a new commander in chief of ability, courage, and energy, the Marquis de Montcalm.

During the early days of 1757, Montreal and Quebec rang with revelry as French officials and military officers vied with each other in the magnificence of their social affairs. Montcalm kept open house three days each week until Lent and entertained at sumptuous dinner parties. The French had reason to be relaxed, for they could count sixty-six hundred seasoned regular troops in New France, and the French Navy was constantly reinforcing Louisbourg. The squadrons there were sufficient to threaten the whole English east coast. The French believed that they would soon cut off the English irrevocably from the interior and deny them access to the Great Lakes. The English might continue to hold a narrow strip east of the mountains, but their hope of an expanding empire in North America was over. No Frenchman and few Englishmen could have foreseen that in three years the tables would be turned.

Although the crisis facing the English colonies at the beginning of 1757 was acute—perhaps the most serious of the eighteenth century—many colonials were unaware of the danger. Indeed, complacency had settled over many areas as merchants, tradesmen, craftsmen, and farmers enjoyed the prosperity that military spending had brought.

Issued to commemorate British victory in America, this English engraving has Quebec in the background, while in unsubtle symbolism France kneels in submission to conquering Britannia.

279

New York and Newport took advantage of the war with France to send out an increasing number of privateers that brought in quantities of money and goods captured on the high seas. The privateer owners, their captains, and the crews all profited, and privateering became so popular that deserters from English vessels in the harbors of New York and Newport hid until they could sign on with a privateer and sail away on a voyage that promised quick and easy money. The sheriff of Newport County asserted that men who enlisted in the army took their first pay and then ran off to sea—"almost as fast as they can be recruited," he added. He estimated that something like ten thousand men who might have been engaged in defending the frontiers had been lured into privateering and related activities. So many deserted in New York that the governor of the province ordered three battalions to surround the city and to make a search of the houses. The rewards of privateering affected nearly everyone, for the money was quickly spent and served to stimulate business. In New York alone, cash and goods brought in by these commerce raiders by 1757 amounted to something like two hundred thousand pounds in value. It is small wonder that privateering created an excitement almost like the gold rushes of later centuries.

But ships bearing letters of marque were not the only vessels that brought a quick profit to port cities, for merchants were not above trading with the enemy. Ship captains loaded sugar and molasses in the French West Indies or traded with French vessels off Nova Scotia for silks, wine, and other luxury products. Winning the war in the back country of North America was of little concern to merchants and skippers whose interests kept their attention focused upon more immediate benefits.

Although most colonials in the old settled areas were unconcerned about the warfare in the interior, every colony had a few clear-sighted people who realized the danger. As in all the earlier wars with the Indians and the French, however, concerted action was lacking. Each colony tried to act in accordance with its special interest. Virginians under Washington were continuing to police as best they could the western frontier of their colony, but in 1757 Washington was despondent over the outlook. In the previous year his men had suffered more than a hundred casualties in some twenty encounters with the enemy. By the summer of 1757, Washington was attempting to guard three hundred and fifty miles of frontier with four hundred men, whom he de-

scribed as "abandoned miscreants," clad in rags, for they had received no issue of clothing since 1754. Raids by French and Indians west of Winchester and Fort Cumberland were frequent, and a move on weakly garrisoned Fort Cumberland failed only because the illness of the French commander stopped the advance. To provide Washington with additional troops, the House of Burgesses passed an act drafting men from each county, but out of four hundred draftees, one hundred and fourteen deserted, and Washington wrote his superior, Colonel John Stanwix, that he had "a Gallows near 40 feet high erected (which has terrified the *rest* exceedingly), and I am determined if I can be justified in the proceeding, to hang two or three on it, as an Example to others." Although Washington actually hanged two deserters on his gallows, defections continued, and he informed Governor Dinwiddie that without reinforcements, he did not expect to see left "one soul living on this side the Blue Ridge the ensuing autumn."

Maryland was even less effective than Virginia in protecting its frontier. Although Fort Cumberland was within Maryland's borders, the assembly of that colony in 1757 objected violently to Lord Loudoun's efforts to have Maryland garrison the fort. Marylanders claimed that since Fort Cumberland was a protection for Virginia territory, Virginia should provide its garrison. Indians, to be sure, were slaughtering settlers on the Maryland frontier, but the merchants and planters in the tidewater region showed little concern. Since both Virginia and Pennsylvania had more exposed frontier than Maryland, they reasoned, let them protect the borders. In the early part of 1757, Maryland could boast only one hundred and fifty men under arms.

Some of the most critical points of danger, such as Fort Duquesne, were in Pennsylvania territory, and her long, exposed border offered a continuing temptation to the French and their Indian allies. In November, 1755, the Indians had massacred the Moravians at Gnadenhütten in the upper Lehigh Valley, and settlers within fifty miles of Philadelphia heard the war whoop of Indians and fell under their tomahawks. Despite the obvious danger, the pacifist Quakers who controlled the Pennsylvania assembly at first refused to take any action whatsoever. The German colonists who were also comfortably established on farms out of danger of Indian attack were likewise pacifists and opposed to any military action. As petition after petition for arms, ammunition, and troops came from the border settlers, non-Quakers in the assembly, led by Benjamin Franklin, tried in vain to move the obstinate Quakers, who merely declared that they would investigate causes of discontent among the Indians. Fearful that the assembly might vote funds for military purposes, Quaker preachers, male and female, harangued crowds on the streets of Philadelphia on the iniquity of war; it was better to suffer, they insisted, than to take a life.

Some of those who had suffered in fact rather than in theory brought a wagonload of scalped and mutilated corpses to the very doors of the assembly to let the Quakers see what really happened on the frontier. Faced with the threat of mob action, the assembly made a concession. It voted a militia act that exempted Quakers and merely affirmed that it would be lawful for others to volunteer, form companies, and elect officers by ballot. Articles of war would be drawn up with the approval of the governor, but unless an officer or enlisted man, after three days' consideration, agreed in the presence of a justice of the peace, he need not be bound by them.

If George Washington complained about the ease with which the Virginia militia evaded their duties, at least he was spared the frustration of trying to raise troops under the futile act of the Pennsylvania assembly. Finally, after much trial of soul, the Quaker-dominated assembly appropriated fifty-five thousand pounds "for the King's use," without mentioning war; the Proprietary office contributed five thousand pounds more on the same vague basis; and the frontiersmen were left to fend off the Indians as best they could with the hope that some of the money for the king's use might be spent for guns and ammunition. Eventually the Pennsylvanians managed to erect a chain of forts and strongpoints from the Delaware to the Potomac while the Quakers salved their consciences by calling these fortifications simply "posts."

The situation on the New York frontier was even more critical than elsewhere during the winter and summer of 1757. The Earl of Loudoun had placed the command of regular troops in the area under Brigadier General Daniel Webb, a hypochondriac and an incompetent. Loudoun himself and his second-in-command, Major General James Abercromby, were devoting their attention to a plan that obsessed Loudoun: an assault on the heart of New France. All through the early part of 1757 Loudoun talked of an attack on Quebec, but on orders from London he changed his objective to Louisbourg. Meanwhile the disposition of the regular troops available in New York was left to Webb's discretion. The two key fortresses in the north were Fort William Henry on Lake George and Fort Edward a little to the south, near the portage on the upper Hudson. From these bases, Webb might have advanced against the French at Fort Ticonderoga, which pointed like a dagger at the English settlements. In fact, the French thought he had such an attack in mind when Captain Robert Rogers led a group of his famous Rangers on a reconnaissance of Ticonderoga in January, 1757. Rogers' men captured some prisoners and gained information about the strength of the French strongholds at Ticonderoga and Crown Point, but Webb failed to follow up with any action.

Instead, the French took the initiative. An expedition of some fifteen hundred French and Indians advanced across Lake George and Lake Champlain and on March

The Earl of Loudoun was a capable organizer of military supply and transport, but he was no diplomat, for his dictatorial manner and temper outbursts antagonized colonial leaders. He was relieved as commanding general at the end of 1757, after a year and a half of failures.

19 appeared before Fort William Henry and began an attack. The fort, defended by five hundred regulars and a small detachment of Rogers' Rangers, was under the command of a regular army officer, Lieutenant Colonel William Eyre, who withstood the onslaught as best he could. Although he could not prevent the enemy from destroying all outlying buildings and a ship under construction on the lake, he held the fort itself until the cold weather and lack of supplies compelled the French to withdraw.

The winter attack on Fort William Henry was the prelude to a successful summer campaign by Montcalm. Before the end of July, he brought together at Ticonderoga an army of six thousand, reinforced by two thousand Indian allies, and was ready for an advance on the English fort. Ferrying his troops down Lake George in barges and canoes during the last days of July and the first two days in August, Montcalm completed the envelopment of Fort William Henry by August 3. Lieutenant Colonel George Monro, now in command at the fort, had only about twenty-one hundred men to resist the army of French and Indians. Although Brigadier General Webb, with headquarters at Fort Edward, had made an inspection of Fort William Henry a few days before the arrival of the French, he had sent only inadequate reinforcements, and after the French began their siege, he took no effective action to aid the beleaguered fort. Webb contented himself with notifying Monro that he could not send relief from Fort Edward, since he had only twenty-five hundred troops in that garrison, and reinforcements of colonial militia were not yet forthcoming. He suggested that Monro might surrender on the best terms he could get from Montcalm.

At last, outnumbered and outgunned, Monro accepted, on August 9, Montcalm's offer for an honorable capitulation. The members of the garrison would be allowed to keep their arms, and, to protect them from the Indians who were eager for scalps, French troops would escort them to Fort Edward. Unhappily the French were unable to control the Indians, who that night fell on the English and massacred more than two hundred, including a few women and the wounded troops. Some four hundred others were carried away by the Indians to Canada.

After systematically destroying Fort William Henry and leveling the neighboring entrenchments, the French withdrew to Ticonderoga and Crown Point without venturing to attack Fort Edward. Troops from New

York and New England were by this time converging on Fort Edward, and Montcalm was unwilling to risk the laurels of his recent victory in an attempt to take this stronghold. He had already brought English prestige to its lowest ebb and had kept many Indians from allying themselves with the English. Meanwhile, the prestige of France in North America was never higher.

While disaster was overtaking the English on the New York and other frontiers, Loudoun received orders from London to proceed against Louisbourg and at once began organizing a land force to operate with the Royal Navy. In the meantime, transports embarked troops in England and Ireland. By mid-July, more than five thousand regular soldiers had reached Halifax to swell the total number of trained soldiers in Nova

Nova Scotia to prevent a counterattack by the French, Loudoun embarked the remainder and sailed for New York and New England ports. The British fleet, which continued to cruise off Nova Scotia, barely missed complete disaster in a hurricane on September 24. One ship was lost, many were damaged, and some had to throw overboard their cannon and heavy supplies to survive the storm. The worst-battered ships eventually struggled home, but eight remained in American waters on orders from Loudoun. Thus ended Loudoun's dream of striking at the heart of French strength in Canada. He had done little more than march up the hill and down again, and the year 1757 played out to an inglorious end for British arms. On December 30, 1757, William Pitt recalled the Earl of Loudoun and appointed Major General Abercromby in his place.

William Pitt was resolved that the long sequence of disasters to British arms in North America had to end, and he began a vigorous effort to recruit sufficient strength to crush the French once and for all. No longer would defeat result from a policy of too little and too late. Pitt authorized the arming and payment of provincial troops by the British government; he gave orders that the rank of provincial officers should be recognized by regular army officers; he ordered to America thousands of regular troops; and he brought pressure on the provincial governments to raise at least twenty-five thousand militia.

Though Abercromby was nominally commander in chief of all troops in North America, Pitt specified that he was to concentrate upon an invasion of Canada, after the capture of Ticonderoga and Crown Point, and leave the direction of campaigns against Fort Duquesne and Louisbourg to others. Brigadier General John Forbes, whom Abercromby placed in charge of the southern provinces, was given the responsibility of marching on Fort Duquesne and redeeming Braddock's defeat. Colonel Jeffery Amherst, a British aristocrat and a soldier who served on the Continent under the Duke of Cumberland, was named a major general and instructed to take Louisbourg. He was to lead the land forces and to coordinate the campaign with a naval attack led by

Scotia to nearly fifteen thousand men. Seventeen ships of the line with about the same number of auxiliary vessels were also ready for action.

But the French had not been idle, and their naval force at Louisbourg now numbered eighteen ships of the line with adequate supporting vessels. Before the end of July, at least four more warships sailed into Louisbourg harbor to strengthen the French flotilla. When British intelligence at long last brought news of the naval and land forces ready to repel an attack on Louisbourg, Loudoun, with the concurrence of Rear Admiral Francis Holburne, who commanded the English fleet, decided that the British had no hope of success and that the attempt to reduce Louisbourg would have to be abandoned. Leaving sufficient troops in

Vice-Admiral Edward Boscawen. Pitt assigned to Amherst's command a talented young brigadier general, James Wolfe.

In no other colonial campaign had such a force been sent against the French as now moved against Louisbourg. By the end of May, 1758, an armada of one hundred and fifty-seven warships and transports headed toward Nova Scotia. On June 8 General Wolfe led a landing party that gained a foothold on Cape Breton Island at Gabarus Bay and began the siege of Louisbourg. For the next seven weeks, the English bombarded the French fort from land and sea. Defending French vessels were sunk, burned, or blown up in the harbor. English shells destroyed storehouses, hospitals, and barracks inside the fort. Though the great stone walls withstood blasts of the artillery, the British fire eventually knocked out all but four guns in the French batteries. On July 26, with the town in ruins, and with many of the defending troops dead or wounded and the rest exhausted, the French commander had to surrender. With this victory the tide turned, and British morale rose. Never again, as in 1745, would the key fortress to Canada be restored to the French to gain some political advantage elsewhere. The English two years later systematically destroyed the fortress. They left only a barren and devastated landscape, the haunt of gulls and of the ghosts of hundreds of dead.

While Amherst and Boscawen were besieging Louisbourg, General Abercromby was making an effort to get on with his campaign against Canada. But provincial troops were slow in responding to his call, and supplies and arms from England were delayed in reaching him. By July 1, he had only twelve thousand men concentrated on Lake George instead of the twenty-seven thousand that Pitt had planned for him to use in the attack on the French forts at Ticonderoga and Crown Point. By July 5, however, additional militia had arrived to increase his force to sixteen thousand of all sorts: regulars, rangers, boatmen, and raw militia. Embarking his men and artillery in a vast armada of bateaux, rafts, and whaleboats, Abercromby crossed Lake George on the night of July 5–6 and landed them in a cove three or four miles southwest of Ticonderoga. An advance party under young Lord Howe encountered and routed a group of French who had been sent out to reconnoiter, but Howe was killed in the first burst of fire. The army moved up the next day and camped near Ticonderoga.

Abercromby learned from captured French soldiers

Titled "Britain's Glory, or the Reduction of Cape Breton,"
this print of the siege of Louisbourg was circulated in 1758,
soon after the fall of the fortress. In the picture, the British
fleet (foreground) appears unscathed by French batteries at
the left, the right, and in front of the town, while at least one
of the French ships huddled in the left background is afire.

that Montcalm had only six thousand troops for the defense of the fort but that reinforcements of at least three thousand men were expected. Speed therefore was necessary, and Abercromby did not wait to bring up all his artillery from the rafts or to mount guns on a hill commanding the fort. In his haste, the British commander on July 8 ordered an attack on French troops entrenched some distance in front of the fort, protected by an abatis —freshly cut trees felled so that their sharpened limbs faced the attackers and made a barrier difficult to climb through even without the fire from soldiers hidden in the trenches beyond. With proper artillery preparation, the British could have demolished this barrier, but Abercromby neglected to use his artillery, a piece of stupidity that was incomprehensible to his own officers.

Regular troops, including a body of picked Scottish Highlanders, charged against the tangle of sharpened tree limbs and died by the hundreds in the murderous fire as they tried to crawl through the maze. Some of the provincial troops, particularly the militia from Connecticut, gave a good account of themselves, but others immediately began to retreat. Soon the retreat was a rout, and the British force, which in the beginning outnumbered the French five to one, fell back to the site of ruined Fort William Henry. Abercromby had had enough and did not attempt to renew the fight, though one of his officers complained that Abercromby had men and equipment sufficient to march through Canada

Remarks on the French Memorials, 1756

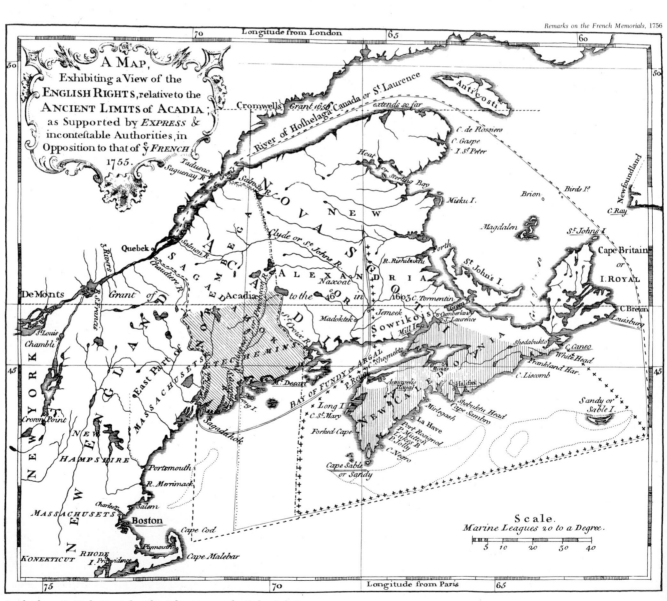

In the long British-French colonial wars, much of the fighting occurred in the area included in this map, and there the issue was finally decided. Once the British won Lake Champlain (above Crown Point, far left) and Louisbourg (far right), the situation of Quebec became precarious. The map shows old grants and treaties in an attempt to prove English rights to Acadia.

if he had made proper use of them. He reported the loss of 464 killed, 29 missing, and 1,117 wounded.

General Amherst notified Abercromby that he was sending six battalions so that a second attempt on Ticonderoga could be made, but after a council of war this attack was postponed and the troops went into winter quarters. This bitter defeat was too much for Pitt. He ordered Abercromby home and gave supreme command of British forces in North America to Amherst.

The humiliation of the defeat at Ticonderoga was eased somewhat by the brilliant action of Lieutenant Colonel John Bradstreet in capturing and destroying the French stronghold at Fort Frontenac on Lake Ontario at the headwaters of the St. Lawrence. Bradstreet assembled a flotilla of bateaux, whaleboats, and rafts, recruited more than three thousand men, and quietly ferried his force across the lake. Unlike Abercromby, he brought up his artillery and began a bombardment of the fort before attempting an assault. So effective was his fire that on August 27 the French surrendered. Fort Frontenac was an important supply depot for the whole Northwest, and its warehouses were loaded with munitions, foodstuffs, and furs. Bradstreet's men took what they could carry away and destroyed the rest, along with the fort itself. No longer would this fortification protect the entrance to the St. Lawrence and serve as a distributing and supply point for the French. Slowly the English were drawing a noose around the French.

Braddock's defeat before Fort Duquesne at the forks of the Ohio still rankled, and Pitt was determined to avenge that catastrophe. Early in 1758 he ordered Brigadier General John Forbes to begin preparations to move against Fort Duquesne. Forbes was a methodical man with an understanding of the value of careful planning. He did not intend to take an army into the wilderness and lose it. After studying Braddock's route from Fort Cumberland to the Ohio, Forbes concluded that a shorter and safer way led across Pennsylvania.

Making Raystown on the Juniata River his supply base, he gradually built a string of strongpoints across the province until he felt that his communications were secure. After much persuasion and some threats, he managed to induce the Pennsylvanians to supply sufficient wagons and horses to transport supplies, munitions, and artillery. And his frontiersmen hacked a road through the wilderness toward Fort Duquesne.

Forbes had as his second-in-command Lieutenant Colonel Henry Bouquet, a Swiss officer of immense competence, and to him is due part of the credit for the ultimate success of the expedition. Bouquet served as Forbes's executive officer, and he was in charge of cutting the road through the wilderness and building forts along the route, an activity that consumed the summer and part of the autumn. In early September, the British had begun a fort at Loyalhanna, to be named Fort Ligonier, and Bouquet decided to send ahead an advance party of Scottish Highlanders under Major James Grant to reconnoiter in the vicinity of Fort Duquesne. He was anxious to discover, among other things, the strength of the Indian allies of the French. Grant's Highlanders with a body of provincial militiamen reached the outskirts of the French fortified area before the enemy discovered them, but they made the mistake of beating their drums to stir their men to action. This alarm aroused the French, who made a sortie from Fort Duquesne with sufficient numbers to surround Grant's men. Grant himself was captured, and of his 800 men, 275 were either killed or captured.

But conditions favoring the British were taking shape. Indians who until now had cast their lot with the French were becoming disenchanted. The destruction of faraway Louisbourg and the British interception at sea of French supply ships were having an effect on the French relations with the Indians. The French were unable to deliver presents as promised, and trade goods were not forthcoming. The Indians learned that those who traded with the English were bountifully supplied, and they heard about the handsome presents that the English lavished on their own redskin allies. Gradually the French found that their allies were melting away.

By November 2, Forbes had concentrated five thousand men, including Washington and his regiment of Virginians, at Loyalhanna ready for a final advance upon Fort Duquesne. In pursuit of a French raiding party ten days later, Washington brought in prisoners who revealed that the Indians had deserted the French and that the Canadian militia had also departed. Forbes pushed forward slowly and on November 24 was readying his men for a final attack when the French blew up the fort and vanished in the direction of Canada. Before departing, Indians who still remained loyal to the French had massacred prisoners from Grant's detachment. Outside the ruined fort they had placed a row of poles on which they stuck the heads of the Scots with their kilts attached to the bottoms of the poles.

Forbes, a desperately sick man at the time of the

fall of Fort Duquesne, died in March, 1759. To replace him, General Amherst appointed Brigadier General John Stanwix and ordered him to fortify the forks of the Ohio by rebuilding Fort Duquesne. The new stronghold was called Fort Pitt. Washington, who was engaged to a well-to-do widow, Martha Custis, and had been elected to the Virginia House of Burgesses, resigned his commission and was succeeded by Colonel William Byrd III.

Though British successes had forced the French to retreat, they had not given up hope. They still held forts in the West and North that remained a threat to the British. Near the western end of Lake Ontario they retained Fort Niagara; Venango, between Pittsburgh and Lake Ontario, was a potential staging area for offensive action in the Ohio Valley; Ticonderoga and Crown Point were still dangerous strongholds in northern New York; Quebec of course remained unassailed and, the French thought, invincible. The capture of all these French strongholds was Pitt's objective for 1759.

The elimination of Fort Niagara as an outpost protecting French trade routes to the western Indians would cripple French influence in that region. Already British relations with the Indians had undergone a profound change since 1757, when even the Mohawks, the most loyal to the British of any of the Six Nations, had seemed to be wavering. Now Sir William Johnson could assure General Amherst that the greater part of the Iroquois would rally to an attack upon Fort Niagara, or upon almost any other objective that he selected. The Iroquois, as well as other Indians, were doing some hard thinking about the future. They all wanted to be on the winning side, and British victories over the French made the future look different from the way it had looked two years earlier, when no Indian allies could be found to defend Oswego.

The rebuilding of Oswego began in the spring of 1759 under the over-all direction of Brigadier General John Prideaux. Prideaux let the French and Indians believe that his whole interest at the moment was in the restoration of that British post. But he was also busy assembling men and boats for a descent upon Fort Niagara. During the first week of July, leaving one thousand soldiers to garrison Oswego, he moved two thousand troops and one thousand Indians up Lake Ontario to within three miles of Fort Niagara. By July 6 he was in position to lay siege to the fort, and for the next nineteen days the British kept up constant artillery fire upon the French fortifications. On July 17 Prideaux himself was accidentally killed by one of his own gunners, and Sir William Johnson took over the command.

The French at Venango had been planning to march against the British at the forks of the Ohio in an attempt to recover the ground they had lost at Fort Duquesne, but after a desperate plea from Captain François Pouchot, the commander at Niagara, they sent a column of six hundred French soldiers and one thousand Indians to attempt to raise the siege. This diversion forced the French to abandon the effort to counterattack on the Ohio. Sir William Johnson learned of the approach of the relief column in time to fortify his rear with an abatis of fallen trees. To make matters worse for the French, their Indian allies, now fearful of antagonizing the Iroquois with Johnson, deserted rather than attack the tribesmen from the Six Nations. Although the six hundred French made a desperate charge upon the British, hidden behind the fallen trees, musket fire mowed them down, and they were forced to flee, with the Iroquois in hot pursuit. The Indians slaughtered many of them, but the British managed to save about one hundred prisoners, including seventeen officers. With the relief force defeated, Captain Pouchot gave up hope and surrendered. Ontario was now an English lake. Since regular officers did not like to take orders from Johnson, whom they regarded as merely a leader of Indians, Amherst sent Brigadier General Thomas Gage to command all the Lake Ontario operations.

Gage busied himself with rebuilding the fort at Oswego, but he reported to Amherst that he did not have the manpower to move on the French stronghold of La Galette, on the site of modern Ogdensburg, New York. For the time being the French would be left to hold that fort. In the meantime Amherst himself was leading an army against Ticonderoga and Crown Point. Since the French had only a few hundred men left in the Lake George area, on July 26 they blew up Ticonderoga and retreated to Crown Point, which they also evacuated and blew up five days later. They were shortening their lines of communication, and their defense perimeter against invasion from the south now extended only from La Galette on the St. Lawrence to Fort Isle-aux-Noix on the Richelieu River (connecting Lake Champlain and the St. Lawrence).

The bastion that had been the goal of colonial and British hopes in all the previous wars, Quebec, remained a bulwark that had to be taken before victory could be complete. In February, 1759, Pitt ordered General Wolfe and Vice-Admiral Charles Saunders to proceed to Halifax to begin the campaign. The Army and the Navy would begin convoying transports down the St. Lawrence as soon as the ice melted.

Wolfe would be in command of the forces mobilized to take Quebec. Because of ill health, he had returned to England after the fall of Louisbourg and was not happy over having to go back to America, even in so responsible a post, and complained that he was "cursed with American service." To support Wolfe, Pitt assigned to him a number of young officers, so young in fact, that old heads called it "the boys' campaign."

The fleet and troops gathered at Halifax and Louisbourg, and by June 4 the great flotilla moved into the Gulf of St. Lawrence preparatory to its descent upon Quebec. Wolfe had an army of some nine thousand regulars and four companies of American rangers (whom he regarded as ill-disciplined and uncertain soldiers). The flotilla consisted of nearly two hundred vessels, including warships, transports, and supply ships. Included in the armament was a heavy train of artillery. This time the assault on Quebec would not fail for lack of men or firepower. With captured French pilots to guide them, the ships neared Quebec on June 26 and the next day cast anchor within five miles of their objective.

On the night of June 28, the French attempted to send fireships against the closely packed English transports, but the wind was not favorable. One ship blew up; others went aground; and British sailors in boats managed to grapple others and tow them away.

On the last day of June, Brigadier General Robert Monckton made a landing on Point Lévis, on the opposite side of the river from the town, and began the emplacement of artillery. Since bombardment of the town, perched high above the river, was ineffective from the English ships, far below the level of the walls, it was important to have batteries high enough to throw shells into the city.

Montcalm had his army strongly entrenched down-

Lord Jeffery Amherst—here caricatured in later years—
was a hero of the French and Indian War but was recalled to
England in 1763 for lack of success during the Pontiac
Conspiracy. His insistence on using Continental tactics
against Indians was a common failing of British officers.

river from the town all the way to the falls of the Montmorency River. Up the St. Lawrence, he had thrown a log boom across the St. Charles River and had thin defenses between the Plains of Abraham and the city walls. To make a frontal attack on Montcalm's entrenched army by assault from the beaches below was unthinkable. Consequently, Wolfe decided to try to reach his flank by landing troops below the Montmorency, which plunged through a chasm to the St. Lawrence but could be forded farther inland. Accordingly, he landed troops across the chasm from the French trenches and began firing into their lines. Through the month of July the British kept up a bombardment from the batteries across the river and from artillery on the other side of the chasm of the Montmorency. Monckton's artillery destroyed many houses and even the cathedral inside the town, but shells alone could not conquer Quebec.

Meanwhile the French had fortified the ford of the Montmorency to prevent a flanking attack by Wolfe. Despite the devastation caused by Monckton's and Wolfe's artillery, Montcalm could not be persuaded to take the offensive. Instead he declared that he would follow the tactics of Fabius and let the enemy wear himself out. It was Wolfe, on the last day of July, who finally tried an assault on the French lines from the flats where the Montmorency empties into the St. Lawrence. At low tide the mouth of this stream could be waded,

and Wolfe attempted to lead his men across the ford and up the embankments beyond. At best this was a desperate undertaking, and the intrepid Wolfe was depending upon the superior courage and discipline of his regulars to overcome the French militia and Indians who, he believed, held this portion of the French lines. But the assault failed. The French counterattacked in force, and a terrific rainstorm wet the powder of both forces. The British were forced to withdraw with the loss of four hundred and forty-three in killed, wounded, and missing. Each side claimed that the rainstorm had saved the other from a decisive defeat. Wolfe had learned that some stratagem other than a frontal attack from the mud flats would be needed to take Quebec. The French, on their part, were so elated that they boasted that Quebec would never be taken.

Through the month of August, the two armies lay watching each other. The British laid waste portions of the countryside, but still Montcalm would not venture out of his fortified positions to attack marauders. The destruction of houses inside Quebec was distressing but not sufficiently disastrous to be decisive. The scarcity of food was becoming critical and might in time force capitulation, but a few supply boats continued to get through the net of British vessels.

If anything, the morale of the British troops was lower than that of the inhabitants of Quebec. Wolfe

Quebec lies across the St. Lawrence River to the right of center in this bucolic scene. Beyond the seated woman is Wolfe's Cove, where the British landed and climbed to the Plains of Abraham (above and to the left of the cove). The structures to the right of the Plains of Abraham are the fortification called the Citadel and its outworks.

himself had been ill during the last days of August, and the troops were aware of it. Furthermore, autumn was coming on, the season of storms, to be followed by freezing weather, and Admiral Saunders and his ship captains were getting fidgety over the delays. Both soldiers and sailors were talking about the failure of the campaign and the need to raise the siege and be gone.

But Wolfe was not yet ready to give up. He studied the shoreline for a possible landing place that might make an assault on Quebec something other than a slaughter. Sweeping the north shore with a telescope, he observed a path up the river from Quebec, leading to heights that seemed to be thinly defended. The path led from a little cove called Anse du Foulon, known ever since then as Wolfe's Cove. Legend says that Major Robert Stobo, who had earlier been held a prisoner at Quebec, pointed out the path to Wolfe; at any rate, Wolfe decided that this trail up the slope might offer a chance for a surprise attack.

On September 7, Wolfe sent transports loaded with troops up the river to Cap Rouge, some distance beyond the Anse du Foulon, to make a feint at landing. Soldiers in their boats rowed back and forth along the heavily fortified beaches as if looking for a place to land. Night came on, and for the next two days rain squalls prevented further efforts. The British troops then landed on the south shore and took up quarters in the village of

St. Nicholas. For the next few days, their vessels again cruised along the river well above the Anse du Foulon pretending to look for a landing spot. The French, confused by these tactics and not knowing where the enemy might attempt to come ashore, were forced to march back and forth to be ready to repel them.

Finally, on September 12, Wolfe quietly embarked the troops that were resting at St. Nicholas and issued a general order for all soldiers and sailors to be ready for action. The first troops to reach the opposite shore were to drive directly upon the enemy's outpost and attempt to hold it while reinforcements with artillery could come up. Wolfe planned to force Montcalm to leave his entrenched positions and commit his army to battle on a site where the French commander had not intended to fight. Wolfe had a total of about forty-eight hundred men available for action. Montcalm had nearly twice that number, but Wolfe counted on surprise to help him. Furthermore, he had scant respect for the French provincials who made up part of Montcalm's army.

On the night of September 12, the British sent warships to bombard the shoreline at Beauport, downriver from Quebec, where the French had their strongest entrenchments. This feint gave the impression that the British were going to attempt another assault, perhaps at the mouth of the Montmorency. Montcalm was fooled and massed troops to repel an attack there.

Then, about 4:00 A.M. on September 13, when the river was still enveloped in darkness, Wolfe with about eighteen hundred men landed along the shore in the vicinity of the Anse du Foulon. To a sentry who heard noises and challenged, the reply was made in French that supply boats were trying to evade the British. That answer was satisfactory, and the landings went on unmolested. A group of Scottish Highlanders scrambled up the path and again a sentry challenged. Again a French voice answered, explaining that the detachment had been sent to protect the heights and that the sentry should notify the guard of that fact. The ruse worked. For a brief time—long enough for British troops to gain the top of the cliffs—they were undisturbed. But soon the little French garrison at the top realized what had happened and opened fire. Within a few minutes Wolfe's men overpowered them and gained a foothold from which they could protect the ascent of the remainder of the troops.

Wolfe gave the order for troops in the boats to disembark and advance to the top of the cliffs. He himself scrambled up, followed by battalion after battalion. When morning came a red-coated army held the Plains of Abraham, a fairly level tract of grass and cornfields, named after a river pilot, Abraham Martin, who had once owned part of the land. Wolfe carefully chose his battlefield. Between him and the walls of Quebec, about a mile to the east, stretched a low, bush-covered ridge, which obscured the view of the town. Wolfe deployed his men facing Quebec in three ranks. Although the plateau at this point is less than a mile wide, with the cliffs of the St. Charles River on the north side, Wolfe did not have enough men to stretch across the whole plateau. Anchoring his men at the point where they ascended, he sent two battalions toward the St. Charles to station themselves at right angles to the main battle line in case the French tried to make an end run around their left flank. To protect his rear from the army under Louis Antoine de Bougainville that had been watching the movements of the British transports up the river, Wolfe stationed light infantry detachments in the woods behind the lines to intercept Bougainville's troops should they put in an appearance. Worn out, however, by marching along the river watching the transports, Bougainville's men were now comfortably resting several miles up the river near Cap Rouge.

Montcalm, who had been expecting an attack from Admiral Saunders's ships downriver at Beauport, heard the ominous news of the British landing early on the morning of September 13. At first, the French disbelieved these reports. A fugitive came into camp in the early hours of the morning with a tale of the English landing, but Montcalm's aide-de-camp dismissed him as crazy. The noise of gunfire in the first encounter was plainly heard, but everyone thought that the British were firing on supply boats. Not until after daylight was the British occupation of the heights confirmed. Montcalm ordered a general alarm and dispatched his best battalions to defend the city. Mounting his horse, he rode through the town; stopped to discuss the development with the Marquis de Vaudreuil, governor general of Canada, whom he roused from his sleep; and then rode off to the scene of action. From an eminence he could see lines of red-coated soldiers drawn up in battle array, supported by Scottish Highlanders in tartans, with their bagpipes already sounding.

Montcalm had to decide whether to order an immediate attack before the British entrenched themselves more thoroughly, or to wait for Bougainville to come up and attack the rear. The French commander already had on the field some forty-five hundred men, while his opponent had only about four thousand. As yet Wolfe had brought up only two small pieces of artillery. But Montcalm knew that Wolfe could land more fieldpieces and would soon be solidly entrenched. He decided to attack at once without waiting for Bougainville's army of some two thousand men or for reinforcements that the Marquis de Vaudreuil had promised to bring out of Quebec, along with a train of artillery.

Believing that his troops were more than a match for the British, Montcalm ordered them to charge the enemy's position. With cheers from the French and screaming war cries from Indian allies and provincial woodsmen, the army charged forward, firing as they ran. The silent British waited in their triple ranks until the enemy was within gunshot distance and then slaughtered the advancing men with musket fire. Unused to such massed firepower, the French gave way and began a disorderly retreat. Seeing this, Wolfe ordered a bayonet charge and quickly sent the French reeling toward the gates of Quebec in utter rout. The Scots with their broadswords swinging went screaming after the fleeing Frenchmen and wreaked havoc among them. Montcalm, on horseback, falling back with his troops, was shot through the body but managed to keep his seat. Troopers supported him on each side until he was safe within the gates of the city, but he was mortally wounded. Wolfe too received fatal wounds as he led a charge on the right wing. Soldiers picked him up and carried him to the rear. As he lay on the ground, he refused to have them send for a surgeon, for he said it was "all over with him." When messengers reported that the French were in full retreat, he remarked to one of his officers, "Now, God be praised, I will die in peace."

Wolfe, an intrepid officer, had premonitions of his death before the battle. Telling a former schoolmate, John Jervis, that he did not expect to survive, he gave him a small picture of his fiancée and asked him to return it to her. As he and some of his officers waited in the boats before the landing, he recited lines from Gray's "Elegy Written in a Country Churchyard":

> The boast of heraldry, the pomp of pow'r,
> And all that beauty, all that wealth e'er gave,
> Await alike th' inevitable hour:
> The paths of glory lead but to the grave.

"Gentlemen," he said, "I would rather have written those lines than take Quebec."

The Battle of the Plains of Abraham was won by the sheer audacity of the commanding general and the heroism and discipline of his troops. Wolfe risked everything in a great gamble and won the victory. He might easily have lost and seen his men decimated. Had Montcalm waited until Bougainville came up with his elite army of two thousand well-trained regulars to attack Wolfe's rear while Montcalm made a frontal assault, supported by artillery available in Quebec (which he did not wait to bring into play), the battle almost certainly would have been a French victory. Wolfe's audacity won; Montcalm's lost. Such is the fate of military decisions.

But Quebec was still in French hands. The British, like their opponents, had lost their commander. Since Monckton, the second-in-command, was disabled by wounds, Brigadier General George Townshend took charge. He immediately ordered the army to fortify its camp and prepare for further action against Quebec. Guns were hauled up and emplaced ready for action. Admiral Saunders also stood by with his warships to continue the attack.

Meanwhile, inside Quebec, the French were in a state of panic. Vaudreuil, listening to this one and that one, believed the last advice that he received. The provincials had had enough of English musket fire, and their commanders claimed that they could not be driven into ac-

"The Storming of Quebec" was the name of this 18th-century English textile print. However, the spirited battle shown in such detail has little relation to what really occurred.

tion again. Food was even scarcer than before, and refugees from the countryside were pouring into the city demanding to be fed. After a council of war, Vaudreuil concurred in the decision of his officers to retreat around the English by crossing the St. Charles River; they hoped to make a stand if possible on the Jacques Cartier River farther up the St. Lawrence. In short, Quebec would be abandoned to its fate.

While these discussions were taking place, Montcalm lay dying. When the examining surgeon told him he had about twelve hours to live, he replied that he was glad he would not live to see the surrender of Quebec. One of his last acts was to send a message to the British commander, General Townshend, asking him to protect the

OVERLEAF: *An English artist, Richard Short, made this painting of British soldiers drilling before the Quebec cathedral in 1759, shortly after the capture of the city. Cathedral, Jesuits College (center), and Recollet Friars Church (right) show effects of the British bombardment.*

French prisoners in the tradition of humanity that the English customarily displayed. Montcalm then received the last sacraments and died early on September 14.

The command of the French armies passed to the Chevalier François Gaston de Lévis, whom Vaudreuil now recalled from Montreal. The unhappy responsibility of surrendering Quebec would fall to Jean Baptiste de Ramezay, whom Vaudreuil had appointed commandant of the city. Vaudreuil himself fled with the retreating troops and met Lévis near Three Rivers. The new commander, hearing that Quebec had not yet fallen, urged Vaudreuil to turn back and march with the reorganized troops to the relief of the city. The army was on the way when Lévis received news that Ramezay had surrendered Quebec. The fate of New France was sealed.

Although Vaudreuil condemned Ramezay for the capitulation, the poor man had no choice. The army—and Vaudreuil—had deserted the capital, leaving the commandant with only garrison troops and a few provincials who refused to fight any longer. General Townshend had pushed his entrenchments closer to the walls, and his heavy guns were trained to begin a bombardment. The people inside the town were panic-stricken, hungry, and ready to give up. When Ramezay asked for terms, Townshend promised that military personnel could surrender with the honors of war and be transported to France and that civilians would be protected in their persons and property and would be free to exercise their religion without interference. Under these generous terms, on September 17, 1759, Ramezay ran up a white flag; on the eighteenth Townshend marched in. The capital of New France, now firmly held by the British, would never be relinquished.

Although some eighteen hundred regulars and sailors —composing the garrison at Quebec—had surrendered and were shipped out to France on transports soon after the capitulation, the French still had a formidable army. Bougainville's battalions lay encamped at Cap Rouge. Lévis, an able commander, had reorganized the shattered troops who had retreated to the Jacques Cartier and had already begun the construction of a fort there. The French also had some ships of war on the upper St. Lawrence. Vaudreuil had fled to Montreal, where he established the new capital. Clearly the French would try to recapture Quebec, and the British hurried to strengthen its fortification. Admiral Saunders, eager to be gone before ice made the St. Lawrence impassable, sailed away with his men-of-war on October 18. The British garrison at Quebec would have to hold out until spring against any siege that the French might mount.

Since Townshend was anxious to return to England, General Monckton, now recovering from his wounds, appointed Brigadier General James Murray to be governor of Quebec and commander of the troops there, with Colonel Ralph Burton as lieutenant governor. Murray was left with some seven thousand men to hold Quebec and lower Canada.

The winter was cold, food and fuel were scarce, and the garrison was tense with rumors that the French were

COLONIAL WILLIAMSBURG

When American artist Charles Willson Peale went to London in 1768 to paint a portrait of William Pitt, he felt that it would be "indecorous" to ask the great statesman to sit for him and instead used a recent bust as a model. This engraving was made from the portrait that resulted.

296

going to try a surprise attack. Indeed, Lévis and Vaudreuil were planning a winter advance on Quebec; they had requisitioned quantities of long ladders and were drilling their troops in scaling operations. But they too suffered severely from lack of food and eventually decided to put off the attack. During the late winter and early spring, disease struck the British in Quebec, and before the return of warm weather Murray lost more than a thousand in dead. Two thousand more were incapacitated by sickness.

The French finally made their attempt to retake Quebec in late April. Lévis had sent an urgent message to France requesting ten thousand fresh soldiers with supplies and munitions before the British could send relief to Quebec or blockade the entrance to the St. Lawrence, but neither troops nor supplies arrived. Nevertheless, the French commander organized an expedition of thirty-nine hundred regulars and three thousand militia to advance on the former capital. On April 27 they reached St. Foy on the outskirts of Quebec, not far from the battlefield where Wolfe and Montcalm had fought the previous September. Although Murray had fewer than half as many men fit for action as Lévis commanded, he, like Montcalm at the Plains of Abraham, chose to attack rather than wait to stand a siege. He believed that his superior artillery would give him the advantage. Accordingly, early on the morning of April 28, he sent three thousand men against the French. Although his men fought valiantly, the French crushed his flanks, and the British had to take refuge within the walls of Quebec; Murray lost in killed, wounded, and captured nearly a third of his men, and he was left to defend Quebec with the remnant of his army. Everything would depend on whether the British or the French Navy first swept up the St. Lawrence.

Luckily for British arms, their Navy succeeded in denying the river to the French, and by the middle of May relief ships arrived in the basin opposite Quebec. Their arrival ended Lévis's hopes of taking the city, and, with little food left and gunpowder scarce, he had to fall back toward Montreal.

The final conquest of Canada depended upon crushing the remaining French forces on the upper St. Lawrence in the region around Montreal. To this end General Amherst now devoted his energies. He himself chose to lead an advance down the serpentine St. Lawrence from Lake Ontario; Murray would push up the river from Quebec; and Brigadier General William Haviland would lead a force from Lake Champlain against Fort Isle-aux-Noix. With these three pincers, the French not only would be defeated, but no corridor would be left for the escape of troops to wilderness redoubts.

The colonial governments had received instructions from Pitt early in 1760 to recruit militia to aid in this final drive against the common enemy. From the colonies north of Pennsylvania Amherst received some fifteen thousand men, but the other colonies raised fewer than four thousand troops for the Canadian expedition because the southern colonies had troubles nearer at hand. The Ohio Valley had to be held, and the Cherokees were carrying on a war on the southern frontier.

The advance against Montreal moved slowly but inexorably. By late August, Haviland had reached Fort Isle-aux-Noix, now defended by Bougainville; with supplies and munitions for only two days left, Bougainville concluded that he could not hold out. Evacuating the fort on August 28, he retreated with most of his men toward Montreal; he left a remnant of gunners to run up the white flag when the rest of the soldiers were clear of the fort. In the meanwhile, Murray was advancing from Quebec, and Amherst was moving down the rapids of the St. Lawrence from Lake Ontario. The defenses of the upper St. Lawrence—Fort La Galette and a hastily erected structure on an island, Fort Lévis—fell to Amherst. By September 6 he had his army in sight of Montreal. Murray had marched past Three Rivers and had procured the submission of the French in each parish as he advanced. Haviland had arrived from the south. The French were cornered. Although Lévis still breathed fire and brimstone, Vaudreuil knew the end had come, and on September 8 he signed a capitulation that surrendered all Canada on condition that his troops would be treated as prisoners of war, that the persons and property of civilians would be safe, and that individuals would be guaranteed freedom of worship.

The long years of war for possession of North America were over. France, it is true, still held the lower portion of Louisiana, but the final disposition of that territory would be made around council tables, not on the battlefield. The British were supreme from Florida north to the Arctic Ocean and west to the Mississippi River. To be sure, the frontiers were not yet safe, nor would they be for many years, for brush-fire wars would break out with the Indians; but the mortal conflict with France was over, and Pitt could look upon his handiwork and take pleasure in the outcome.

Social and Intellectual Life

By 1760 the original thirteen British colonies in North America all had settled governments, a well-established citizenry, a degree of economic strength, and the beginnings of a sophisticated society. Only Georgia, the latest of the colonies to be settled, remained an exposed frontier region, but by the Treaty of Paris in 1763, England took possession of Florida and removed the Spanish threat from the south. The same year, Georgia settled its troubles with the Creek Indians and established its borders to include most of the territory later incorporated into the states of Alabama and Mississippi. With rich lands beckoning, settlers from the older colonies and from overseas began to pour into Georgia.

In the other colonies, settlers were also pushing farther into the interior. Indian wars in the 1760's and British efforts to preserve Indian hunting grounds beyond the Alleghenies only temporarily halted the drive westward. Between 1760 and 1775 the back country began to fill up as settlers filtered over the mountains into fertile valleys beyond. With the French threat removed from Canada and the Spanish no longer a danger in Florida, frontiersmen had to contend only with Indians and such restrictions as Parliament in London might try to enforce.

Although postwar adjustments caused a temporary depression, the thirteen colonies continued to make advances in the decade and a half preceding the outbreak of hostilities with the mother country. The colonies now included a wide variety of peoples, trades, skills, and occupations. No longer were the inhabitants of British North America homesick Englishmen, eager to make money out of the products of the New World and return home. They were now Americans, with few emotional ties to the mother country. Many families in Virginia, Maryland, New England, New York, New Jersey, Pennsylvania, and the Carolinas had been there for several generations. They farmed the land, sailed the seas, fished commercially, and engaged in many businesses, crafts, and trades. A few acquired great fortunes and established themselves as a proud and aristocratic gentry.

Although the economic planners in London might imagine that they had created a

During the 18th century, Philadelphia became the cultural center of the colonies, and the corner of Second and Market Streets (left) was the heart of the city. The spire is on Christ Church.

closed mercantilist empire, with overseas possessions supplying raw material and the mother country furnishing manufactured products, the economic picture was not so simple as that. In spite of restrictive regulations and official disapproval, manufacturing on an increasing scale was flourishing in most of the colonies. For example, the manufacture of beaver hats was so successful in Boston, New York, Newport, and Philadelphia that it threatened the hat industry in England and resulted in orders to customs officers to watch for hats, manufactured in defiance of regulations, that were being shipped to the West Indies.

Some manufacturing in the colonies was carried on in violation of the Acts of Trade; some was encouraged by the British authorities. The production of pig iron, for example, was favored, but in 1750 Parliament forbade the colonies to set up slitting mills for making nails and iron rods, or forges for the making of steel or finished iron products. This law, however, was more honored in the breach than in the observance. The production of raw iron increased to such an extent that in 1775 the colonies produced thirty thousand tons, or about one seventh of the world's iron.

The colonies of course were not economically independent, but they had all developed substantial economic resources of a wide range and variety that promised ultimate prosperity. Farseeing individuals in all the colonies realized the immense undeveloped potential; a few had already taken advantage of the opportunities offered, while others were preparing to reap the benefits of the vast natural resources spread before them.

The colonies were still essentially rural, even those whose lifeblood was trade. Cities were small, and farming country lay just beyond their outskirts. A man could live in the center of Boston, New York, or Philadelphia and operate a farm nearby without much inconvenience. The largest city in the American colonies was Philadelphia—which was also one of the two or three largest cities in the British Empire—yet Philadelphia's population in 1760 was only 23,750. In the same year New York had a population of 18,000; Boston, 15,600; Newport, 7,500; and Charles Town, South Carolina, 8,000. By 1775 these populations had increased so that Philadelphia had 40,000; New York, 25,000; Boston, 16,000; Newport, 11,000; and Charles Town, 12,000. No other towns in the colonies numbered as many as 9,000 inhabitants before the Revolution. With two exceptions, all the towns that had shown material growth were ports.

The largest town in the interior was Lancaster, Pennsylvania, with between 5,000 and 6,000 inhabitants. The total population of the thirteen colonies in 1760 has been estimated at 1,695,000; by 1775 it had grown to 2,418,000, according to one estimate, and 2,803,000, according to another.

Immigration into the colonies increased rapidly with the coming of peace in 1763. The long wars with France had made sea travel even more hazardous than usual; furthermore, passage across the Atlantic was not easy to get when transports were required for troops and military supplies. The end of the wars caused economic maladjustments in Europe, a depression, and unemployment, all of which led to emigration to the New World. England had many unemployed people who saw no future at home. Scotland, a country poor in natural resources but rich in courageous men, had eager emigrants ready to try a new life overseas. Ireland had surplus populations of both native Irish and more recent settlers who had come from Scotland to occupy Ulster. In the Rhineland and other areas of Germany, prospective emigrants had heard of the opportunities many of their countrymen had found in Pennsylvania.

The emigration of Scots was particularly significant, for they had a far-reaching influence upon the civilization of the new land. Three strains of Scots came to America, with three distinct sets of characteristics: Ulster Scots from Northern Ireland, Lowland Scots, and Highlanders. The first to make a marked impression were the Ulster Scots, who began emigrating in large numbers in the early eighteenth century and continued to come until the end of the colonial period.

These Scots, usually described in American histories as "Scotch-Irish," were Presbyterians who had occupied much of Northern Ireland, lands earlier confiscated from the rebellious native Irish. They had developed a thriving linen and woolen industry, and many had fine herds of cattle. Their diligence had been their undoing, for their linen, wool, and cattle offered such competition to the English that Parliament passed various acts to restrict production in Ireland. Added to these restrictions was the so-called Test Act of 1704, which required all officeholders to subscribe to the Established Church, something the Presbyterians were not willing to do. Depression and bitter resentment among the Ulster Scots induced them once more to set out in search of a better life, this time in America. They came with a hatred of the English that they retained

Bethlehem, Pennsylvania, was only sixteen years old when an unknown artist painted this view in 1757. The Moravian founders of Bethlehem were only one of the many industrious groups that helped build the prosperity of Pennsylvania.

until the Revolution gave them an opportunity to vent their hostility in overt rebellion.

The number of Ulster Scots who came to America in the colonial period is difficult to ascertain, but one of the most thorough investigators of this movement estimates that they numbered approximately 200,000. The emigration from 1763 until the beginning of the Revolution was particularly heavy. During three years, from 1771 to 1773, some 28,600 left Ireland for the colonies. It is conservatively estimated that by the first census in 1790, a little over 14 per cent of the total white population, or something approaching 450,000 people, were Scotch-Irish.

The propaganda that William Penn and his agents carried on convinced the early emigrants that Pennsyl-vania offered greater opportunities for fertile land and for freedom of worship than any of the other regions. The experiences of the first Ulster Scots confirmed this, and they urged their fellow countrymen to come to Pennsylvania. Philadelphia, Chester, and Newcastle became the principal ports of entry for them, but obviously they could not settle in the region around Philadelphia, already occupied by earlier arrivals. Nor could they settle on the rich lands that the Germans had taken up in the Lancaster and York areas. Consequently they had to push on beyond the settlements into frontier zones.

Thus the Ulster Scots became the typical frontiersmen of the eighteenth century. Hardy and courageous, convinced that they had God on their side, they equated

301

the Indians with the Amalekites of the Old Testament and were ever ready to smite them hip and thigh and take their land. Although the Pennsylvania Quakers had made treaties with the Indians that they tried to observe meticulously, the obstreperous Ulster Scots frequently made trouble on the frontier and showed no scruples about squatting on Indian land. In time the land became theirs by right of occupation.

Ulster Scots, at first welcomed by Pennsylvania, soon became a problem for the Quaker colony. They did not get along with their neighbors of other stocks, either in Pennsylvania or elsewhere. The Germans disliked and avoided them. The English and the Welsh in Pennsylvania found them invariably troublesome. They showed little regard for land patents and simply settled where no authority existed to keep them out. A restless, ever-moving group, by the end of the colonial period they were found in clearings on the frontiers of most of the colonies, but chiefly from Pennsylvania to Georgia. A clannish people, they kept to themselves and did not mix easily with other groups.

An Anglican preacher, one Charles Woodmason, bitter and bigoted himself, made a journey in the back country of South Carolina in 1766 and commented on the Scotch Presbyterians whom he found there. One region on the Pee Dee River he described as "occupied by a set of the most lowest, vilest crew breathing— Scotch-Irish Presbyterians from the north of Ireland." Violently hostile to other faiths, Woodmason inveighed against the efforts of the South Carolina assembly to attract immigrants from Ulster instead of thinking of the interests of the Church of England: "Hence it is that above £30,000 Sterling have lately been expended to bring over 5 or 6000 Ignorant, mean, worthless, beggarly Irish Presbyterians, the Scum of the Earth, and Refuse of Mankind, and this, solely to ballance the Emigrations of People from Virginia, who are all of the Established Church."

These Scots from Ulster, for all of Woodmason's invectives, played an important role in the colonies. They spearheaded westward expansion and helped to open up the back country. They were the most ardent patriots when war broke out with England. Although bigots like Woodmason accused these Scots of shiftlessness, they produced educational leaders who set about establishing schools in order to ensure an adequate supply of Presbyterian preachers.

As for the Highlanders, a few arrived after the Jaco-

David Dove, here sketched by the noted early American artist Benjamin West, was one of the great schoolmasters of the colonies. Crotchety and forceful, Dove taught in the Philadelphia area from 1751 until his death in 1769. Besides his regular pupils, he trained a number of teachers who carried on his high standards of scholarship.

WEST, Sketchbook, 1779, PENNSYLVANIA HISTORICAL SOCIETY

bite rebellion of 1715, but the real influx began after the rebellion of 1745 and their defeat at Culloden in 1746. Then thousands of Highlanders accepted the king's offer of a pardon to rebels who would take the oath of allegiance and emigrate to America. Most of these refugees came to North Carolina and settled in the Cape Fear Valley. (The town now called Fayetteville was originally named Campbelltown because of its Scottish settlers.) Highlanders who had arrived in North Carolina earlier were largely responsible for persuading late-comers to settle in this region. This movement, continuing until the Revolution, gave North Carolina the largest body of Highlanders in the thirteen colonies. Other Highlanders, veterans discharged from Scottish regiments in the wars against the French, settled in upper New York. Most colonies had some Scottish Highlanders. At the Revolution, many of the Highlanders remained loyal to Great Britain, and the Battle of Kings Mountain in North Carolina was fought almost entirely by Scots on both sides.

Of the third group of Scots, the Lowlanders, many settled in towns and became traders and merchants. In fact, few colonial towns in the second half of the eighteenth century were without Lowland Scots engaged in trade, either in their own interests or representing merchants in Glasgow. After the mid-eighteenth century much of the tobacco processing industry of Great Britain centered in Glasgow, and many agents came from Glasgow to Virginia and Maryland and set up tobacco-buying stations at Norfolk, Annapolis, Baltimore, and at such inland points as Tappahannock. Scottish merchants and traders were also an important element in the economic life of New England, New York, Pennsylvania, the Carolinas, and Georgia in the period just prior to the Revolution. Some Lowland Scots settled in the back country and became farmers, but they are hard to trace, for they soon mingled with the Scotch-Irish and cannot be easily distinguished from them. The Scots, because of their toughness, tenacity, industry, and intellectual qualities, had an influence upon the colonies that far transcended their numerical strength.

The immigration of English settlers, as one could expect, increased enormously after the Peace of Paris in 1763. These immigrants were of all classes, but most were workmen, artisans, and farmers who helped to swell the labor force in those colonies where African slavery had not taken hold. Among the other increments of population arriving in the decades just prior to the

Revolution were large numbers of Germans (chiefly Lutherans but including some Moravians), a few Swiss, Italians, and French, and a scattering of Jews.

Negro slavery had become an institution in the agrarian colonies of the South and supplied the principal body of unskilled labor, but every colony had some slaves, even Georgia, where slavery at first had been outlawed. By 1770, out of a total population of something like 2,312,000, Negro slaves numbered 462,000. The greatest number were in the South, where they could work productively on the tobacco and rice plantations, but even New England had some slaves. Massachusetts in 1763 had 5,214 Negroes; Connecticut in 1774 had 6,464; Rhode Island, 3,761. In New York in 1774, out of a total population of 182,247, Negroes numbered 21,149. Most of these were held as slaves. In the southern colonies the numbers were much greater. Maryland in 1761 had 114,332 white inhabitants and 49,675 Negroes. A rough estimate of the population of Virginia in 1774 gave 300,000 whites and 200,000 Negroes; an estimate in South Carolina in 1775 listed 60,000 whites and between 80,000 and 100,000 Negroes.

Many Southerners were distressed over the institution of slavery, not only on moral grounds, but for economic and social reasons as well. In the eighteenth century Virginia and South Carolina lived in fear of slave insurrections, and South Carolina suffered several uprisings. What is more, Negro slavery discouraged white craftsmen and artisans and made skilled work in the South costly and hard to come by. But all efforts to curb the influx of slaves failed. Human greed was too powerful. The great rice planters in South Carolina needed slaves to work their fields, as did the tobacco planters of Virginia and Maryland. And the authorities in London would listen to no plea for the curtailment of a traffic that had proved immensely profitable to English traders and merchants for more than a century. New England merchants and shipowners were also deeply involved in the slave trade, and slavers from Boston and Newport regularly brought their cargoes of human freight to the West Indies or to mainland ports in the southern colonies.

In addition to black slaves from Africa, the colonies received large numbers of white bondsmen, known as indentured servants. Many came in the seventeenth century to the agrarian colonies, and until the end of the colonial period they continued to arrive by the shipload. Most of these immigrants could find no other way to pay their passage except to agree to serve a master for a stated period, usually four years but sometimes longer. At the expiration of a servant's period of servitude he received certain specified benefits, which varied from time to time and from place to place. These might consist of a sum of money, clothes, tools, or a piece of land.

Another kind of indentured servant was the "redemptioner," one who got to a port bound for America and could not raise sufficient money to pay for his passage. Captains of immigrant vessels would take such a passenger aboard and land him at an American port with the proviso that if he could not find friends or relatives who could raise the balance due on his passage, the captain could indenture him to a master for a sufficient time to reimburse the passage money.

An unwilling type of indentured servant who came to America was the convict, male or female, condemned to "transportation." These immigrants were unwelcome —Benjamin Franklin suggested sending back cargoes of rattlesnakes in retaliation. But though from time to time colonial legislatures passed laws to prevent convicts being shipped to them, London disallowed the laws. The northern colonies were fairly successful in keeping out convicts because they could provide less employment than the agrarian colonies. Although some convicts were sent to New Jersey, Pennsylvania, the Carolinas, and occasionally to other colonies, Virginia and Maryland received the greatest number of these undesirables. According to shipping returns, more than nine thousand convicts arrived in Maryland between 1748 and 1775. But, weak from jail fever and malnutrition, the death rate among them was phenomenally high.

The indentured servants who served out their time usually acquired land and became farmers or took up some trade or craft. In any case, if they survived the period of their indenture, the world was before them and ample opportunities beckoned. Many who arrived as indentured servants prospered and founded families that flourished in later years. Little or no stigma was attached to this means of getting across the Atlantic. The tide of immigration of servants of this type, chiefly Germans and Scots, greatly increased after 1765 and continued until the Revolution. It has been estimated that between 1750 and 1775, Pennsylvania alone probably received over fifty thousand indentured servants.

Scottish schoolmasters were quite common in Virginia and in other colonies. Indeed, planters were accustomed to buy indentured servants for this purpose, to the disgust of competing tutors. Jonathan Boucher, a Virginia tutor, complained in 1773 that "at least two thirds of the little education we receive are derived from instructors, who are either INDENTURED SERVANTS, OR TRANSPORTED FELONS. Not a ship arrives either with redemptioners or convicts, in which schoolmasters are not regularly advertised for sale, as weavers, tailors, or any other trade; with little difference, that I can hear of, excepting perhaps that the former do not usually fetch so good a price as the latter."

Because so many Scots served as tutors in Virginia, planters complained that their children learned to speak with a Scottish accent. Philip Vickers Fithian, a Princeton graduate who served as a tutor in the household of Robert Carter of Nomini Hall, notes in his diary for April 6, 1774, that Carter told him he preferred "a Tutor for his Children who has been educated upon the Continent [American], not on a supposition that such are better Schollars, or that they are of better principles, or of more agreeable Tempers; but only on account of pronunciation in the English Language."

Throughout the colonial period, skilled labor was in short supply, and those artisans and craftsmen with special talents enjoyed steady employment and good wages. In the more industrialized northern colonies, a wide variety of craftsmen flourished. Shipbuilding, for example, which was one of the most important industries in New England, required many different specialties: carpenters, joiners, sailmakers, shipwrights, blacksmiths, ropemakers, caulkers, painters, and related artisans. The flourishing iron industry gave work not only to foundrymen but to various subsidiary artisans: stone diggers, miners, limestone workers, charcoal burners, furnacemen, forgemen, drivers, and loaders. Flour milling, which flourished in the wheat-growing areas, especially in Pennsylvania and in Delaware on the Brandywine, required millers, watermen, mechanics, millrace tenders, and warehousemen. The variety of skilled trades in the days before machines took the place of men was endless, and a new country required skills and specialties that were rarely sufficient for the demand.

Every region needed carpenters, joiners, cabinetmakers, plasterers, slaters, brickmasons, sawyers, and painters—the craftsmen who made possible the houses that have survived as testimonials to their high standards of construction and design.

In the South, where Negro slaves were more abundant, some learned to be skilled craftsmen, and their competition served to discourage free white craftsmen—and to arouse considerable hostility among competing white labor. Even in New England, where some slaves were held, the competition with white free labor caused discontent and hostility. In fact, the threat of slave competition was in a large measure responsible for the virtual elimination of slavery in New England. John Adams said in 1795, "If the gentlemen had been permitted to hold slaves, the common white people would have put the slaves to death, and their masters too, perhaps."

Some colonial craftsmen were the equal of those found on the other side of the Atlantic. American silversmiths turned out excellent silverware in most of the principal cities of the coast. Although Paul Revere is perhaps the one most widely remembered today, other silversmiths from Boston to Charles Town, South Carolina, gained fine reputations. Silver served as a sort of savings bank for colonials who invested money in plate that had a steady value, could be identified by its markings, and served both useful and ornamental purposes. Every householder who could afford silver bought a little, even if only a few rat-tailed spoons.

The prosperity of colonial craftsmen depended upon the increase of wealth and the demand for their services. By the mid-eighteenth century, and even before, the colonies all had some families who lived in fine houses,

had sufficient servants, and could afford the luxuries available to the wealthy anywhere. Many of the objects that supplied the amenities of a prosperous life were from England, but there was also a demand for home manufactures. Although Robert Beverley could complain at the beginning of the eighteenth century that Virginians imported everything, even their woodenware, conditions in the next few decades altered materially. Philadelphia developed into a center where many crafts flourished, and Philadelphia furniture was widely distributed. Philadelphia also sent out to other towns in the colonies journeymen trained to carry on their trades. Benjamin Franklin sent a printer to Charles Town to start a printing office and newspaper. Cabinetmakers in Charles Town, advertising their skills, recommended themselves as "from Philadelphia." At Newport some of the finest cabinetmakers plied their crafts. Furniture made in the colonies ranged in quality from crude puncheon benches to excellent imitations of Chippendale. The best craftsmen, of course, were in the larger cities, but hardly a town of consequence in the later eighteenth century lacked some skilled workers capable of supplying the basic items needed in homes.

Many folk arts flourished. Even in frontier cabins, women developed distinctive styles for quilts and coverlets. The Pennsylvania Germans evolved decorated pottery, fancy needlework and embroidery, wood carving, wood painting, and their own distinctive forms of decorative arts.

One of the most important contributions of the Germans was the long squirrel rifle, manufactured by gunsmiths at Lancaster and elsewhere in the German districts of Pennsylvania. These rifles, sometimes with decorative devices carved on the stocks or engraved on steel panels, showed precise technical skill. The Germans were also responsible for building the great Conestoga covered wagons, which served as a great land fleet conveying farm products from the interior to the port of Philadelphia.

Colonial Americans took pride in their houses and built as well as their resources permitted. Not even the most ascetic Puritan could condemn a man for erecting a commodious house for an ever-growing family—and some of the Puritans were noted for the large number of their children. By the late eighteenth century, Boston merchant princes already lived in substantial mansions on Beacon Hill, furnished with handsome furniture, waited on frequently by black slaves far better trained

BOSTONIAN SOCIETY

This "Painters' Arms" sign, whose date of 1701 was altered from 1697, hung outside the shop of Thomas Child in Boston. The coat of arms is that of the painters' guild of London; Child apparently brought it over to America with him, as there was no similar guild in the colonies.

305

Williamsburg 1765

This is Williamsburg, capital of colonial Virginia, about as it was May 29, 1765, when Patrick Henry denounced the Stamp Act and George III to cries of "Treason!" from many of the burgesses. At the west end of Duke of Gloucester Street, the town's main axis, is the College of William and Mary (upper left), its buildings grouped in a triangle with the large Wren

Building at the apex. At its east end is the Capitol (lower right), where the House of Burgesses met and Patrick Henry spoke. The large edifice with spire at top center is the Governor's Palace, residence of the royal governor. The cross-shaped building where the avenue in front of the Governor's Palace intersects Duke of Gloucester Street is Bruton Parish Church (the steeple familiar to visitors to the Williamsburg of today was not built until 1769). The octagonal structure almost in the center of the view is the Magazine, where powder and arms were stored. Many of the houses shown here exist in today's restored Williamsburg only as foundations covered by grass or lost under the asphalt of parking lots.

This painting was commissioned to commemorate a very successful voyage by the slave brig Marie Séraphique, which in a crossing of five months in 1772–73 lost only seven of 340 slaves. The picture shows the ship anchored at Haiti while planters and their wives examine the Negroes or dine under the awning. Most slaves bound for the colonies passed through the West Indies.

than the servants in most southern plantation houses. The houses of lesser folk in New England were well and compactly built. Tradition and weather demanded good buildings, and the country had carpenters and brickmasons capable of this work. The majority of houses were of wood, the most plentiful building material, although from time to time, because of the fire hazard, municipal authorities tried to discourage wooden structures in favor of brick.

The Quakers, for all their talk about simplicity, built impressive mansions in Pennsylvania. James Logan, as early as 1728, erected in the country outside Philadelphia a magnificent brick house that he named Stenton. It was three stories high and had a great parlor and state dining room in addition to a smaller family dining room, living rooms, and a library. Isaac Norris, another rich Quaker, built a great country house, Fair Hill, not far from Logan's estate. One influence that helped to foster good architecture in Philadelphia was the establishment of the Carpenters' Company, a guild of master carpenters, who published their own manual and insisted upon standards of good construction.

Philadelphia, the wealthiest of the colonial cities, took pride in its public buildings, which followed the style now called Georgian, an adaptation of classical lines and proportions to the needs and the materials of the day. The American Philosophical Society building, the State House, and Carpenters' Hall all exemplify the best of this style of architecture in public buildings.

Professional architects were not generally available, even for the most imposing public buildings. Peter Harrison, an English ship captain who settled at Newport in the mid-eighteenth century, has been called the first American architect. Harrison was responsible for designing King's Chapel in Boston, and in Newport the Redwood Library, the Touro Synagogue, Freemason's Hall, and the Brick Market. William Buckland, who eventually settled down in Annapolis, was another of the early architects. He was responsible for designing and building George Mason's house, Gunston Hall, which was completed in 1759, and for the design of many houses in Maryland. But most houses in British America before the Revolution were planned and built by carpenters with only the help of books of designs and plans imported from England.

That so many houses from New England to Georgia were well designed and well built testifies to the skill of master craftsmen. The best carpenters had a high de-

gree of competence and were able to follow the designs found in a number of books ranging from recent editions of Andrea Palladio of Vicenza to that ubiquitous manual for ordinary builders, Batty Langley's *The City and Country Builder's and Workman's Treasury of Designs* (1740). A master carpenter, faced with a commission to erect a mansion for a Boston merchant or a plantation house on the James River, had a variety of books to help him and the owner select the kind of house desired.

Only the well to do, however, could afford the skills supplied by the best trained of the master carpenters, and they frequently complained of the dearth of experienced workmen. This scarcity was greatest in the South, where slave labor tended to drive out free artisans. Slaves attained a considerable degree of skill and readily learned from craftsmen brought in to teach them or to work independently. Slaves did much of the building in Maryland, Virginia, and the Carolinas.

On the frontier, and in isolated areas, buildings had to be such as a settler could erect with his own hands and the help of family and friends. From the Germans and the Swedes, British immigrants learned the art of making log cabins, pigpen style, and by the eighteenth century the log cabin had become the characteristic wilderness structure. With notched logs, and mud for caulking the cracks, a tight and substantial house could be built with relative ease.

Although wars and depressions might cause temporary halts to development, not even the threat of a French victory during the eighteenth century stopped for long the growth of the colonies or the promise of advancement and ultimate prosperity they offered the settlers. Since labor was always in demand, no ablebodied man need want for work that would pay enough for him to save something and get ahead. Since land was abundant and could be had on reasonable terms, every man, even the day laborer, could look forward to a time when he might be a landowner. The possession of land has always conferred a certain status, and even though land in America was not so scarce as in Europe, its possession continued to carry with it both material and intangible assets.

In the South, the great planters, possessing sometimes thousands of acres, developed a landed aristocracy that succeeded in monopolizing much of the economic and political power. In Virginia, planters like the Carters, Byrds, Burwells, Randolphs, Fitzhughs, and scores of others owned the best lands in the tidewater region and held the most important offices in the province. They were vestrymen in the Anglican Church—the established state church. They served as justices of the peace, sheriffs of the counties, colonels of the militia, members of the Council of State, and members of the House of Burgesses. At meetings of the council and the House of Burgesses the flower of this planter aristocracy gathered in the little capital of Williamsburg to attend to political business and to enjoy social contacts that they missed on distant plantations. They entertained each other at dinners and balls and created a lively social "season." Some of the planters maintained town houses in Williamsburg.

In their origins these planters were usually men whose immigrant forebears had had sufficient capital to acquire land with servants enough to cultivate the tobacco that made them prosperous. Few of these families can be traced with certainty to aristocratic families in England. The Byrds, for example, got their start from a goldsmith, John Byrd, who married the daughter of a ship captain named Thomas Stegg engaged in the Virginia trade. The son of this match, the first William Byrd, came to Virginia to help his uncle, also named Thomas Stegg, in trade he had developed with the Indians. William Byrd I became a prosperous Indian trader, inherited land and bought more, and joined the ranks of the top planter class.

These planters, intent upon getting ahead, worked hard at the tasks of management. Although they enjoyed the social amenities, and some wasted their substance in gaming and horse racing, most of them devoted themselves with singular concentration to making their plantations pay. Landon Carter, who lived for many years at Sabine Hall and kept a diary from 1752 to 1778, reports in minute detail the routine of a busy planter. Carter emphasizes the wastefulness of slave labor, the incompetence of overseers and their charges, the everlasting oversight required of the landowner, and the frequency of disaster and loss. No planter who achieved wealth could afford to live in indolence and the silken ease pictured in popular romance. These were hard-working aristocrats.

Maryland had an upper planter class much like that of Virginia, some of whom acquired great tracts of land and established family dynasties of power and continuing influence. Families like the Carrolls, Chews, Hammonds, Lloyds, Taskers, and Dulanys dominated colonial Maryland. The Dulanys are a conspicuous example

of self-made aristocrats who achieved wealth and power. The founder of the family, Daniel Dulany the elder, arrived from Ireland in the early eighteenth century as a redemptioner. At Port Tobacco, where he landed in April, 1703, he was lucky enough to find a lawyer, Colonel George Plater, who needed an apprentice capable of serving as clerk. Plater paid the passage owed to the ship captain and took Dulany as an indentured apprentice until he worked out his time. This apprenticeship gave Dulany the experience needed to qualify as a lawyer, and in time he rose to wealth and eminence, holding the offices of attorney general, commissary general, and member of the Governor's Council. His son, Daniel Dulany the younger, attended Eton and Cambridge, married an heiress, Rebecca Tasker, and became one of the most influential landowners in Maryland.

South Carolina had an upper class whose fortunes

New England merchant James Tilley had his portrait painted by John Copley in 1757, when he was fifty years old and had attained success. Tilley was only one of many merchants to become affluent in that time of flourishing commerce.

came from rice planting, sometimes combined with trade and merchandising. In this colony, too, many of the prominent aristocrats at the end of the colonial period traced their origins back to simple workmen who managed to capitalize upon opportunities to buy land and make a profit from trade. Some of the early settlers in South Carolina came from Barbados, where they had made enough money in sugar plantations to enable them to get a start in the new colony. Few aristocratic families in Charles Town in the late eighteenth century exceeded the grandeur of the Manigaults. The first of the name was Pierre, a craftsman who arrived in Charles Town about 1695, tried farming, and eventually opened a tavern. As he prospered he established a brandy distillery, which did well, and set up a shop for making barrels. Soon Pierre Manigault was the owner of a second distillery and of warehouses on the Charles Town docks. His son Gabriel Manigault followed in his father's footsteps, added to the business, and became the richest man in the province. Gabriel's son Peter, born in 1731, went to London to finish a classical education, became a member of the Inner Temple, and was admitted to the English bar. One of the most prominent lawyers in South Carolina and a polished aristocrat, he took his place in the provincial assembly and eventually was elected its speaker. Thus the line of Pierre Manigault, craftsman, tavernkeeper, and distiller, prospered.

Henry Laurens, Revolutionary leader, was another self-made South Carolina aristocrat who combined business and planting. Son of a Huguenot saddler who made a comfortable fortune in his saddlery business, Henry Laurens branched out as a commission merchant exporting rice, indigo, deerskins, and furs, and dealing in imports of wine and slaves. He bought up rice plantations and was soon one of the wealthiest and most influential men in the colony. Before the Revolution, Laurens, who never liked selling slaves, gave up that part of the business and concentrated upon his rice plantations.

South Carolina grandees of the tidewater region combined trade and farming and made a profit in both. Charles Town was a convenient port for West Indian traffic and for trade with the coast of Africa, which offered a good market for rice. The great planters had town houses on the riverfront now known as "the Battery," where sea breezes could cool them in summer. In the winter they lived on their plantations bordering the Cooper, the Ashley, the Santee, or some other river, but heat, mosquitoes, and malaria made the river houses uninhabitable in the summer. It was then that the planters withdrew to their town houses in Charles Town for a social season that included concerts given by the St. Cecelia Society, plays at the Dock Street Theatre, and balls and social gatherings of many sorts. Savannah, Georgia, and Wilmington, North Carolina, had a similar social structure.

All the colonies developed an upper crust of wealthy planters, merchants, or shippers who quickly assumed the airs and trappings of an aristocracy. The planter aristocracy of the agrarian colonies approximated English county families more nearly than any other social group in America, but the merchant grandees of New England were fully as proud of their accomplishments and status. The richest pre-Revolutionary merchant in Boston was Thomas Hancock, who at thirteen was apprenticed to a bookseller. By the time he received his freedom, he was able to set up as an independent bookseller himself and later married Lydia Henchman, daughter of the leading bookseller of Boston. Hancock traded thriftily and expanded from bookselling into other businesses, including a mercantile establishment that dealt in fish, whale oil, rum, and general merchandise. Hancock became a partner with Charles Apthorp, another noted merchant of the day; between them they supplied the British army in Nova Scotia under generous contracts that added to their wealth. In 1755 Hancock furnished seventeen vessels used in transporting the Acadians to their places of exile. Like many merchants of the day, Hancock looked upon smuggling as an honorable occupation and was noted for his success in evading the law.

Having no son to inherit his wealth, Thomas Hancock adopted his nephew, John Hancock, who became a vocal patriot, a signer of the Declaration of Independence, and, as the richest merchant on the patriot side, a substantial contributor to the cause of liberty. But John Hancock had the temperament and manners of a *nouveau riche*. He flaunted his wealth, lived ostentatiously, annoyed honest John Adams, and himself was annoyed because the Continental Congress did not make him commander in chief of its army.

Boston had many great merchants who lived luxuriously but avoided the flamboyance of John Hancock. Their ships sailed to ports in Europe, the Wine Islands, Africa, the West Indies, and to coastal ports of British America. Their cargoes were varied, sometimes legal, sometimes illegal, but usually profitable. They transported vast quantities of rum and traded some of it for slaves on the Guinea coast. Peter Faneuil accumulated a great fortune in trade and was known in his time as a highly successful smuggler. He is also charged with making part of his fortune in the slave trade. A bachelor himself, he named one of his best ships *The Jolly Bachelor*. When news reached him of this vessel's safe arrival in Boston harbor with a human cargo, Faneuil is said to have gone piously to church to thank God for making him the instrument by which so many heathen souls were brought to salvation. Since he donated to Boston Faneuil Hall, called "the Cradle of Liberty" because of the many patriotic meetings held there, a current saying was that "the Cradle of Liberty rocks on the bones of the Middle Passage."

No Virginia aristocrat managed to reach such eminence as a fisherman of Kittery, Maine, William Pepperrell. His father, also named William, as a small boy was apprenticed to the captain of a fishing vessel. Pepperrell the elder worked hard and became a successful fish and lumber dealer. Young William became a partner in his father's business, accumulated a competence, married the granddaughter of Judge Samuel Sewall, and was made commander of the expedition against Louisbourg. Grateful for the capture of Louisbourg, the British government in 1746 created Pepperrell a baronet, the first American to receive such a high honor. Sir William's son and heir died before his father, and for a time the title lapsed; but Sir William made his grandson, William Pepperrell Sparhawk, heir to his estate on condition that he drop his last name; and in 1774 the king made him a baronet.

In the later colonial era, Rhode Island had some of the most prosperous and enterprising merchants in all New England. They engaged in a highly diversified commerce that extended from New England to Europe, Africa, the West Indies, and the mainland colonies south to Georgia. Never meticulous about obeying the Acts of Trade, the Rhode Islanders found their coast admirably suited to evading British revenue cutters, and they managed to smuggle in quantities of molasses from the French West Indies. Most of this molasses went into the manufacture of rum, in great demand on the Guinea coast, where it could be exchanged for slaves.

Newport was the first town in Rhode Island to develop an important merchant aristocracy. By the middle of the eighteenth century, merchants such as Daniel Ayrault, John Channing, Henry Collins, Abraham Redwood, William Ellery, Godfrey and John Malbone, and Samuel Vernon had created a golden age for Newport. Many made their fortunes in the slave trade.

Few mercantile dynasties anywhere in America exceeded the Browns of Providence in the diversity and the magnitude of their interest. The first of the name, Chad Brown, who arrived in New England in 1638, fathered a line that continues unbroken to the present day. In the later eighteenth century the Browns controlled fleets of vessels trading to the ends of the earth; they engaged in varied mercantile and manufacturing activities that included the production of spermaceti candles, the distilling of rum, and the smelting of pig iron. Hardly a profitable activity in Rhode Island failed to enlist the interest of the Browns. Obadiah Brown, business leader of the family after 1739, was responsible for developing new enterprises, including a "chocklit" mill where he ground chocolate beans brought back by shippers from the West Indies. He also began the making of candles, and as a young man, in the sloop *Mary*, he made the initial voyage of the Browns to the Gold Coast in search of slaves. After Obadiah's death in 1762, the business was continued by four Brown brothers under the name of Nicholas Brown and Company. Melancholy after the death of his wife in 1773, one of the brothers, Moses, disturbed by thoughts of the horrors of the slave trade, which had added to the company's prosperity, withdrew from active participation in commerce to lead a contemplative life. He later became a Quaker and joined the Rhode Island Abolition Society. Not all consciences were comfortable about the nefarious Guinea trade.

Rhode Island saw the rise of a number of prominent Jewish merchants. Some were Sephardic Jews whose ancestors had fled to Holland from Spain and Portugal; others were Jews who had reached Holland from Germany. Ultimately some of these Dutch Jews emigrated to the colonies, principally to New York, Philadelphia, Newport, Charles Town, and Savannah. In the decades preceding the Revolution, the Jews of Newport were among the most prosperous in North America. The leading Jewish merchant was Aaron Lopez, who had a fleet of more than thirty ships trading wherever a profit could be made; he was described by a contemporary, Ezra Stiles, as "a merchant of the first eminence, for honor and extent of commerce probably surpassed by no merchant in America." Jacob Rivera, father-in-law of Lopez, is sometimes credited with the introduction of

the technique of making spermaceti candles, though Obadiah Brown may also claim that distinction. The first castile soap appears to have been manufactured in Rhode Island by James Lucena. Although the Jewish merchants of Rhode Island were not numerous, they played a conspicuous part in the commercial development of the area.

New York had an aristocracy of wealthy and influential families, some of whom held vast tracts of land, while others depended upon the Indian trade and a variety of commercial activities. From the time of the Dutch occupation of the Hudson Valley, a few individuals had carved out great estates, and wealthy families frequently intermarried and consolidated fortunes already substantial. The Van Cortlandts, the Livingstons, the Schuylers, the De Lanceys, and a few other families owned vast tracts of land, lived like princes, and exerted great political influence in the colony. They also interested themselves in developing commercial enterprises, in acquiring still more land, and in adding to their wealth as best they could. Philip Schuyler, for example, went to England on business in 1761 and returned with fresh ideas for improving his property. What he had seen in England made him eager to live like an English country gentleman. To his patrimony he added thousands of acres of land in the Mohawk Valley and erected on its streams grist mills, flour mills, and the first water-powered flax mill in the country.

A numerous clan of Livingstons (descended from a wellborn Scot, Robert Livingston, who was the first of his family in New York) wielded great power in the province. In the legislative assembly of 1759, out of twenty-seven members, four were Livingstons. Presbyterians, they led a popular faction opposed to Lieutenant Governor James De Lancey, head of the Episcopal party. Philip Livingston, later one of the signers of the Declaration of Independence, was not only a man of wealth, but he also had many cultural and intellectual interests. In 1737 he had received an A.B. degree from Yale, and he retained a concern for higher education throughout the rest of his life.

With opportunities for the acquisition of land and a chance to participate in profitable trade, a few enterprising men in all the colonies managed to outstrip their less energetic or less fortunate contemporaries. They rose to positions of power, had the status of grandees, and were sometimes proud, autocratic, disdainful of the multitude, and forgetful of their own origins. But many

Next only to the Bible, Poor Richard's Almanack *was the most popular book in the colonies. At left is a portion of a printed "Poor Richard's handkerchief." A portrait of Benjamin Franklin is in the center; at top and bottom are scenes that illustrate maxims from the* Almanack.

of the self-made aristocrats in the colonies, both in New England and the South, had a keen sense of social obligation and a belief that privilege carried with it responsibility. That concept helps to explain the leaders who had a part in creating a nation after 1776. Throughout the colonial period—as later—America offered a chance for the man of intelligence and diligence to rise through his own efforts.

The prominence of the men of wealth, the houses they built, the furniture and silver they left for posterity, and the records of the grand life they lived tend to obscure the fact that the bulk of the population in all the colonies were hard-working folk who plied their trades, farmed their own land, sailed their fishing craft, and owned no slaves to save them from the burden of labor. These were independent people, some of whom in time would save, invest, and pull themselves up the economic and social ladder, for such was the process in a new country. Others were content to live out their lives in the stations to which God had called them, getting a satisfaction out of their skills and crafts, their farms and trades. Not every colonial aspired to be a great planter or a rich merchant. But while many were satisfied with the simple life in which they found themselves, others burned with a zeal for self-improvement and an ambition to rise in the world, traits that have always characterized Americans. The best colonial expression of this ambition for self-improvement can be found in the works of Benjamin Franklin, who set forth prescriptions for advancement in his own *Autobiography* and in *Poor Richard's Almanack*.

An epitome of Franklin's advice on how to get ahead in the world was compiled by himself in 1757 for the *Almanack* of 1758 and is known as "Father Abraham's Speech," or by its more usual title, "The Way to Wealth." Few if any other writings by an American have been so widely disseminated and so often quoted. Under the fiction of an old man delivering an impromptu bit of advice at an auction sale, Franklin gathered up his best proverbs and wove them into a fable full of sly humor and shrewd counsel. There, crystallized for all time, are adages that are still commonplaces in American thinking: *Sloth, like Rust, consumes faster than Labour wears, while the used Key is always bright. . . . The sleeping Fox catches no Poultry. . . . Early to Bed, and early to rise, makes a Man healthy, wealthy and wise. . . . Industry need not wish. . . . At the working Man's House Hunger looks in, but dares*

not enter. . . . God gives all Things to Industry. Then plough deep, while Sluggards sleep. . . . Three Removes is as bad as a Fire. . . . Keep thy Shop, and thy Shop will keep thee. . . . A Ploughman on his Legs is higher than a Gentleman on his Knees. . . . Pride breakfasted with Plenty, dined with Poverty, and supped with Infamy. . . . The second Vice is Lying, the first is running in Debt. . . . 'Tis hard for an empty Bag to stand upright. These proverbs and many others in the same crisp idiom are a part of the little narrative of Father Abraham's speech, which warns near the end that "this Doctrine, my Friends, is *Reason* and *Wisdom*; but after all, do not depend too much upon your own *Industry*, and *Frugality*, and *Prudence*, though excellent Things, for they may all be blasted without the Blessings of Heaven; and therefore ask that Blessing humbly, and be not uncharitable to those that at present seem to

In *Adam*'s Fall
We finned all.

Thy Life to mend
This Book attend.

The Cat doth play
And after flay.

A Dog will bite
A Thief at Night.

The Eagle's Flight
Is out of Sight.

The idle Fool
Is whipt at School.

The New-England Primer, *of which this is one page, was like other schoolbooks of its time in that it tried to inculcate religious and moral precepts along with the ability to read. This Primer was published in 1769.*

want it, but comfort and help them. Remember Job suffered, and was afterwards prosperous."

This little tract, which combined worldly prudence with a dash of piety as a proper formula for success, quickly gained an international audience. Franklin himself was astonished, and not a little proud, of its reception. As he pointed out in the *Autobiography*, English newspapers printed it widely, householders bought broadside versions and stuck them up in their houses, the clergy and gentry distributed large quantities to their parishioners and tenants, and publishers in France brought out two translations. "In Pennsylvania, as it discouraged useless expense in foreign superfluities," Franklin observed with satisfaction, "some thought it had its share of influence in producing that growing plenty of money which was observable for several years after its publication." The popularity of "The Way to Wealth" has gained momentum from that day to this. More than a thousand editions have been recorded in English, and some three hundred in foreign languages. Franklin's essay, which served as a manual of success, sums up the American belief that the little man, by his own efforts and merits, can become the captain of his fate. This doctrine, derived from experience and observation by one of the wisest of colonial Americans, profoundly influenced the social attitudes of many Americans in Franklin's own time and ever since.

From Maine to Florida, the conditions of colonial life bred an independence of spirit and a sense of freedom unlike anything that Europeans had known. No tenant felt bound to the land; no artisan thought himself confined to one employer or even to one locality. If he did not like life as he found it, he could go somewhere else. The mobility that has always characterized American life had its beginning at the very start of civilization on these shores. All the colonies had groups among their population who were constantly on the move in search of conditions more to their liking. For example, the intractable and hard-bitten Scots who moved into the back country of the Carolinas, Virginia, Maryland, and Pennsylvania were not easily governed or influenced by the men of entrenched wealth and position in tidewater regions. These Scots had come to America to escape both poverty and tyranny, and they had no notion of being subservient to any established class of men.

A quality that most of the back-country folk had in abundance, particularly those of Scottish derivation, was a determination to maintain their freedom and to resist encroachments upon any rights that the new country offered. Political acumen was not a monopoly of the well to do and the privileged; backwoodsmen developed a degree of political skill and utilized these political talents in a continuing contest with the powers in authority. In Pennsylvania, Virginia, and the Carolinas the division between seaboard society and an interior group that grew steadily more discontented and aggressive is particularly marked in the three decades preceding the Revolution. The readiness of frontiersmen to demand their rights and fight for them, to insist upon equality of representation, and to protest the encroachment of vested interests represented by older, more secure, and more conservative elements had an important influence in the colonies from Pennsylvania southward. Lines drawn between the upcountry folk and the conservative groups in tidewater regions persisted for generations after independence. Most of the people in the back country in the 1760's and the early 1770's were less concerned about the tyranny of King George III than about the oppression of their own lawmakers, who paid little heed to their complaints about taxes and fees exacted for every legal transaction.

So acute was the unrest in North Carolina in 1768 that the dissidents, calling themselves "Regulators," formed an organization to resist high taxes, unjust laws, and exorbitant fees. A petition presented to the legislature by thirty citizens of Orange and Rowan counties declared that the "poor Petitioners" had been "continually squez'd and oppressed by our Publick Officers both with Regard to their fees as also in the Laying on of Taxes as well as in Collecting together with Iniquitous appropriations, and wrong applications." "Money is very scarce," they added, and though "to gentlemen Rowling [rolling] in affluence, a few shillings per man, may seem triffling yet to Poor people who must have their Bed and Bed clothes yea their Wives Petticoats taken and sold to defray these charges, how tremendious." They could come by neither paper money nor coins with which to pay taxes, and they craved redress from the legislature, which gave no relief.

The Regulators at first tried to influence the provincial government by petitions and pamphleteering, but when protests proved vain, they drifted into a state of open rebellion. On May 16, 1771, Governor William Tryon with a force of militia met more than two thousand Regulators a few miles from Hillsboro in an engagement that ever since has been known as the Battle

315

of Alamance, from the name of a nearby creek. Each side lost nine men killed and a number wounded. Later twelve Regulators were tried for treason and six were hanged. The Regulator movement broke up, but discontent remained. Although the resistance of North Carolina's back-countrymen was more overt than that elsewhere, similar animosities had developed in the interior regions of most of the colonies.

Yet it would be an oversimplification to say—as some historians have attempted to show—that the American Revolution was an internal conflict between classes as well as an external struggle against British rule. Social relations in all the colonies were complex, and they varied from colony to colony. A generalization for North Carolina will not fit precisely conditions in New York. Nevertheless, no colony was without groups unhappy over the status quo. The British missed a chance to capitalize upon frontier antagonism toward the well-to-do cliques of the provincial ruling classes.

The modern concept of class structure is easy to overemphasize in discussing the stresses and strains in colonial society. If we read into the complaints of artisans in Philadelphia, New York, or Boston in the 1760's the incipient unrest of a proletariat, we shall misinterpret the facts of colonial life. Nor were discontented back-countrymen necessarily the precursors of Western radicals. Indeed, frontiersmen were more conservative in some respects than tidewater folk. Cultural conservatism, for instance, is often more manifest in frontier societies than in older settled regions. Nowhere is this more evident than in efforts in frontier communities to reproduce the best of the older societies that settlers had known. Preachers and teachers labored to re-establish religious observances, a sense of decorum, and at least elemental opportunities for education.

Few were more concerned about education than the Presbyterian ministers who carried both the gospel and literacy to the Scotch-Irish on a far-flung frontier. Although one modern historian has termed the Scotch-Irish "shiftless" because of their restlessness and mobility, they were responsible for some of the most significant educational developments in the back country. The Reverend William Tennent, Sr., a graduate of the University of Edinburgh, founded, as early as 1726, an institution of higher learning at Neshaminy, Pennsylvania, which became known as the Log College. Here he turned out Presbyterian preachers, trained in Greek and Latin, for it was a cardinal belief of the Presby-

William Bartram, like his father John, was a leading naturalist of the 18th-century period that saw a flowering of the arts and sciences. The pictures at left resulted from a trip during the 1770's to Florida and the southern colonies and are, from top: the marsh pink (Sabbatia), *a coppernosed bream, and snails* (Polygyra albolabris).

terians that the password to Heaven must be uttered in one of the classical tongues. John Blair and Samuel Finley, two early presidents of Princeton, were graduates of the Log College. Princeton, founded in 1746, sent out a steady stream of preachers and teachers who carried not only a message of Calvinistic theology but instruction in the elements of literacy and often some contact with classical culture.

For Americans, education has always been regarded as the road to social advancement. Faced with the disintegrating forces of the frontier, settlers in America very early set about establishing schools or otherwise providing for the education of their children, "lest they grow up barbarous in the wilderness." They soon established the doctrine that education supplied a way to rise in the world. Not every father, of course, eagerly sought to send his children to school; many were content that their children should help in the fields or should be bound out to work at a trade. Few communities, however, were without influential citizens concerned over the need for educational facilities. Boston, and Massachusetts Bay generally, set an example from the seventeenth century onward by establishing schools free to those unable to pay. Even in the backward parts of North Carolina, from the middle years of the eighteenth century some effort was made to provide at least minimal instruction in reading, writing, and ciphering for those who wanted to learn.

But the acquisition of even rudimentary learning was not easy in rural areas where settlements were sparse and the people poor. Parents had to be responsible for seeing that children learned to read and write. If the parents were illiterate, children might inherit their illiteracy unless they picked up a little knowledge from a passing circuit rider or an itinerant schoolmaster. The wonder is that colonial Americans in the back country acquired even the rudiments of an education and developed a respect for learning. In some fashion most of them got at least a little book learning, enough at least to read the King James version of the Bible, often the only book in their possession.

The story was different in the older and more sophisticated regions. Here were schools and opportunities for association with enlightened folk. Philadelphia could offer instruction in a wide range of subjects from surveying and navigation to draftsmanship and painting. Everyone is familiar with Benjamin Franklin's description in his *Autobiography* of the interest of young craftsmen and businessmen of Philadelphia in book learning—and the practical use to which they put it. Franklin organized a club "for mutual improvement," the Junto, and later the same group established a subscription library for the purchase of improving books— "the mother of all the North American subscription libraries," Franklin declared. And he added: "These libraries have improved the general conversation of Americans, made the common tradesmen and farmers as intelligent as most gentlemen from other countries, and perhaps have contributed in some degree to the stand so generally made throughout the colonies in defence of their privileges."

Franklin's words are significant. For by the beginning of the controversies with Great Britain, the colonies could boast a mature citizenry, many of whom were well read and well educated for their day. Opportunities for higher education existed at Harvard College (1636), the College of William and Mary (1693), Yale (established in New Haven in 1716), Princeton (founded in 1746 as the College of New Jersey), Columbia (chartered in 1754 as King's College), and Pennsylvania (first called the College, Academy, and Charitable School of Philadelphia under a charter revised in 1755). Two other colleges were chartered in the colonial period but were slow in getting organized: Brown (first created as Rhode Island College in 1764) and Rutgers (first chartered as Queen's College in 1766).

Every colony also had a few booksellers, book collectors, and libraries. The Reverend Cotton Mather in Boston and William Byrd II in Virginia accumulated two of the best private libraries, each consisting of something over thirty-six hundred volumes. No two individuals could have been more different than Mather and Byrd, yet both bought and read many of the same books: the classics, scientific treatises, political tracts, legal works, philosophic works, practical manuals, sermons, and devotional books. Byrd, worldly and sophisticated, was an inveterate sermon-reader: "In the evening I read a sermon in Mr. Norris but a quarrel which I had with my wife hindered my taking much notice of it," he observes in his diary for December 25, 1710. Not many book buyers of the eighteenth century could boast libraries like those of Mather and Byrd, but the demand for books increased as the century wore on, and by the end of the period the book trade was flourishing, particularly in Boston and Philadelphia. The best book market in the South was Charles Town.

Another evidence of intellectual maturity was the widespread interest in science. Americans accepted the Baconian belief that in science one could find a means for the relief of man's estate, a belief that grew from generation to generation. Benjamin Franklin was instrumental in founding a scientific society "for the promotion of useful knowledge," which in 1744 took shape as the American Philosophical Society and in 1769 merged with another organization, the American Society, which had developed from the old Junto.

Franklin's own investigations of electricity, which had the practical result of encouraging the use of lightning rods, gave him an international reputation. The first account of his experiments was published in London in 1751 with the title: *Experiments and Observations on Electricity, made at Philadelphia in America, by Mr. Benjamin Franklin.* Translations into French, German, and Italian attracted widespread attention and let the world know that natural philosophy was not the exclusive monopoly of the Old World.

Scientific contacts between the Old World and America were not new, for colonial observers had conscientiously reported their findings to the Royal Society in London and to other scientific groups. Botany, zoology, and mineralogy were naturally the subjects of greatest interest; many Europeans had believed that cures for the ills of mankind might be found in plant, animal, or mineral materials from the New World. Eighteenth-century collectors appointed agents in America to search for specimens and material of interest, beauty, or utility. Peter Collinson, a London merchant and himself a member of the Royal Society, made arrangements with a Philadelphia Quaker, John Bartram, to collect botanical specimens and seeds for him and his friends. The letters between them, which continued until Collinson's death in 1768, reveal the keen observations of the Quaker naturalist, who established a botanical garden on the banks of the Schuylkill River. A self-trained scientist, Bartram learned Latin so that he could study the work of European contemporaries like Linnaeus, the Swedish botanist. So great was Bartram's fame that Linnaeus sent one of his own research students, Peter Kalm, to Philadelphia to study with him.

Naturalists, observant physicians, and inspired amateurs of natural philosophy flourished in the second half of the eighteenth century. Dr. Alexander Garden, a physician of Charles Town, for whom the gardenia is named, typifies the community of scientific interest that

existed in the colonies. In 1754 he traveled to New York, where he met Dr. Cadwallader Colden, who had written on botany, anthropology, physics, mathematics, and various medical problems including yellow fever, cancer, and diphtheria. Returning from New York, Garden stopped in Philadelphia to see Bartram and his plants. Soon Dr. Garden was corresponding with Colden, Bartram, John Clayton of Virginia, and with the leading scientists in Europe: Linnaeus of Uppsala, John Frederick Gronovius of Leiden, and others. In 1763 Garden was elected to the Royal Society of Uppsala, and in 1773 to the Royal Society of London.

Although colonial colleges followed traditional curricula fairly closely, they did not altogether neglect science; in a few instances distinguished scientists

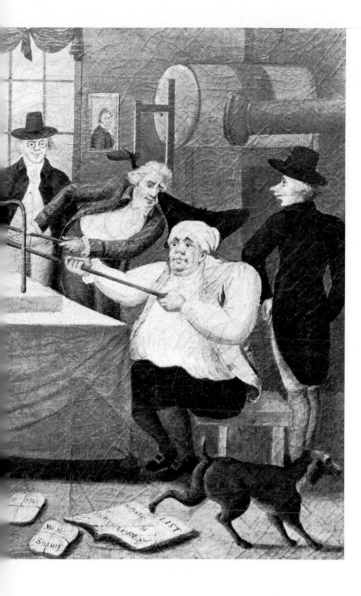

enough to win a medal from the Royal Society. Eliot encouraged Stiles in his scientific pursuits. Stiles made many scientific observations, one of the most interesting being an experiment with silkworms to test the practicality of silk culture in New England. During the summer of 1763, while preaching at Newport, he hatched about three thousand worms—two of the fattest and most voracious he named General Wolfe and Oliver Cromwell—and kept detailed notes on their progress. Stiles and his Negro slave spent a part of every day except Sunday foraging for mulberry leaves for the worms. The summer's work produced less than a pound of raw silk and showed the difficulties of silk production in New England. Stiles's notes, which have been preserved, reveal a high quality of observation.

Because of the activities of the American Philosophical Society and the intellectual curiosity of many enterprising young craftsmen (some of whom we today would call technologists), Philadelphia early became a center of lively scientific interest and of the application of new techniques. In 1730 Thomas Godfrey, a glazier by trade and a member of Franklin's original Junto, invented a navigating instrument called a quadrant that came to be known as Hadley's quadrant because of the simultaneous invention of the instrument by James Hadley in England. James Logan, a wealthy Quaker official and a scientist himself, wrote to the Royal Society in 1734 to establish Godfrey's claim to the invention.

David Rittenhouse was one of the most versatile and talented of the self-taught scientists of Philadelphia. Brought up on a farm near Germantown, he taught himself mathematics and physics and acquired a remarkable knowledge of astronomy. In 1751 he opened an instrument shop on his father's farm. In 1767 he constructed an orrery that attracted much attention, and in the following year he gave a paper before the American Philosophical Society on the transit of Venus that was to occur in 1769. His calculations, and his later observations of this phenomenon, gave him contemporary fame and are still regarded as remarkably advanced for their time. Rittenhouse later became a professor of astronomy at the University of Pennsylvania.

flourished within academic precincts. For example, John Winthrop IV, Hollis Professor of Mathematics and Natural Philosophy at Harvard from 1738 until 1779, encouraged the study of theoretical science and mathematics and gained an international reputation for his observations in physics and astronomy. His excellence was rewarded with an honorary degree from the University of Edinburgh and election to the Royal Society.

Ezra Stiles, one of the most learned men in New England, who became president of Yale in 1778, had wide scientific interests—often with a practical focus. He was an intimate friend of Jared Eliot, clergyman and physician, who in 1762 published an *Essay on the Invention, or Art of Making Very Good, If Not the Best Iron, from Black Sea Sand*, which was impressive

319

His were not cloistered talents, for he proved himself a practical engineer as well as a theoretical scientist.

An intellectually alert group of physicians in Philadelphia established a highly advanced school of medicine in 1765 at the College of Philadelphia (later the University of Pennsylvania). The two chief promoters of this enterprise were Dr. John Morgan and Dr. William Shippen, Jr., both of them graduates in medicine from the University of Edinburgh. In 1769 Dr. Benjamin Rush, who later became one of the foremost teachers of medicine, was elected professor of chemistry in the new medical school.

In the later colonial period, scientific speculation occupied the attention of many of the best minds of the day, as theological speculation had dominated thinking in the previous century. Many an eighteenth-century theologian combined scientific investigation and theological writing, and occasionally a scientist also turned his mind to theology. Since the time of Cotton Mather and Jonathan Edwards, theologians had found science attractive, and by the second half of the eighteenth century science was proving an alluring mistress, attracting all types of colonial minds, from preachers in their pulpits to apprentices in their shops.

The way in which scientific-minded people were able to keep up with the experiments and observations being made by kindred spirits scattered throughout the colonies indicates the improvement that had taken place in intercolonial communications in the eighteenth century. In the early days of settlement, little direct communication was possible between individual colonies. South Carolina found it much easier to communicate with London than with Boston. But by the mid-eighteenth century, conditions had vastly changed. In 1756 Charles Town was cheered by the arrival of the first regularly established postal carrier from Boston, the beginning of an official fortnightly service. Already Benjamin Franklin and William Hunter, who had taken over the post office in 1753, were improving the service between northern cities and the South as far as Williamsburg. An increase in coastal shipping made communication by water easier.

The means of communication between the colonies and with Europe continued to improve. Military needs had stimulated the institution of a regular packet-boat service with England. Intercolonial mail service was now improved by packet boats connecting the principal American ports. One packet service in New York plying

to Florida advertised in 1767 accommodations for both passengers and slaves. Overland mail service between Charles Town and Boston still took ten weeks, but the time between New York and Boston by 1764 had been reduced to six days. A network of private carriers further stimulated travel and the delivery of mail and parcels. Aroused by the action of British agents who opened private mail, the Sons of Liberty instigated the establishment of a subscription postal service that bore the name "Constitutional Post." Begun in August, 1774, by William Goddard of Baltimore, it had an immediate success, soon putting the old post out of business.

The relative ease of communication during the years of controversy made it possible for agitators to carry on their propaganda with an efficiency that would have been impossible a century or even a half century before. Newspapers flourished, and few regions were so backward or so distant that they could not be reached by paper or pamphlet. It is significant that even in the interior of North Carolina, the Regulators had carried on much of their agitation through the printed word. Since the seventeenth century, when Governor Berkeley of Virginia had boasted that the colony was afflicted with neither printing presses nor free schools, much had happened. From Charles Town to Portsmouth, printers now prospered. Benjamin Franklin himself made a good living in the printing trade, as did some of his competitors. Between the years 1761 and 1776 the printing presses of the British colonies turned out 5,862 titles that have been recorded. Many other titles must have been lost to history. The printers were a busy lot, and they had a vast influence on developing political events. Furthermore, between 1763 and 1775 the total number of newspapers in the colonies doubled, a fact that indicates the demand for news and comment on the politics of the day. Americans had already become insatiable consumers of newspapers. British America had produced a reading public that eagerly bought the latest books from Europe as well as the most recent pamphlet from the local printer.

By the end of the colonial period the thirteen British colonies had come of age. They all could boast a mature citizenry who could read, think, and discuss the problems that faced them. This citizenry was diverse in its interests and attainments, but it was neither naïve nor untrained for responsibility. It was ready for the burdens of nationhood when its leaders cut the ties that bound them to Great Britain.

THE
Royal *American* Magazine,

OR UNIVERSAL
Repository of Instruction and Amusement.

For JANUARY, 1774.

CONTAINING,

With the following EMBELLISHMENTS, viz.

No. I. A VIEW of the TOWN of BOSTON, with several Ships of War in the Harbour.
No. II. The THUNDER STORM, an affecting historical Piece, very neatly engraved.

BOSTON: Printed by and for I. THOMAS, near the MARKET. Sold by D. FOWLE, in Portsmouth, New-Hampshire; THOMAS & TINGES, in Newbury-Port; S. and E. HALL, in Salem; J. CARTER, Providence; S. SOUTHWICK, Newport, Rhode-Island; E. WATSON, Hartford; T. and S. GREEN, New-Haven; T. GREEN, New-London; J. HOLT, New-York; T. and W. BRADFORD, Philadelphia; A. GREEN, Maryland; R. WELLS, and C. CROUCH, in South-Carolina.

In Their Words...

The Colonies Mature

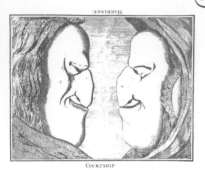

Courtship's doting sours in marriage; reversible cartoon of mid-1700's by Nathaniel Hurd

As an author, Benjamin Franklin is best remembered for the homely maxims of Poor Richard's Almanack. A less rustic side of the man now called the most cosmopolitan American of his day is seen in the excerpt below. Some scholars think the addressee —"My dear Friend"—to have been Franklin's fourteen-year-old son William: however, the letter may have been written simply as a literary exercise.

June 25. 1745

My dear Friend,

I know of no Medicine fit to diminish the violent natural Inclinations you mention; and if I did, I think I should not communicate it to you. Marriage is the proper Remedy. It is the most natural State of Man, and therefore the State in which you are most likely to find solid Happiness. Your Reasons against entring into it at present, appear to me not well-founded. The circumstantial Advantages you have in View by postponing it, are not only uncertain, but they are small in comparison with that of the Thing itself, and being *married and settled*. It is the Man and Woman united that make the compleat human Being. Separate, she wants his Force of Body and Strength of Reason; he, her softness, Sensibility and acute Discernment. Together they are more likely to succeed in the World. A single Man has not nearly the Value he would have in that State of Union. He is an incomplete Animal. He resembles the odd Half of a Pair of Scissars. If you get a prudent healthy Wife, your Industry in your Profession, with her good Economy, will be a fortune sufficient.

But if you will not take this Counsel, and persist in thinking a Commerce with the Sex inevitable, then I repeat my former Advice, that in all your Amours you should *prefer old Women to young ones.* You call this a Paradox, and demand my Reasons. They are these:

1. Because as they have more Knowledge of the World and their Minds are better stor'd with Observations, their Conversation is more improving and more lastingly agreable.

2. Because when Women cease to be handsome, they study to be good. To maintain their Influence over Men, they supply the Diminution of Beauty by an Augmentation of Utility. They learn to do a 1000 Services small and great, and are the most tender and useful of all Friends when you are sick. Thus they continue amiable. And hence there is hardly such a thing to be found as an old Woman who is not a good Woman.

3. Because there is no hazard of Children, which irregularly produc'd may be attended with much Inconvenience.

4. Because thro' more Experience, they are more prudent and discreet in conducting an Intrigue to prevent Suspicion. The Commerce with them is therefore safer with regard to your Reputation. And with regard to theirs, if the Affair should happen to be known, considerate People might be rather inclin'd to excuse an old Woman who would kindly take care of a young Man, form his Manners by her good Counsels, and

Churches in New England show influence of Sir Christopher Wren, who made plan above for an English church steeple.

prevent his ruining his Health and Fortune among mercenary Prostitutes.

5. Because in every Animal that walks upright, the Deficiency of the Fluids that fill the Muscles appears first in the highest Part: The Face first grows lank and wrinkled; then the Neck; then the Breast and Arms; the lower Parts continuing to the last as plump as ever: So that covering all above with a Basket, and regarding only what is below the Girdle, it is impossible of two Women to know an old from a young one. And as in the dark all Cats are grey, the Pleasure of corporal Enjoyment with an old Woman is at least equal, and frequently superior, every Knack being by Practice capable of Improvement.

6. Because the Sin is less. The debauching a Virgin may be her Ruin, and make her for Life unhappy.

7. Because the Compunction is less. The having made a young Girl *miserable* may give you frequent bitter Reflections; none of which can attend the making an old Woman *happy.*

8[thly and Lastly] They are *so grateful!!*

Thus much for my Paradox. But still I advise you to marry directly; being sincerely Your affectionate Friend.

Benjamin Franklin

Most colonial architects had little formal training, but their accomplishments were formidable. One of the most accomplished was Peter Harrison, an English sea captain who settled in Newport, where he designed the Redwood Library. In this letter he reports to the Reverend Henry Caner on his plans for King's Chapel in Boston.

Newport, September 15th, 1749

Sir,—Since I first undertook to draw a Design for the New Church, many things has unexpectedly occurr'd to prevent me from finishing it in the time you requested. However have at last compleated it; and now send you per the Post Rider all the Plans and Elevations (as mentioned below) which I should be glad to hear answer your expectations, and that no material Alteration is made in the Execution, as it is very possible by that means the Symmetry of the Whole may be destroy'd.

The Body of the Building (as you directed) is as Plain as the Order of it will possibly admitt of; but the Steeple is fully Decorated, and I believe will have a beautifull effect. The Inside is likewise design'd Plain, and as regular as can be contriv'd from the Dimensions you limited me to. From these hints, you may perhaps be able to answer the Objections of such the Committee and others, who may not be conversant with Drawings, or have not a Taste in Things of this Nature. I am, Sir,

Your most humble Servt.
Peter Harrison

Around the middle of the 18th century Charles Hansford, a largely self-educated blacksmith from York County, Virginia, wrote four poems comprising nearly 2,000 lines of heroic verse. He called them "A Clumsey Attempt of an Old Man to turn Some of his Serious Thoughts into Verse," but in many respects they were surprisingly pol-

A blacksmith at his anvil

ished and skillful. The last of the four poems, "My Country's Worth," was written in praise of Hansford's state and its people, climate, commerce, and geography. As these lines indicate, however, the blacksmith-poet did not hesitate to show Virginia's "gloomy" as well as its "bright and shining" side.

Thus far I have with pleasure gone; but now
A melancholy broods upon my brow.
For, oh, my country, it would not be right
Nor just for me only to show thy bright
And shining side! I fear thou hast a dark
And gloomy one. Attend thee! Do but hark!
The dice-box rattles; cards on tables flow.
I well remember, fifty years ago
This wretched practice scarcely then was known.
Then if a gentleman had lost a crown
At gleek or at backgammon, 'twere a wonder,
And rumbled through the neighborhood like thunder.
But many now do win and lose pistoles
By fifties—nay, by hundreds. In what shoals
Our gentry to the gaming tables run!
Scoundrels and sharpers—nay, the very scum
Of mankind—joins our gentry, wins their cash.
O countrymen! This surely would abash
Our sleeping sires! Should one of them arise,
How would it shock *him*! How would it surprise
An honorable shade to see his boy
His honor, time, and money thus employ!
How could he bear to hear that Sacred Name
From whose dread presence he so lately came
Profan'd and trifled with, their *frauds* to screen?
Methinks he'd wish his son had never been;
Methinks he'd wish for power to destroy
Such wretches and annihilate his boy!

Pardon such warm expressions from a father.
Who would not choose annihilation rather
Than into everlasting flames be press'd?
Oh, hideous thought! O gamesters, think the rest!

Charles Hansford
"My Country's Worth," 1752

The first issue of the New-England Magazine *appeared in Boston in August, 1758. Its announced purpose was to "collect and amplify old and new and entertaining and useful Remarks." History does not tell us whether readers felt that "remarks" such as those below fulfilled this admirable credo, but it does record that only three issues of the magazine were published.*

A *learned Method* to roast EGGS.

1. Bodies of a *black* colour are found more inflammable than other Bodies, by reason the rays of light falling on them are not reflected outwards, but enter the Body, and are often reflected and refracted within it, till they be stifled and lost.

2. A Virtuoso of unsuspected credit assured mr. Boyle, that he had, in a hot climate, by carefully blackening the shells of eggs, and exposing them to the sun, seen them thereby well roasted in a short time.

Queer Notions

One *John Scot*, famous for Learning, being asked, by a young Gallant, (who thought to have put him out of Countenance as he sat at Table) What Difference there was between a *Scot* and a *Sot*? answer'd suddenly, *Mensa tantum (The Table's Breadth)* for the other sat over-against him.

One Mr. *Bull* went to visit Mr. *Hide*: *Hide* said smilingly, *Bull, where's your Horns*, O Sir, replied he, they always *go with the Hide*.

A Braggadocia swore that he met with two great Enemies at one Time, and he tost one so high in the Air, that if he had had a Baker's Basket full of Bread, he would have starved in the Fall; and the other he struck so deep into the Earth, that he left Nothing to be seen but his Head and one Arm, to pull his Hat off to thank him.

New-England Magazine, No. 1, August, 1758

On September 8, 1760, France surrendered Montreal and all Canada to Great Britain. Major Robert Rogers, whose famous Rangers had fought the French from Detroit to Nova Scotia, helped to occupy the city. As this excerpt from his journal shows, he clearly saw the enormous strategic and commercial significance of the French defeat.

By the time I came to Longville, [about four miles below Montreal] the army, under the command of Gen. Amherst, had landed about two miles from the town, where they encamped; and early this morning Monsieur de Vaudreuil, the governor and commander in chief of all Canada, sent out to capitulate with our General, which put a stop to all our movements till the 8th of September, when the articles of capitulation were agreed to, and signed, and our troops took possession of the town-gates that night. Next morning the Light Infantry, and Granadiers of the whole army . . . with a company of the royal artillery, with two pieces of cannon, and some hobitzers, entered the town, retaking the English colours belonging to Pepperel's and Shirley's regiments, which had been taken by the French at Oswego.

Thus, at length, at the end of the fifth campaign, Montreal and the whole country of Canada was given up, and became subject to the King of Great Britain; a conquest perhaps of the greatest importance that is to be met with in the British annals, whether we consider the prodigious extent of the country we are hereby made masters of, the vast addition it must make to trade and navigation, or the security it must afford to the northern provinces of America, particularly those flourishing ones of New England and New York, the irretrievable loss France sustains thereby, and the importance it must give the British crown among the several states of Europe: all this, I say, duly considered, will, perhaps, in its consequences render the year 1760 more glorious than any proceeding.

Journals of Major Robert Rogers, 1765

Mortar (left) and field gun, from a Treatise on Artillery *of 1768*

The first native American botanist was John Bartram, whose observations on the natural history of the colonies gained him an international reputation. In 1765, in his capacity as royal botanist, he explored the St. Johns River in Florida with his son William (see page 316). This excerpt reveals his meticulous eye for detail, and also a fascination with tastes and smells.

[January] 10th. Pleasant morning; thermometer 50. The wolves howled, the first time I heard them in Florida; here we found a great nest of wood-rat, built of long pieces of dry sticks, near 4 foot high and 5 in diameter, all laid confusedly together; on stirring the sticks to observe their structure, a large rat ran out, and up a very high saplin with a young one hanging to its tail. . . .

14th. . . . We landed on the west side [of the cypress swamp], which was low and rich for 100 yards back, rising gradually from the water to 4 or 5 foot perpendicular, then comes to a level, looking rich and black on the surface for an inch or two, then under it a fine sand to a great depth; this level produceth red-bay, great magnolia, water and live oaks, liquid amber, hiccory, and some oranges, but no large trees . . . Our hunter killed a large he-bear supposed to weigh 400 pounds, was 7 foot long, cut 4 inches thick of fat on the side, its fore-paw 5 inches broad, his skin when stretched measured 5 foot and a half long, and 4 foot 10 inches in breadth, and yielded 15 or 16 gallons of clear oil; two of us had never eaten an ounce of bears meat before, but we found it to our surprize to be very mild and sweet, above all four-footed creatures, except venison; although it was an old he-bear, his fat, though I loathed the sight of it at first, was incomparably milder than hogslard, and near as sweet as oil of olives; it was not hunger that engaged us in its favour; for we had a fat young buck and three turkeys fresh shot at the same time, and some boiled with the bear, but we chose the last for its sweetness. . . .

17th. A few miles below the lake we came to a fine rich low dry bluff 4 foot above the water; it declined gradually to a fine marsh, near half a mile wide to the pinelands, and a very extensive prospect to the Indian side over marshes and large swamps; this is the finest piece of rich dry ground I observed since we left the head of the river; it produced very good rich grass, palms and live-oaks, the dry ground may be 8 roods wide and 40 long; here we cut down three tall palm or cabbage-trees, and cut out the top bud, the white tender part, or the rudiments of the great leaves, which will be six or 7 foot long, when full grown, and the palmed part 4 in diameter; this tender part will be three or 4 inches in diameter tapering near a foot, and cuts as white and tender as a turnip; this they slice into a pot and stew with water, then, when almost tender, they pour some bears oil into it, and stew it a little longer, when it eats pleasant and much more mild than a cabbage: I never eat half so much cabbage at a time, and it agreed the best with me of any sauce I ever eat, either alone or with meat: Our hunters frequently eat it raw, and will live upon it several days; the small palmetto or chamaerops yields a small white bud no bigger than one's finger, which is eaten by men, bears, and horses, in case of great need; this situation pleased me so much we called it Bartram's Bluff, and for an industrious planter with a few hands may be a pretty estate. . . .

24th. Moderate clear morning; rowed early by a bank of pine-land for several miles and some cypress-swamps, then came to a large creek called Johnson's Spring. . . . we came at last to where the cattails and bullrushes grew so thick that we could not force the battoe through them . . . we landed to search the head-springs, and passed through

Ruellia flowers, drawn by William Bartram near the coast of Georgia during the 1770's

an orange-grove and an old field of the Florida Indians, then came to the main springs, where a prodigious quantity of very clear warm brackish water boiled up between vast rocks of unknown depth . . . we examined the composition of the rocks, and found some of them to be a concrete redish sand, some whitish mixed with clay, others a ferruginous irregular concrete, and many a combination of all these materials with sea-shells, clams, and cockles; we found in the bank an ash-coloured tenacious earth, and a strata of yellow sand beneath; near here my son found a lovely sweet tree, with leaves like the sweet bay, which smelled like sassafras, and produced a very strange kind of seed-pod, but the seed was all shed, the severe frost had not hurt it; some of them grew near 20 foot high, a charming bright evergreen aromatic. . . . We then steered our course to Bryan's Island, on which there is some good land and rich swamp, with pretty much pine-land, it is supposed to contain about 1500 acres; here we encamped on a rocky rising ground, and found numbers of great and small oyster-shells, clams, perriwinkles, seamuscles, and cockles, all cemented together with broken fragments, some ground as fine as coarse sand; they were all confusedly mixed up and jumbled together as upon our sea-coast; first a strata of shells, then a strata of shells and fragments fill up the least cavity; it is remarkable that we never found any scallops to the south of Carolina, either on the coast or up in the country.

A Journal Kept By John Bartram of Philadelphia,
Botanist to His Majesty for the Floridas, 1765–66

The October 31, 1765,
Pennsylvania Journal
used this symbol to
mock stamps required
by the Stamp Act.

In 1765, in the Virginia House of Burgesses, Patrick Henry made his famous speech against the Stamp Act, closing (according to some accounts) with the words: "If this be treason, make the most of it." At the same time, he introduced seven resolutions asserting that only the Virginia legislature could tax Virginians. (Five passed, and all seven subsequently were publicized throughout the colonies.) Afterward Henry jotted down these notes on the back of the original draft of the resolutions.

The within Resolution passed the House of Burgesses in May, 1765. They formed the first Opposition to the Stamp Act and the Scheme of Taxing America by the British Parliament. All the Colonys either Thro Fear, or want of Oppertunity to form an Opposition, or from Influence of some Kind or other, had remained Silent, I had been, for the first Time elected a Burgess a few Days before, was young [29], inexperienced, unacquainted with the Forms of the House and the Members that composed it, Finding the men of Weight averse to Opposition, and the Commencement of the Tax at Hand and that no person was likely to step forth. I determined to venture and alone, unadvised and unassisted, on a blank Leaf of an old Law Book wrote the within. Upon offering them to the House, violent Debates ensued, Many threats were uttered and much Abuse cast on me by the Party for Submission, After a long and warm Contest the Resolution passed by a very small Majority, perhaps of one or two only. The Alarm spread throughout America with astonishing Quickness and the ministerial Party were overwhelmed. The great Point of Resistance to British Taxation was universally established in the Colonys. . . .

Patrick Henry
Memorandum on the back of the original draft of the
resolutions introduced in the Virginia House of Burgesses, 1765

The paintings of Benjamin West and John Singleton Copley reflect the growing sophistication of colonial culture after 1750. In 1766 Copley wrote to West, who had a studio in London, thanking him for his advice and voicing a desire to see Europe.

Boston, Novr. 12, 1766.

Sir,

Your kind favour of Augst. 4, 1766, came to hand. It gave me great pleasure to receive without reserve Your Criticisms on the Picture I sent to the Exibition. Mr. Powell informd me of Your intention of wrighting, and the handsom things You was pleas'd say in praise of that little performance, which has increased my estamation of it, and demands my thanks . . . It was remarkd the Picture was too lind. this I confess I was concious of my self and think with You that it is the natural result of two great presition in the out line, which in my next Picture I will indeavour to avoid, and perhaps should not have fallen into it in that, had I not felt two great timerity at presenting a Picture to the inspection of the first artists in the World, and where it was to come into competition with such masterly performancess as generally appear in that Collection. In my last I promis'd to send another peace. the subject You have sence pointed out, but I fear it will not be in my power to comply with Your design, the time being two short for the exicution of two figures, not having it in my power to spend all my time on it, and the Days short and weither cold, and I must ship it by the middle of Feby. at farthest, otherwise it will come too late for the exibition. but I shall do something near what you propose. Your c[a]utioning me against doing anything from fancy I take very kind, being sensable of the necessity of attending to Nature as the fountain head of all perfection, and the works of the great Masters as so many guides that lead to the more perfect imitation of her, pointing out to us in what she is to be coppied, and where we should deviate from her. In this Country as You rightly observe there is no examples of Art, except what is to [be] met with in a few prints indiferently exicuted, from which it is not possable to learn much, and must greatly inhanch the Value of free and unreserved Criticism made with judgment and Candor.

It would give me inexpressable pleasure to make a trip to Europe, where I should see those fair examples of art that have stood so long the admiration of all the world. the Paintings, Sculptors and Basso Releivos that adourn Italy, and which You have had the pleasure of making Your Studies from would, I am sure, annimate my pencil, and inable me to acquire that bold free and gracefull stile of Painting that will, if ever, come much slower from the mere dictates of Nature, which has hither too been my only instructor. I was allmost tempted the last year to take a tour to Philadelphia, and that chiefly to see some of Your Pictures, which I am informd are there. I think myself peculiarly unlucky in Liveing in a place into which there has not been one portrait brought that is worthy to be call'd a Picture within my memory, which leaves me at a great loss to gess the stile that You, Mr. Renolds, and the other Artists pracktice. I shall be glad when you write next you will be more explicit on the article of Crayons, and why You dis[ap]prove the use of them, for I think my best portraits done in that way. . . .

I shall be exceeding glad to know in general what the present state of Painting in Italy is, weither the Living Masters are excellent as the Dead have been. . . .

I am Sir with all Sinceri[t]y Your friend and Humble Sert.

J: S: Copley.

Sketch by John Copley of an officer leading troops; this was a study for one figure in a painting of a battle scene.

$\mathcal{P}$erhaps no man worked harder to avoid an open conflict with England than John Dickinson, a conservative lawyer from Pennsylvania. Yet his carefully reasoned statements on liberty and freedom in the colonies helped to precipitate the final break with the mother country. Here, in an excerpt from the first of a series of essays later issued in pamphlet form, Dickinson calls attention to the act that suspended the New York legislature in 1766.

My Dear Countrymen,

I AM a FARMER, settled after a variety of fortunes, near the banks, of the river *Delaware*, in the province of *Pennsylvania*. . . .

From infancy I was taught to love humanity and liberty. Inquiry and experience have since confirmed my reverence for the lessons then given me, by convincing me more fully of their truth and excellence. Benevolence towards mankind excites wishes for their welfare, and such wishes endear the means of fulfilling them. Those can be found in liberty alone, and therefore her sacred cause ought to be espoused by every man, on every occasion, to the utmost of his power: as a charitable but poor person does not withhold his *mite*, because he cannot relieve *all* the distresses of the miserable, so let not any honest man suppress his sentiments concerning freedom, however small their influence is likely to be. Perhaps he may "touch some wheel" that will have an effect greater than he expects.

These being my sentiments, I am encouraged to offer to you, my countrymen, my thoughts on some late transactions, that in my opinion are of the utmost importance to you. Conscious of my defects, I have waited some time, in expectation of seeing the subject treated by persons much better qualified for the task; but being therein disappointed, and apprehensive that longer delays will be injurious, I venture at length to request the attention of the public, praying only for one thing,—that is that these lines may be *read* with the same zeal for the happiness of British America, with which they were *wrote*.

With a good deal of surprise I have observed, that little notice has been taken of an act of parliament, as injurious in its principle to the liberties of these colonies, as the STAMP-ACT was: I mean the act for suspending the legislation of New-York.

The assembly of that government complied with a former act of parliament requiring certain provisions to be made for the troops in America, in every particular, I think, except the articles of salt, pepper, and vinegar. In my opinion they acted imprudently, considering all circumstances, in not complying so far, as would have given satisfaction, as several colonies did: but my dislike of their conduct in that instance, has not blinded me so much, that I cannot plainly perceive, that they have been punished in a manner pernicious to American freedom, and justly alarming to all the colonies.

If the BRITISH PARLIAMENT has a legal authority to order, that we shall furnish a single article for the troops here, and to compel obedience to that order; they have the same right to order us to supply those troops with arms, cloaths, and every necessary, and to compel obedience to that order also; in short, to lay *any burdens* they please upon us. What is this but *taxing* us at a *certain sum*, and leaving to us only the *manner* of raising it? How is this mode more tolerable than the STAMP ACT? . . .

John Dickinson
Letters from a Farmer in Pennsylvania, 1768

Portrait of John Dickinson, probably a later version of a 1771 woodcut by Paul Revere

Even his more celebrated contemporary, Benjamin Franklin, could not compete with David Rittenhouse, a self-educated clockmaker of Philadelphia, in mechanical ingenuity. In Jefferson's judgment, Rittenhouse also was "second to no astronomer living." For the transit of Venus in 1769 he built an observatory—including the first telescope to be assembled in the colonies—and although he fainted midway through the transit, he became one of the first to see the Venusian atmosphere.

EARLY in *November*, 1768, I began to erect an *Observatory*, agreeable to the resolutions of the AMERICAN PHILOSOPHICAL SOCIETY; but, thro' various disappointments from workmen and weather, could not compleat it, till the middle of *April*, 1769. . . .

I HAD, however, for some weeks before this, with my 36f. Refractor, observed eclipses of Jupiter's satellites, in such a name that, tho' my equal-altitude instrument was not finished, and consequently I could not set my timepiece to the true noon, I should nevertheless be able to tell the time of those eclipses afterwards, when the instrument should be ready. For this purpose, I observed, almost every fair evening, the time by the clock, when the bright star in Orion disappeared behind a fixed obstacle, by applying my eye to a small sight-hole, made thro' a piece of brass, fastened to a strong post. . . .

MAY 20th, in the morning, the clock was set up for the last time, pretty near the mean time. It had no provision for preventing the irregularities arising from heat and cold; nor could I find leisure to apply any contrivance of this sort. . . .

At 2^h. $11'.39''$ per clock, [on June 3] the Rev. Mr. *Barton* of *Lancaster*, who assisted me at the Telescope, on receiving my signal, as had been agreed, instantaneously communicated it to the counters at the window, by waving a handkerchief; who walking softly to the clock, counting seconds as they went along, noted down their times separately, agreeing to the *same second*. And three seconds sooner than this, to the best of my judgment, was the time when the least impression made by *Venus* on the Sun's limb, could be seen by my Telescope.

WHEN the Planet had advanced about one third of its diameter on the Sun, as I was steadily observing its progress, my sight was suddenly attracted by a beam of light, which broke through on that side of *Venus* yet off the Sun. Its figure was that of a *broad-based pyramid*; situated at about 40 or 45 degrees on the limb of *Venus*, from a line passing through her center and the Sun's, and to the left hand of that line as seen through my Telescope, which inverted. About the same time, the Sun's light began to spread round *Venus* on each side, from the points where their limbs intersected each other.

As *Venus* advanced, the point of the Pyramid still grew lower, and its circular Base wider, until it met the light which crept round from the points of intersection of the two limbs; so that when half the planet appeared on the Sun, the other half yet off the Sun was entirely surrounded by a semicircular light, best defined on the side next to the body of *Venus*, which continually grew brighter, till the time of the internal contact.

IMAGINATION cannot form anything more beautifully serene and quiet, than was the air during the whole time; nor did I ever see the Sun's limb more perfectly defined, or more free from any tremulous motion; to which his great altitude undoubtedly contributed much.

David Rittenhouse

Observations at Norriton, before and after the Transit of Venus, June 3d, 1769

On March 5, 1770, a detachment of British regulars under the command of Captain Thomas Preston was provoked into firing into a crowd in Boston. Five men were killed, and the so-called Boston Massacre, publicized by Sam Adams and others, aroused indignation and anger throughout the colonies. When Preston was put on trial for murder, John Adams and Josiah Quincy, Jr., courageously agreed to defend him. In the first letter below, Quincy's father reproaches him for undertaking to help "criminals." The second letter is Quincy's eloquent reply to his father, reminding him of the cardinal principle of English jurisprudence—that a man is innocent until proved guilty. And as it turned out, Preston was acquitted.

Braintree, March 22, 1770.

My Dear Son,

I am under great affliction at hearing the bitterest reproaches uttered against you, for having become an advocate for those criminals who are charged with the murder of their fellow-citizens. Good God! Is it possible? I will not believe it.

Just before I returned home from Boston, I knew, indeed, that on the day those criminals were committed to prison, a sergeant had inquired for you at your brother's house; but I had no apprehension that it was possible an application would be made to you to undertake their defence. Since then I have been told that you have actually engaged for Captain Preston; and I have heard the severest reflections made upon the occasion, by men who had just before manifested the highest esteem for you, as one destined to be a saviour of your country.

I must own to you, it had filled the bosom of your aged and infirm parent with anxiety and distress, lest it should not only prove true, but destructive of your reputation and interest; and I repeat, I will not believe it, unless it be confirmed by your own mouth, or under your own hand.

Your anxious and distressed parent,

Josiah Quincy.

Boston, March 26, 1770.

Honoured Sir,

I have little leisure, and less inclination, either to know or to take notice of those ignorant slanderers who have dared to utter their 'bitter reproaches' in your hearing against me, for having become an advocate for criminals charged with murder. But the sting of reproach, when envenomed only by envy and falsehood, will never prove mortal. Before pouring their reproaches into the ear of the aged and infirm, if they had been friends, they would have surely spared a little reflection on the nature of an attorney's oath and duty;—some trifling scrutiny into the business and discharge of his office, and some small portion of patience in viewing my past and future conduct.

Let such be told, Sir, that these criminals, charged with murder, are *not yet legally proved guilty*, and therefore, however criminal, are entitled, by the laws of God and man, to all legal counsel and aid; that my duty as a man obliged me to undertake; that my duty as a lawyer strengthened the obligation; that from abundant caution, I at first declined being engaged; that after the best advice, and most mature deliberation had determined my judgment, I waited on Captain Preston, and told him that I would afford him my assistance; but, prior to this, in presence of two of his friends, I made the most explicit declaration to him of my real opinion on the contests (as I expressed it to him) of the times, and that my heart and hand were indissolubly at-

Coffins by Paul Revere embellished a 1770 Boston Massacre broadside. Initials denote Samuel Maverick and Samuel Gray, two victims.

tached to the cause of my country; and finally that I refused all engagement, until advised and urged to undertake it, by an Adams, a Hancock, a Molineux, a Cushing, a Henshaw, a Pemberton, a Warren, a Cooper, and a Phillips. This and much more might be told with great truth; and I dare affirm that you and this whole people will one day REJOICE that I became an advocate for the aforesaid 'criminals,' *charged* with the murder of our fellow-citizens.

I never harboured the expectation, nor any great desire, that all men should speak well of me. To inquire my duty, and to do it, is my aim. Being mortal, I am subject to error; and, conscious of this, I wish to be diffident. Being a rational creature, I judge for myself, according to the light afforded me. When a plan of conduct is formed with an honest deliberation, neither murmuring, slander, nor reproaches move. For my single self, I consider, judge, and with reason hope to be immutable.

There are honest men in all sects,—I wish their approbation;—there are wicked bigots in all parties,—I abhor them.

I am, truly and affectionately,

Your son,

Josiah Quincy, Jr.

John Harrower, an impoverished Scottish merchant, sailed for Virginia as an indentured servant and found employment as a tutor to the family of a planter. In this letter to his wife in England he reports on the life he found and, with considerable prescience, suggests that the British tax on tea may lead to "a total revolt."

Belvidera 14th. June 1774

My Dearest Life

I wrote you from London on Wednesday 26th. Jany. last which Im hopefull came safe to hand, and found you and my dear Infants in perfect health, and am hopefull this will find both you and them in the same state. . . . I am now settled with on[e] Colonel Wm. Daingerfield Esqr. of Belvidera, on the Banks of the River Rappahannock about 160 Miles from the Capes or sea mouth, and seven Miles below the Toun of Fredericksburgh. My bussiness is to teach his Childreen to read write and figure. Edwin his oldest son about 8 years of [age] Bathurest his second 6 years of age & William his youngest son 4 years of age. He has also a Daugher whose name is Hanna Basset. I came to this pleace on Thursday 26th. May and next morning I received his three sons into my charge to teach, the two youngest boys I got in A:B:C, and the oldest just begun to syllab and I have now the two youngest spelling and the oldest reading. I am obliged to teach in the English method which was a litle aquard to me at first but now quite easy. I am also obliged to talk english the best I can, for Lady Daingerfield speacks nothing but high english, and the Colonel hade his Education in England and is a verry smart Man. As to my Agreement it is as follows Vizt. I am obliged to continue with Coll. Daingerfield for four years if he insists on it, and for teaching his own Childreen I have Bed, Board, washing and all kinds of Cloaths during the above time, and for what scholars I can get more than his Childreen I have five shillings currancy per Quarter for each of them which is equall to four shillings Sterling. . . .

As to my living I eat at their own table, & our witualls are all Dressed in the eng-

Schoolroom scene from a "morality" story: one pupil studies diligently in a room of idlers.

lish taste. We have for breakfast either Coffie of Jaculate [chocolate] and warm loaf bread of the best flour. . . . For Dinner smoack'd bacon or what we cal pork ham is a standing dish either warm or cold. When warm we have greens with it, and when cold we have sparrow grass. . . . As for Tea there is none drunk by any in this Government since 1st. June last, nor will they buy a 2d. worth of any kind of east India goods, which is owing to the difference at present betwixt the Parliament of Great Brittan and the North Americans about laying a tax on the tea; and I'm afraid if the Parliment do not give it over it will cause a total revolt as all the North Americans are determined to stand by one another, and resolute on it that they will not submit. . . .

John Harrower
Journal, 1773–76

hysician Benjamin Rush believed firmly in the efficacy of bleeding his patients, and his medical theories would be considered primitive today, yet his studies in certain branches of experimental physiology were remarkable for their time. A signer of the Declaration of Independence, Rush also wrote on social and political topics. As this excerpt indicates, he was one of many thoughtful colonists who realized that liberty and slavery cannot endure together.

Official symbol of an English abolitionist society, also supported by American Quakers

. . . Slavery is so foreign to the human mind, that the moral faculties, as well as those of the understanding are debased, and rendered torpid by it. All the vices which are charged upon the Negroes in the southern colonies and the West-Indies, such as Idleness, Treachery, Theft, and the like, are the genuine off-springs of slavery, and serve as an argument to prove that they were not intended, by Providence for it.

Nor let it be said, in the present Age, that their black color (as it is commonly called) either subjects them to, or qualifies them for slavery. The vulgar notion of their being descended from Cain, who was supposed to have been marked with this color, is too absurd to need a refutation. . . .

The first step to be taken to put a stop to slavery in this country, is to leave off importing slaves. For this purpose let our assemblies unite in petitioning the king and parliament to dissolve the African company. It is by this incorporated band of robbers that the trade has chiefly been carried on to America. . . . Let such of our countrymen as engage in the slave trade, be shunned as the greatest enemies to our country, and let the vessels which bring the slaves to us, be avoided as if they bore in them the Seeds of that forbidden fruit, whose baneful taste destroyed both the natural and moral world. . . .

Ye men of SENSE and VIRTUE—Ye ADVOCATES for American Liberty, rouse up and espouse the cause of Humanity and general Liberty. Bear a testimony against a vice which degrades human nature, and dissolves that universal tie of benevolence which should connect all the children of men together in one great Family.—The plant of liberty is of so tender a Nature, that it cannot thrive long in the neighborhood of slavery. Remember the eyes of all Europe are fixed upon you, to preserve an assylum for freedom in this country, after the last pillars of it are fallen in every other quarter of the Globe.

Benjamin Rush
*An Address to the Inhabitants of the British Settlements
in America upon Slave-keeping, 1773*

Thomas Jefferson—a pencil drawing by Benjamin Latrobe

Thomas Jefferson was serving in the Virginia House of Burgessess when he wrote A Summary View of the Rights of British America, *his first published political work. Jefferson denied parliamentary authority over the colonies and acknowledged royal sovereignty only when the king promoted the interests of the colonists. In this excerpt he bases his argument on rights "derived from the laws of nature" and reminds George III that "kings are the servants, not the proprietors of the people."*

That these are our grievances which we have thus laid before his majesty, with that freedom of language and sentiment which becomes a free people claiming their rights, as derived from the laws of nature, and not as the gift of their chief magistrate: Let those flatter who fear; it is not an American art. To give praise which is not due might be well from the venal, but would ill beseem those who are asserting the rights of human nature. They know, and will therefore say, that kings are the servants, not the proprietors of the people. Open your breast, sire, to liberal and expanded thought. Let not the name of George the third be a blot in the page of history. You are surrounded by British counsellors, but remember that they are parties. You have no ministers for American affairs, because you have none taken from among us, nor amenable to the laws on which they are to give you advice. It behoves you, therefore, to think and to act for yourself and your people. The great principles of right and wrong are legible to every reader; to pursue them requires not the aid of many counsellors. The whole art of government consists in the art of being honest. Only aim to do your duty, and mankind will give you credit where you fail. No longer persevere in sacrificing the rights of one part of the empire to the inordinate desires of another; but deal out to all equal and impartial right. Let no act be passed by any one legislature which may infringe on the rights and liberties of another. This is the important post in which fortune has placed you, holding the balance of a great, if a well poised empire. This, sire, is the advice of your great American council, on the observance of which may perhaps depend your felicity and future fame, and the preservation of that harmony which alone can continue both to Great Britain and America the reciprocal advantages of their connection. It is neither our wish, nor our interest, to separate from her. We are willing, on our part, to sacrifice everything which reason can ask to the restoration of that tranquillity for which all must wish. On their part, let them be ready to establish union and a generous plan. Let them name their terms, but let them be just. Accept of every commercial preference it is in our power to give for such things as we can raise for their use, or they make for ours. But let them not think to exclude us from going to other markets to dispose of those commodities which they cannot use, or to supply those wants which they cannot supply. Still less let it be proposed that our properties within our own territories shall be taxed or regulated by any power on earth but our own. The God who gave us life gave us liberty at the same time; the hand of force may destroy, but cannot disjoin them. This, sire, is our last, our determined resolution; and that you will be pleased to interpose with that efficacy which your earnest endeavors may ensure to procure redress of these our great grievances, to quiet the minds of your subjects in British America, against any apprehensions of future encroachment, to establish fraternal love and harmony through the whole empire, and that these may continue to the latest ages of time, is the fervent prayer of all British America!

Thomas Jefferson
A Summary View of the Rights of British America, 1774

On June 15, 1775, the Continental Congress unanimously elected George Washington commander in chief of the Army. Three days later Washington wrote this letter to his wife Martha at Mount Vernon. It reveals his great reluctance to accept a call to duty that he knew would be long and arduous; it also reflects the courage and resolution that enabled the colonies to survive seven years of conflict with the most powerful nation of the 18th century and, finally, to prevail.

My Dearest,

I am now set down to write to you on a subject, which fills me with inexpressible concern, and this concern is greatly aggravated and increased, when I reflect upon the uneasiness I know it will give to you. It has been determined to Congress, that the whole army raised for the defence of the American cause shall be put under my care, and that it is necessary for me to proceed immediately to Boston to take upon me the command of it.

You may believe me, my dear Patsy, when I assure you, in the most solemn manner, that, so far from seeking this appointment, I have used every endeavour in my power to avoid it, not only from my unwillingness to part with you and the family, but from a consciousness of its being a trust too great for my capacity, and that I should enjoy more real happiness in one month with you at home, than I have the most distant prospect of finding abroad, if my stay were to be seven times seven years. But as it has been a kind of destiny, that has thrown me upon this service, I shall hope that my undertaking it is designed to answer some good purpose. . . . I shall rely, therefore, confidently on that Providence, which has heretofore preserved and been bountiful to me, not doubting but that I shall return to you in the fall. I shall feel no pain from the toil or the danger of the campaign; my unhappiness will flow from the uneasiness I know you will feel from being left alone. I therefore beg, that you will summon your whole fortitude, and pass your time as agreeably as possible. Nothing will give me so much sincere satisfaction as to hear this, and to hear it from your own pen. My earnest and ardent desire is, that you would pursue any plan that is most likely to produce content, and a tolerable degree of tranquillity; as it must add greatly to my uneasy feelings to hear, that you are dissatisfied or complaining at what I really could not avoid.

As life is always uncertain, and common prudence dictates to every man the necessity of settling his temporal concerns, while it is in his power, and while the mind is calm and undisturbed, I have, since I came to this place (for I had not time to do it before I left home) got Colonel Pendleton [a delegate from Virginia to the Continental Congress] to draft a will for me, by the directions I gave him, which will I now enclose. The provision made for you in the case of my death, will, I hope, be agreeable.

I shall add nothing more, as I have several letters to write, but to desire that you will remember me to your friends, and to assure you that I am, with the most unfeigned regard, my dear Patsy, your affectionate, &c.

Letter to Martha Washington, Philadelphia, June 18, 1775

Martha and George Washington both had portraits made in 1776 by Charles Willson Peale.

A CURE FOR THE REFRACTORY

OTETOURT

TOBACCO.
A PRESENT
For
JOHN WILKES
Esq.
LORD MAYOR OF
LONDON

The Number of the conspir—

Non Importation

LIBERTY

Eve of Revolution

With the fall of Quebec and Montreal, the war with France in North America was over so far as it concerned the mainland colonies, and citizens from Maine to Florida believed that life would be easier. For more than a century, the mention of the fleur-de-lis had been enough to give nightmares to thoughtful residents of the British colonies. Now French flags were furled, and a British regime was taking control of Canada and the western outposts. The Seven Years' War in Europe still had more than two years to run before its final solution, and the British Navy still had work to do in the Caribbean and the Pacific, but for a brief interval the thirteen colonies relaxed. No longer would French officers lead marauding Indians against their frontier outposts. Peace would reign in the West, and settlers in that region could move at will into the lands beyond the Alleghenies and stake out their holdings without interference. Or so they believed. Speculators were already counting the profits they hoped to make from land grants in the Ohio Valley.

King George II, who had waged incessant war against the French and had led his army in person at the Battle of Dettingen, lived to see the fall of Canada, but on October 25, 1760, while walking in his garden, he had a heart attack and died. His troublesome son Frederick Louis had died nine years before, and George II was succeeded by Frederick Louis's son, who was crowned George III. The new king, a man of strict morality, was determined to give his country an efficient and honest government. He was also determined to strengthen the authority of the sovereign and to rule without adherence to any political party. His personal views on government would ultimately have a profound effect upon his empire across the seas; in less than a decade and a half, the sovereign who was hailed on his accession as a patriot king would be anathema to his American subjects. Convinced of his own wisdom, stimulated by his mother's injunction "to be a king," and unwilling to listen to advice, George III became an arbitrary ruler and unnecessarily alienated his subjects in the colonies, who at first never dreamed of independence. Before independence became the goal of any appreciable number of Americans, the colonies

An English cartoon of 1775 shows Virginia loyalists being forced
by lumpish patriots to choose between difficult alternatives:
either sign an agreement not to trade with Great Britain, or get
a coating of the tar and feathers displayed on the gallows.

would have to be stirred by controversies and quarrels that came as an aftermath of the settlement of the war with France.

The Seven Years' War, waged on the continent of Europe, in America, Asia, Africa, and on the high seas, was the costliest war in Great Britain's history. By 1766 her national debt amounted to more than £133,000,000. It was not unnatural that George III should contemplate the sums spent to protect the colonies and conclude that they should assist in paying off the debt accumulated in their behalf. However just taxes for this purpose might seem to the king, the efforts to procure revenue from the thirteen colonies stirred endless controversies and helped to bring about the ultimate fall of the empire that the war had won.

The colonies as a whole had flourished during the war, and the authorities in London were well aware that they could afford to contribute to the imperial revenue. The colonies themselves could not deny their prosperity, but they found reasons to label all revenue measures as unjust. The legislative assemblies of the several colonies from the beginning had asserted their right to tax, and the colonials now maintained that only their own legislative bodies had the right of taxation. Although the cry of "no taxation without representation" was to come a little later, the idea was implicit in the earliest controversies. The colonials were determined not to admit the right of any governmental body across the seas to impose taxes upon them.

The end of the North American phase of the Seven Years' War plunged the colonies into an era of readjustment that soon dispelled the euphoria that peace had brought. Colonials soon realized that peace did not mean plenty; that wartime prosperity was vanishing; and that the departure of British soldiers and sailors, whom they had not always welcomed, would cause the loss of trade. As frequently happens after a war, a depression followed in the 1760's; it did not affect all regions with equal severity but was sufficiently widespread to upset the economic progress of all the colonies in some degree.

Most of the port towns in the years immediately preceding 1760 had enjoyed unusual prosperity. Soldiers and sailors spent money freely, and the British government paid for housing, food, and such equipment as the colonies could provide. Shipyards struggled to supply the demand for craft of all sorts—the Army required a vast swarm of supply vessels of every type from bateaux

to ocean-going ships. Farmers in the back country also found a ready market for grain, hay, hogs, cattle, flour, and cured meats as Army contractors sought supplies for both men and horses. Rum distilleries worked overtime to produce the enormous quantities of drink that both soldiers and civilians consumed. Tanyards could hardly cure enough hides for the leather needed to make shoes, harnesses, saddles, straps, cartridge boxes, jerkins, leather breeches, and countless other items. Hardly a trade failed to respond to the demand for goods and services during the years immediately preceding the fall of Canada. The economy was inflated, and the end of the war and the departure of troops to other areas saw a diminished demand for commodities and services. The collapse was neither immediate nor general, but the boom was over, and some businesses faced bankruptcy.

Merchants and shipmasters from Boston, Newport, New York, and other port towns had never been squeamish about smuggling or trading with the enemy, and the focus of the war after 1760 drove many of them to illicit trade. Cargoes of grain, flour, meat, fish, and even guns, powder, and lead found their way from the colonies into French hands.

One of the favorite ways of trading with the enemy was for a shipmaster to obtain a flag of truce to sail to a French West Indian port ostensibly for the exchange of prisoners. Frenchmen were sometimes hired to pose as prisoners in order to make the application for flags of truce more credible. But Governor William Denny of Pennsylvania did not bother to inquire into the details if a shipmaster could pay twenty pounds for a blank flag of truce. Other colonial governors were equally venal. Frequently not a single British prisoner was brought back, but the ships, which outward bound had carried foodstuffs, returned deeply laden with sugar, molasses, tea, wine, silks, and other French luxury goods. Sometimes the ships cleared for one of the neutral islands controlled by the Dutch, Danes, or Spaniards. Monte Cristi, on the northern coast of Spanish Santo Domingo, commonly called "the Mount" in colonial parlance, was a favorite haven for illicit trading ships. A report to the British government in February, 1760, asserted that as many as one hundred British flag vessels had been counted at one time at Monte Cristi. In the summer of 1760 Pitt wrote to governors of the British colonies urging them to do all in their power to curb the "illegal and most pernicious Trade ... by which the enemy is ... supplyed with Provisions,

Boston artist Nathaniel Hurd created this piece in 1762 to extol George III, then quite new to his throne. Hurd also pictures William Pitt, friend to the colonies but ousted as minister by the king a year before, and James Wolfe, dead hero of Quebec.

and other Necessaries, whereby they are . . . enabled to sustain, and protract, this long and expensive war."

Colonial governors, however, found cutting off a lucrative source of profits no easy task. Just as rum-running flourished during the prohibition era in the face of official opposition, so did trade with the French find popular support in the colonies despite laws prohibiting it. So widespread was the traffic, and so entrenched were the traders, that when news got around New York that a certain George Spencer was about to expose their practices, he was mobbed and thrown into jail. In a complaint to General Amherst, Spencer claimed that he was kept in prison because he had information about the illegal business of two justices of the New York Supreme Court.

The authorities in London were not so easygoing as they were in the days of George II, however, and they began tightening up the administration of colonial affairs and keeping a sharper watch over colonial legislation and the actions of colonial governors. No longer would the colonies profit from salutary neglect. Trouble was brewing, not only from new regulations but from the enforcement of imperial laws long on the books. Not only would the British Navy do its utmost to stop trading with the enemy, but both the Navy and customs officers would enforce the Acts of Trade and Navigation.

Great Britain, like other nations in the seventeenth and eighteenth centuries, regarded colonies as useful if they could supply raw materials and absorb manufactured products of the mother country. This mercantilist viewpoint resulted in regulations under James I and Charles I that later, under the Commonwealth in 1651,

339

culminated in the first of a series of Acts of Trade and Navigation. From this time onward, successive Trade and Navigation Acts were enacted until the very eve of the Revolution, all designed to bring prosperity to British shippers and merchants and at the same time to provide a market for the products of American fields, waters, forests, and mines.

The early Navigation Acts were aimed primarily at the Dutch, who had developed a vast carrying trade. The laws made it illegal for foreign ships to trade with the British colonies unless specially licensed to do so. All goods from the colonies had to be transported in British-owned ships (colonial vessels, of course, were included), with crews at least 75 per cent of whom were to be of British or colonial birth. The Navigation Act of 1660 specified that certain "enumerated" commodities,

including tobacco, sugar, and indigo, could be shipped only to England or to other English colonies. Over the years, as the production of profitable commodities increased, the list of enumerated items grew longer until it included such things as rice, beaver pelts, deerskins, naval stores, copper ore, molasses, pig iron, and hemp. The Navigation Act of 1663 further tightened restrictions to make it illegal to import into the colonies all except a few specified commodities from foreign sources unless they had first been transported to England and a duty had been paid there. In 1673 Parliament passed an act levying a duty equal to the duty charged in England on enumerated articles shipped from one colony to another. At the same time, certain exceptions were made over the years to encourage colonial commerce. For example, fish and barrel staves could be shipped to the

An unknown artist painted the schooner Baltic *of Salem as she came into "Cape fare" (possibly Cape Fear, North Carolina) on February 16, 1766, with the pilot boat going out to meet her. This is the earliest known contemporary view of a Salem vessel. Much of the commerce bringing prosperity to the colonies at that period was being carried in small vessels like the* Baltic.

Madeira and the Canary Islands and wine imported from them directly. Salt could be imported directly from Spain to benefit the Newfoundland fisheries. Fish, grain, rum, barrel staves, woodenware, and a few other non-enumerated articles could be shipped to any market.

One of the purposes of the Navigation Acts was to ensure that the mother country maintained a favorable balance of trade, and that she did not have to export bullion or coins to pay for raw products. The export of British specie to the colonies was illegal, and since the colonies were forbidden to coin money, the dearth of hard money was a serious problem in every colony. Foreign coins found their way into the colonies, frequently through illegal avenues. The commonest form of this foreign money was the Spanish dollar, usually referred to as a "piece of eight." Because coins were hard to come by, Virginia and Maryland established a system of payments in tobacco. Each of the colonies had a system of legalized money of account, referred to as "lawful money," which meant money based on bookkeeping. Actual transactions were conducted with bills of exchange, warehouse receipts, personal notes, and sometimes by barter of commodities.

In 1690, after the futile effort to capture Quebec, Massachusetts issued paper money to pay her soldiers. This was the first paper money issued in British North America, but other colonies soon followed Massachusetts' example. Some "loan banks" were established in the early eighteenth century and issued money based on land mortgages. South Carolina, for example, had for a time a flourishing "Land Bank," and Massachusetts had another, which was suppressed in 1741 by Parliament under the so-called Bubble Act of 1720, a measure passed to correct the abuses of the South Sea Bubble. One of the soundest of colonial paper currencies was that advocated by Benjamin Franklin and issued by Pennsylvania.

But throughout the colonial period, the scarcity of hard money created a serious economic problem. The colonies' imports exceeded their exports, and the balance of payments was always against them. Planters in the tobacco colonies might be rich in land, and merchants in New England might do a flourishing business, but they were invariably hard pressed for specie required for the payment of debts that could not be settled in colonial currencies or by credits accumulated with their factors overseas. The shortage of hard money constantly plaguing the colonies became particularly acute after the close of the war against Canada in 1760.

Modern scholars lean to the view that the Acts of Trade and Navigation on the whole benefited the North American colonies. For one thing, they gave the colonies a virtual monopoly of a number of raw materials sold to the mother country, which processed them and exported them to the rest of the world. Tobacco from Virginia and Maryland offers the best example of the monopoly enjoyed by a raw product in the English market. Some industries also flourished as a result of the restrictions of the Navigation Acts. For example, New England shippers and shipbuilders profited enormously from the requirement that ships in the British carrying trade had to be of colonial or British construction. By the Revolution, it is estimated that approximately 30 per cent of all commercial ships owned by Great Britain were of colonial construction.

Even though the Navigation Acts in theory bore hard upon some sections of colonial society, the easygoing attitude of officials responsible for their enforcement until the succession of George III kept them from becoming a great burden. The passage of the Molasses Act of 1733, designed to protect the British West Indies from competition of the French sugar islands, placed a tax of six pence a gallon on foreign molasses and also taxed foreign rum and sugar. If the law had been strictly enforced, the rum distilleries in New England would have suffered, trade in fish and barrel staves would have declined, and merchants in New England and elsewhere would have gone without Spanish and French money that they badly needed. Actually, trade with the French, Spanish, and Dutch islands suffered little interference.

Colonial shipmasters also sailed to Amsterdam and other European ports where they exchanged American goods for luxury products in demand at home. Boston shippers, British officials charged, supplied the colonies with contraband European goods that should have been imported from England. Honest Quaker merchants in Philadelphia, respectable Baptists in Newport, and earnest Puritans in Boston made a handsome profit from the illegal traffic. They salved their consciences by arguing that the laws were unjust, and that they had to raise cash by foreign trade in order to pay their just debts, since Parliament would not allow the export of English money to the New World. Whatever benefits the colonies may have reaped from the Navigation Acts, most colonials thought the acts oppressive.

And however right the British authorities may have

been in insisting upon the enforcement of the laws, the new policies under George III inevitably reaped the whirlwind. One of the most provocative measures was the use of writs of assistance—general warrants without the name of any informing witness—granting customs officers the right of search and seizure. These writs had been authorized by a Massachusetts court in 1755 as a means of combating the flag-of-truce ruse for trading with the enemy, and in 1769 they were again employed in an attempt to run down smugglers, for Pitt had ordered the strict enforcement of the Molasses Act of 1733. Incensed when the king's officers broke down their warehouse doors and opened casks and cases of suspected goods, Boston merchants hired an eloquent lawyer, James Otis, to defend them against such "tyranny." Otis was the king's advocate general in the Boston court of vice-admiralty, and normally it would have been his duty to prosecute offenders against the Navigation Acts who were required to appear in the admiralty courts. Instead, Otis resigned his lucrative office and in February, 1761, argued against the legality of the writs of assistance. He lost his case, but five years later the attorney general upheld his position.

Otis based his argument on natural law. The fundamental law governing all Britons, he reasoned, was based upon natural law, which contravened acts of Parliament. He also maintained that British subjects in America had the same rights as Englishmen at home. These arguments were frequently repeated in the next fifteen years. Concerning Otis's eloquence in arguing against the writs of assistance, John Adams declared: "Otis was a flame of fire! . . . American independence was then and there born; the seeds of patriots and heroes were then and there sown."

While the king's officials were struggling with recalcitrant merchants in Boston and other towns in the colonies, the king's navy and army elsewhere in the world were continuing the fight against France. Belatedly, in 1761, Spain had agreed to come to the aid of France, and on November 3, 1762, by the secret Treaty of Fontainebleau, France ceded to Spain all the Louisiana territory, an act that would have important later repercussions for America. But the Spanish alliance was of little help to France. Everywhere the British were victorious. Within two years, most of the French and Spanish islands in the Caribbean were under British control, and the Philippines had fallen to a British naval force. On the Continent and in India, the British continued to add to their victories. By the end of 1762 the allies had to sue for peace, which was settled by the Treaty of Paris, signed on February 10, 1763.

By the terms of the treaty, France formally ceded to Great Britain all Canada and all lands she had previously claimed east of the Mississippi River except New Orleans. Unrestricted navigation of the Mississippi River was guaranteed to British subjects. Great Britain allowed France to keep two small unfortified islands in the Gulf of St. Lawrence, St. Pierre and Miquelon, so that her fishermen in Newfoundland waters might have a place to dry their nets. But French ships were forbidden to come within three leagues of British possessions in the Gulf of St. Lawrence and were not allowed to come within fifteen leagues of Cape Breton Island. Although some English merchants would have willingly traded all French Canada for the rich sugar island of Guadeloupe, Great Britain restored this island and Martinique to the French. Spain was obliged to cede to Great Britain East and West Florida, and in return the British gave back to Spain Cuba and the Philippines.

With the war at last settled throughout the world, and with a vast empire under her control, Great Britain could once more turn to the business of solidifying her position and welding all the parts together. That task proved beyond the power of the king's ministers. Instead of acquiescing in what London regarded as reasonable demands, the colonies resisted every assertion of imperial authority. Self-interest that had kept them more or less obedient to imperial authority during the long periods of war no longer operated with the same validity. Now the colonies found that their self-interest did not always coincide with the interests of the empire.

Two interrelated problems brought on crises soon after the Treaty of Paris had proclaimed an era of peace. They concerned the disposition of the western lands and the readjustment of Indian affairs. From London it appeared that a simple formula establishing mutually exclusive territories for Indians and white settlers might be a satisfactory solution to perennial complaints from the Indians about interlopers in their hunting grounds. Restlessness and open warfare on the part of Indian tribes formerly loyal to France indicated that drastic action was required. Some headway already had been made. In October, 1758, Pennsylvania made an agreement with the western Indians in the Treaty of Easton to respect their hunting grounds west of the Alleghenies and to keep settlers east of the mountains.

*The signers of this private note for ten pounds in 1740
promised to pay Isaac Winslow in Boston ten ounces
of silver or an equivalent value in gold by the end of 1755.*

But, despite the treaty, emigrants swarmed into the region around Fort Pitt, on the site of Fort Duquesne. So numerous were these intruders that Colonel Henry Bouquet, the military commander in the region, on October 13, 1761, issued an order requiring the observance of the Treaty of Easton.

In the meantime, the western Indians were growing more and more disenchanted with the British who had replaced the French in Detroit and in other western outposts. Trade goods were scarce, and English traders demanded higher prices than the French. Some items were lacking altogether. Powder and lead, for example, were now almost unobtainable, and the Indians pointed out that they needed ammunition for hunting. Some of the Indian leaders charged that the British debauched their tribesmen with rum and then cheated them out of their furs. More and more whites were filtering across the mountains, and the Indians foresaw their land occupied and their game driven away.

Hostilities broke out in the spring of 1763. In May an Ottawa chief named Ponteach, or Pontiac, attempted to take Detroit by treachery, but his scheme was revealed and he had to lay siege to the fort. In the meantime, Delawares, Shawnees, and Senecas went on the warpath and captured most of the British outposts between Fort Pitt and Detroit; these were the only two western outposts that the Indians failed to take. Detroit held out five months before Pontiac retreated in November. Severe fighting occurred at Bloody Ridge, Bushy Run, and at other points during the summer and autumn of 1763. General Jeffery Amherst was so angry over the Indians' treachery that he wrote Colonel Bouquet suggesting that he spread smallpox among the tribesmen. Bouquet replied that he would be glad to distribute germ-bearing blankets among them but for the danger of exposing good men to the disease. Although the worst of the war was over by the beginning of the next year, Pontiac himself did not make peace until 1766.

The danger on the western frontier and the loss to the fur traders from constant Indian disturbances forced the British government to take steps to settle the troubles. In June, 1763, Lord Shelburne, president of the Board of Trade, recommended that land west of the Appalachians, except for a portion of the upper Ohio Valley, be set aside for an Indian reservation, and that emigration be forbidden west of the mountains. Shelburne reasoned that this action would force settlers to move into the newly created provinces of Quebec, West Florida, and East Florida, where Englishmen were needed. Before Shelburne could complete the plan he had worked out, the Earl of Hillsborough replaced him as president of the Board of Trade. The new president, rash and precipitate, revised Shelburne's plan by eliminating the provision to permit settlers in the upper Ohio Valley and forthwith issued the Proclamation of 1763, establishing the crest of the Appalachians as the line beyond which emigrants could not pass. Furthermore, Hillsborough ordered settlers already on the west side of the mountains to remove themselves immediately.

The Proclamation Line, which the British government looked upon as a temporary expedient pending some more permanent solution of the Indian problem, succeeded in exasperating Americans of all types. Although emigrants disregarded it and continued to push across the mountains, they could not be certain of their rights to land in the wilderness, for they were now merely squatters in forbidden territory. The land companies and land speculators were also at a loss to know what to do. Since the 1740's speculators and investors had looked upon western land as a potential source of wealth waiting only to be exploited. Governors of colonies like Virginia, which claimed land all the way to the Pacific Ocean, had been accustomed to authorize surveys and to issue patents to western lands. The Proclamation of 1763 removed this authority from the governors and transferred it to the king acting through the Privy Council and the Board of Trade, a longer and more cumbersome procedure. The whole western land problem was left in a state of confusion.

Land speculators, however, did not lose hope. Many land-hungry Virginians, Pennsylvanians, and others continued to explore the trans-Appalachian country and to pick out territory they hoped to make their own. Dozens of land companies, often composed of wealthy merchants or planters, were organized to establish baronies west of the mountains. A few individuals sought to carve out vast estates for themselves, among them George Washington, who kept emissaries busy investigating lands in the Ohio Valley, and George Croghan, Pennsylvania Indian trader and agent.

For a decade after 1763, the land fever raged. Between 1764 and 1765 George Croghan organized a group known as the "Suffering Traders"—Indian traders who had suffered as a result of Pontiac's Conspiracy—and other prospective landholders (including Benjamin Franklin and wealthy Philadelphia merchants) into the Illinois Company, which sought more than a million acres bordering the Mississippi River. Croghan and Franklin were both involved in another syndicate known as the Indiana Company, which tried to get a tract just west of the Proclamation Line between the Monongahela, Little Kanawha, and Ohio rivers. The hunter and explorer Daniel Boone lent his services to a North Carolinian, Richard Henderson, who was trying to get land for himself and associates in Kentucky. These were only a few of the organizations seeking western land despite the prohibitions of the Proclamation of 1763. In fact, pressure from the speculators and land companies soon forced the British government to alter the line of demarcation and shift it westward.

Shifting the line involved high politics, for the boundaries affected investments of members of Parliament

CANTONMENT of *HIS MAJESTY'S FORCES in* N. AMER. *ACCORDING TO THE DISPOSITION NOW MADE & TO BE COMPLEATED AS SOON AS PRACTICAB* taken from the General Distribution dated at New York 29. March 1766. *By Dan.Paterson, As.I Qur.* with the alteration to Summer 1767 lins in yellow.

who had speculated in land, territories that the Board of Trade had promised land companies, tracts that powerful speculators hoped to get once a new line was established, and the interests of a number of Indian tribes whose lands had to be avoided or purchased. To placate the Indians, speculators showered them with presents and made promises of continued gifts. Many Indians gave up their lands believing that the white men would subsidize them forever. Finally, in a series of Indian treaties negotiated at Hard Labor Creek with the Cherokees in October, 1768, at Fort Stanwix with

344

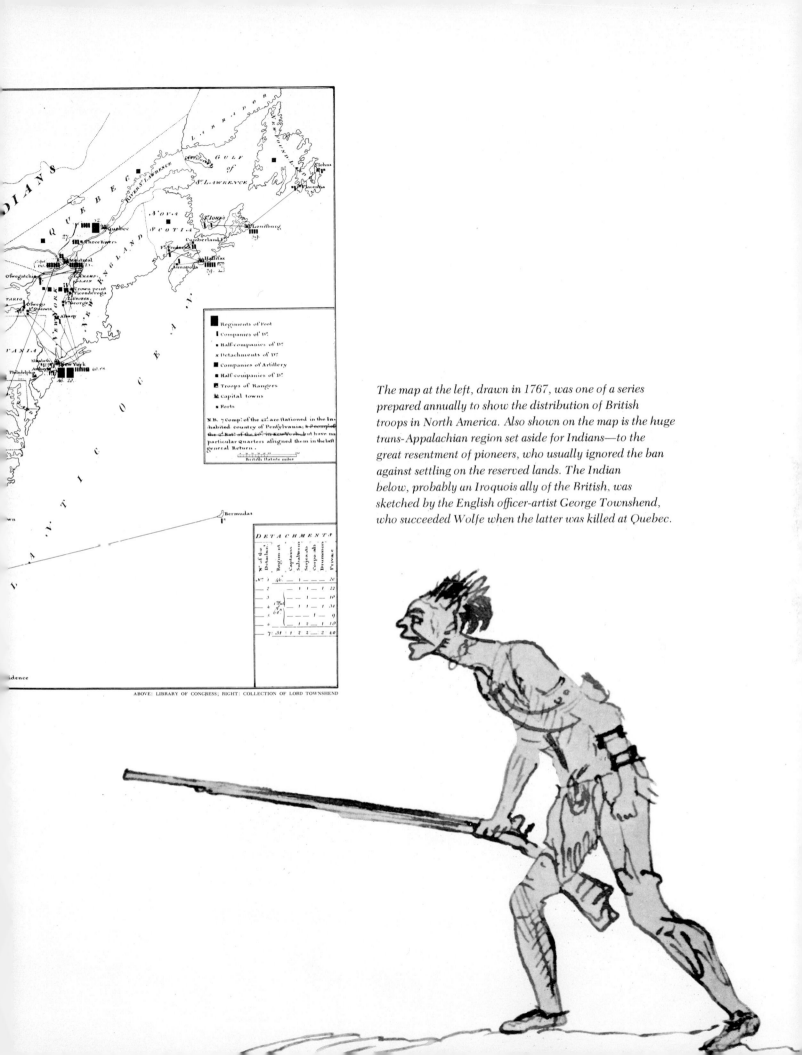

Regiments of Foot
Companies of D?
Half-companies of D?
x Detachments of D?
Companies of Artillery
Half-companies of D?
Troops of Rangers
Capital towns
Forts

N.B. 7 Comp? of the 42? are stationed in the In-habited country of Pensylvania; & 2 comp? of the 2? Bat: of the 60? in New York but have no particular Quarters assigned them in the last general Return.

British Statute miles

| DETACHMENTS |
N? of the Detacht.	Regiment	Captains	Subalterns	Serjeants	Corporals	Drummers	Privates
N? 1	46?	1	—	—	1	—	20
2		—	1	1	1		22
3		—	1	—	1		10
4	1 Bat? 60?	1	1	—	1	1	30
5		—	—	1		—	9
6		—	1	2	—	1	19
7	31	1	2	2	2		80

The map at the left, drawn in 1767, was one of a series prepared annually to show the distribution of British troops in North America. Also shown on the map is the huge trans-Appalachian region set aside for Indians—to the great resentment of pioneers, who usually ignored the ban against settling on the reserved lands. The Indian below, probably an Iroquois ally of the British, was sketched by the English officer-artist George Townshend, who succeeded Wolfe when the latter was killed at Quebec.

the Iroquois and other northern Indians in November of the same year, and later in the Treaty of Lochaber with the Cherokees in October, 1770, the British managed to shift the line farther west and to provide vast territories for speculation. But despite the lavish distribution of presents, farsighted Indians were not pleased. They realized that their days in ancestral hunting grounds were numbered.

An effort to bring some order into the British relations with the Indians was made by a plan that George Croghan took to London for submission to the Board of Trade and got tentatively adopted in July, 1764. This provided for maintaining a division already made into a northern and a southern district separated by the

During Pontiac's War, British Colonel Henry Bouquet moved from Fort Pitt westward to the Muskingum River to subdue the Shawnee and Delaware Indians and to free white captives. Below is the scene, as artist Benjamin West pictured it, as the Indians gave up to Bouquet some of the two hundred captives that were released. Many white children did not want to leave their Indian foster parents and friends.

Ohio River. Sir William Johnson was superintendent of the northern region (with Croghan as his second-in-command), and Colonel John Stuart was superintendent of the southern region. The Plan of 1764 called for the establishment south of the Ohio of many small trading posts among the various tribes, with a blacksmith shop at each post where Indians could sharpen their tools. An interpreter would also be available to help both traders and Indians. The resident agent at each post would set fair prices and arbitrate disputes between traders and Indians. This plan was good in theory, but it broke down in practice because the governors of Georgia, South Carolina, and Virginia licensed a horde of traders, many of them greedy rascals, who swarmed into the back country and cheated the Indians.

In the Northwest, Sir William Johnson decreed that all trade must be concentrated at two main posts, Detroit and Mackinac, an inconvenient arrangement for both Indians and traders. Illegal French traders and unlicensed Americans traveling among the tribesmen bought up furs and conveyed them down the rivers to profitable markets in St. Louis and New Orleans. The British fur companies saw their profits dwindle as trade fell off by more than a third in the years between 1764 and 1768. The British attempt to eliminate the French from the fur trade and to make new regulations called for many adjustments that were long in coming. In the meantime, the Indians were discontented, and many traders were losing money and grumbling over interference from London. The imperial effort to settle the twin problems of western land and the Indian fur trade succeeded only in alienating thousands of colonials.

The restlessness of the Indians and their persistent threat—and, it was whispered, the growing recalcitrance of the colonists themselves—influenced the British government in 1763 to set up for the colonies a military establishment of ten thousand regulars. In the government's view, the incapacity of the colonies during the Seven Years' War to unite in their own defense or to provide adequate support for a war on the frontier had made evident the necessity of this action. No one, of course, openly said anything about coercing the colonies. A few cynics complained that the establishment was primarily designed to provide soft assignments for British officers. But the official assertion was that the regulars were needed to defend the country against the Indians or a foreign aggressor. And since it was for the defense of the thirteen colonies, George III's govern-

ment thought that they might pay part of the upkeep.

Logical and reasonable as this viewpoint appeared in London, it did not meet with favor on the American side of the Atlantic, and the revenue measures put into effect in the next few years drove the colonies further along the road of stubborn opposition to Parliament. The actions of George Grenville, first lord of the treasury, chancellor of the exchequer, and prime minister from 1763 to 1765, particularly antagonized the colonists. Grenville pushed through Parliament the Revenue Act of 1764, commonly known as the Sugar Act, which imposed new taxes and provided for the enforcement of the Navigation Acts. Although it reduced the tax on molasses in effect since 1733 from six pence to three pence a gallon, provisions were made for the actual collection of the new tax, something that had not occurred before with any regularity. Enforcement made a difference, and importers screamed that they were ruined.

The very next year, Grenville got another even more unpopular act through Parliament, the Stamp Act of 1765. If Grenville had lain awake nights trying to devise a measure to annoy the colonists, he could not have found a better means than the Stamp Act, which had the earmarks of having been deliberately designed to irritate everyone, rich and poor. No one could escape the new tax, the first direct tax ever levied on the colonists, for every document required for any transaction had to be written or printed on special paper embossed with the tax stamp, and the paper had to be procured from special stamp tax offices. Furthermore, the stamps had to be paid for in sterling instead of colonial currency, and sterling was worth a third more than most colonial money. Hardly a scrap of paper used in the colonies escaped the tax. Every legal paper, every paper in commerce, licenses of every kind, newspapers, almanacs, college diplomas, playing cards, and even dice required a stamp, which might range in cost from four pence for an almanac to four pounds for a liquor license. Not only were the stamps costly; they were also inconvenient, for no business could be transacted until someone had gone to the stamp office and got the right sort of paper embossed with the right sort of stamp. Since everyone was affected by the stamp tax, all could unite in condemning it. And since the most articulate members of society, the lawyers and the newspaper publishers, suffered the most expense and inconvenience, their outcries were the loudest.

OVERLEAF: *When word was received in Boston in mid-May of 1766 of repeal of the Stamp Act, an obelisk was set up under the Liberty Tree and unveiled with fireworks. Paul Revere made this engraving showing all sides of the obelisk. The portraits are of "worthy patriots," English friends of the colonies, and include even George III.*

AMERICAN ANTIQUARIAN SOCIETY

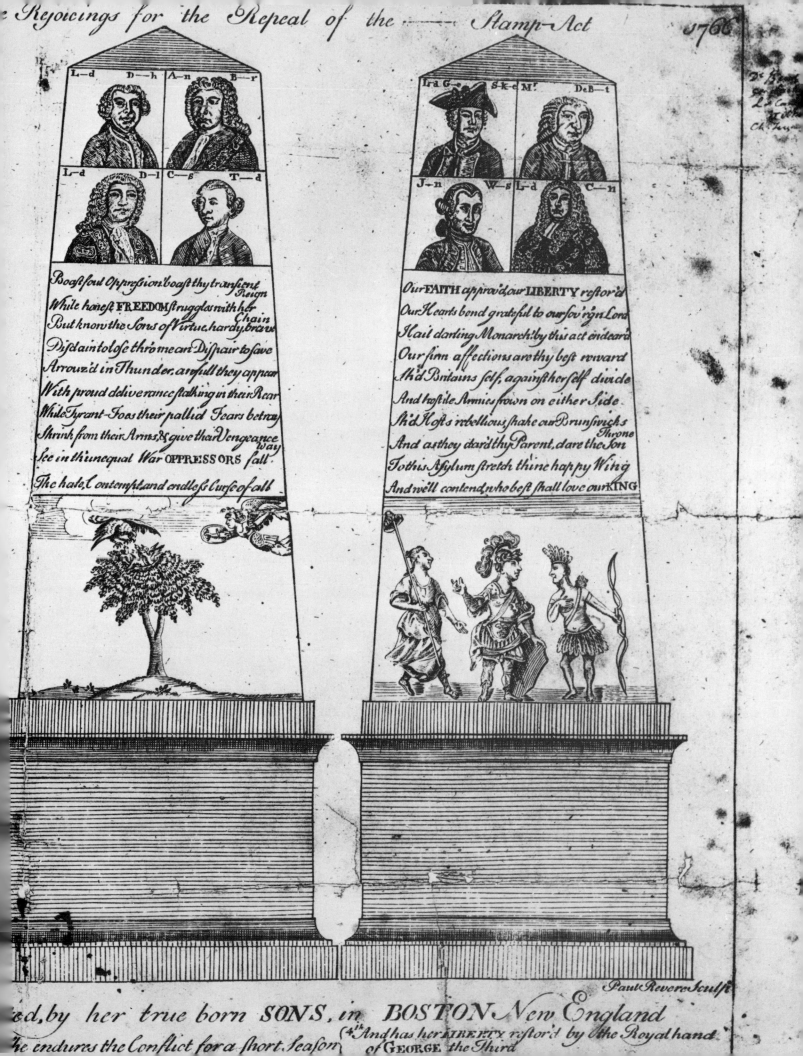

The Revenue Act of 1764 had prepared the way for the furor that the Stamp Act precipitated, for the new duties in the Revenue Act raised prices and attempted to change the habits of both men and women in the interest of English merchants. For example, the colonists had developed a taste for Madeira wine, which from the beginning they had imported duty-free direct from the islands. The new act placed a prohibitive tax on Madeira in an effort to make wine drinkers in the colonies turn to port or sherry, which had to be imported from England. The act also put a heavy duty on French fabrics, especially lawns and linens, and on silks and cottons. This duty was designed to help English manufacturers at the expense of Continental sources.

The Revenue Act of 1764 and the Stamp Act of 1765 created a furor such as the colonies had never before seen. The newspapers published diatribes against the king's ministers, whom they chose to blame for the iniquity, and agitators began to clamor for repeal of the detested acts. Hardly a town of consequence failed to organize a group who took the name of "Sons of Liberty." In most towns the Sons of Liberty were respectable citizens determined to circumvent laws that they regarded as violating the rights of freeborn Englishmen. Mobs in New York, Newport, Charles Town, and elsewhere stormed the stamp tax offices, burned the embossed paper, or forced the officials to destroy paper and stamps. Never had the colonies seen such unity of purpose and action.

The Stamp Act brought into prominence two leaders, Samuel Adams and Patrick Henry, one in Massachusetts and the other in Virginia, who were to serve as firebrands of revolution. Both became the voices of the nonaristocratic elements in society, and both were con-

cerned about encroachments upon what they considered the constitutional rights vouchsafed to colonists no less than to native residents of Great Britain.

Samuel Adams, a distant cousin of John Adams, who was to become the second President of the United States, was born with a genius for politics—and for political agitation. Throughout his life, he was ever ready to neglect his own business for the public good as he saw it. After taking a bachelor's and a master's degree at Harvard, he entered his father's brewery, where, a historian has commented, "he did little good for lack of capacity, and little harm from lack of responsibility." By 1763 he was expressing his talent for local politics as a member of the Caucus Club, a group of Boston politicians who met in Tom Dawes's attic. He had found his milieu, and the enactment of the Stamp Act gave him an opportunity to stir up popular re-sentment against the governing clique in Massachusetts.

In Virginia Patrick Henry, himself a fairly prosperous planter in a backwoods county, first gained prominence in 1763 in a famous case known as "the Parson's Cause." The clergy of the established church in Virginia had traditionally received their pay in tobacco. But after poor crops in 1755 and again in 1758, the House of Burgesses fixed the rate of pay for the clergy at two pence a pound of tobacco, and salaries could be paid in cash at that rate instead of in tobacco as formerly. The clergy complained that it was unfair not to let them receive their pay in high-priced tobacco during years of scarcity, and they carried their cause to the Privy Council, which disallowed the Virginia law. In a suit brought in Hanover County by a clergyman asking for back pay in tobacco, Patrick Henry undertook to plead the case for the defending vestry. With flaming

When British troops landed in Boston in 1768 to help keep the increasingly defiant people of that city in check, artist Christian Remick made a record of the event. Remick —not a well-known figure—was a mariner as well as an artist.

351

oratory, Henry argued that the action of the King's Privy Council in vetoing a law passed by the House of Burgesses was tyranny. Moved by Henry's eloquence, the jury awarded the clergyman precisely one penny. From this time onward, Henry's reputation was made as a spokesman against the king's prerogative. In May, 1765, as a member of the House of Burgesses, he argued that the Stamp Act was illegal and unconstitutional, and he offered seven resolutions that asserted, with rising indignation, that Virginia's legislative assembly alone had the right to tax Virginians. In the course of the debate, Henry made his famous declaration: "Caesar had his Brutus—Charles the First, his Cromwell—and George the Third"—and he paused dramatically—"may profit by their example." On May 30 the House of Burgesses passed the first five of Henry's "Resolves," and all seven were published in the newspapers. They helped to stir the other colonies to action.

The legislative assembly of Massachusetts, prodded by Samuel Adams and other Sons of Liberty, passed a resolution early in June that called upon all the mainland colonies to join in a congress to protest the new tax. The Stamp Act Congress convened in New York City from October 7 to October 25, 1765, and was attended by representatives from all the colonies except Virginia, New Hampshire, North Carolina, and Georgia. The Congress passed fourteen resolutions that stated the position already taken by Virginia in Henry's "Resolves," namely that the colonists had all the rights and privileges of any of the king's subjects, that no taxes could be legally imposed without representation, and that since the colonies could not be represented in Parliament, their own assemblies had the sole constitutional right to tax them. Since the Stamp Act provided that violations should be tried in the admiralty courts without juries, the resolutions complained particularly of this violation of the rights of British subjects.

The language of the resolutions was not revolutionary, but it showed the trend of colonial thought. Opinion was rapidly crystallizing around the doctrine that traditional liberties were in danger and that the colonists should be vigilant to defend the constitutional rights enjoyed by British subjects anywhere. Soon scores of pamphleteers and writers in the newspapers would be citing examples from republican Rome and quoting tracts written during the Glorious Revolution of 1688 to justify their opposition to "tyranny." The Stamp Act Congress, having passed its resolutions and drawn up petitions to the king and to Parliament, adjourned, and the delegates went home to continue their agitation against a law that they had convinced themselves was aimed at their basic freedoms.

No village or settlement in North America was too distant to escape the propaganda against the Stamp Act, the most unpopular measure affecting the colonies that Parliament had yet passed. Town meetings in New England and county courts in the agrarian colonies of the South argued about the injustice of the law. Contributors to the newspapers wrote about the iniquity of the tax, and already a few were describing the law as the beginning of the enslavement of free men.

From Maine to Georgia the public clamor against the Stamp Act echoed until even Whitehall heard. More effective than resolutions, however, was a boycott of British goods sufficiently widespread to cause alarm to British merchants. A severe dip in exports to the colonies frightened London merchants into petitioning the House of Commons on January 17, 1766, to repeal the act, "in order," they declared, "to secure themselves and their families from impending ruin [and] to prevent a multitude of manufacturers from becoming a burthen to the community." The petition of the merchants made an impression, and the House of Commons began an investigation. Sitting as a committee of the whole on February 3 and for the following ten days, the House of Commons called witnesses, many of whom had been suggested by the merchants, to testify on the effect of the Stamp Act. Among these witnesses was Benjamin Franklin, who was in London as agent for the colony of Pennsylvania. Franklin made a reasoned defense of the American opposition to taxation by pointing out the huge amounts that the colonies had spent in their own defense. He also argued that Americans were entitled to the "common rights of Englishmen" guaranteed by the Magna Carta and set forth in the Petition of Right. In conclusion, in answer to a question about the present attitude of Americans toward British goods, he declared that Americans no longer took pride in wearing British garments but now wore "their old clothes over again till they can make new ones."

In July of 1765, Grenville's ministry had been replaced by one headed by the Marquess of Rockingham. Faced with opposition to the Stamp Act at home and abroad, Rockingham in March, 1766, moved for repeal. The Commons were willing, but the House of Lords opposed this action, because, they maintained, repeal

Paul Revere engraved this portrait of his fellow revolutionary, Sam Adams, in 1774. A mediocre artist, Revere copied a portrait by one artist and the frame by another.

Royal American Magazine, APRIL, 1774; SPENCER COLLECTION, NEW YORK PUBLIC LIBRARY

would display a weakness and lack of authority in Parliament. Finally, after pressure from the king, a bill repealing the act passed both houses and received the royal approval on March 18. To save face, however, Parliament felt obliged on the same day to pass the Declaratory Act, which asserted Parliament's superiority over colonial legislative assemblies in all matters. Any laws passed in the colonies "whereby the power and authority of the Parliament of Great Britain to make laws and statutes as aforesaid is denied, or drawn into questions, are, and hereby declared to be, utterly null and void to all intents and purposes whatsoever."

Overjoyed at the repeal of the Stamp Act, most colonials were in no mood to quibble over face-saving declarations of Parliament. William Pitt, who had opposed the act, was a great hero, and even King George, who had used his influence to end the law, was again hailed as a noble sovereign. In an excess of zeal, the New York assembly voted to erect statues of both Pitt and King George. Everywhere bells rang and the people celebrated the annulment of a measure that had stirred all thirteen colonies and had come closer to uniting them than even the threat of conquest by the French.

But here and there a few dissidents took no joy in the celebrations. The fundamental issues affecting the liberties of the colonies remained unchanged. The Declaratory Act firmly announced the subjection of the colonies to Parliament. Sam Adams, displeased at the foolish jollity of his townsmen over the repeal, set about fanning the embers of discontent lest the colonies grow complacent and forget the dangers of tyranny.

If wisdom had ruled Parliament, the damage done by the Stamp Act and the Revenue Act of 1764 might have been repaired. Even Sam Adams might have been converted from his radical opposition. But wisdom was not evident at either Westminster or Whitehall. The foolish pride of Englishmen could not brook the insolence of a parcel of backwoods colonials who chose to flout the king's authority, question Parliament's right to control them, and set themselves up as philosophers and students of the ancient laws of England.

The Rockingham ministry fell in August, 1766, and the king once again turned to William Pitt (now the Earl of Chatham) to form a government. This turn of events might have changed the course of American history had not Pitt's illness soon afterward forced him to relinquish the leadership of the government to the young and incompetent Duke of Grafton. Grafton allowed Charles Townshend, the chancellor of the exchequer, to push through Parliament a new set of revenue laws known as the Townshend Acts, which became effective November 20, 1767.

The colonists had complained that the Stamp Act imposed a direct internal tax contrary to their constitutional rights; by implication at least they had indicated that indirect external taxes in the form of duties were less objectionable. Acting on this hint, Townshend contrived to put import duties on glass, lead, paint, papers, and tea and revised the laws to enforce the collection of the duties. Under the Townshend Acts, judges again were instructed to issue writs of assistance to enable customs officers to search suspected premises. The new laws also expanded the admiralty courts, where offenders against the customs ordinances were brought to trial.

While these actions were being taken by Parliament, trouble of another sort was brewing in New York as the result of the Quartering Act, which had become effective on March 24, 1765. This act, passed at the request of General Thomas Gage, required the colonies to provide housing and supplies for British troops on station, and in 1766 added a provision permitting commanders

n Account of a late Military Maſſacre at Boſton, or the Conſequences of Quartering Troops in a populous well-regulated Town, taken from the -ſton-Gazette, of March 12, 1

BOSTON, March 12, 1770.

THE Town of Boſton affords a recent and melancholy Demonſtration of the deſtructive Conſequences of quartering Troops among Citizens in a Time of Peace, under a Pretence of ſupporting the Laws nd aiding Civil Authority; every conſiderate and nprejudic'd Perſon among us was deeply impreſt ith the Apprehenſion of theſe Conſequences hen it was known that a Number of Regiments ere ordered to this Town under ſuch a Pretext, ut in Reality to inforce oppreſſive Meaſures; to we and controul the legiſlative as well as executive Power of the Province, and to quell a Spirit f Liberty, which however it may have been baſe- oppos'd and even ridicul'd by ſome, would do onor to any Age or Country. A few Perſons mongſt us had determin'd to uſe all their Influ ace to procure ſo deſtructive a Meaſure with a iew to their ſecurely enjoying the Profits of an merican Revenue, and unhappily both for Bri- in and this Country they found Means to effect it It is to Governor Bernard, the Commiſſioners, eir Confidents and Coadjutors, that we are in- ebted as the procuring Cauſe of a military Power this Capital—The Boſton Journal of Occur- nces, as printed in Mr. Holt's York Gazette, om Time to Time, afforded many ſtriking In- ances of the Diſtreſſes brought upon the Inhabi- nts by this Meaſure; and ſince thoſe Journals ave been diſcontinued, our Troubles from that uarter have been growing upon us: We have own a Party of Soldiers in the face of Day fire f a loaden Muſket upon the Inhabitants, others ave been prick'd with their Bayonets, and even r Magiſtrates aſſaulted and put in Danger of eir Lives, when Offenders brought before them ave been reſcued; and why thoſe and other bold d baſe Criminals have as yet eſcaped the Pu- ſhment due to their Crimes, may be ſoon Matter Enquiry by the Repreſentative Body of this eople—It is natural to ſuppoſe that when the habitants of this Town ſaw thoſe Laws which ad been enacted for their Security, and which ey were ambitious of holding up to the Soldiery, uded, they ſhould more commonly reſent for emſelves—and accordingly it has ſo happened; any have been the Squabbles between them and e Soldiery; but it ſeems their being often worſt- d by our Youth in thoſe Rencounters, has only rv'd to irritate the former—What paſſed at Mr. ray's Rope-walk, has already been given the ublic, and may be ſaid to have led the Way to e late Cataſtrophe—That the Rope-walk Lads hen attaked by ſuperior Numbers ſhould defend emſelves with ſo much Spirit and Succeſs in the lub-way, was too mortifying, and perhaps it ay hereafter appear, that even ſome of their Of- cers were *unhappily* affected with this Circum- ance: Divers Stories were propagated among e Soldiery, that ſerv'd to agitate their Spirits; articularly on the Sabbath, that one Chambers, Serjeant, repreſented as a ſober Man, had been iſſing the preceeding Day, and muſt therefore ave been murdered by the Townſmen; an Of- er of Diſtinction ſo far credited this Report, that e enter'd Mr. Gray's Rope-walk that Sabbath; d when required of by that Gentleman as ſoon he could meet him, the Occaſion of his ſo doing, e Officer reply'd, that it was to look if the Ser- ant ſaid to be murdered had not been hid there; s ſober Sergeant was found on the Monday hurt, in a Houſe of Pleaſure—The Evidences ready collected ſhew, that many Threatnings d been thrown out by the Soldiery, but we do t pretend to ſay that there was any preconcert- Plan, when the Evidences are publiſhed, the orld will judge—We may however venture to clare, that it appears too probable from their onduct, that ſome of the Soldiery aimed to draw d provoke the Townſmen into Squabbles, and at they then intended to make Uſe of other eapons than Canes, Clubs or Bludgeons.

Our Readers will doubtleſs expect a circumſtan- al Account of the tragical Affair on Monday ght laſt; but we hope they will excuſe our be- g ſo particular as we ſhould have been, had we t ſeen that the Town was intending an Enquiry d full Repreſentation thereof.

On the Evening of Monday, being the 5th Cur- nt, ſeveral Soldiers of the 29th Regiment were en parading the Streets with their drawn Cut- ſſes and Bayonets, abuſing and wounding Num- ers of the Inhabitants.

A few minutes after nine o'clock, four youths, amed Edward Archbald, William Merchant, rancis Archbald, and John Leech, jun. came own Cornhill together, and ſeperating at Doctor oring's corner, the two former were paſſing the arrow alley leading to Murray's barrack, in hich was a ſoldier brandiſhing a broad ſword of uncommon ſize againſt the walls out of which e ſtruck fire plentifully. A perſon of a mean coun- enance armed with a large cudgel bore him com- any. Edward Archbald admoniſhed Mr. Mer- ant to take care of the ſword, on which the ſol- er turned round and ſtruck Archbald on the arm, puſhed at Merchant and pierced thro' his oaths inſide the arm cloſe to the arm-pit and azed the ſkin. Merchant then ſtruck the ſoldier ith a ſhort ſtick he had, and the other Perſon ran the barrack and bro't with him two ſoldiers, e armed with a pair of tongs the other with a ovel: he with the tongs purſued Archbald back ro' the alley, collar'd and laid him over the head ith the tongs. The noiſe bro't people together, d John Hicks, a young lad, coming up, knock'd e ſoldier down, but let him get up again; and ora lads gathering, drove them back to the bar- ck, where the boys ſtood ſome time as it were to ep them in. In leſs than a minute 10 or 12 of em came out with drawn cutlaſſes, clubs & bay- ets, and ſet upon the unarmed boys and young lks, who ſtood them a little while, but finding the equality of their equipment diſperſed.—On hear- g the noiſe, one Samuel Atwood, came up to ſee hat was the matter, and entering the alley from ck-ſquare, heard the latter part of the combat d when the boys had diſperſed he met the 10 or ſoldiers aforeſaid ruſhing down the alley towards e ſquare, and aſked them if they intended to mur- r people? They anſwered Yes, by G—d, root d branch! With that one of them ſtruck Mr. twood with a club, which was repeated by ano- er, and being unarmed he turned to go off, and ceived a wound on the left ſhoulder which

The BLOODY MASSACRE perpetrated in King-Street BOSTON on March 5th 1770 by a party of the 29th REGt

Unhappy BOSTON! ſee thy Sons deplore,
Thy hallow'd Walks beſmear'd with guiltleſs Gore:
While faithleſs P—n and his ſavage Bands,
With murd'rous Rancour ſtretch their bloody Hands;
Like fierce Barbarians grinning o'er their Prey,
Approve the Carnage and enjoy the Day.

If ſcalding drops from Rage from Anguiſh Wrung
If ſpeechleſs Sorrows lab'ring for a Tongue,
Or if a weeping World can ought appeaſe
The plaintive Ghoſts of Victims ſuch as theſe;
The Patriot's copious Tears for each are ſhed,
A glorious Tribute which embalms the Dead.

But know, FATE ſummons to that awful Goal,
Where JUSTICE ſtrips the Murd'rer of his Soul:
Should venal C—ts the ſcandal of the Land,
Snatch the relentleſs Villain from her Hand,
Keen Execrations on this Plate inſcrib'd,
Shall reach a JUDGE who never can be brib'd.

*The unhappy Sufferers were Meſs*rs *SAM*l *GRAY, SAM*l *MAVERICK, JAM*s *CALDWELL, CRISPUS ATTUCKS & PAT*k *CARR Killed. Six wounded; two of them (CHRIST*r *MONK & JOHN CLARK) Mortally*

reached the bone and gave him much pain. Retreating a few ſteps, Mr. Atwood met two officers and ſaid, Gentlemen, what is the matter? They anſwered you'll ſee by and by. Immediately after, thoſe heroes appeared in the ſquare, aſking where were the boogers? where were the cowards? But notwithſtanding their fierceneſs to naked men, one of them advanced towards a youth who had a ſplit of a raw ſtave in his hand, and ſaid damn them here is one of them; but the young man ſeeing a perſon near him with a drawn ſword and good cane ready to ſupport him, held up his ſtave in defiance, and they quietly paſſed by him up the little alley by Mr. Silſby's to Kingſtreet, where they attacked ſingle and unarmed perſons till they raiſed much clamor, and then turned down Cornhill ſtreet, inſulting all they met in like manner, and purſuing ſome to their very doors. Thirty or forty perſons mostly lads, being by this means gathered in King ſtreet, Capt. Preſton, with a party of men with charged bayonets, came from the main guard to the commiſſioners houſe, the ſoldiers puſhing their bayonets, crying, Make way! They took place by the cuſtom-houſe, and continuing to puſh to drive the people off, pricked ſome in ſeveral places; on which they were clamorous, and, it is ſaid, threw ſnow-balls. On this, the Captain commanded them to fire, and more ſnow-balls coming, he again ſaid, Damn you, Fire, be the conſequence what it will! One ſoldier then fired, and a townſman with a cudgel ſtruck him over the hands with ſuch force that he dropt his firelock; and ruſhing forward aimed a blow at the Captain's head, which graz'd his hat and fell pretty heavy upon his arm: However, the ſoldiers continued the fire, ſucceſſively, till 7 or 8, or as ſome ſay 11 guns were diſcharged.

By this fatal manœuvre, three men were laid dead on the ſpot, and two more ſtruggling for life; but what ſhewed a degree of cruelty unknown to Britiſh troops, at leaſt ſince the houſe of Hanover has directed their operations, was an attempt to fire upon or puſh with their bayonets the perſons who undertook to remove the ſlain and wounded!

Mr. Benjamin Leigh, now undertaker in the Delph Manufactory, came up, and after ſome converſation with Capt. Preſton, relative to his conduct in this affair, adviſed him to draw off his men, with which he complied.

The dead are Mr. Samuel Gray, killed on the ſpot, the ball entering his head and beating off a large portion of his ſkull.

A mulatto man, named Criſpus Attucks, who was born in Framingham, but lately belonged to New-Providence, and was here in order to go for North-Carolina, alſo killed inſtantly; two balls entering his breaſt, one of them in ſpecial goring the right lobe of the lungs, and a great part of the liver moſt horribly.

Mr. James Caldwell, mate of Capt. Morton's veſſel, in like manner killed by two balls entering his back.

Mr. Samuel Maverick, a promiſing youth of 17 years of age, ſon of the Widow Maverick, and an apprentice to Mr. Greenwood, Ivory-Turner, mortally wounded, a ball went through his belly, and was cut out at his back: He died the next morning.

A lad named Chriſtopher Monk, about 17 years of age, an apprentice to Mr. Walker, Shipwright; wounded a ball entered his back about 4 inches above the left kidney, near the ſpine, and was cut out of the breaſt on the ſame ſide; apprehended he will die.

A lad named John Clark, about 17 years of age, whoſe parents live at Medford, and an apprentice to Capt. Samuel Howard of this town; wounded, a ball entered juſt above his groin and came out at his hip, on the oppoſite ſide, apprehended he will die.

Mr. Edward Payne, of this town, Merchant, ſtanding at his entry-door, received a ball in his arm, ſhattered ſome of the bones.

Mr. John Green, Taylor, coming up Leverett's Lane, received a ball juſt under his hip, and lodged in the under part of his thigh, which was extracted.

Mr. Robert Patterſon, a ſeafaring man, who was the perſon that had his trowſers ſhot through in Richardſon's affair, wounded; a ball went thro' his right arm, and he ſuffered great loſs of blood.

Mr. Patrick Carr, about 30 years of age, who work'd with Mr. Field, Leather-Breeches-maker in Queen-ſtreet, wounded, a ball enter'd near his hip and went out at his ſide.

A lad named David Parker, an apprentice to Mr. Eddy the Wheelwright, wounded, a ball entered in his thigh.

The People were immediately alarmed with the Report of this horrid Maſſacre, the Bells were ſet a Ringing, and great Numbers ſoon aſſembled at the Place where this tragical Scene had been acted; their Feelings may be better conceived than expreſs'd; and while ſome were taking care of the Dead and Wounded, the Reſt were in Conſultation what to do in thoſe dreadful Circumſtances.—But ſo little intimidated where they, notwithſtanding their being within a few Yards of the Main-Guard, and ſeeing the 29th Regiment under Arms, and drawn up in King-Street; that they kept their Station and appear'd as an Officer of Rank expreſs'd it ready to run upon the very Muzzles of their Muſkets.—The Lieut. Governor ſoon came into the Town-Houſe, and there met ſome of his Majeſty's Council, and a Number of Civil Magiſtrates; a conſiderable Body of the People immediately entered the Council Chamber, and expreſſed themſelves to his Honor with a Freedom and Warmth becoming the occaſion. He uſed his utmoſt Endeavours to pacify them, requeſting that they would let the Matter ſubſide for the Night, and promiſing to do all in his Power that Juſtice ſhould be done, and the Law have its Courſe; Men of Influence and Weight with the People were not wanting on their part to procure their Compliance with his Honor's Requeſt by repreſenting the horrible Conſequences of a promiſcuous and raſh Engagement in the Night, and aſſuring them that ſuch Meaſures ſhould be entered upon in the Morning as would be agreeable to their Dignity, and a more likely way of obtaining the beſt Satiſfaction for the Blood of their Fellow Townſmen.—The Inhabitants attended to theſe Suggeſtions, and the Regiment under Arms being ordered to their Barracks, which was inſiſted upon by the People, they then ſeparated and returned to their Dwellings by One o'Clock, at 3 o'Clock Capt. Preſton was committed, as were the Soldiers who fir'd, a few Hours after him.

Tueſday Morning preſented a moſt ſhocking Scene, the Blood of our Fellow Citizens running like Water thro' King-Street, and the Merchants Exchange the principal Spot of the Military Parade for about 18 Months paſt. Our Blood might alſo be track'd up to the Head of Long-Lane, and through divers other Streets and Paſſages.

At eleven o'clock the inhabitants met at Faneuil-Hall, and after ſome animated ſpeeches becoming the occaſion, they choſe a Committee of 15 reſpectable Gentlemen to wait upon the Lieut. Governor in Council, to requeſt of him to iſſue his Orders for the immediate removal of the troops

The Meſſage was in theſe Words:

THAT it is the unanimous opinion of this meeting that the inhabitants and ſoldiery can no longer live together in ſafety; that nothing can rationally be expected to reſtore the peace of the town and prevent further blood and carnage, but the immediate removal of the Troops; and that we therefore moſt fervently pray his Honor that his power and influence may be exerted for their inſtant removal.

His Honor's Reply, which was laid before the Town then Adjourn'd to the Old South Meeting-Houſe, was as follows,

Gentlemen,

I AM extremely ſorry for the unhappy differences between the inhabitants and troops, and eſpecially for the action of the laſt evening, and I have exerted myſelf upon that occaſion that a due enquiry may be made, and that the law may have its courſe. I have in council conſulted with the commanding officers of the two regiments who are in the town. They have their orders from the General at New-York. It is not in my power to countermand thoſe orders. The Council have deſired that the two regiments may be removed to the Caſtle. From the particular concern which the 29th regiment has had in your differences, Col. Dalrymple who is the commanding officer of the troops has ſignified that that regiment ſhall without delay be placed in the barracks at the Caſtle until he can ſend to the General and receive his further orders concerning both the regiments, and that the main guard ſhall be removed, and the 14th regiment ſo diſpoſed and laid under ſuch reſtraint that all occaſion of future diſturbances may be prevented.

The foregoing Reply having been read a conſidered—the queſtion was put, Whether port be ſatisfactory? Paſſed in the Negativ 1 diſſentient) out of upwards of Vo

It was then moved & voted that John H Eſq; Mr. Samuel Adams, Mr. William Mo William Phillips, Eſq; Dr. Joseph War ſhua Henſhaw, Eſq; and Samuel Pemberto be a Committee to wait on his Honour the Governor, and inform him, that it is the mous Opinion of this Meeting, that the Repl to a Vote of the Inhabitants preſented his in the Morning, is by no means ſatisfactor that nothing leſs will ſatisfy, than a total mediate removal of all the Troops.

The Committee having waited upon the Governor agreeable to the foregoing Vote; fore the Inhabitants the following Vote of received from his Honor.

His Honor the Lieut. Governor laid bef Board a Vote of the Town of Boſton, pa Afternoon, and then addreſſed the Board as

Gentlemen of the Council,

"I lay before you a Vote of the Town ton, which I have juſt now received fro and I now aſk your Advice what you ju ſary to be done upon it.

The Council thereupon expreſſed themſ be *unanimouſly* of opinion, "that it was ab neceſſary for his Majeſty's ſervice, the goo of the Town, and the Peace of the Provin the Troops ſhould be immediately remove the Town of Boſton, and thereupon adv Honor to communicate this Advice of the to Col. Dalrymple, and to pray that he wo der the Troops down to Caſtle-William. Committee alſo informed the Town, that C rymple, after having ſeen the Vote of Coun to the Committee, "That he now gave h of Honor that he would begin his Prepara the Morning, and that there ſhould be n ceſſary delay until the whole of the two Re were removed to the Caſtle."

Upon the above Report being read, the tants could not avoid expreſſing the high S tion it afforded them.

After Meaſures were taken for the Secu the Town in the Night by a ſtrong Watch, the Meeting was Diſſolved.

The 29th Regiment have already left the 14th Regiment are following them, ſo expect the Town will ſoon be clear of Troops. The Wiſdom and true Policy Majeſty's Council and Col. Dalrymple th mander appear in this Meaſure. Two Re in the midſt of this populous City; and th bitants juſtly incenſed: Thoſe of the nei ing Towns actually under Arms upon the port of the Maſſacre, and the Signal only to bring in a few Hours to the Gates of many Thouſands of our brave Brethren Country, deeply affected with our Diſtreſ to whom we are greatly obliged on this —No one knows where this would have en what important Conſequences even to th Britiſh Empire might have followed, wh Moderation and Loyalty upon ſo trying ſion, and our Faith in the Commander's A have happily prevented.

Laſt Thurſday, agreeable to a general of the Inhabitants, and by the Conſent o and Friends, were carried to their *Grave* ceſſion, the Bodies of *Samuel Gray, Sam verick, James Caldwell,* and *Criſpus At* unhappy Victims who fell in the bloody of the Monday Evening preceeding!

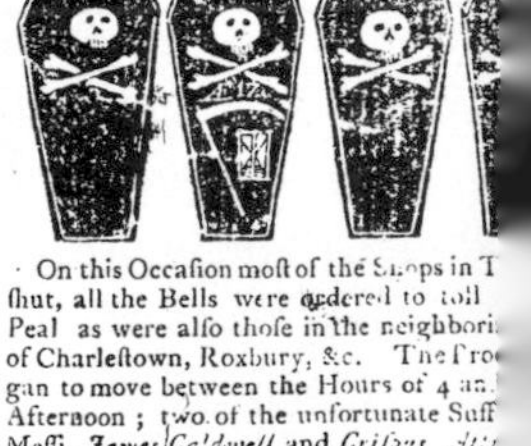

On this Occaſion moſt of the Shops in T ſhut, all the Bells were ordered to toll Peal as were alſo thoſe in the neighbori of Charleſtown, Roxbury, &c. The Pro gan to move between the Hours of 4 an Afternoon; two of the unfortunate Suff Meſſi. *James Caldwell* and *Criſpus Att* were Strangers, borne from Faneuil-Hal ed by a numerous Train of Perſons of a and the other two, viz. Mr. *Samuel Gr* the Houſe of Benjamin Gray, (his Broth North-ſide the Exchange, and Mr. *Maver* the Houſe of his diſtreſſed Mother Mrs. *verick*, in Union-Street, each followed by pective Relations and Friends: The ſeve ſes forming a Junction in King-Street, the of that inhuman Tragedy, proceeded fr thro' the Main-Street, lengthened by an Concourſe of People, ſo numerous as to follow in Ranks of ſix, and brought long Train of Carriages belonging to the Gentry of the Town. The Bodies were in one Vault in the middle Burying-grou aggravated Circumſtances of their Death tears and Sorrow viſible in every Counte gether with the peculiar Solemnity with whole Funeral was conducted, ſurpaſs D

BOSTON, March 19.

Laſt Wedneſday Night *trick Carr*, an Inhabitant of of the Wound he received Street on the bloody and Night of the 5th Inſtant juſt before left his Home, his coming into the Street the fatal Ball in his Hip wh out at the oppoſite Side; fifth Life that has been ſac the Rage of the Soldiery, feared it will not be the laſt, others are dangerouſly languiſhing of thei His Remains were attended on Saturday Faneuil-Hall by a numerous and reſpect of Mourners, to the *ſame* Grave, in wh who fell by the *ſame* Hands of Violence terred the laſt Week.

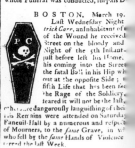

to requisition quarters in inns, alehouses, and unoccupied houses. When General Gage, who had headquarters in New York, demanded that the legislative assembly of that colony implement the act providing for necessary lodging for his troops, he met with only partial acquiescence. Bad blood between regular troops and the citizenry eventually led to rioting. When the legislature continued to refuse to authorize proper quarters and supplies, the royal governor suspended its functions, an action that Parliament later confirmed.

The dismissal of a colonial legislative assembly by administrative and parliamentary action supplied ammunition to the radicals who now fulminated against tyranny and oppression. The indignation aroused by the Townshend Acts, combined with the uneasiness produced by the suspension of the New York assembly, resulted in a fresh wave of propaganda against the action of the British government. In Massachusetts Sam Adams, seeing a new opportunity for action, helped organize the Nonimportation Association of 1768 and kept up a heavy personal correspondence with radical leaders in the other colonies. In the principal ports, organizers of the boycott held demonstrations and aroused public opinion to support the ban on British goods. In the person of John Dickinson of Pennsylvania, a new voice was raised to condemn the action of the British. By nature, temperament, and social milieu Dickinson was really a conservative, but he could not tolerate the contempt displayed by the British government toward the American colonists; in time he came to believe that a conspiracy existed in England to suppress freedom in America. In November, 1767, he began to publish in *The Pennsylvania Chronicle* the first of fourteen essays to which he gave the title, "Letters from a Farmer in Pennsylvania to the Inhabitants of the British Colonies." By the end of the following year, these letters, reprinted as pamphlets, were being widely read throughout the colonies and in Great Britain itself. Dickinson marshaled his eloquence to show the iniquity of the Townshend Acts and the dangers implicit in the suspension of the New York assembly.

The drumbeat of propaganda against British "tyranny" continued to rise. In 1768 Sam Adams composed a "Circular Letter" approved by the Massachusetts House of Representatives to be sent to the legislative assemblies of the other colonies. This letter condemned the Townshend Acts and called upon the other colonies to unite for the common defense of their liberties. The letter particularly warned against attempts by the Crown to make the royal governors and judges independent of colonial authorities. When the Earl of Hillsborough, secretary for the colonies, read the letter, he pronounced it seditious and ordered colonial governors to suspend any legislative assembly that approved it. But the fat was already in the fire, and several colonial legislatures had already endorsed the letter with enthusiasm. Governor Francis Bernard of Massachusetts ordered the General Court (the legislative assembly) to expunge the letter from the record; when it refused, he suspended it in compliance with Hillsborough's orders.

The lives of the customs agents were troubled and difficult. Every device was used to trick and circumvent them, and here and there violence occurred. When Boston customs officers in 1768 asked for armed help in enforcing the laws, the Admiralty ordered the ship of war *Romney* sent from Halifax. On October 1 of that year, two regiments of regular troops equipped with artillery also landed in Boston. This show of force further irritated the inhabitants.

Throughout the colonies, sentiment for the boycott of British goods increased. The nonimportation agreements were so effective that the value of British imports fell from £2,157,218 in 1768 to £1,336,122 by the end of 1769. Since this was an argument understood by Parliament, even by the proud members who wished to punish American upstarts, in 1770 the government, now led by Frederick Lord North, moved to modify the Townshend Acts.

In April, 1770, all the duties were removed except that on tea. Lord North insisted upon the retention of one duty as a symbol of Parliament's continued authority. But the Quartering Act, which had earned the ill will of the colonists, was not renewed. Gradually business began to improve, nonimportation was forgotten, and for a time it looked as if controversies with the mother country might be forgotten.

Indeed, the return of complacence troubled the radicals, and Sam Adams once more took up his pen to keep his correspondents in the other colonies alert to the danger of British usurpation of their liberties. Rows and near riots between citizens and garrison troops in New York and Boston provided some grist for the agitators, and full-scale trouble in Boston on the night of March 5, 1770, was the sort of thing that the radicals needed. When roving bands of rioting workers and soldiers in the streets of Boston met a detachment of troops

The broadside at left appeared some three weeks after the Boston Massacre of March 5, 1770. The account was reprinted from the Boston Gazette *of March 12; the illustration is one of Paul Revere's engravings. Both picture and text are highly inaccurate and give no hint that the patriots were largely a rioting mob.*

under the command of Captain Thomas Preston, a fracas started and someone gave the order to fire. Three civilians were killed outright, and two were so severely wounded that they died.

This was the so-called Boston Massacre that Sam Adams magnified in lurid words and that Paul Revere pictured in an engraving. As the result of the upsurge of indignation, Governor Bernard reluctantly agreed to remove the troops from the town to Castle William and to allow the civil authorities to try for murder Captain Preston and the soldiers of his squad. John Adams, Josiah Quincy, and Robert Auchmuty served as attorneys for the accused and saw to it that they received a fair trial. All were cleared of the murder charge, but two of the soldiers were convicted of manslaughter. When they pleaded benefit of clergy under old English law, they were freed after being branded on their thumbs.

Despite the furor stirred by the riot in Boston, calm soon settled over the colonies as business responded to the removal of the Townshend duties. Merchants imported quantities of goods to replenish depleted stocks; and cargoes of American grain, meat, fish, and other food products found a ready market abroad at higher prices than usual. The Board of Trade was even forced to permit payment in English coins for American exports, a step that helped improve the financial position of the colonials, who had hitherto been short of specie. For two years following the repeal of the Townshend Acts, prosperity reigned, and the agitators found it difficult to maintain a sense of crisis and alarm.

But Sam Adams was equal to the situation. As historian Samuel Eliot Morison has commented: "A middle-class Bostonian, austere and implacable, Adams alone among leaders of the American Revolution was a genuine revolutionary, resembling in several respects the communist agitators of our time. He was certainly the Western world's first orchestra-leader of revolution. He knew that voters are moved by emotion rather than logic. A master of propaganda, he realized that the general run of people prefer drama and ritual to a well-argued exposition." So Adams was not disposed to let the colonies lapse into somnolent complacency under the influence of prosperity. He kept up an incessant correspondence with kindred spirits in the other colonies and waited impatiently for some explosive incident that he could magnify into evidence of British tyranny.

Precisely what Adams wanted occurred in the summer of 1772. On June 9 a customs schooner, the *Gaspee*,

356

This English drawing of about 1770, in which an officer examines three recruits while a sergeant tries to hold them in line, was a satirical observation on the poor grade of men joining the British Army. The colonists spoke of redcoats so poorly paid they had to take spare-time jobs.

ran aground near Providence, Rhode Island, and that night a mob led by a respectable merchant, John Brown, sailed out of Providence, boarded, and burned the helpless customs vessel, which flew the flag of the Royal Navy. This indeed was an affront that London could not brook. When the news reached Whitehall, tempers seethed, and a royal proclamation went out on August 26 offering a reward of five hundred pounds for the identity of the dastardly villains who had dared touch one of the king's ships. Furthermore, when apprehended, they were to be sent to England for trial. It is of interest that the king's commissioners could never discover them. Coincidental with this issue came an announcement from Governor Hutchinson of Massachusetts that henceforth he would not be beholden to the assembly for his salary but would receive it directly from the Crown, as would Massachusetts judges. Here was the beginning, thoughtful colonials decided, of complete control of executive and judicial officials from London. It was easy for Adams and the radicals to alarm even the least excitable of their contemporaries with visions of trials across the seas for infringements of the king's laws, or at best, trials at home before judges in the pay of the Crown.

The *Gaspee* episode and the new scheme for paying royal governors and judges were soon the subjects of conversation in inns, taverns, courthouses, and town markets throughout the colonies. In November Adams got together a twenty-one-man committee in Boston to spread the word throughout the land that American liberties faced a new and present danger. This Committee of Correspondence, soliciting help from the other colonies, soon succeeded in organizing propaganda units elsewhere. In March, 1773, the Virginia House of Burgesses created a Committee of Correspondence with Patrick Henry, Thomas Jefferson, and Richard Henry Lee as its most articulate members. By February, 1774, all of the colonies except North Carolina and Pennsylvania had active Committees of Correspondence busily engaged in distributing propaganda aimed at alerting the populace to encroachments upon American liberties.

As yet the colonies were not demanding independence from Great Britain; indeed, not even the radicals wanted to cut connections with the mother country. They merely wanted to insure against Parliament and the king's ministers usurping rights that they had convinced themselves resided in the legislative assemblies of the individual colonies. As colonial writers continued

357

Cal Sacks

Boston
1774

British warships blockaded Boston in the summer of 1774, for Parliament had closed the port on June 1 to punish the tea-dumping townspeople. British regiments were encamped on the pastures of the Common (top), and troops were stationed at strategic points elsewhere in the town. To the right of the Common is Beacon Hill, and atop it the signal for which it

Overt tro
night of Dec
Captain Rot
bor since No
that the dut
arrival or th
the time ha
seize and lan
zens said mu
held, and Ca
other. The sh
not permit hi
was now liab
a band disg
wharf, boarde
and dumped
chests of tea.
but Boston w
Company's te
back the tea s
the cargoes. C
stored it in a
break with Gr

The destruc
plauded in th
Boston radica
those who had
certain that
waited to see
They were no
choking with ra
manded action
lish newspaper
Finally, beginn
the Commons c
of laws designe
calcitrance. The
history as the C
alienate the mo
Boston Tea Par

A crisis over t
dering frustratio
pride of the hom
the controversie
rights of English
gle between the
The immediate e
sympathy for be

was named: a pole bearing a bucket of tar to be burned as an alarm. Boston's hills were later cut down and used as shoreline fill, completely altering the town's tadpole shape. Extending toward the reader is Long Wharf: directly inland from it in the middle of the street is the Statehouse (the Boston Massacre occurred on the harbor side of the State-house). In the open space to the right of Long Wharf is cupolaed Faneuil Hall. The dammed-up bay is a mill pond; water impounded at high tide flowed out through water wheels at ebb tide. The steeple closest to the near end of the mill dam is on Christ Church, where, legend says, two lamps in the belfry told Paul Revere that the British were coming by water.

colonies would be improved by this punishment or would draw the right conclusions from the discipline. Nor were all Englishmen pleased over the tightening authority exerted by King George and the king's friends over their own liberties. For more than a decade John Wilkes, a member of Parliament and in 1774 Lord Mayor of London, fought the king with satire and invective and on occasion defended the colonies. Though Wilkes's character was something less than savory, the colonists made him a hero and the South Carolina assembly voted fifteen hundred pounds sterling to help pay his debts. Other Englishmen more exalted than Wilkes continued their opposition to policies that they foresaw would lead to disaster. Lord Chatham remained a friend of the colonies, and Edmund Burke lavished his eloquence to defend them.

In the debate in the House of Commons over the Massachusetts Government Act on May 2, 1774, Burke had declared: "If you govern America at all, Sir, it must be by an army; but the Bill before us carries with it the force of that army; and I am of opinion they never will consent without force being used. . . . Repeal, Sir, the Act which gave rise to this disturbance; this will be the remedy to bring peace and quietness and restore authority; but a great black book and a great many red coats will never be able to govern it. It is true, the Americans cannot resist the force of this country, but it will cause wranglings, scuffling and discontent. Such remedies as the foregoing will create disturbances that can never be quieted." Burke spoke truer than he knew.

American moderates had struggled to persuade Englishmen that a little understanding, a demonstration of good sense, and a modicum of forbearance would ease a situation rapidly moving toward catastrophe. One of the most persistent of these Americans was Benjamin Franklin, who had many friends in Great Britain and who had long served as agent in London of the province of Pennsylvania. In 1768 Georgia appointed Franklin to serve as its agent, and by 1770 he was also serving as agent for New Jersey and Massachusetts, a series of appointments that gave him almost the status of colonial ambassador. He used his talents to try to bring about reconciliation and understanding. Until 1774 he continued to believe that moderation on both sides would ultimately result in an adjustment of the problems plaguing both Great Britain and the colonies, but after the passing of the Coercive Acts, he began to despair. Franklin had suffered enough personal abuse in Eng-

land to convince himself of the arbitrary arrogance of those in authority. One episode alone was enough to sour even this benign man. In 1772 he had seen six letters written by Governor Hutchinson to an unnamed English friend, believed to be Thomas Whately, a secretary to Grenville, in which Hutchinson had urged "an abridgment of what are called English Liberties" of the colonists. Franklin obtained these letters in confidence and sent them to Thomas Cushing, speaker of the Massachusetts House of Representatives, with the understanding that they would neither be copied nor printed. But they fell into the hands of Sam Adams, who, in June, 1773, read the letters before a secret session of the House. They were soon printed far and wide, even in London. The disclosure of Hutchinson's views, and the manner in which the letters had come to light, caused a sensation, and Franklin found himself in an embarrassing predicament. At a hearing before the Privy Council in London on January 29, 1774, the solicitor general called him a thief and a rogue, and he lost his post as deputy postmaster general of the colonies. Other abuse, even less merited than this, was heaped upon Franklin, until finally, on March 20, 1775, he sailed for home, convinced that reconciliation was hopeless.

In the meantime, Parliament had enacted other measures that further exasperated and alarmed the Americans. One of these was the Quebec Act, passed on May 20, 1774, which established a highly centralized government in Canada, somewhat analogous to the government that the Canadians had lived under during the French possession of Canada. But since under this act most of the governing authority would be in the hands of appointees of the Crown, the colonists to the south construed this as a sign of what was ultimately in store for them. The Quebec Act had other disturbing features. The Catholic Church was given a preferred status in French Canada, and at once colonial Protestants saw in this a hint of popery that they must resist. Worse still, the Quebec Act declared the boundaries of Canada to be on the Ohio River, which excluded Virginia, Connecticut, and Massachusetts from their long-claimed western lands.

The religious question raised by the Quebec Act was related to one that had long troubled some of the colonists. The connection between church and state had been a matter of contention at one time or another in most of the colonies, and the abolition of an established church would be one of the results of the Revolution.

An English political cartoon of 1775 shows America aflame, while British leaders continue to fan the flames higher with the various measures directed against Massachusetts.

Soon after the Stamp Act controversy, the colonies had heard rumblings of a plan by the Anglican church to appoint an American bishop. Previously the affairs of the church in the colonies had been the responsibility of the Bishop of London. To colonials already excited over the threat to their civil liberties, the specter of prelatical tyranny, of a bishop who would work hand in glove with royal governors to impose the yoke of an established church upon them, was not to be taken lightly. The outcry over an American bishop eventually subsided, but freedom from the domination of Canterbury was one of the requirements of the American Episcopal Church after the Revolution.

By the early summer of 1774 sentiment in the colonies had reached a point of desperation and despair over the ever increasing authority of king and Parliament. On May 13 General Thomas Gage, commander of British troops in America, supplanted Governor Hutchinson as royal governor of Massachusetts. The change was symbolic of the determination of the Crown to rule Massachusetts and the rest of America by force of arms if necessary. Hard on the installation of what in effect was a military government in Massachusetts came the word that on June 2 Parliament had passed another Quartering Act, this time applicable to all the colonies, allowing troops to be quartered not merely in taverns and vacant buildings but in occupied houses as well.

The handwriting was on the wall for even the blindest Tory to read, said the pamphleteers: king and Parliament were determined to suppress the liberties of Americans, and no course was left but to meet force with force. Mass meetings, town meetings, and official bodies of various sorts began to urge concerted action against Great Britain. In Boston the Committee of Correspondence produced a "Solemn League and Covenant" in which the signers agreed to boycott all British goods and to avoid any transactions with Great Britain of any sort. On June 17 the Massachusetts House of Representatives sent out a call to the other colonies to name delegates to a Continental Congress to be held in Philadelphia in September. Other groups elsewhere had also been urging the need for a congress of all the colonies. The call for the First Continental Congress met with favor everywhere except in Georgia, and the twelve other colonies named fifty-six delegates who first met in Carpenters' Hall, Philadelphia, on September 5, 1774. Twelve days later the First Continental Congress approved, not without some misgivings, a set of resolu-

tions known as the Suffolk Resolves. These resolutions, adopted by a convention in Suffolk County, Massachusetts, on September 9, were the handiwork of Dr. Joseph Warren, an ardent patriot of Boston; they had been carried posthaste to Philadelphia by Paul Revere; and their approval by the Congress under the whip of its radical members signified the temper of the times, for the Suffolk Resolves not only declared the Coercive Acts unconstitutional and not to be obeyed, but they called upon the people to arm themselves into organized militia to resist enforcement. They also called for an embargo on British trade.

The Continental Congress's own resolutions were somewhat less belligerent but clearly indicative of a determination to resist the enforcement of laws violating the fundamental rights of the colonists. The Congress enumerated these rights, including a statement "that they are entitled to life, liberty, and property, and they have never ceded to any sovereign power whatever a right to dispose of either without their consent." They also declared that Americans are "entitled to all the rights, liberties, and immunities of free and natural-born subjects within the realm of England." The resolutions passed by the Congress listed their numerous grievances and demanded the repeal of the objectionable acts. In a concluding statement, the Congress declared: "To these grievous acts and measures Americans cannot submit, but in hopes that their fellow subjects in Great-Britain will, on a revision of them, restore us to that state in which both countries found happiness and prosperity, we have for the present only resolved to pursue the following peaceable measures: 1st. To enter into a non-importation, non-consumption, and non-exportation agreement or association. 2. To prepare an address to the people of Great-Britain, and a memorial to the inhabitants of British America, & 3. To prepare a loyal address to his Majesty, agreeable to resolutions already entered into."

The way would be left open for negotiations, but probably not many members of the Congress in their secret thoughts believed that King George and his ministers would relent. The Congress had declared that "for the present only" it would pursue the peaceable but stern measures outlined. Implied was the threat of grimmer action to come. The time of vacillating debate and controversy was drawing to a close. The calling of the First Continental Congress marked the real end of the colonial era; the period of revolution had begun.

Road to Independence

Though most colonists remained loyal Englishmen as 1775 began, the point of separation was nearing. George III, with a little wisdom, could have ended the quarrel with his American subjects; instead he treated them as he would refractory horses whose spirits must be broken. But the colonists were not cowed, chances for compromise slipped away, and rebellion came with the five dramatic episodes pictured on the following pages. To a British cartoonist, the Boston Tea Party of 1773 (overleaf) was the cause of the break; he depicts Father Time with a magic lantern, showing a slide of a teapot exploding in a world gone awry. But though the Tea Party defied the king, it was not revolt. Revolution came April 19, 1775, when minutemen faced British redcoats at Lexington and Concord (in the painting, the British enter Concord). Two months later the chance of reconciliation with England was virtually ended when an American army came to desperate grips with the British at Bunker Hill (the picture is of the death of patriot leader Dr. Joseph Warren). Remaining loyalties to England faded. In New York, the statue of George III was toppled by men tired of kings. And in Philadelphia, on a July day in 1776, brave men pledged their lives and sacred honors in declaring that the colonies were, of right, free and independent.